Blessed By the Lord Led By the Spirit

Eunice Redeker Hausler

Words Matter Publishing
P.O. Box 1190
Decatur, Il 62525
www.wordsmatterpublishing.com

ISBN 13: 978-1-958000-86-1

Library of Congress Catalog Card Number: 2023946308

Table of Contents

Forward

In her first book, *Thank You Lord for the Privilege*, (Words Matter Publishing, 2021) Eunice told the story of her faith and gratitude-filled life of service to her personal Lord and Savior, Jesus Christ. Even as we compiled that book, she had a dream to complete a second book comprised of the decades of letters she had written from New Guinea, letters with much more detail of the day-to-day workings on the mission field and beyond. This is that book, augmented further by many letters before, and following the New Guinea years, both hers and those written to and from family members, co-workers, Lutheran Church-Missouri Synod (LCMS) Board of World Missions Staff, etc. (As a bonus, we've even been able to include the Orders of Worship from some of the milestones in her life).

One of the repeated comments I've heard in response to book one has been: "WOW! What a faith she has!" Yes, indeed! And that faith is not the "faith" of what we have sometimes identified as the faith of a New Testament Pharisee, described and/or demonstrated for "show." Not at all! That faith is a life lived in response to a Savior who has been ACTIVE through the power of the Holy Spirit: daily, hourly, minute-to-minute on some days, of her life. That Holy Spirit: present with her, moving in and through her, leading, guiding, sometimes carrying, and always supporting her through obstacles and joys, through sorrow and isolation, through very challenging situations (professionally and/or personally), through situations of people/family loving and caring for her.

It is our sincere hope and prayer, that our faithful God will further use this book, so that, again, people around the world will see His hand, His power, His Spirit, His love.

Sit back, grab that cup of coffee, or iced tea; grab the yellow highlighter; buckle the seat belt; and *say a prayer*. A prayer that the Holy Spirit might speak to YOU through this book; might lead YOU through this book...to a deeper relationship with God, to clarity in YOUR walk with Him, to ACTION and SERVICE to so many around YOU, so that others might see HIM through YOUR light, through YOUR life!

In Him whose love is boundless,
Charles "Chuck" Redeker

Dedication

This book is dedicated to my family.

My husband, Ray Hausler.

Our daughters, Paula Meister and Charla Hausler-Englebretsen

Our grandchildren: Evan and Anna Price, Aaron, Nathan, and Carlee Englebretsen.

And our sons-in-law: Russell Englebretsen and Jerry Meister

Finally: my nephew Charles Redeker who made this whole effort possible.

Acknowledgements

Special thanks to Charles Redeker and Lisa Fuehne for encouraging me to have this book published. Special thanks to Charles for editing and compiling the many letters from many files, into this book. It was a huge task, but he did it with enthusiasm, zeal, and a joyful spirit. Deep thanks and appreciation.

Vital to this publishing effort was Tammy Corwin, CEO of Words Matter Publishing LLC. Tammy and her staff exuded knowledge, grace, and wisdom in pulling it all together.

Explanation of the book structure

-We have chosen to relate the contents of this book, chronologically, so that the reader can more easily track the evolution of the story. However, in some cases, this "ruins the surprise" as relating to the contents of newsletters subsequently written!

-Given the time span covered by the book, (after all, the author is now in her late 80's!), we have chosen to simply relate the chapters to the decades within which Eunice has lived.

-Entries, for the most part, have been related per the original texts. In some cases, an ellipsis (...), will indicate information has been left out.

-Information in parenthesis indicates further clarification for the reader. Generally, one line at the beginning of each entry has some information to delineate a new entry. However, when a parenthesis exists within most longer entries or BEFORE or AFTER entries, they may stretch for several lines and thus are being used to help you, the reader, understand more of the content. In Eunice's original letters, parenthesis was not frequently used.

When the information in the () is the same font as the surrounding narrative, this information accompanied the original writing. When the information in the () is a different font style, this information is to give the reader additional insight.

-We have chosen to add a to assist with the delineation between entries.

-Abbreviations: Following the first use of a particular place or group, etc., for example, Concordia Teacher's College, we will note the abbreviation (CTC), which will then be used thereafter.

Introduction

A special thanks to Charles Redeker, my nephew, who along with my friend, Lisa Fuehne when they saw the letters I had saved from my life's work and adventures (these included letters I wrote, and letters written to me), decided that they needed to be published because they show God at work. Also, a great "thank you" to all the wonderful people who wrote letters to me during my life. These have always been received with joy while being uplifting and genuinely appreciated.

Every step I made and every adventure, were all given to me by my Heavenly Father, the God of the Bible: Father, Son, and Holy Spirit. Despite my sinfulness, God led me each day, even as a child. I saw Him walking with me every day. I was always talking to Him and He gave me answers, strength, and wisdom. I never felt I could do anything on my own, but I always prayed, and God gave me the courage to move ahead. He inspired my every thought. Now my prayer is that anyone who reads this book will read their Bible and trust in God to give them everything they need to move forward in life.

Especially I pray children who can read will see how Jesus led people in the Bible and led me, and how He will do the same for them. I pray that all adults who have not read their Bible and seen Jesus will be filled with the Holy Spirit to read their Bible and move forward in life with strong faith in Jesus, with the courage and fortitude only He can give. Then life will not be a misery, but a great joy as the love of Jesus fills you. "The love of Jesus, what it is, none but His loved ones know." This is a note a friend once put in my pocket when I was leaving for New Guinea, and it has filled me with joy and courage all my life. If you see how Jesus loved, and it soaks into your heart and soul, then you will want to spread His love around to everyone you meet. God grant this to each one of you. Great joy will fill your life as you: See Jesus more clearly, Love Him more dearly, Serve Him more surely, and Thank Him more heartily.

(The following was written by Eunice during Mission School at Concordia Seminary, in July 1959, before leaving for New Guinea.)

Why a Missionary-teacher?

"Eunice A. Redeker to be Commissioned a Missionary-teacher to New Guinea" on May 24", was the column headline of our Philadelphia Lutheran, May issue. The headline, when seen in actual print, was a little shocking. Here was a long-time desire in fulfillment. A desire I had never dreamed could come true.

*Now that it is true, I will tell you about myself and how it all came about. I grew up on a farm near Shattuc, IL, with my parents, three sisters and three brothers. A public school was attended until I was nine years old. Then I transferred to our Bethlehem Lutheran School, Ferrin, IL. It was while in religious instruction at this school that I received the inspiration to become a full-time worker in the Lord's kingdom. My high school years were spent at Carlyle Community High School, Carlyle, IL. During these years I was active in our Walther League activities, as well as school functions. I met many Christian and other friends and acquaintances during these years. During my final year at high school, my girlfriend and I made the decision to apply at Concordia Teachers College (CTC), River Forest (RF), IL, for admission since we were both interested in going into full time church work. CTC was chosen because for girls, our pastors advised us, there was a great need in the teaching profession. Also, one of our friends was attending college at Seward, NE at this time. (*Also, a CTC*). One of the fellows in our high school class also accompanied us to CTC after some influence from us.*

The years at college were exciting, inspirational, as well as educational. I had to work my way through since my parents could not pay for my schooling. I worked as a waitress. The tips were good, so I made out wonderfully. For His rich blessings in helping me secure enough finances, I praise God. I took my courses four years in three. Since I stayed at RF during the summers, summer school was convenient. My years at CTC were fruitful in mission work. As a member of our Missions Activity Group, I heard several foreign missionaries present a slide lecture, and many opportunities for canvassing in the local area presented themselves. A desire to bring Christ to others became strong. My supply teaching year was spent at Hope Lutheran School, Westcliffe, CO. This church and school were in a mountain valley below the Sangre De Cristo Range. (The New Guinea area sounds similar). After I arrived there, our pastor was with us two weeks and then accepted a call and left. Here I was! The only teacher for all eight grades, no fellow worker for fifty miles! Complete dependence on the Lord was my source of strength and encouragement. Besides, the congregation was not too favorable toward keeping the school open. I went ahead with the Lord's guidance and our school moved forward so that when I left the following May, the people were enthusiastic towards getting another teacher. They were also busy calling a pastor. My year at Westcliffe was a tremendous experience in many phases: Sunday School leadership, Walther League, counseling, personal counseling, and visitation, plus the organ bench on Sunday A.M.

After this year, I returned to RF to finish my schooling and graduated with a B.S. in Ed. Degree on August 2, 1956. It was also at this time that I had met a friend, who it seemed would be my life-mate, but the Lord showed us differently later. My assignment by the Board of Assignments after graduation, was to start a school in Levittown, PA; Rev. Walter A. Maier, Jr., pastor. Levittown, the assignment said, was a booming city of 17,000 homes, 80,000 population. Again, I was faced with a real challenge. I prayed the Lord for His grace, guidance, and wisdom. I never at the time realized what a mission challenge was also awaiting me in this assignment. I really appreciated my Westcliffe experience now and dug into school organization and administration materials at RF that last summer.

I arrived in Levittown, August 4, and found a wonderful pastor and people to work with. School was started in the Parish Building *basement. Along with school again, leadership in Walther League was needed, as well as in Sunday school. Then there was organ playing and my experience in personal counseling was a real help and need in Levittown also. Through the children I reached many families very closely. My three years at Levittown led me to a real desire to tell of Christ to people, who never had the opportunity to hear of Him. Here at Levittown much canvassing and calling was done to people, who knew Christ, yet would not accept Him. Last October 1958, during our Eastern District Teacher's Conference, the congregation advised me to go home to recover from a physically run-down condition. It was during this week that I visited Dr. O.H. Schmidt, Secretary of our Board of Foreign Missions, to inquire about Foreign Missions. I had planned to go into nurses training to prepare myself for this work. I had always had a strong desire to be a nurse. I did not think teachers were able to go into the mission field as such. Through my conversation with Dr. Schmidt, I learned New Guinea needed a teacher badly to open a girl's school for the natives. Dr. Schmidt invited me to his home that evening to view slides on New Guinea. I was very much impressed. He told me to pray and think about it. They would contact me, also they had other people who had applied, so nothing was definite. The questions kept running through my mind: "Am I ready to go <u>now</u>? Do I really want to leave my family, this school, and people I love dearly, as well as my friends? Am I willing to give up the opportunities of meeting someone with whom to share my life?" Through much struggling in prayer, the Lord clearly pointed out to me, "I gave My life for thee, what hast thou given for Me?" His call: "Go ye into all the world and preach the Gospel to every creature, and lo I am with you always even unto the end of the world," kept ringing in my ears. His words "Give and it shall be given unto you," kept coming to me. Yes, physical conditions were keeping me here, but the Lord kept calling me away. I decided if the Lord directed the appointment to me, I would say, "Here I am, send me, send me." My parents were quite upset at first but understood. All moved ahead, the Appointment came in February, I accepted and so it is I have the opportunity and privilege to bring the Gospel to the heathen, to people whom Christ dearly loved and for whom He also died. Unless I go, these people may never have* *the opportunity to hear of our Savior. What a joy, what a privilege! I praise God that He would use a person like me, who often feels so inadequate, for such a great challenge. My assignment is to start a girl's school for the native girls in New Guinea. Once again, I plead to the Lord for His mercy, guidance and wisdom, His love and patience. I feel similar to the way I did when I went to Levittown. Before me lies a tremendous challenge. I would say I can not do it, but I go in the name of the Almighty God, the all-powerful and merciful God, in Him all things are possible. "I can do all things through Christ, who strengtheneth me." (Philippians 4:13) The joy, the inner peace, the dependence on the Lord, the blessings that have already come to me since I accepted this assignment is overwhelming.*

My congregation at Levittown, PA, gave me a wonderful, inspiring farewell. The Lord has blessed our work there. Last year we received our second teacher from RF. I was acting principal. Our kindergarten teacher was a member of our congregation, holding a degree from the Heidelberg University in Germany. She taught German to our third and fourth grades also. Our school grew so that we now have an enrollment of 120. We started with grades one and two, three years ago. This fall we will have added up to grade five. We are now constructing the first unit of our school building, four classrooms. God answered our prayer and sent us a man principal to replace me, another blessing which made me feel free to go. In all my life, I can only say: "How great and manifold are the mercies and riches of God!" May His name be glorified throughout the earth amongst men until we sing the eternal praises forevermore in our home.

The following was delivered to the Concordia Historical Institute St. Louis, MO, September 30, 2014

The Lutheran Church—Missouri Synod, Western Highlands,
Papua New Guinea
1948-1972

Blessed By the Lord Led By the Spirit

By Eunice Redeker Hausler,
serving PNG from 1959—1973 as a Missionary Teacher
(While there is some duplication to the above, we are relaying this text in its entirety)

To be a missionary, I have seen one needs a lot of training. God did this for me. I grew up on a farm near Shattuc, IL. This gave me the ability to work hard and live with much, with little, and with whatever was provided. I went to a one room school which gave the skills to have to work on your own and learn as much as you could when other classes were being taught. High School gave me the opportunity to increase my knowledge. I had to work hard in my studies as my grade school background was not the best. I also worked for a family to make enough money to stay in (high) school. College at CTC, RF, greatly expanded my vision and knowledge. CTC was a very Christian place to be and the staff and students helped my faith grow in my Lord and Savior, Jesus Christ. I again had to work various jobs to stay in school and also, stay up late at night to finish my homework. After two years and two summers, I took a call to teach in a one room school in Westcliffe, CO. You could teach without a degree at that time. I had to work hard as an administrator and teacher of Grades one through eight. I returned to CTC at the end of the school year with a lot of experience. I finished college after one year and two summers with a B.S. in Ed. Degree. My Call then was to Hope Lutheran School, Levittown, PA. Rev. Walter A. Maier, Jr., was the Pastor. With God's guidance and pastor's help we started a school with 32 students in Grade 1 and 2 and 18 in kindergarten. I thanked God for all the past experience as this was a monumental task. After three years we had Kindergarten—Grade 5, with 120 students and were building a school. We had started in the basement of the church. All this was because of God's great blessing on this place.

Then the Call came for me to go to the Western Highlands of New Guinea to start a Girl's School. The Lord led me to accept this Call. I went to summer school at Concordia Seminary, St. Louis, Missouri (STL), and was on the mission field in New Guinea by September 1959. Landing in a very primitive culture was a shock to my system. I began by learning the language. We learned Pidgin English first as it was a good in-between language. I learned some Enga (the native language), but my teaching was to be in English so I did not become proficient in it. We were going to start the school at Yaibos, where Rev. Ian and Enid Kleinig, missionaries from Australia, were stationed. I lived in their home. Enid helped me a lot to learn the new culture and the education going on at the Yaibos boy's school. I learned customs of the Enga people which was so unlike anything I had ever experienced. The first weekend I was there, we walked up one mountain then to the top of another mountain and down to the valley where we had a baptism of over 200 people. They were dressed in white and what an inspiring experience that was! Praise God that the work our missionaries before me, had done a lot of preaching and teaching the Word of God and that was bearing fruit. Hundreds of people were coming to the Lord and being baptized. They preached from 1948—1957 before they had the first baptism, because they wanted to be sure the people were grounded in the Spirit of the true God, the Holy Spirit, and not still thinking of Him as one of their animalistic spirits.

After summing up the situation about girls having a separate school from boys, I asked Dr. Willard Burce, chairman of the Mission, who along with Rev. Otto Hintze were the first missionaries there in 1948, about combining our girl's school with the boys' school at Pausa. Pausa had been started about three years earlier. He sent me to the coast to investigate what the other Lutheran Missions were doing. I found they were putting their girls into boys' schools as a saving on staff and school buildings. So I was sent to Pausa to work with Ken Bauer and Dale Busse at the boys school. We were adding girls to the student body. I lived in the Busses' living room for 8 months until a small house was built for me. During this time, I had a severe bout with malaria, but recovered after some complications. It was difficult to add girls to our school as girls were to marry and bring pigs to the tribe. The dowery for girls was many pigs and pigs were the wealth of the tribes. If the girls went to school, they may not marry but do other work. We got three girls the first year, then 14 the second year, but it was a struggle. Thanks to our LCMS Missionaries, in conjunction with the New Guinean Pastors, who helped encourage their congregations to send us girls.

Life in New Guinea was hard in those days. New Guinea at that time was separated from Papua. Not until 1981, when they received independence did the two countries unite as one, PNG. We had jeeps as our transportation and the roads were not good. Jeeps were not to be used for personal pleasures, so we were pretty isolated and I used to walk to the hospital to mingle with the nurses there. (This was about a 5 mile walk one way.) *We lived in bush houses, no running water, and outhouses. Thank God, I could adjust easily as I had that as a child. At first, I had a hard time seeing the natives as people. They lived in bush houses with dirt floors and no furnishings, only a fire in the center and women had pigs living in the back of their houses. Their conditions were worse than our animals in the US. The first year was hard adjusting to such a different way of life, but as ever, I prayed a lot and trusted God that He was using me to bring the Gospel to these people. After a while, the students and people became very dear to me. I have found wherever you go, "love" is only given us by Jesus. His love flows into us and then out of us. As we see His great love for us by coming to earth, suffering and dying for us, we can share this love, which is beyond human understanding, with any peoples. Loving them broke down barriers and helped us reach these people where they were. I have to say, God gave wisdom also, because we kept pleading at His throne for it. We often came to blocks in the road, not knowing how to turn, and He supplied our needs. There were no textbooks so we wrote books and they had to meet the needs of our students. Later the government had some books, especially in English. After 13 years there, I can truly say that our Pausa School which became St. Paul's Lutheran High School, was a good school with high standards, and well known amongst the Highland schools.*

Now how does all this connect to CHI? Well, our goal here at CHI is to record the history of our church for people now and for generations to come, so they can see and hear how God has worked among His people and through His people. The people of PNG are part of the great band of people whom God claims as His own. The great number of people that came to the Lord during the 13 years that I was there, resounds as a great number that learned to praise and believe in our marvelous God by the power of the Holy Spirit. These people will join you and me before the throne of God on the last day. The singing and praising they do resounds like a mighty chorus before the throne of God. In 2013, we had a delegation of 17 people come from PNG to our PNG reunion. Our Mission staff still get together every other year. These 17 people came to thank us for having brought the Gospel to them. Ten of them were our former students, who now are doctors, nurses, lawyers, pastors, teachers, and leaders in government. They informed us that their government is very Christian and their parliament begins with prayer every morning. One of our men from the Western Highlands is the leader in the parliament. You should have heard the witnessing and praising of our God that they did! They were witnesses to us and together we lifted up songs, hymns and beautiful encouraging messages in the Lord to each other. This is the legacy of PNG has at CHI—that a people who did not know God, now know Him and beautiful music is rising to heaven from that remote island. This in the archives of CHI will be an inspiration to future generations to not be afraid, but with joy and confidence in the Lord, they might continue to carry the Gospel to wherever the Lord calls them – because God will go before them and He will bless His Word on the hearts of people everywhere and then these people also can praise the wonderful God that we know. This God reveals Himself in His Word and wherever this Word is proclaimed. It has power to save people everywhere. We must "go," that is the secret!

The archives of CHI will reveal this to generations yet to come and encourage them on to spread the "Good News" of the Gospel to all the world. A cloud of witnesses will bear this out on the last day when our Lord and Savior returns to take us all to our eternal home.

Chapter 1

The 1950's

(The following give us an idea of Eunice in the years preceding her mission to New Guinea.)

Annual Declaration

August 4, 1952

I solemnly declare that I purpose to serve my Lord and His Church as a Christian Day School Teacher.

In order to prepare myself for this high calling I have enrolled at:

CONCORDIA TEACHERS COLLEGE, 7400 AUGUSTA St., RIVER FOREST, ILL.

If at any time my purpose should change or circumstances make it impossible for me to continue in this resolve, I will immediately give written notification of this fact to the president of the college and I will comply with the regulations of the Synod concerning payment of tuition.

Signed: Eunice Redeker
Countersigned: Mrs. Anna Redeker

(As we researched material to include in this book, the reader will see a large number of entries directed to Eunice's brother Richard, his wife Florence, and son Charles. Given the number of extant letters communicated with them, they are included to give a fuller picture of Eunice and the circumstances in her life. There is no reason to believe Eunice communicated with them any more frequently than other members of her family, however, very few of those communications were able to be accessed).

CTC, RF
(Postcard - 2-cent stamp)

September 10, 1952

To Richard and Florence,

Finally getting around to writing to you. Concordia is really wonderful: I like it so much here already. Everybody is so nice. We have 10 girls in our room. We just got back about an hour ago from a Camping Picnic in the Forest Preserves. Last night we had a Choral Fest in front of the Ad. Building, then a short devotion. Monday night I baby sat and Sunday night we had chapel. The days have been kept busy with tests and Tues. noon the women of Grace church served us a delicious luncheon after which we toured Grace School. How are you both and Charles? Will write more later. You write too.

Love, Eunice

CTC-RF
(Card–3 cent stamp)

Oct. 18, 1952

Dear Richard, Florence and Charles,

I suppose by now you are thinking I had forgotten about you but that's not it. I have been so busy with studies, work etc., I just haven't been writing any letters. Sorry I forgot your birthday (Richard) *but I hope you had a Happy one and wish you many, many more. Too bad I couldn't "pinch" you.*

By now I like it here fine. I've been seeing a little of Chicago lately and I sure didn't imagine Chicago to be as big as it is and I've only seen a small portion. Last Sunday we went to the Museum of Science and Industry, very interesting but we didn't get to see as much as we would have liked too. Wednesday was tour day and I went with the group that went to the Oriental Institute and University of Chicago. I got to see an Egyptian mummy, something I have always wanted to see. The Rockefeller Chapel is enormous but really beautiful. Florence, I suppose you've seen all these places already.

Today Agnes (Carlyle high school friend who also attended CTC) *and I went to the Field Museum and Shedd Aquarium. We again didn't get to see nearly all of it but it's really amazing and educational to visit these.*

I've been studying quite hard this week as I had several tests. I also work at Gabriel's Tea Room on Sunday or three nights a week as Waitress. I like it there as the tips are real good.

Next weekend is Homecoming. Friday night Bonfire Party, Saturday morning Parade, and Saturday evening the Banquet. Also Saturday afternoon Homecoming football game, Concordia vs. Aurora. I like to watch football since I've learned a little about the game.

Last night we had a Spook Party. Had a swell time. Everybody dressed up and there were some wonderful costume ideas. Three movies were shown and the last one was a Halloween one as it was filled with ghosts and skeletons. We also went through the spook house and I was really hoarse when I got out of there, screamed all the way through.

Grace Lutheran Church is celebrating its Golden Anniversary this week. They're having a Pageant in our gym. I like Dr. Giesemann very much but I like Pastor Erwin Paul at St. John's, Melrose Park a little better so we've been going to church there the past two Sundays and are going to communion there tomorrow.

How are you all? I hope fine. I also hope Charles is well again as mother wrote he had a bad cold and you had to give him shots. I guess you've gotten your wheat all sowed by now.

Well, I had better close as I have a lot of things to do besides all of my ironing.

Bye for now and write soon.

Love your sis, Eunice

P.S. I was sorry to hear your Dad (Florence's father and Eunice's 7th & 8th grade teacher at Bethlehem, Ferrin) *fell and broke 3 ribs. Hope he's getting well again.*

CTC, RF

June 29, 1953

Dear Florence,

Well, I finished the workshop course. It was very interesting. Now Summer School which of course will require more studying. How's everything? I guess you're kept plenty busy with the garden, the house and taking care of Charles. Tell him and Rich "Hello." I guess he's really getting big and doesn't remember me. Well, I must close and will see you soon.

Love your sis, Eunice

Westcliffe, CO

September 18, 1954

Dear Richard, Florence, and Charles,

Well, how's all with you? I'm fine and like it here very much. The mts. are so beautiful especially now the aspen are turning yellow. Amongst the green balsam and pine, it is very beautiful. Everyone says, however, it is much more beautiful when the mts. are snowcapped.

I have a lovely place to stay, with two widows next door to school. I like teaching fine. I have 15 pupils. It isn't a life of roses, but it is very enjoyable and such a thrill to work with little ones. Pastor Kretzmann is leaving to Oxford, NE so that makes it kind of rough for me. They are so nice to me and I will miss them. Not to have a Pastor is hard up here because Pastor Riske of Canon City, our nearest Pastor, who is our vacancy pastor, is 40 miles away. We went there today for Mission Festival since we didn't have services. It certainly is a scenic drive. We drove up to the Royal Gorge bridge, the world's highest swinging bridge, also we drove over the skyline drive from which we could see Canon City. It sure is amazing and beautiful. You can sure see the Almighty God's wonderful handiwork and He is still the best artist.

I've been up in the mts. several times, twice fishing. I love to climb them and the altitude doesn't bother me. I take advantage of all chances I get to see something.

The train ride here was a real thrill. I slept all night, however, on the Missouri Pacific. About froze with the air conditioner on. I had my circle skirt so covered up with half of it. Pueblo is a pretty big place. What I saw looked like an Indian settlement. Their houses were built up on little mounds-like.

How's Charles? Tell him "Hi." How's your sis, Edith? Did she arrive in Germany and how does she like it? I guess, -oh yes, today is Ralph's wedding. (Both siblings of Florence's). *I hope it's as nice out there as it is here. Well, bye. Write sometime.*

Loads of Love, Your sis, Eunice

Westcliffe, CO
(Along with a birthday card for Richard, the following:)

October 15, 1954

Dear Richard, Florence, and Charles,

Just a line as I'm kind of busy as usual. I suppose you've heard Pastor Kretzmann is gone now so I'm a "Jack of all trades." All meetings I seem to have to attend. Believe me leading topics is a rather difficult job, but the Lord certainly is with me and helping in every need. I even got stuck with making the Sunday Bulletins. Boy, I must say: I'll be experienced when I'm through here.

Sorry I forgot your Birthday Rich, but I'll try to do better next time. I wish you a belated "Happy Birthday" and many, many more. May God Bless and Keep you through the coming year. I was sorry to hear about your accident. I hope you're well again and no ill effects left to bother you.

Deer season opened here today. All men are in the mts. hunting deer. It's a big occasion as all boys, 14 and over who have a license, got out of school today. Sunday a group of us women are going up in the mts. too. The men are going to cook dinner for us. Let's hope they catch a deer or we'll starve. Ha Ha.

Last Tues. I caught a 9 lb. 2 oz. fish. I could hardly hold him. I just went in and picked him out of the water. Mr. Rankin took a picture of me with it so when it's developed, I'll send it to you. You ought to live here. You can just go in and pick out a big fish like that. Ha Ha.

Last Friday we had our first P.T.A. meeting. The children put on a program. Also 3 of our high school students play band instruments so they gave us a little variety. Then we had refreshments and closed with a vesper service. The parents seemed to have enjoyed it. It certainly is helpful to talk your problems over directly with the parents.

I like teaching just fine. I have a swell group of youngsters. We do so many things, of course they have to study hard too, that comes first. This week I gave I.Q. Achievement and personality tests. Giving them is OK, but oh.... the grading, I still don't have all the percentiles figured yet.

The people are all so helpful and good to me. If it weren't for them, I couldn't do all.

Florence, Mrs. Kretzmann was surprised to hear you were my sister-in-law. She said you were such a swell person and good seamstress. Of course, I told her I knew that better than she did! I hated to see the Kretzmann's leave.

Well, I must close. Write sometime. Rich, I wish you loads of more "Happy Birthdays". Tell Charles "Hi."

I saw Ralph and Ruthie's wedding picture. I imagine it was pretty, would like to have seen it.

Bye now, Love, Your sis, Eunice

Westcliffe, CO

Apr 5, 1955

To Richard, Florence, Charles,

An Easter card: "Wishing you all a Joyous and Blessed Easter."

Love, Eunice

Westcliffe, CO

May 17, 1956

Happy Birthday Little Sweetheart (Charles-age 4)

(In addition to card, a Service folder from the Sunday Worship Service, listing the vacancy pastor and "Miss Eunice Redeker, School Teacher" and the following:)

Just a line to tell you I'm fine and hope you all are too. Sorry I skipped Charles' birthday. Hope he had a very "Happy Birthday." Am anxious to see him and you too.

I am always kept so busy I never get time to write. I'm so far behind now I hate to start answering.

Yesterday we went to Pueblo for Sunday School Teachers Institute. We've been doing some camping in the mts. I love it. I'll miss these mts., my children and the people here, but I'll be anxious to see you all. They're begging the socks off me to stay but I feel I should finish school next year. They are getting a Pastor here so they won't be completely out.

Well, I'll be seeing you soon. Hope you are all fine.

Bye, Bye, and God Bless you, Love, Eunice

CTC, RF

July 12, 1956

Dear Florence,

Tonight I just happened to look through my birthday book and realized I missed your birthday. So sorry but hope you had a very happy one and may God grant you a blessed and happy year ahead.

As usual I'm kept so very busy. Am taking Children's Literature this summer, which will be so helpful. We are required to read and evaluate 100 Children's books. I love it. I also took the Kindergarten-Primary Workshop. Miss Marella Mensing, author of the Christian Kindergarten, was our instructor and was tremendous. Her Christian philosophy of teaching was a wonderful influence.

Was sorry you didn't get to spend more time with us when we were home. Hope Charles is better and full of pep as ever. Betty is getting along fine although getting use to it all was a little hard at first. (Sister Betty attended CTC, RF also).

Pastor Maier has been very faithful about writing and keeping me all informed about Levittown. I'm looking forward to going but realize the great responsibility. One assurance I have though and that is "I can do all things through Christ who strengtheneth me." Philippians 4:13.

Must close for now. Hope you can make it when I graduate. Hope all are fine. God bless you all and grant you many more Happy Birthdays Florence.

Your loving Sis, Eunice

CTC, RF

July 26, 1956

Mr. and Mrs. Richard Redeker and son,

The Graduating Class of Concordia Teacher College announces its Commencement Exercises Thursday evening, August second, Nineteen hundred fifty-six at eight o'clock in The Quadrangle.

Eunice

From the Sunday Bulletin of Bethlehem Lutheran Church, July 29, 1956
Ferrin, Illinois (Home Church of Eunice)

Miss Eunice Redeker, daughter of Mr. & Mrs. Richard Redeker, Sr., will be graduated from Concordia Teachers College, River Forest, Illinois, this coming Thursday evening, August 2nd, at 8:00 p.m. Bethlehem Congregation is invited to attend the commencement exercises. Eunice has received and accepted a call to teach in Hope Lutheran

School, Levittown, Pennsylvania. We ask that God will grant Eunice His choicest blessing in her new field of labor.

August 2, 1956
Concordia Teachers College, River Forest, IL
The Summer Commencement

THE PROCESSIONAL
THE INVOCATION
THE HYMN OF INTERCESSION

1. Dear Lord, to Thy true servants give
The grace to Thee alone to live.
Once bound by sin, but saved by Thee,
They go to set the pris'ners free,
The Gospel message to proclaim
That men may call upon Thy name.
2. They gladly go at Thy command
To spread Thy Word o'er sea and land.
Be Thou with them and make them strong
To heal sin's ills, to right the wrong.
Thou rulest over wind and wave,
And mighty is Thine arm to save.
3. When all their labor seems in vain,
Revive their sinking hopes again;
And when success crowns what they do,
Oh, keep them humble, Lord, and true
Until before Thy judgment seat
They lay their trophies at Thy feet.

THE ADDRESS
THE CHOIR: "What God Does That Is Noble Done".........Luvaas
THE PRESENTATION OF THE GRADUATES

THE AWARDING OF THE DIPLOMAS AND DEGREES
THE MESSAGE OF THE PRESIDENT
THE PRAYERS
THE BENEDICTION
THE HYMN OF PRAISE

1. Praise to the Lord, the Almighty, the King of creation!
O my soul, praise Him, for He is thy Health and Salvation!
Join the full throng;
Wake, harp and psalter and song;
Sound forth in glad adoration!
2. Praise to the Lord, who o'er all things so wondrously reigneth,
Who, as on wings of an eagle, uplifteth, sustaineth.
Hast thou not seen
How thy desires all have been
Granted in what he ordaineth?
3. Praise to the Lord, who hath fearfully, wondrously, made thee;
Health hath vouchsafed and, when heedlessly falling, hath stayed thee.
What need or grief
Ever hath failed of relief?
Wings of His mercy did shade thee.
4. Praise to the Lord, who doth prosper thy work and defend thee,
Who from the heavens the streams of His mercy doth send thee.
Ponder anew
What the Almighty can do,
Who with His love doth befriend thee.
5. Praise to the Lord! Oh, let all that is in me adore Him!
All that hath life and breath, come now with praises before Him!
Let the Amen
Sound from His people again;
Gladly for aye we adore Him.

THE RECESSIONAL

From the Nashville (IL) Journal

August 9,1956

"Mr. and Mrs. Wilbert Redeker of here, Mr. and Mrs. Richard Redeker Sr., Mrs. Paul Tyberendt and Mrs. Richard Redeker Jr., all of Ferrin attended the graduation of Miss Eunice Redeker at Concordia Teachers College of River Forest on Thursday evening. She received her diploma and B. S. in Education in the class of 31 (graduates).

Miss Eunice Redeker left for Levittown Pa. Friday evening where she accepted a call as teacher and organist at the Hope Lutheran church there. She is the daughter of Mr. and Mrs. Richard Redeker Sr. of Ferrin."

Levittown, PA

August 24, 1956

Dear Richard, Florence and Charles,

Really, I haven't forgotten you it's just a matter of being kept so busy not knowing where to turn.

As you probably know I like it here fine. People are wonderful to me. I have a lovely place to stay, a very consecrated Pastor to work with. The Lord is very good to me, I still marvel at the unbelievable blessings. Serving the Lord and especially teaching His little lambs is a great privilege and pleasure.

Florence and Rich, thanks so much for the gift you gave me. Florence how cute of you to put the little doggie in my suitcase. I got a bang out of him when unpacking. Most of all Flo, thanks for your wonderful note, I read it several times on my train ride here. Could only thank God for a sister like you, and above all who understands so well. The past two weeks I've been busy working on things which go with the organization of school.

I'm in a very historical section of the U.S. here. This is George Washington territory. Saw Washington Crossing, Lookout Tower and other historical points. Also got into New York City, was on top of the Empire State building and saw quite a bit of New York. One day we were at Beach Haven on the Atlantic Ocean. Had great fun jumping and diving into the waves. Had to be careful, however, for the undertow.

Pennsylvania is a very beautiful state. We are very close to the Artist's territory here along the Delaware River.

Levittown is quite different. 17,000 homes, almost 80,000 people. The homes are of 4 types, all are simple, have lovely large lawns, and very nice. People here from all over the U.S. which causes it to be a very friendly place.

Florence so glad you came up for graduation. You certainly helped make it a wonderful occasion.

Hope you are all fine and by now your busy summer work should be calming down. Suppose you're in the peach business about now. I remember those days; they're wonderful though when those cold winter days arrive.

Well must close. May He who never slumbers or sleeps keep His watchful eye ever over You and preserve you till we meet again!

Write Soon.

Your loving Sis, Eunice

P.S. Thanks again so much for all.

Levittown, PA
(On personalized stationery!)

October 8, 1956

Dear Richard, Happy Birthday,

Hi! How are you? I'm fine only busy as usual. School is coming fine. The Lord has marvelously guided and directed me. It is quite a responsibility. People here have to be shown the value of a Christian Day School.

People here are very good to me. We've been having real fall weather, lots of rain. The leaves are beautiful now.

Am in a hurry, have a meeting to prepare for this evening so will close.

Hope all of you are well. God bless you and keep you.

Have a "Happy Birthday" Richard. And wishing you many, many more.

Your loving Sis, Eunice

Levittown, PA
(Form Letter-1st part)

December 18, 1956

Dear Friends,

May the joy of our Savior's wonderous birth fill you all with peace and hope this Christmas!

Greetings from the East! I am certainly very happy out here, it's a wonderful experience, and am teaching 20 little lambs in Grades 1 and 2 of our new Christian Day School. With a large "Building for Christ" program in action, we hope to, the Lord willing, soon build a new school, parsonage and church, which we need very much due to the fact that we now only have our Parish Building. There are many souls to win here, the harvest is white, since Levittown is an entirely new city, with people many of which are without a church. Pastor Walter A. Maier, Jr., is a man filled with great zeal to do the Lord's work and is by God's grace bringing in many people. At present he has 30 in his Adult instruction class and in his last class were 34 who were confirmed, some baptized. Since Levittown is populated with young couples we have many, many children, very few teenagers. Our Walther League (LCMS Youth Organization), *however, in three or four years will be well on its way.*

The Levittown homes are quite different, there are four types. They were built in mass production, therefore are not as sturdy as those I was use to, however, they are very comfortable.

We are now busy on our Christmas Program which is Friday, 8:00 P.M. December 21. The children are quite excited and really in the Christmas spirit at this time. Our Sunday School program is Sunday, December 23. 400 children are enrolled in our Sunday School.

Due to the very crowded schedule yet a most interesting one, I find it impossible to write to all of you individually, therefore to give you a brief insight into work here am sending this little note.

Wishing all "A Blessed Christmas – a Joyful and Happy New Year"!

(Personal note added)
Hi Rich, Flo, and Charles!

How are you? Fine here only loaded down with duties, will be glad to shove some of them on Tom Friday. He's playing the organ for me which is a big help.

We've been having a lot of rain, today was the first sunshine this week. No snow yet.

How's Charles? Can imagine he's a big boy by now.

Must close for now. God bless you and keep you.

We'll be thinking of you all Christmas!

Much love, Your Sis, Eunice

Levittown, PA
Greetings at Christmas (Form Letter)

December 9, 1957

Once again may the good news of our Savior's birth fill your hearts with peace, hope, comfort and joy this blessed Christmas tide.

My desire is to write to all of you with a personal note, but since this is not possible at this time I will try to include some of our Levittown news in this way.

We are now in the second year of our Hope Lutheran School. By God's grace we now have three grades and an increased enrollment. We have our classes in the basement of our Parish Building and our kindergarten meets in the back of the church auditorium, which is the upstairs of our Parish Building. Plans are now underway for our new school building which we pray and hope will be partially completed by September, 1958. Our Sunday School now numbers an enrollment of five hundred, and here also we very much are in need of added space. We are now calling our second teacher and so are moving forward to the upbuilding of our hoped for eight-grade school.

All of you most likely heard about our colored family, who moved into Levittown during August. My folks were visiting me at this time. It was quite an unusual uproar and the mob action very unnecessary. As of now all is very calm and the family is still living here.

During October we had the Preaching-Teaching-Reaching Mission here in the Philadelphia area. Hope had very inspiring results. 247 calls were completed and 478 persons contacted by 155 of our lay visitors. 30 persons were gained for adult instruction; 14 desired membership by transfer or profession of faith. 43 children for Sunday School and 9 persons for baptism. This was a busy but most blessed week. We called on the unchurched five evenings, October 6-10. We who know our Lord and Savior can only thank and praise Him for this knowledge and pray that we will be preserved in this faith until He calls us to be with Him in our eternal home.

On November 1, I left 23 Peachtree Lane, where I had stayed alone in one of our member's home while they were in Texas on duty for a year. Now I'm living in our larger Levittown homes with five public school teachers. As you can imagine, there's never a quiet moment here. It's most helpful to be able to talk over the day's school experiences with fellow teachers.

During the latter part of November, Dr. Paul Maier and his mother were here visiting Pastor Maier and family. Paul had just returned from his studies at the Old Heidelberg in Germany. We *reviewed many of his slides of Europe and the Holy Land. Maybe you remember his articles in <u>This Day</u> during the spring of '55.*

May all of you enjoy a truly blessed Yuletide season and a happy, successful, and joyous New Year.

Sincerely, Eunice

Thought this might have some news you didn't get! Will see you soon! (Personal note added).

(The following is concerning the incident mentioned in Eunice's Dec. 9, 1957, letter as reported in the Baltimore Sun, August 20, 1997 edition. Due to licensing restrictions, we can only relay the first 10% of the article here. The reader is HIGHLY encouraged to Google the title and read the entire article. It is highly pertinent to the world of 2023 and the racism of today.)

Trauma of Levittown Integration Remembered History: In August 1957, an African-American family moved to Deepgreen Lane and was greeted by a mob screaming racial epithets and making threats.

By Lacy McCrary

PHILADELPHIA—PHILADELPHIA - Daisy Myers vividly remembers the rocks through the windows, the taunts and name-calling and cross-burnings and the day-and-night blaring of "Old Black Joe" that greeted her arrival as a member of the first African-American family in Levittown, Pa., 40 years ago.

Memories of nights, more than a week of them, in which a mob that was estimated from 200 to 1,000 people gathered along Deepgreen Lane in the Dog Hollow section screaming racial epithets, throwing Molotov cocktails and yelling threats.

But she quickly dismisses those memories. She says that she prefers to remember the positives that came out of those violent summer days in August 1957.

"I look back on it as not a bad time in my life. With all of my schooling [two master's degrees], I would never have learned as much about human nature as I did then, and I wouldn't have met such fine people like Martin Luther King, Pearl Buck and Jackie Robinson." …

Pub Date: 8/21/97

(Envelope and Stationery: Letter head of Hope Lutheran Church-handwritten letter)

March 23, 1957

Dear Florence, Richard, and Charles,

Was so happy for your detailed letter today, so good to really know what's going on. Mother's letters have been very vague as she seems to be in such a hurry. Certainly, you have had many trials, illnesses, and bereavements lately. Was so shocked to hear of (…) (a very close friend and neighbor to Richard & Florence) *sudden death, just doesn't seem possible. All I can say is, "Let us glory in the Lord, our Maker, Creator, who has made us and whose we are, certainly, He knows all things best." We don't understand now but we shall some day when we shall be with Him. What a time for this to happen-while we are celebrating our Savior's suffering and death for us, He has removed our sins and then by His glorious resurrection we know that we to shall someday live, forever with Him in that bliss. Certainly, it happening at this time should add comfort, courage, and strength.*

My prayers have been with (niece) *and that the Lord would do what He sees best. Will she require a kidney operation? Am also concerned about the very high temperature.*

Was quite surprised to hear about (…) and Aunt (…) . We never know what life holds but we must through much trial and tribulation enter into the kingdom of God.

I received a Call this past Wednesday, to teach grades 3 and 4 in Danville, IL. We're having a meeting tomorrow on it. I haven't made up my mind definitely as yet. A letter from Tom this P.M. gave me very little help. As I see it, the Lord is telling me to stay here.

I'm living in a lovely home, all furnishings were left while the (...) went to Texas for a year. Mr. (...) is an engineer and was called there for a year to construct a building. Have lots of room so come see me!

Yes, Florence, I am most happy here., the Lord has been with me, wondrously sustained and guided me. School is coming along well, and certainly look forward to being with my 26 little ones each day, leading them closer to Him who loves them.

As you can imagine I'm very anxious to see you all. My family is still very dear to me, and I think of you all every day. Living out East here is quite different, so compact, rush, rush, and very expensive. I prefer the West. Many souls here to be won, a Great mission challenge! People are wonderful, very hospitable.

Am so anxious to see Charles, can imagine he has grown so much. Will also be looking forward to seeing my little nephews I've never seen.

We had a taste of spring but this week it's been back to wintery weather. We really have had a mild winter, however.

And so thanks again Florence for your wonderful and most welcome letters. Sorry I didn't write sooner but am just kept so busy. Will be telling you all in a few weeks—God-willing. A big hug for Charles and you all. Excuse handwriting-am perked up here in a chair writing on a book!

My love to you all, Eunice

Levittown, PA
(With Birthday card)

July 1, 1957

Dear, Florence, Richard, and Charles,

Happy Birthday, Flo, just hope you have a very happy day and wishing God's richest blessings in the year ahead.

How's everything? Have been hearing of all the rain and tornado weather you've been having. Have you been able to get any crops in at all?

We finished Vacation Bible School last Friday. Had an enrollment of 355 children. Pastor was gone last week for a conference at Camp Pioneer, N.Y., so I was left in charge. Am happy it's all over, truly an experience and a wonderful mission opportunity. I also have been doing some calling on the unchurched, but will more fully this month. This is certainly so necessary; our prospect file is filled. How dark and hopeless are the lives of those who don't know the Lord Jesus.

Was in Bronxville, N.Y. this weekend for Meg's, my roommate last year, wedding. Enjoyed it much, saw many old friends, and saw our prep school there. Meg's father is Pres. of Concordia, Bronxville.

We've been having very hot and humid weather until Sat. A cool breeze hit us and has stayed. The humidity is terrific here.

How's Charles? Such a wonderful little boy, wish I could see you all more often. Probably won't get home in Aug., since I'm going to be at camp as Walther League Counselor one week and also two of my girlfriends are coming out. Why don't you come too?

Am busy now getting rid of (or trying to) Japanese beetles, they're so destructive. Otherwise, I'm keeping up with house and lawn fairly well, keeps me hopping.

Well have 37 children next year in Grades 1-2-3. Am struggling to hold the enrollment down to that amt.

The Lord cares for you!

Much love to you all, Eunice.

(Postcard of the Liberty Bell, Philadelphia, PA)
(Below are other letters {See Chapter 2} written by Eunice's mother with an explanation of her language background).

August 22, 1957

Dear Richard, Florence, and Charles,

We here at Eunice. We all OK. The plane ride was nice. We got dinner on plane. It was real nice.

With love, Mom, Dad, Luther (Redeker)

Levittown, PA

July 18, 1958

Dear, Florence, Richard, and Charles,

(With Birthday card-With note on the card:) *The reason I'm thinking of Birthdays is because three of the families-with the family I'm staying with, gave me a surprise party last night. They said I'd never tell them when my birthday is, they were just going to surprise: so nice of them. They gave me a lovely Concordance Bible and half-slip.*

Greetings from me. It seems so long since I've heard from you or written to you. Time just flies by so fast. So sorry I skipped your birthdays, but guess I just haven't been giving any thought to what day it is. Each day seems to hold so many things to be done.

Am enjoying school very much. I am taking two helpful courses. Elementary School Guidance and School Administration. It's a new experience to be attending a University. Guess I'm prejudice, but CTC has so much more in every way.

The Voter's approved a plan for a 4-room school last Monday PM, so now we're looking forward to the real thing which should be ready for use fall of '59. Our teacher, Bessie Pakan, will be here Aug. 1. I knew her at CTC so look forward to her being here.

We've having lovely weather, a little humid at times but nothing to complain about. My classes are in an air-conditioned building so that means a lot.

Have been a little concerned about our situation in the Middle East. Russia certainly has herself set and is watching cautiously. Certainly, pray they will settle the whole thing without actual fighting.

The Lord again called home so suddenly one of your neighbors. It's so hard to believe, but the Lord knows all things best.

Can imagine you've been quite busy. How was the harvesting this year? Is Charles enjoying it? Certainly would be a joy to see you all, but I felt I needed the schooling this summer and that doesn't leave any free time. We had VBS immediately after school was out, then Summer School and the day after school, I go to Walther League Camp for a week. I am a counselor for it, they always need them so I felt I should help. I love the activities. After camp only a week to get ready for school as we have Principal's conference in Buffalo, NY the last week in Aug.

Well, I must close for now. I do hear how you are occasionally from mother. Hope you have a very "Happy Birthday" Florence, and may the Lord grant you His richest blessing through the coming year. Also, Charles, by now he will wonder about getting a birthday greeting. The Lord be with you and keep you in His loving care.

Much love, Eunice

Levittown, PA (Form Letter)

December 1958

Greetings on our Savior's Birthday!

As once again we raise our hearts and voices in praise and thanks to God for His abundant grace and mercy in showing His great love for us by sending His only Son into the world to redeem us, we pray that God will give to us a deeper understanding, greater joy and brighter Christmas than we have ever known. As the Shepherds, let us worship Him and tell of Him to others; as the angels, let us sing praises; and as the Wisemen, let us worship, adore and offer to Him our gifts.

During this year many rich experiences as well as abundant blessings have been enjoyed. Hitting some of its highlights are these: ---The last of our '56-'57 school-year was a busy time since we worked on an operetta, "The Children of Mother Goose." It was given at the auditorium of a neighboring school and the children had a good lesson on co-operating and working together. In April we received the good news that our Synod's Board of Assignments, through the Lord's direction, was sending to us Miss Bessie Pakan of Boyceville, Wisconsin, graduate of CTC, RF, to be added to our school staff. Through this blessing we were able to add grade four this year. We also, through the Lord's direction, came into contact with Mrs. Edith von Kornya, a teacher from Germany last spring when she came to visit our school and observe our teaching. She enrolled her two children in our school and consented to teach our P.M. Kindergarten session this year as well as teach German to Grades three and four one-half hour a day. Through her efforts we are able to sing three Christmas carols in German at our Children's Christmas Program this year. ---On June 5, our congregation celebrated its fifth anniversary. The Lord blessed this congregation richly in five years. A membership of 350, Sunday School of 500 and Christian Day School of Kindergarten and three grades was the count on this day. ---On June 6, the Concordia Seminary Chorus of Springfield, Illinois, presented a choral concert, stopping here the day before they boarded a plane in New York for England, where along with other European countries they were on tour this year. ---Finally, school was out on June 12, and we entered upon a busy two week Vacation Bible School. Then I attended Temple University, Philadelphia, for five weeks, taking administration courses to help in leadership here this year. During this time I was moving around since, we, the six of us teachers, who lived together last school year, broke up our little home. I stayed with a wonderful Christian family in Yardley, Pa., members of our church. After summer school I was counselor at our Eastern District Walther League Camp, in the Poconos near Arendtsville, Pa. ---After a busy week finishing school preparations for '58-'59, welcoming Bessie, setting up our new home, (four of us teachers rented a home which the congregation has wonderfully furnished for us), I hiked off to Principal's conference at Buffalo, New York, the final week of August. ---Now came a busy September, school starting with an enrollment of ninety-nine, an increase of forty-four children. Trying to fit them in our Parish Hall and basement was a little task but it all is working out. Four teachers now are on our staff. Then in October we rejoiced greatly when our Building for Christ Committee went forward with definite plans on our school building. Four rooms will be completed by fall '59. Also during this month, a series of short illnesses forced me to a little rest after which I was able to fly home to visit my family for a week. It was a beautiful time of the year to be home, the autumn colors, busy harvesting period and being with the folks again, did much to send me back here to continue the work that was waiting. It was also during this time that I was given the opportunity to go into one of our foreign mission fields next year. This is a great joy for me because the Lord is giving me the opportunity to tell His Word to people in foreign lands, who yet do not know Him. At present I am still praying for the Lord's guidance in this endeavor. -----Over the Thanksgiving holidays I toured the New England states, going up to Presque Isle, Maine, with one of my roommates. We also traveled into Canada crossing the St. John's River. The trip was wonderful and the scenery was beautiful. Snow blizzards and 4 degrees below temperatures gave us an experience of real winter, but only added the beauty of snow covered hills, evergreen branches and frozen lakes. This was real Christmas tree country, Aroostook County potato country, as well as a hunter's ideal spot. ---Now our busy Christmas preparation is underway and in all these we rejoice because the Lord has made all this possible by showing us His great love first. Each gift reminds of His great gift; each light of He, Who lights our sin-darkened hearts; each Christmas tree draws our eyes up to Him. ---May you all enjoy a blessed Yuletide season, a joyous and blessed New Year.

Sincerely, Eunice

(Personal note added:)

Hi! Well, here it is Christmas already! Quite busy here, our program is coming along plus many other activities. Our Walter League is giving a pageant.

Will be thinking of you all, esp. Christmas but hope you all have a very "Merry Christmas." Would love to hear Charles say his piece (in the Lutheran day school program). *"God bless you,"*

Much love, Eunice

LCMS, Bd of Missions, STL, MO

2/19/59

Dear Miss Redeker,

I am very happy to inform you that the Board for Missions in Foreign Countries at its meeting on February 16 resolved to issue to you an appointment as teacher in New Guinea. The document is enclosed herewith for your prayerful consideration.

Since you have had the opportunity to speak with Mr. Hinlicky at length about the assignment I shall not add anything regarding it.

You will, of course, be interested in the material considerations provided by the Board. These are stated in the "Missionary Manual" on page 13 ff. It will be good to give the whole Manual a careful reading. Salaries are currently paid at 70% of the U.S. scale. A single person begins at $144.50 a month, but this beginning is figured from the time of your graduation from teachers' college. If we have correct information you will have completed four years of teaching in June and this will entitle you to the first increment, raising the salary to $151.75. While you are still in the U.S.A. this will be $216.50.

One necessary item in your review of this position will be your health. We ask you to have a complete physical examination before you give us your word on the call. Have the doctor send the bill and his examination results to us. The latter will be submitted to our medical examiner for action.

We are also enclosing some personnel information sheets. We are sending you two copies which we ask you to make out and return to us. When it comes to listing the higher schools which you have attended would you, please also indicate the years in which you were at these schools?

Should you accept this appointment, and we sincerely hope you shall, you will be expected to attend the School of Missions this summer. This extends five weeks, ending July 24. During the time of this school there is also excellent opportunity to receive any necessary "shots" and other treatment. We shall begin our paper work required to get into New Guinea then also. We hope that by September 1 you will be able to get underway.

I know you will have many questions and both our business manager, Mr. A. G. Erdmann, and I stand ready to help you in any way we can. We shall be eager to keep in touch with you.

May the Lord then direct your prayerful thinking on this matter.

Very cordially yours,
Herman H. Koppelmann
Acting Executive Secretary

DIPLOMA OF APPOINTMENT

In the name of the Holy Trinity, Father, Son and Holy Ghost. Amen.

THE BOARD FOR MISSIONS IN FOREIGN COUNTRIES OF THE LUTHERAN CHURCH-MISSOURI SYNOD, exercising the authority which God has vested in His Church on earth and which by said Synod is vested in the aforementioned Board, has resolved to appoint you,

Miss Eunice Redeker
of Levittown, Pennsylvania
to be a missionary teacher in New Guinea.

BY THIS APPOINTMENT YOU ARE AUTHORIZED AND OBLIGATED:

To carry on the work of a Christian missionary teacher as this shall be specifically allocated to you by the New Guinea Conference and the Board;

To proclaim the Word of God wherever possible in this your work in its full truth and purity as recorded in the canonical writing of the Old and New Testaments and as professed in the confessional writings of the Evangelical Lutheran Church as contained in the Book of Concord of 1580;

To execute your high calling with all faithfulness and sacrifice, by the gracious help of God, and to show Christ to young and old among the non-Christians and Christians with whom you may come in contact as the only Savior of the fallen human race;

To discharge the functions of your office as a missionary teacher in an evangelical manner, working for the Christian education of the youth, maintaining Christian discipline in accord with Holy Scripture and within the bounds of Christian reason and justice;

To extend your missionary work beyond the school where possible to as many non-Christians as you can reach within the province of your designated missionary labors;

To live in a consistently Christian manner, thereby commending the Gospel of Jesus Christ to every man;

And, as God is a God of peace and good order, the Board pledges you at all times to observe and cultivate true fraternal and friendly relations with your collaborators, being intent upon keeping the unity of the Spirit in the bond of peace; also to co-operate conscientiously with the Board by complying with, and carrying out, the rules now existing, and such as may from time to time be formulated, for the regulation and advancement of our Foreign Mission enterprise.

ON THE OTHER HAND, we, THE BOARD OF MISSIONS IN FOREIGN COUNTRIES, will at all times be mindful of our duty and responsibility to advance the cause of Foreign Missions to the best of our ability and to provide faithfully for your decent maintenance as the conditions in New Guinea and the homeland demand and permit.

God, our Savior, who bought also the heathen with His precious blood and commanded us to preach the Gospel to every creature, make you willing and joyous to go to New Guinea as His messenger of Peace.

May He bless you and make you a blessing unto many according to the riches of His grace! Amen.

In the name and by the authority of THE BOARD FOR MISSIONS IN FOREIGN COUNTRIES OF THE LUTHERAN CHURCH-MISSOURI SYNOD.

Herman H. Kopplemann
Acting Executive Secretary
St. Louis, Missouri
February 19, 1959

Levittown, PA (Form Letter)

February 28, 1959

Greetings to all,

Since many of you have written and asked me to write when I knew and had made a decision on my appointment to one of our foreign mission fields, I am writing this little note to all of you so that you might know my decision and remember me in your prayers. Through much prayer and the Lord's direction I have accepted the appointment to open our first school for girls in our mission field, New Guinea. It is with a heart filled with gratitude to God for this blessed opportunity, that I report to you. At present I feel very inadequate and have many questions but I am working for my Savior, and He, Who has so abundantly blessed me thus far, will go with me to New Guinea. I am only an instrument in His hand, and know, "I can do all things through Christ, Who strengtheneth me." Philippians 4:13

I will be here in Levittown, until June. June 14, a commissioning service is being planned here at Hope Church, where I will retain my membership. Then for five weeks I will attend our school for missionaries at Concordia Seminary, St. Louis, and should be ready to go about, September 1.

Since I still have a very busy schedule here, I knew I would not find the time to write to you all individually, but I do extend to you my cordial greetings, hoping you are all well. It is a joy hearing from many of you and it will be a real joy to hear from you all. May the Lord hold His protecting hand over you.

Very cordially yours, Eunice

Also enclosed was the Hope Lutheran Messenger (The Sunday Church Service Folder) for March 1, 1959 with the following:

<u>MISS REDEKER</u> this past week received and accepted a call to become missionary-teacher at one of our Synodical mission stations among the aborigines in New Guinea, the large island in the Pacific north of Australia—a position for which she made application last fall. Thursday evening she presented to the Board of Parish Education her resignation as teacher in Hope School, effective at the close of the current term, June 5. A service of commissioning for Miss Redeker has been tentatively scheduled at Hope Church for Sunday, June 14. Thereafter she will attend foreign missions' school for five weeks at Concordia Seminary, St. Louis, then leave for New Guinea about September 1. Hope congregation regrets to see our first teacher go from our midst but we commend Miss Redeker for her willingness to undertake this missionary service and pray God will use her mightily in bringing Gospel doctrines to the young in a primitive, pagan South Pacific society.

Board for Missions in Foreign Countries *March 3, 1959*
The Lutheran Church—Missouri Synod
210 North Broadway
Saint Louis 2, Missouri

Attention: Doctor Herman Koppelmann,
Acting Executive Secretary
Gentlemen:

It is with deep humility, heartfelt joy, and sincere gratitude to Almighty God, that I received and now accept the appointment as missionary-teacher in our foreign mission field, New Guinea. I have given the appointment prayerful consideration. Many days, even before I received the appointment, I struggled with the Lord in prayer. Now He has very clearly and plainly shown me to accept this appointment. I pray daily that He will give me the needed abilities, wisdom, knowledge, understanding, courage, health, and strength I will need to carry on the work to which He has called me. I am thankful the Lord is giving me the privilege and opportunity to witness of Him to these people for whom He also died. I trust Him and can say with Paul, "I can do all things through Christ, who strengtheneth me."

I have had my physical examination; the report should reach your office soon.

A letter containing questions of information will be sent your office in the near future.

Thank you for all your help. May the Lord be with you as you carry on in this great work for Him.

In His service,
Miss Eunice A. Redeker, Principal
Hope Lutheran School

(Form Letter) (Letter to Greater Philadelphia area congregations)

Hope Lutheran Church
Mill Creek Parkway & Haines Road
Levittown, Pennsylvania

May 12, 1959

Dear Brother,

Miss Eunice A. Redeker, teacher and acting principal of Hope Lutheran School, Levittown, for the past three years, has accepted a call to become Lutheran missionary-teacher to New Guinea and will be commissioned for this work at a special service in Hope Church on May 24, beginning 4:00 p.m. The Reverend Doctor Herman H. Koppelmann of St. Louis, acting Executive Secretary of Synod's Board for Missions in Foreign Countries, will be speaker on this occasion and officiate at the rite of commissioning.

Hope congregation extends to you and the members of your congregation the cordial invitation to be present at the commissioning service and for the social hour following. Perhaps you will be kind enough to make mention of this service and invitation in your church bulletins the next two Sundays. Thanks much for this courtesy.

This notice is being sent also to our area day school principals, whom the congregation also herewith invites to the commissioning service. We respectfully request that the principals inform the other day school teachers on their staffs about the service and that all teachers who can attend the special worship on May 24 kindly gather in the Hope Church basement by 3:45 p.m., where they may take positions for the formal processional of teachers into the church auditorium at the beginning of service.

At an appropriate place during the rite of commissioning, principal Roy Eberle of Saint Luke's Lutheran School, Croydon, will be asked to offer a few words of greeting and remarks of Christian farewell to Miss Redeker in behalf of the area school teachers (who will be sitting together at the front of the church). Following this, Teacher George Hinlicky—home on furlough from New Guinea—will be asked to address Miss Redeker in behalf of our New Guinea missionary force and relative to the work Miss Redeker plans to undertake in the South Pacific this fall.

It is our hope that the commissioning service will provide a stimulating spiritual experience for all worshipers in attendance. Thank you in advance for your assistance in "getting the people out" on May 24.

In the Savior's service,
Walter A. Maier, Jr. Pastor

(Rev. Maier also apparently had these letters sent to family members, to which Eunice added the following:)

P.S. Wish you could be here. Pastor is sending these to you and area cong.

Will see you soon. Love, Eunice

"Girl Accepts Mission Call to New Guinea" May 23, 1959

(Newspaper Heading in Levittown Newspaper with article similar to that on the Commissioning Service folder {below} with her picture)

Hope Lutheran Church Sunday Bulletin May 24, 1959

"A special service at which Miss Eunice Redeker will be formally commissioned as Lutheran Missionary-Teacher to New Guinea will be held at Hope Church today, beginning 4:00 p.m. Speaker and officiant at the rite of commissioning will be the Reverend Doctor Herman H. Koppelmann of St. Louis, Acting Executive Secretary of the Board for Missions in Foreign Countries, Lutheran Church—Missouri Synod. All our members and friends are invited to participate in the worship on this memorable occasion and to remain for the social hour following in the church basement."

The Service of Commissioning for Miss Eunice A Redeker

May 24, 1959

Hope Lutheran Church, Levittown, Pennsylvania

The Order of the Service

The Prelude: "Solemn Prelude "Gloria Domine"......Noble

The Processional Hymn.........."Come, Thou Almighty King"

1. Come, Thou almighty King,
   Help us Thy name to sing.
   Help us to praise.
   Father all-glorious,
   O'er all victorious,
   Come and reign over us,
   Ancient of Days.

2. Come, Thou Incarnate Word,
   Gird on Thy mighty sword,
   Our prayer attend.
   Come and Thy people bless
   And give Thy Word success;
   Stablish Thy righteousness,
   Savior and Friend!

3. Come, holy Comforter,
   Thy sacred witness bear
   In this glad hour.
   Thou, who almighty art,
   Now rule in ev'ry heart
   And ne'er from us depart,
   Spirit of Pow'r!

4. To the great One in Three
   Eternal praises be
   Hence evermore!
   His sov'reign majesty
   May we in glory see
   And to eternity
   Love and adore! Amen.

The Versicles

Pastor: O Lord, open Thou my lips.
Cong: And my mouth shall show forth Thy praise.
Pastor: Make haste, O God, to deliver me.
Cong: Make haste to help me, O Lord.

The Gloria Patri

The Anthem by the Grade School Children: "Jesus Shall Reign Where'er the Sun"......... Hatton

The Lection.................................... Matthew 28: 16-20

The Versicle

Pastor: But Thou, O Lord, have mercy upon us.
Cong: Thanks be to Thee, O Lord!

The Hymn of Missions...................."Soldiers of the Cross, Arise"

1. Soldiers of the Cross, arise,
Gird you with your armor bright.
Mighty are your enemies,

Hard the battle ye must fight.

2. O'er a faithless, fallen world
Raise your banner in the sky;

Let it float there wide unfurled;
Bear it onward, lift it high.

3. Mid the homes of want and woe,

Strangers to the living Word,

Let the Savior's heralds go,
Let the voice of hope be heard.

4. Where the shadows deepest lie,
Carry truth's unsullied ray;
Where are crimes of blackest dye,
There the saving sign display.

5. To the weary and the worn
Tell of realms where sorrows cease;
To the outcast and forlorn
Speak of mercy and of peace.

6. Guard the helpless, seek the strayed,
Comfort troubles, banish grief;
In the might of God arrayed,
Scatter sin and unbelief.
Amen.

The Sermon: "A Teacher Come From God"...........John 3:2 & 20:21

The Offering (The offering will flow into the mission treasury of the Lutheran Church—Missouri Synod)

The Senior Choir Anthem:
"Jesu, Priceless Treasure"............... ....Crueger-Bach

The Rite of Commissioning

The Hymn of Consecration.................."Take My Life and Let it Be"

1. Take my life and let it be
   Consecrated, Lord, to Thee;
   Take my moments and my days,
   Let them flow in ceaseless praise.

2. Take my hands and let them move

   At the impulse of Thy love;
   Take my feet and let them be
   Swift and beautiful for Thee.

3. Take my voice and let me sing
   Always, only, for my King:
   Take my lips and let them be
   Filled with messages from Thee.

4. Take my silver and my gold,
   Not a mite would I withhold;
   Take my intellect and use
   Ev'ry pow'r as Thou shalt choose.

5. Take my will and make it Thine,
   It shall be no longer mine;
   Take my heart, it is Thine own,
   It shall by Thy royal throne.

6. Take my love, my Lord, I pour
   At Thy feet its treasure store:
   Take myself, and I will be
   Ever, only, all, for Thee. Amen.

The Versicle

Pastor: Let my prayers be set forth before Thee as incense:
Cong: And the lifting up of my hands as the evening sacrifice.

The Nunc Dimittis

Lord, now lettest Thou Thy servant depart in peace according to Thy Word; for mine eyes have seen Thy Salvation, which Thou hast prepared before the face of all people, a Light to lighten the Gentiles and the Glory of Thy people Israel. Glory be to the Father and to the Son and to the Holy Ghost; as it was in the beginning, is now, and ever shall be: world without end. Amen.

The Prayers

The Kyrie

Lord, have mercy upon us.
Christ, have mercy upon us.
Lord, have mercy upon us.

The Lord's Prayer

The Salutation

Pastor: The Lord be with you.
Cong: And with thy spirit.

The Collect for Peace

Cong: Amen.

The Benedicamus

Pastor: Bless we the Lord.
Cong: Thanks be to God.

The Benediction

Cong: Amen.

The Announcements

The Recessional Hymn..............."Hark! The Voice of Jesus Crying"

1. Hark! The voice of Jesus crying,
"Who will go and work today?
Fields are white and harvests waiting,
Who will bear the sheaves away?"
Loud and long the Master calleth,

2. Let none hear you idly saying,
There is nothing I can do,"
While the souls of men are dying
And the Master calls for you.
Take the task He gives you gladly,

Rich reward He offers thee;	Let His work your pleasure be;
Who will answer, gladly saying,	Answer quickly when He calleth,
"Here am I, send me, send me"?	"Here am I, send me, send me!" Amen.

The Postlude: "Triumphal March"..............................Morrison

The Preacher and Officiant at the Rite of Commissioning: The Reverend Doctor Herman H. Koppelmann of Saint Louis, Acting Executive Secretary of the Board for Missions in Foreign Countries, Lutheran Church—Missouri Synod.

The Liturgist: The Reverend Walter A. Maier, Jr., Pastor of Hope Lutheran Church.

The Organist.................................. Mr. Ralph E. Brown

The Directress of the School Children's Choir.........Miss Bessie M. Pakan

The Senior Choir Director.....................Mr. Ernest C. Kosan

A social hour in honor of Miss Redeker will follow in the basement immediately after the close of the service. Everyone in attendance at the commissioning service is invited to be present.

MISS EUNICE A. REDEKER

Miss Eunice A. Redeker was born on a 160-acre farm near Shattuc, Illinois, August 22, 1934, one of eight children, to Mr. and Mrs. Richard G. Redeker. She received her elementary schooling through the fifth grade at Flaherty Public School in Carlyle, and through grades six to eight at Bethlehem Lutheran School in Ferrin, Illinois (Miss Redeker's home congregation is Bethlehem Lutheran Church); obtained her secondary education at Carlyle Community High school in Carlyle; and was student at Concordia Teachers College, River Forest, Illinois, from September 1, 1952, to August 2, 1956, the day she graduated from this institution with a Bachelor of Science Degree in Education. During the academic year 1954-1955 Miss Redeker served as supply teacher at Hope Lutheran School, Westcliffe, Colorado.

Immediately after college graduation Miss Redeker came to Hope Lutheran Church, Levittown, Pennsylvania, where on September 9, 1956, she was inducted into office as instructress of the first two grades (One and Two) with which Hope Lutheran School opened that fall. This June she will have completed her third year as teacher and acting principal at the school, which has grown under the blessing of God to an enrollment of 100 pupils in the Kindergarten and first four grades and is presently served by three staff members.

Miss Redeker plans to leave Levittown after the close of school early next month, spend several weeks visiting with her parents in Illinois, and then attend Foreign Missions School in mid-summer on the campus of Concordia Seminary, Saint Louis, Missouri. Arrangements will be made to have Miss Redeker flown to our New Guinea mission field some time after the first of September.

Miss Redeker's specific assignment in the highland region of New Guinea where our Church conducts it's missionary program (see enclosed folder) is to establish a school for native girls and married women of the Enga tribe at Yaibos. Her address will be: c/o Mr. Edward Dicke, Wapenamanda W.H.D., Box 56, Madang, New Guinea. For the first year she will spend two hours a day in the study of Pidgin English—the language of missionary-native communication. Miss Redeker will begin her work by gathering women from the backwoods and teaching them habits of health and personal hygiene, games, gardening, nutrition, and the Pidgin English. As the natives' confidence is gained, the instruction in the truths of God's Word will follow.

The importance of the initiation of a program for female education in New Guinea has been indicated by Dr. Koppelmann, as follows: "The reason why we consider the placement of Miss Redeker so urgent is this, that, while the men are being educated, the women are not. Experience in other missions indicates that the uneducated woman will be a hindrance to her husband, while possible even dragging him back into heathen practices, simply because she doesn't know any differently."

The members of Hope congregation regret to see Miss Redeker leave their midst but commend her for her willingness to undertake this missionary service. Their interest and intercessory prayers surely will follow her to the new area of Kingdom endeavor, especially also since she will retain her membership with Hope congregation. May God use Miss Redeker mightily in bringing Gospel doctrines to young and old in a primitive, pagan South Pacific society!

June 25, 1959

To Whom It May Concern:

This is to certify that Miss Eunice A. Redeker is a missionary under appointment to the Board for Missions in Foreign countries of The Lutheran Church, Missouri Synod for service in New Guinea, where she will be engaged primarily as a teacher. Miss Redeker comes well qualified for this position, having graduated from Concordia Teachers College in June of 1956, with a B.S. in Education. She has also completed two courses in school administration at Temple University, Philadelphia.

Miss Redeker is an American citizen, having been born in this country.

The Board for Missions in Foreign Countries assume full responsibility for the support and maintenance of Miss Redeker while she is on the field and en route, and also the cost of any repatriation should that become necessary.

Any courtesy shown Miss Redeker in the granting of a passport will be greatly appreciated by us.

Sincerely yours,
BOARD FOR MISSIONS IN FOREIGN COUNTRIES,
The Lutheran Church–Missouri Synod
A. G. Erdmann Business Manager

July 17, 1959

Dear Miss Redeker,

We are now ready to proceed with final application for entry into Australia and the Territory of Papua, New Guinea. Enclosed you will find form #47, a yellow copy, which is to be completed as much as possible and then you will find two form #1, application for registration, this copy is in duplicate and must be completed and signed. Then we have a white medical examination sheet. Even though you have had a previous medical examination, it will be necessary to present this blank to the physician and have him insert the findings and sign the copy where necessary.

Might I suggest that, if at all possible, you make arrangements with the Grandel Clinic to have this medical examination and include a chest X-ray. Dr. Stindel or his associate will complete the examination. In addition to that white sheet, we will need a mental health clearance certificate signed by the doctor. We will also need from the Clinic a certificate of chest X-ray examination giving negative findings for tuberculosis. Please bear in mind it is not necessary for you to have in your possession the X-ray films but we will need the certificate from the Clinic.

If you should have difficulty completing the green and yellow forms, I will be pleased to lend every assistance possible. I will be available most any day if you will just give the office a ring to make sure.

When you come to the office you should have with you the following items

1) *Form #47 – yellow application sheet*
2) *Form #1 – (in duplicate) application for registration*
3) *Completed medical examination sheet*
4) *Mental health clearance certificate*
5) *4 passport size photographs*
6) *Certificate from T.B. Clinic or Public Health Authority of chest X-ray examination giving negative findings for T.B.*

After all this information has been completed and gathered, we will send them to the Australian Consulate General's office in New York along with your passport where they will examine the documents and stamp the visa permit in your passport book. When we send the documents and papers along with your passport to New York we should have your passport book back in about 10 days therefore I would urge you to make reservations for your medical examination at your earliest opportunity.

While you are in the office we will complete form #2031 for your Social Security. I think that will just about complete all the details with the exception of final travel arrangements. Since the time is fast approaching for your departure to New Guinea, I would appreciate it very much if you would get in touch with me by telephone at your earliest convenience so that definite arrangements can be made for transportation taking into consideration any stopovers you would like to have us include.

Cordially yours,
A.G. Erdmann
Business Manager
Board For Missions in Foreign Countries

July 22, 1959

Dear Dr. Kopplemann:

I appreciate very much the opportunity to see Miss Redeker about whom we have had previous correspondence. You will recall that she is a teacher who is planning to leave on August 23, 1959, for our field in New Guinea. I went over her completely here at the office the afternoon on July 20, 1959.

This young lady is age 24 (…). Her occupation is a teacher and she graduated from River Forest in 1956. For the past three years she has been teaching in Pennsylvania. Her father is a farmer near here in Illinois and the health of the family is good, she has always been single, she states that her health now is excellent, and had appendix (...) surgery (...) in 1946.

I checked Miss Redeker completely and found her excellent throughout (...). The laboratory work was entirely within normal limits, which information we had before. Her chest x-ray was essentially negative and her EKG as well.

I would recommend Miss Redeker for the foreign mission field, she is a personable young woman and possesses great zeal for the work. Even though she is single I felt certain that she will be able to stand the work in the foreign field (...) and felt that in her case special psychiatric interview was not necessary (...).

Many thanks for letting me see this young lady personally since I do think that it means more than a brief resume of examination which I had previously received from the doctor in Pennsylvania.

Kindest person regards,

C.E. Stindel, M. D.

(Eunice had no knowledge that Mr. Erdmann sent this and the following letter. In retrospect, it seems that he knew he had a young single female traveling alone and wanted to ensure that there were friendly faces to meet her along the way).

South San Francisco, Ca.

July 30, 1959

Dear Rev. Wyneken,

Final preparations are being made for Miss Eunice Redeker to go to New Guinea. Miss Redeker in the past three years has been teacher and acting principal of Hope Lutheran Church in Levittown, Pennsylvania and has now accepted a call to teach the school for native girls in New Guinea. Even though she has no personal acquaintances in San Francisco she would like to spend a few hours on the West Coast before departing for New Guinea. We have made travel arrangements which call for her arrival in San Francisco at 9:00 P.M. abroad T.W.A. flight #203 on August 25th and her departure from San Francisco the next night, August 26, at 11:59 P.M. aboard Pan American Airways flight 865 for Hawaii.

I felt sure that some ladies in San Francisco would enjoy spending a day with Miss Redeker. Any arrangements you might make would be greatly appreciated by us.

Thanks in advance for your very good help.

With Christian greetings,
A.G. Erdmann

Honolulu, Hawaii

July 30, 1959

Dear Rev. Schroeder,

You no doubt are aware that Miss Eunice Redeker has been assigned by our Board to teach a school for native girls in New Guinea. For the past three years Miss Redeker has been teacher and acting principal of Hope Lutheran School in Levittown, Pennsylvania. For the past six weeks she has been attending Mission School here in St. Louis and is now making final preparations for her visit to New Guinea.

In her travels to New Guinea, she had hoped to spend a day in Honolulu even though she tells me she has no personal acquaintances there. I indicated to her that I was sure arrangements could be made to show her a few interesting places while she was visiting your city. For this short visit we have arranged her schedule to arrive from San Francisco aboard Pan American Airlines flight #865 at 6:40 A.M. on

August 27th and she is scheduled to leave Honolulu that same evening at 6:30 P.M. aboard Pan American Airways flight #811 for Sydney.

I am sure that any arrangements made for Miss Redeker will be greatly appreciated.

With Christian greetings,
A.G. Erdmann

(The writer of the following letter was Rev. Ian Kleinig, a missionary in New Guinea when Eunice arrived. {Eunice lived with him, his wife Enid, and their four children from August to January until she moved to Pausa to teach the girls, and thus coeducation was started. They were wonderful to her}. A further few words about things in this letter. The full names of the other three missionaries noted in the letter are: Rev. Harold Freund, Rev. Willard Burce, and Rev. Otto Hintze. Rev. Harold Freund was a missionary from the Australian Lutheran Church who was initially serving on the island of Siassi, and later he and his family went further inland in New Guinea to help the Evangelical Lutheran Church. His son Roland started the agricultural program in the mission at Mukuamanda. {Further down in this letter, it states he was at Yaibos, that is where he did his initial training, so as to eventually be able to open his agricultural program at Mukuamanda. In 1959, Mukuamanda did not exist as a station}. Given that the native New Guineans left their pigs forage anywhere, it was thus necessary to build fences around the school and other buildings. The "cargo boys" mentioned were younger native men/boys who would generally carry supplies for the missionaries, especially when a new station was being founded. They also helped to clear and break the ground for the buildings being constructed. The "interpreters" or "interrupters" were New Guinea men who had learned English and helped the missionaries learn Enga. Missionaries who had learned the Enga language and then were able to help interpret the Bible to the New Guineans were Rev's.: Burce, Hintze, Kleinig and later Leroy Eckert and Harley Koptzke. The Wycliffe Bible Translators are a Bible translator organization that is still in operation in 2023. They go into mission fields around the world to help the missionaries learn the languages used by the local natives and help to interpret the Bible into those languages. The boys won "tinned meat" at the sports day. "Tinned meat" was brought inland from the coast of New Guinea. Things that were "tinned": cheese, small wieners, chicken pieces, and lamb pieces. The cans were about half the size of the regular 15 oz can of today. And finally, the "lovely oval at Amapyak" included the kickball field in the oval, surrounded by the children's dorm, two of the staff's homes, and the school.)

(Form Letter)
Lutheran Mission, Wabag, W.H.D.
New Guinea

September 1959

Dear Christian Friends,

It is just 11 years since Pastor Freund and my brother-in-law, Armin Kleinig, first came into the Wabag area and decided that it was a promising field for mission work. After they had been here several months, they were joined by Missionaries Burce and Hintze. Recently statistics showed that there are now 3,319 baptized Christians among these Enga natives, 2,179 of these being communicant members. The Yaibos circuit has a communicant membership of 475.

Sometimes, especially in the early years, we wondered if we were making any progress at all. Even now, newer missionaries opening up outlying areas and setting up new stations feel discouraged at times as they seem to have so little to show for their efforts. But when we look back over the past ten years it is not difficult to see what a marvelous change and growth there has been in the lives of many of these Enga people, and we are most thankful to God for the wonderful way He has brought these people to the knowledge of Christ their Saviour, and we feel privileged and humbled to have been allowed to have a part in this work.

Now that there are a number of Christian congregations in various parts of this Wabag valley, there is a need for a training centre for indigenous evangelists. In May delegates from the different congregations met with the missionaries at Yaramanda, and among other things decided to establish an evangelists' school at Birip, an out-station in the Yaibos circuit, where a large class of catechumens were baptized last year. Eventually Missionary Burce will be in charge of this school where selected men from the congregations, with some background in reading and writing, will attend for a certain period to learn how to make their work of preaching the Gospel more effective. They will be taught such subjects as doctrine, Bible study, how to present the Gospel to the heathen, how to instruct catechumens; and they will discuss such matters as the practical application of the Gospel in the lives of Christians, and problems they may already have encountered in their work or congregational life.

This school will be supported by the Enga congregations each communicant member contributing one shilling for the project. Besides this the Yaibos congregation will be supplying the materials for and building the school, a really big task for them. The Birip congregation too will be kept busy, preparing the site for the school and building fences and ditches to keep out pigs. This school will represent a real step forward in the growth of this native church, with the congregations cooperating and working together to set up this training programme and we pray that they may derive much blessing from it. Later on, when the school is well established, and there are young men with higher educational qualifications available, from our secondary schools, the natural development will be, we hope, a seminary for native pastors.

Last letter we wrote to you, I believe we mentioned how great the need is for a qualified woman teacher to organize a school programme for the native girls. Now we are very happy to report that the wanted teacher is right here, having arrived from the States just a week ago. Miss Eunice Redeker, originally from Illinois, will be starting the school for native girls next February. Cargo boys have been busy these past weeks clearing the ground at the back of our house for the new school and Eunice's bush house. The school will be a kind of secondary school, drawing on the other stations for pupils who have had 4 or 5 years of schooling. Eunice is already putting in as much time as she can studying pidgin English and Enga, and there are plenty of school children about the place only too anxious to air their knowledge and act as interpreters, or "interrupters" as some people call them. Soon she will be visiting the other stations to see how the schools are run and to gather information about the curriculum, special problems, and so on.

Another branch of the work which is receiving a boost by the arrival of a new worker is in the agricultural line. There has been an agricultural committee comprising Ian and another member of the staff living in this area, for some years but their main concern has been with the mission cattle, seeing to the breeding and distribution of milk cows, care of calves and butchering of steers---mainly for the benefit of the white staff on the field. The men have realized however that there is scope for a trained agricultural worker to help and teach the natives how to improve their gardens and pigs. An important part of his work too will be to investigate ways in which the natives can develop cash crops, for as they come more into contact with our civilization, they will want to improve their standard of living and their traditional subsistence economy cannot provide much more than the bare essentials for living.

About three months ago, Mr. Roland Freund, son of the first missionary in this area, arrived from Australia to undertake the work of an agricultural missionary. He is stationed at Yaibos and is at present working on setting up a programme of work that will be of most benefit and instruction to the natives. He has already visited the government agricultural station and other outfits near Mt. Hagen and Banz to enquire about coffee growing, and the trials and tribulations of raising sheep and pigs in these parts. He had two good young sows brought from Hagen to set up a kind of model piggery here. The natives do not take special pains with the food and housing for their pigs but allow them to forage in the bush and swamps for what food they can find. Consequently most of their pigs are little runts, subject to worms, pneumonia and sometimes anthrax. Roland has built a sty and enclosure from roughhewn timbers such as are available to the natives, and keeps the two sows there feeding them only the kind of food that the natives themselves would be able to give their pigs, so that they cannot argue, if his project is successful, that he has the advantage of food and materials which are readily available to the white man. He wants to show the natives that by keeping their pigs in enclosures away from other pigs, and feeding them regularly, they can more easily check the spread of worms and sickness among their pigs, and promote faster growth.

It seems that there may be a good market on the coast for coffee beans and shelled corn and natives are excited at the prospect of being able to grow cash crops, and in all this they will need help and direction from someone who has the time to look into the handling, transport and marketing of these crops. We hope that this new phase of mission work will be of real help to the natives. This agricultural programme is being linked closely with the evangelistic and congregational work in the hope that it will serve the cause of the Gospel by making the native Christians more and more aware of their stewardship obligations and privileges and enable the young growing church to become less and less dependent on outside funds.

Some of you may be interested to hear of a shipment of heifers that was flown by DC3 charter direct from Cairns in North Queensland (Australia), to *Wabag in June. Although the mission has a good herd of dairy cattle, there has been an unusually high percentage of bull calves among the offspring of our first batch of cows, and there are not enough cows to go to all the mission households. A number of Sunday schools and other groups in the States responded generously to an appeal for funds to buy young heifers from Australia, and this money combined with some funds held by the Agriculture committee paid for the purchase of 18 young heifers and a pedigreed bull calf with the impressive title of Soleigh's Ethel Chief. We hope now that in a couple of years there will be plenty of milk for all the staff.*

The native language still is a big problem to the missionaries in this field, and a tremendous amount of study in analysis and description needs to be done before any grammars or translations can be finalized. For some time it was realized that tone plays an important role in the language, and to help with the analysis and study of this problem we sought the valuable assistance of the trained linguist, Mr. Allan Healey, of the Wycliffe Bible Translators who are now working in New Guinea. From his investigations it is quite clear that tone does play a very significant role in the Enga Language, and anyone working in this language will need to master this aspect of speech if he wishes to speak the language correctly, and to understand its function if he wants to produce a correct translation of the Word of God. It is difficult to explain this tone problem in a simple way but this may give you some idea what it is about. There are many words, long and short, in Enga, which are spelled alike and sound alike but differ totally in meaning. The correct meaning in many instances can be determined only by the tone of the word or by the tone of a single syllable in the word, and for a person reading the language to know what is meant there must be some indication mark to tell whether the tone is high or low. For instance, the word "angga" can mean 1. A cold, 2. A pandanus nut, 3. A noose. For a reader or listener to know what is meant, the correct tones must be symbolized in the printed word---there may be one high tone, or one low tone, or both, or two of a kind or neither. The discovery of this feature in the language now means that each missionary must learn the tonal value of every word, and the considerable amount of vernacular language material must all be revised to include the correct tone markings.

This letter is becoming rather lengthy and so I must touch only briefly on other matters. The medical work at Yaibos is still being capably handled by Es Janetzki and a number of serious and urgent cases have come into the clinic during the past year, requiring immediate transfer to the hospital ten miles away. In August the annual sports day for native boys and girls was held at Yaibos and Amapyak. The Yaibos boys carried all before them, winning the track and field event and the soccer, for all of which they received the sports shield, a case of tinned meat and a new soccer ball. The field sports were held on the lovely oval at Amapyak where the European school is, and as we learned something from last year's mistakes and experience, the programme this year was better organized and those of us who helped during the show enjoyed having the girls on the team.

Our children just this term moved into the permanent European School building and are very thrilled with everything in this modern well-equipped school. The dormitories for the boarding children have been completed for some months but we had some difficulty in finding a matron to take charge. But it won't be long now, as Miss Dawn Jericho, from Gawler in South Australia has agreed to take on the job and should be here soon. I have such a little space left now to thank all our friends for letters, greeting cards, contributions, gifts, and especially your prayers and good wishes. We are all enjoying very good health and are very content in our work here.

With Christian Greetings, Eunice Redeker

October 4, 1959

Dear, Florence, Richard, and Charles,

Greetings from New Guinea! And what a beautiful place it is. I've just been visiting most of our stations and all are very beautifully laid out and the beautiful mts. and vegetation around. Of course, as you look over the valley and mountainsides, you also think of the thousands of natives living there and many still in heathenism. These natives are quite the people, so different. I'm trying to learn Enga so I can communicate more freely with them and learn more about their daily lives and what they think. In my newsletters I'm going to try to tell you about them from time to time. I'll be sending pictures too.

I guess Mom told you I had a wonderful trip out. I sure enjoyed every minute of it. Wish you all could have an opportunity to see so much. Australia was really fascinating. I felt as if I were back in the 1920's. People were very friendly though, and showed me around. When first arriving in New Guinea, I really felt strange, the sudden overabundance of strange people. I'm still not use to them fully but certainly am much more so. I pray daily for the Lord to help me to increase in love for these people, whom He also loves.

By the way I really appreciated you coming to the airport when I left. I won't ever forget that day! Sure think of you all often but know our Heavenly Father loves and cares for you. I sat with a man from

Chile all the way to San Francisco. Our conversation got quite interesting soon after we left St. Louis, so my tears dried up and I enjoyed the rest of the trip, as I had prayed I would.

Since I don't have a birthday card, Richard, I will have to wish you a "Happy Birthday" in this letter. May God be with you through the coming year and grant you His peace and joy. I'll be thinking of you October 15, throw a kiss to the East, be sure to catch it!

How does Charles like school? Does he enjoy his new teacher? Will be anxious to hear how all is coming along.

In two weeks, I'm going to be visiting our girls schools at the coast. Will be good to be in civilization again. Ha! The Kleinig's are sure swell. I'm going out with them as they go out for their vacation.

My newsletter will tell you much of the details of my last month's experiences. Write soon. Charles, hope you like school, be a good boy.

God be with you.

Love and kisses,
Eunice

Board for World Missions

October 9, 1959

Dear Friend,

In order to get our records up-to-date we are coming to each and every one of our missionaries for help. The category we have reference to at the present time, which we feel is in many cases outdated, is the names and addresses of the parents of our missionaries.

So would you, please, give us the names and present address of your parents? If one or the other, or both, have deceased, mention that also.

Then, in case you have someone else to be notified of any important events, date of arrival, etc., instead of your parents, give us the name and address of that person also. In the cases where both parents have passed away, it will of course, be imperative that you give us the name and address of another close relative or friend.

We would appreciate having this information in our office no later than October 30. Your help in this will be very much appreciated.

Cordially yours,
Herman H. Koppelmann
Acting Executive Secretary

P.S. ANNUAL REPORTS will again be due on December 31, 1959. We would appreciate having these in our office by January 15, 1960. The reports should include chronology, health of self and family, official position, activities, report on vacations, appraisal of activities of the past year, and plans and prospects for the forthcoming year.

(The below is the first "official" newsletter sent through Hope Lutheran, Levittown, written by Eunice.)

New Guinea Lutheran Mission
Western Highlands, Wabag, New Guinea

October 1959

Greetings from New Guinea!

Now that I have been here in New Guinea for a month so many things have happened and it hardly seems possible that I've been here that long. I'm becoming well initiated and my heart is filled with thanks to God for His wonderful protection, guidance, & abiding presence as I made the exciting trip here, as well as during the first days here. Life is quite different here and it was only the knowledge that my Savior was with me as well as knowing that He has much work for me to do which made adjusting not quite so difficult. To all of you, relatives and friends, I am most grateful for your prayers and letters. Just to know your prayers and thoughts were with me was a great comfort. Also I enjoyed every minute as I knew it was through your gifts of Christian love that this privilege is possible for me.

Now a few highlights of my trip and first month here. I left a hot, humid, 97 degree St. Louis at 4 p.m., August 25. The flight over the Rockies was very beautiful; we followed the going-down sun and saw a colorful sunset as it went down beyond the mountains. We arrived in San Francisco at 9:30 p.m. The temperature was 61 degrees, and quite chilly after St. Louis. Mr. & Mrs. Hildebrand, representing the Southern California Lutheran Women's Missionary League (LWML), met me at the airport and I spent the night with them in their lovely new home in San Bruno, California. The next day I spent seeing much of San Francisco, really enjoyed Fisherman's Wharf and Chinatown. A ride in the one cable car left in San Francisco was quite a thrill. Mr. & Mrs. David Raff also of San Bruno were my host and hostess Wednesday evening. They took me on a tour of San Francisco at night. Our Southern California L.W.M.L. is to be commended for their wonderful hospitality to us. At 11:00 p.m., Mrs. Raff saw me off from the San Francisco airport. I wondered what lay ahead! The night would be spent above the ocean. I was filled with anxiety but soon calmed down as I knew our heavenly Father watches and cares for us. Our hostess and host showed us how to use the life jackets. The hostesses were dressed in mumus, a full Chinese dress, very popular in Hawaii. The flight over the ocean was very smooth. Bright and early, 6:45 a.m., we landed at the Honolulu airport. A former friend and classmate of CTC, RF, Eunice Schumann, and two other teachers teaching at Redeemer Lutheran School, Honolulu, met me. They greeted me with nine beautiful lei. The flowers were simply gorgeous and to think that they were real. I enjoyed a most exciting day. Eunice rented a car and we drove around part of the island. The scenery and flowers, vegetation, beaches, and 70-degree temperature make this island of Oahu almost a paradise. At. 6:45 p.m. I boarded Pan American again for Sydney, Australia. Again I wondered what the Lord would let me enjoy seeing next. During the night we stopped at Fiji, a small island, to refuel. We saw very little except that it was my first meeting with natives. Their bushy hair, dark skin, and small stature impressed me even though it was in the middle of the night.

We arrived in Sydney at 10:00 a.m., Saturday. Having crossed the international date line, I skipped a day, Friday, August 27. Sydney has a very beautiful harbor and the bridge over it reminded me so much of the Pennsylvania Turnpike bridge over the Delaware River. Sydney's many red brick homes impress you from the air. After getting through medical inspection and customs, I was greeted by Mr. Hamer of the Nelson and Roberts Company. His Holden car fascinated me, it was strange sitting in the left front and not driving, then driving along on the left side of the streets was most unusual, but it's the safe way in Australia and also in New Guinea. The cars were mostly small cars, very few American made. The Hamer's were wonderful to me, treating me to a delicious dinner, showed me a little of Sydney as we drove back downtown to the hotel, where I was to stay till Monday p.m. The people in Sydney were very friendly. Each day I met someone, who was so kind as to show me around to see the places of interest. Sydney is built on hills. At the zoo I saw many of the animals I would soon see in New Guinea. On Sunday afternoon I attended the services at our Lutheran church. The service reminded me of the German services we had at my home church when I was a little girl. I also enjoyed seeing several of Sydney's beautiful beaches; however, since it was winter and the temperature 61 degrees, not too many people were in the water, but many were enjoying sunbathing. I also enjoyed seeing "South Pacific," my last movie for a while. Through Nelson & Roberts Company I got my record player, Master's voice, three speed, battery. It is a treasure to me here. Many thanks to my fellow teacher co-workers in the Philadelphia area for it. I also made arrangements to get a short-wave transistor radio, which the parents of my school children at Hope, Levittown, are making possible for me. I'm quite anxious for it to arrive. Then on Monday evening the Hamer's took me to the airport and now I was finally on my way to New Guinea. We landed at Port Moresby at 6:45 a.m. There were the natives, the people the Lord was giving me an opportunity to bring the Gospel to. I tried to get a good glimpse of them and observe them closely. They were small in stature, and were watching me and every move I made too! Their shyness seemed almost unbelievable, but they were friendly: large smiles, beautiful teeth. Since this was Port Moresby, the natives here were more developed and wore clothing. At 7:30 a.m. we boarded a DC-3 for the Highlands. It was an old Army plane and quite crude after the luxury I had on all the other planes, but it was fun and I also was able to see more area below. The scenery was just so beautiful, the native straw huts, and well-kept gardens could be seen at spots under the camouflage of tall grass and vegetation. After stopping at two small stations we arrive at Minj, where I was to board a piper cub, our American Lutheran Mission's plane, to get to our mission station at Wapenamunda. When I got off the plane at Minj there were just oodles of natives all around, really looking us over. We must be funny specimens to them with all our paraphernalia. Anyway it's quite an experience to have many people around gazing at you, and not being able to say a word to them, just smile, and then a few brave ones ventured over to shake my hand. I was wearing a peacock-feathered hat, and this was quite an attraction; they "awed" and "ahed." They love beautiful feathers for decoration in their hair. After about thirty minutes the piper cub came. We climbed in and now I was really getting anxious to get to my destination. From the cub I got a beautiful all-around view of the area and some of our mission stations. We landed at our station, Pawari, to pick up Pastor Struckbein, who was going to a language conference (they have now found that after all the work they have put into the language, most of it will have to be revised as tone is playing a great part in the language. An example is: a word can mean two or three different things depending on where the accent falls). We landed at our station, Yaramanda, where the conference was held. From here we flew over our higher school for boys, Pausa, and one of our hydroelectric plants, from which our hospital receives its power in the Lae River. We got a beautiful view of Mt. Hagen, the highest mountain in this range. Our next stop was Wapenamanda, where Mr. Dicke, our business manager, met me with his motorbike. In two seconds there were at least fifty natives around all gazing to see what the piper cub was bringing in now. By now I was getting used to greeting them and just enjoying myself observing their curiosity. They were so friendly and so helpful in carrying my baggage to Dicke's. My first motorbike ride took me to the Dicke's home, a bush home, but very comfortable. After a delicious lunch I was anxious to see our supply store, more of the natives and the scenery. Then I was so sleepy I welcomed a long nap. That evening the Rev. and Mrs. Ian Kleinig picked me up with the jeep. They had been at the language conference too. We enjoyed a bumpy ride up the mountains, over some most unique and rickety covered native-made bridges, to the station where I'll be setting up our girls' school, Yaibos. Rev. Kleinig, of Australia, is the missionary here. They have five children and I'm enjoying my stay with them as I await the completion of my bush house in their back yard. It is being built by our agriculturalist, Roland Freund. He came here in June to investigate what can be done in the way of growing things here. If something could be developed it would help economically.

The Janetzkis', a builder from Australia, are also living here, and down the road ¼ mile, Amapyaka, is our Highland Lutheran School, a wonderful set up which the LWML has made possible for our missionaries' children. Mr. Don Gerber is doing a wonderful job as administrator and teacher. The Heppners, Mr. a mechanic from Australia, are also at Amapyaka. Missionaries going up and down the valley usually stop in so we have a little more activity here than at most stations.

I have been busy since arrival here, getting acquainted with the natives, their language, and observing our schools. I feel very inadequate but am praying for wisdom and guidance. Pidgin is coming along fairly well, not too difficult to pick up, but I'm also trying to learn the native Enga language, which is quite difficult. I really feel a need to learn Enga so that I might communicate with these people directly rather than through an interpreter. In your prayers, please remember to ask the Lord to grant that I might learn the language quickly.

At first the filth and odor of the natives bothered me considerably, but now I have become quite used to them as I hardly notice. Their personalities and individuality are shining through. They are likeable and kind. At times, I hear, they like to be friendly because it may mean the kone (as they call us white people) will come forth with something for them. So far, I haven't experienced this. Their houses are low, for warmth, and are made of kunai, a hard grass. A fire-

place is in the center of the house and the smoke inside is very intense, sometimes I wonder how they stand it. The man's house is round. The woman's house is oblong, larger than the man's since she has the children with her, and the pigs in the back room. What impressed me was that they have little or no equipment or clothing in their home. Daily the women get food from their gardens, mostly mapu (sweet potato), although they are growing some vegetables now as they can buy seeds from our trade store. Money has been introduced and they are earning it by doing jobs for the mission as well as working for the government, building roads, etc. They also bring in vegetables and sell them to the Europeans. We get some fine carrots, cabbage, beans, peas, and tomatoes. Pineapple, bananas, passion fruit, lemons, grapefruit, oranges, and limes grow here but not as well as farther down the valley. Coffee grows fairly well and peanuts, very well.

The past three weeks I've been visiting our various stations. I spent a week at Sirunki, where Pat and Joe Neubacher, from CTC, RF, came to teach last year. It was a thrill to see a school running so smoothly in a bush building and very little in equipment and materials. Sirunki is about 8,700 feet above sea level and it gets quite cold there. The natives there also wear no clothing, and there is no fire in the school but they still enjoy school tremendously. Pat and Joe gave me much help as to materials available, problems they've encountered and just general information.

From Sirunki I decided to hike with several New Guinea boys as guides to our farthest station, Papayuk, which is twelve miles. Hiking is great sport here with the adventurous trails and beautiful scenery. Pastor and Mrs. Erwin Spruth are stationed at Papayuk. They are quite isolated from the rest of us but are very happy and have a beautiful station in the Lakaip valley.

My stays at the homes of our missionaries have been spiritually very uplifting. These men are men of prayer, they realize complete dependence on the Lord. We also are in need of your prayers. Only by the grace of God has the preaching of the Gospel here been effective. Our mission now numbers 3,656 baptized souls.

This week I'm in Irelya, our most centrally located station. We have two missionaries, a missionary teacher and builder living here.

This is our most densely populated area. I'm staying with Mr. & Mrs. George Hinlicky. Some of you may remember them as the ones who interviewed me last January. Mr. Hinlicky teaches the boys school here now. He will be opening a higher school for boys, our second, next year at Kubilitz, about 10 miles up the valley from here, if all works out as planned.

Pastor Willard Burce is planning to open a lay evangelists training school at Birup, a station about 10 miles down the valley from here. At present the buildings are being constructed. This school's purpose will be to train deacons and congregational officers so they might more effectively carry on the work of spreading the Gospel.

At present our girls school is also being built at Yaibos. We hope to start school on February 1. So far, I haven't done much in the way of setting up a curriculum, only observing and collecting materials. I am planning to visit our American Lutheran Missions Girls School at the coast soon, as well as our Higher School for Boys at Pausa. Teaching here will be so different. We try to dig into the background and daily lives of these people and build from there. Their experiences and backgrounds are very limited. These people are not to be pitied, however, they have homes, food and God's wonderful creation is very close to them. The Word of God has already been brought to many but the challenge is still great. As you look over the valley and mountainsides you realize there are thousands of people who have never been brought the Gospel message, and then as you follow the mountainsides up, your eyes are lifted to Him from whom comes all our help and we pray that He will show us the way that we might be guided in doing His work most effectively, that His glory might be revealed to these people, and His Kingdom come to them.

This letter has gotten rather lengthy, but it seems when one first arrives here there is so much to observe and all is most interesting and fascinating and I did want to share a little of it with you. It is a tremendous joy to know you are making it possible for me to be here.

In closing I want to extend my heartfelt thanks to you for your prayers, letters, and words of encouragement before I left the States as well as since I'm here in New Guinea. Your prayers are my constant need, only by the grace of God through the Holy Spirit's guidance can our work here go forward. Your letters are much looked forward to. I would like to answer each one individually but since this is impossible, I am thankful for this way of reaching you all. If at any time your address changes and you still wish to receive my letters, kindly notify Mrs. Lennord Pitney, 38 Thornyapple Lane, Levittown, Pennsylvania.

To the boys and girls at Hope Lutheran School and Sunday School I say a special word of thanks for your cards and letters. It's always a thrill to hear from you.

Hope Walther League: my watch is working like a charm—so thankful to have it and wear it constantly. Often think of you as I check our fleeting time.

My shipment of goods isn't to arrive till about December 1. I'll sure be happy when it does come—living from a suitcase gets a little tiresome.

In order that you might get more of an idea as to the life and work here, in each future letter I will try to tell you about a phase of it.

Our Father in heaven bless and keep you all. The distance between us is short when we realize our God is everywhere.

In Christ,
Eunice A. Redeker

Please note my address: New Guinea Lutheran Mission, Western Highlands, Wabag, New Guinea

(Most of the letters stating "Form Letter" sent through Hope Lutheran, Levittown, had a concluding paragraph or two, generally similar in content to the below {we will only include it this one time. While this is an actual addition to a newsletter written much later during her time in PNG, we thought it most representative.)

This Newsletter is duplicated and distributed through the courtesy of Hope Lutheran Church, Levittown, Pennsylvania, where Miss Redeker holds her membership. Miss Redeker was the first principal-teacher of Hope Lutheran School, coming to Levittown in 1956. She left the parish the spring of 1959 and went to New Guinea where she established the first school for girls. She is presently teaching at St. Paul's Lutheran High School in Wapenamanda, New Guinea. She will be due for a furlough in the fall of 1966.

Please send additions, changes of address, etc., for Miss Redeker's mailing list to Mrs. Lennord Pitney, 38 Thornyapple Lane, Levittown, Pennsylvania.

Our gracious thanks to all those who have contributed toward the postage for the mailing of the Newsletter.

(One other note in regard to the mailing of the Newsletters by Hope: while the extant mailing lists are somewhat difficult to examine, it would appear each Newsletter was mailed to approximately 300 addresses {individuals, Churches, Schools, LWML's, etc.} including many states in the USA, as well as foreign counties including, at a minimum: Canada, Japan, China, Nigeria, Australia, Germany, Wales and Hong Kong.)

November 9, 1959

Dear Wilma, Willard and Darrell,

(Wilma was Eunice's oldest sister and like a mother to her, Wilma's husband, and son).

Hi! How are you? Well now this is my second letter to you, how about one from you pretty soon?

Have been quite busy lately. Spent two weeks at the coast. Was really hot there but very beautiful also. The coconuts, bananas and other tropical fruit trees and all the flowers are just gorgeous.

Well, I found that Teaching Certificate, it was with my stuff I sent from PA. Sorry I caused you so much trouble.

The pictures I took that day in St. Louis before I left, turned out real good, so I can see you very often.

Wilma, the Board asked us to make a will just in case we blink out. Well, I made mine out to you. One copy is kept in the Bd. of Foreign Missions file and I'm sending you a duplicate copy. Thought maybe you'd like to know about it.

Really nice here, so warm during the day, nice and cool at night. Seems strange we're not getting any fall and winter weather. Can't believe Christmas is so close. Can you imagine having beautiful green grass, gorgeous flowers (also poinsettias), and 70 degree weather for Christmas, well that's what I'll have this year!

Well, hope you are fine. Write soon. Have a very Merry Christmas.

God bless you and keep you.

How's Darrell? Tell him "Hi" for me.

Much love,
Eunice

(The following was included with the above letter).

THIS IS THE LAST WILL AND TESTAMENT of me, Eunice Anna Redeker, of New Guinea Lutheran Mission-Missouri Synod, Western Highlands, Wabag, New Guinea, in the Territory of Papua and New Guinea, serving as a school teacher.

I HEREBY REVOKE ALL former Wills and Testamentary Dispositions heretofore made by me.

I APPOINT the Business Manager of the New Guinea Lutheran Mission-Missouri Synod, Western Highlands, New Guinea, to be the executor of this my Will. After payment of all my just debts and funeral and testamentary expenses, I GIVE DEVISE AND BEQUEATH the whole of my estate both real and personal of whatsoever nature and wheresoever situated unto Mrs. Willard Maschhoff of Hoyleton, Illinois, R.R.#2, U.S.A.

DATED this 7th day of November in the year of our Lord One thousand nine hundred fifty nine.

SIGNED and DECLARED by the said Eunice Anna Redeker, the Testator as and for her last Will in the presence of us both present at the same time who at her request in her presence and in the presence of each other have hereunto subscribed our names as witnesses.

Witness: Ian Kleinig
Occupation: Clergyman
Address: Wabag, New Guinea

Witness: C. L. Janetzki
Occupation: Builder
Address: Wabag, New Guinea

Signed: Eunice Anna Redeker

December 3, 1959

Dear Eunice,

A blessed Christmas to you, our mission representative in the territory of New Guinea! All of us here at Hope Lutheran Church praise God for your presence in the highland region, along with other faithful workers, as representative of us all in carrying out the Savior's Great Commission to evangelize the world. May the Lord of the Church strengthen you for your arduous tasks and make you a blessing to many among whom you labor! This is a prayer of your many friends in the Hope Lutheran parish, Levittown, Pennsylvania, U.S.A., during the holiday season which will soon be upon us.

Enclosed please find a Christmas remembrance from Hope congregation—a $25-check. We have sent this directly to you, rather than <u>via</u> Saint Louis, that you may put the funds to immediate and good use.

May Christ, the blessed companion of each of us who confess His name, accompany you with His presence and benediction throughout the new year of 1960!

In the Savior's service,
Walter A. Maier, Jr
Pastor

Christmas 1959

Dear Florence, Richard and Charles,

Merry Christmas! My time has really flown. Doesn't seem possible Christmas is so near. Sort of miss all the excitement and decorations but we have beautiful weather and gorgeous flowers. I've been teaching some and so have had the boys singing Christmas carols. Will spend Christmas with the nurses at the hospital, all the young, single ones get together for festivities. Now I'm living at Pausa, where our higher school for boys is. I'm living with the Dale Busse's. I knew him at CTC. Ken Bauer is also here. After all my visiting I brought up the matter of co-education, it seemed separating boys and girls was not helping this society at all, they need to learn to live with one another and cooperate. So our Executive Committee decided on co-education. We're moving our girls here to Pausa, they're building us a dorm and me a little permanent house; the boys have the school laid out campus style, a lovely job of landscaping. They just finished the large 2-room classroom here, plus workshop, cookhouse, and Bauer's permanent house. It sure is a help to me to not have to worry about all the Administrative work, especially since scouting for materials is such a necessity here. Had a wonderful hike last Sunday, hiked 7 ½ hrs. up 3500 ft. It's so beautiful, we've got a wonderful view of our Lae Valley here. Well must close for now, hoping you are all well. Remember you in my prayers. Hoping you have a very Merry Christmas, a Blessed and Joyous New Year. Charles how is school? So happy to hear you have a Pastor.

Much love, Eunice

Chapter 2

The 1960's

(A couple of explanations about the letter below: "relics from World War II"-parts of New Guinea were invaded by the Japanese. They practically had all of New Guinea and then were on to Darwin, Australia. They also bombed Darwin, doing a lot of damage there as well. "Records arrived from friends at home" -Eunice was fortunate to have a record player, thus friends sent records with hymns and music mainly by Bach, Mozart, and Handel. And a word about the missionary arrivals: in 1886-German missionaries started mission work, built schools, and built hospitals in bigger, {more coastal} towns of Madang, Lae, Finchhafen, and Port Moresby. Later the American Lutheran Church came and then eventually the Australian Lutheran Church came to New Guinea.)

(Form Letter)

February 1960

Greetings from the second largest island in the world!

Since my last letter many changes have been made, many new experiences enjoyed, and I've become a little more familiar with the people and language of New Guinea. Our greatest joy during this time has been the celebration of our Savior's birthday and the adding of many more souls to the kingdom of God through Holy Baptism.

The last two weeks of October 1959, I spent at the coast visiting our American Lutheran Church's schools. It was a very informative and interesting stay. Much was observed of educational methods and materials available. It was very hot and humid at the coast, really the tropics! The vegetation, flowers, and birds were very colorful and beautiful. I was fortunate in that the "Simbang", a small ship belonging to the American Lutheran Mission, was making a trip down the coast to Finschafen and Lae at the time and I was able to see these places also. We witnessed the dedication of a new hospital at Finschafen. This is also where the first missionaries to New Guinea landed in 1886. In our studies of New Guinea at Concordia Seminary last summer, we had learned about many of these places, and so it was most interesting to see them in reality. At the coast many relics of World War II are still visible, however, most of the areas destroyed have been rebuilt and are back to normal.

Through my visits to our schools here in the Highlands and at the Coast, it was realized that co-education could be possible and also that it would be advantageous to the natives in helping them to learn to live and work together more harmoniously. This was brought to the attention of our Executive Committee, who unanimously approved the resolution. Our Board of World Missions is at present considering this matter. Meantime, I have been moved here to Pausa, where our Boy's Higher School is. Mr. Dale Busse and Mr. Kenneth Bauer started this school two years ago. It's a joy working with them and their experience will help me over many obstacles. We are departmentalizing and I will be teaching English, Reading, and Spelling to all students; Physical Education and Home Economics to the girls. Since our buildings are not yet completed, we have delayed opening school until February 29. This school was started two years ago, and until now the school buildings were made of bush materials. Because of their quick deterioration, they are economically more costly, and so permanent buildings are being constructed. At present a two-room classroom, large, spacious rooms, and three-room girl's dormitory is completed. A workshop, cookhouse, three boy's dormitories and the Bauer's house is still in construction. A little permanent house will be built for me here, most likely by June. In the meantime, I am living with the Busse's in ½ of their living room behind a shower curtain.

On November 15, a large baptism of 560 communicants was held at our station, Sirunki. On November 29, seventy were baptized at one of the outstations of our Yaibos station. December 15, seventy were baptized at our newest station, Kunditz, and January 31, 1960, 360 were baptized at our station, Raiakama. What a tremendous blessing from Almighty God that so many have been added to His kingdom! These baptisms are very impressive, and inspiring. Our Missionaries and Evangelists spend several years instructing the catechumens. Several weeks before the baptism they are examined, each one individually, in their knowledge of the catechism and Bible stories. These examinations are very thorough as the Missionary wants to be very sure they are really giving up their former superstitions and heathen practices and are accepting Jesus as their Savior from sin. The natives then make preparations also physically for this big occasion. They at first often brought in much food and would celebrate with a feast after the service, but this is no longer done, since the large crowds are very difficult to serve. The morning of the baptism, they wash very thoroughly at the stream or river, and dress in a white lap-lap, (a piece of white cloth draped around their body, purchased in the trade store). They started this custom of themselves, the idea probably coming from the coastal natives. Very early they come and form a line, while in this line they sing the few hymns they know, in their own language, until the service begins. These services are held outside, usually on the kick ball field. Every station has one of these as kick-ball is their favorite sport. Logs are laid in pew-like fashion on the ground for those to be baptized to sit on, the rest of the congregation sits on the ground. A little shelter of logs covered with kunai, (a tough grass), *is put up for the altar. A loud speaker is put up, getting power from a jeep engine. When the service starts the Missionaries lead the procession into the kickball field, they march in two at a time. They are singing all the while. When there is a large baptism, this procession takes from fifteen to twenty minutes. After they are seated the service proceeds, the native elder(s) being the liturgists and the station missionary delivering the sermon. A simplified order of service is followed. The service is in the native language. After the service those to be baptized, come up in groups of from fifteen to fifty and kneel at the altar. Several Mission-*

aries usually officiate. Many buckets of water are sitting at the altar and the missionaries fill pans with water and baptize as the people are kneeling. Then a group is going back to their seats and the new group is going up while the congregation sings. During the administering of the sacrament all is quiet so the words spoken by the Missionary can be heard. After they have been baptized, they all go up again in the same groups and receive Holy Communion, excepting the small children. Wine and bread wafers, as used in our churches in America, are used. The wine comes from Australia. After the service all the communicants march out first and form a line, and the congregation shakes hands with each one, wishing them God's blessings. Many Christians from other congregations and many who are curious attend the service, a wonderful opportunity to reach many more people with the Gospel message. At the Sirunki baptism it was estimated that about 8,000 to 10,000 people were present. The service lasted about four hours and in the sun it got very hot. The smaller baptisms are conducted in the same manner only they are accomplished in a shorter period of time.

On November 25, we were saddened when Donnie Gerber, 5, and Ivan Heppner, 8, sons of our teacher at Highland Lutheran School, Don Gerber, and our mechanic, Louis Heppner, were drowned. They had been playing in a small stream and wandered down to the Lae River, which has some very swift and treacherous currents. They were taken by one of these. The families were much saddened but found comfort in knowing that their little ones were now with their Savior, enjoying the bliss of heaven.

Christmas here was quite different, but the joys of our Savior's birth were with us. The warm weather and beautiful, clear evening on Christmas Eve, brought us very close to the way it must have been that evening in Bethlehem, long ago. All was calm and still here. The simple bush homes of our people here, made you realize that in just such a simple abode was our Savor born. They made you realize more deeply that Jesus also loves these people and wants them in His eternal kingdom. The natives celebrated Christmas with a service Christmas Eve and Christmas Day. They decorated their bush churches very beautifully with fresh flowers, poinsettias, a Christmas tree, (the casuarina, a type of pine tree), *and they used branches of these trees to hang over the doors, and on the center posts. They do nothing in their homes. They never kept records of their birthdays until our Missionaries and the government came in, so it must have seemed very strange to them at first that we celebrate birthdays.*

I spent Christmas Eve with the Kleinig's and our Missionaries stationed at Yaibos and Amapyak. Christmas Day the nurses invited us to their home at the hospital. They had ordered a turkey from the coast and we certainly enjoyed it, the first fowl we'd had since here. We had a very nice Christmas tree, and on Christmas Eve two boxes of records arrived from a friend, Elvin Simshauser, at home. We certainly are enjoying them. We heard very few Christmas carols over the radio here.

My deepest thanks also to all of you for the many cards, and letters. It was such a joy hearing from you. I hung up each card, forming a Christmas tree on the wall in my room. I read and enjoyed them all often. Letters mean much to us here. We get our mail once a week.

At present we are in the rainy season and the rains are very heavy every afternoon. Lately, it has also rained all night. It isn't depressing, however, since the mornings are beautiful and sunny.

January 19-24, we had our Annual Missionary Conference. It was very interesting to hear about and discuss the whole mission program here. Since the government will be opening new areas soon, (this is amongst tribes where no white man has been before), we are asking the Mission Board for three pastors, so we might enter these areas right away. We also are in need of teachers to relieve our Missionaries of their teaching obligations, so they might be able to give more time to the evangelistic work. We're praying that it will be possible to get the three teachers we've asked for to arrive here this year.

Language study is progressing slowly. Since the government requires us to teach only English in our higher Standards I will not need to know the language for teaching. However, it is important to know in our contacts with the people here.

I am especially grateful at this time to the Lord that He saw it in His all-wise providence to see my Mother through serious surgery, on January 14. She is recovering progressively.

My thanks to you for your prayers in our behalf. Our Lord hears and by them you are doing much to help our work for Him here. We ask you to continue to remember us and all our Missionaries in your prayers. We can do nothing of ourselves, but with the Lord's guidance, and Holy Spirit working, some are being brought to our Savior every day.

God's rich blessings be with you in 1960.

A worker in Christ's kingdom,
Eunice Redeker

(While Eunice was in New Guinea, Wilma, took care of Eunice's banking.)

Feb. 27, 1960

Dear Wilma, Willard and Darrell,

Hi! How are you? Seems like ages since I've seen you but guess it'll be ages longer yet before I will. How's Darrell? Bet he's really growing and enjoying all those Christmas toys. Bet it was nice having mom around. Wilma, a million thanks for taking care of mom the way you did. God bless you for all you're doing. Sure hope mom takes it easy now that she's home. Thanx for getting those flowers for mom. Now I hope you wrote the check from my account for them. You be sure you do it that way.

Thanks too Wilma for sending me a telegram right away. I was sort of upset until I got it that Monday morning – 3 days after the operation, pretty fast not? Really only 2 days as there's a day's difference between here and the U.S.A. We're 16 hours ahead of you.

I'm sending you a statement of my account. Hope you can understand it. You'll have to send me a list of the checks you wrote and we should have the same balance. Subtract the $78.00 I wrote out in checks from your balance and add the $112.50 I deposited and our balances should click. I think the amount I deposited is $112.50, it *may be a little less because of the exchange rate. (I deposited 50 pounds* {the Australian money system} *which should be about $112.50). You can tell me what the bank statement has. Wilma, I want to pay you the rest I owe you. I'll wait till I make my next deposit then I can pay you it all at once. I still owe you $350.00 – right?*

Well, all here is coming fine. We hope to open school next week. Our school is really nice, the other buildings aren't finished though. Dr. Koppelmann and Mrs. were here this past week. He gave the O.K. to build me a little permanent house. It'll be real nice and I'll be so happy when it's finished so I can get all my things together. I'm living with the Busse's now and they are so good to me. I think Edith Casson, a nurse, is coming over tomorrow. Sure good to have them (she and Marge) out here.

Sure rains here. We've had over 40 inches since January!

We cooked some food native style, in a pit in the ground 2 Sunday's ago. Really delicious and so unusual. Well must close for now. Hope you are all fine. A big hug for Darrell! And <u>*write*</u> *sometime. God's blessings be with you.*

Much love, Eunice

Banking sheet attached:

When I left Shattuc 9/1959, left in bank:	$246.80
Gave you in St. Louis	88.00
I deposited now about-Feb. 1960	<u>$112.50</u>
	Total $447.30

I wrote these checks:

1. Nov. 21, '59 <u>No. 17</u> to Ruth Pitney, Levittown, Pa. Hope Church Contribution — $20.00
2. Feb. 3, 1960 <u>No. 18</u> to Hope Church — $30.00

3. Feb. 13, 1960 No. 19 to Richard Redeker Sr.		$3.00
4. Feb. 16, 1960 No. 20 to Elvin Simshauser		$25.00
	Total	$78.00

$447.30
-78.00
$369.30 Balance

(The following letter is from a student at Rooke Island whom Eunice met when she went there to observe the teaching being done on a co-ed basis and is an example of how quickly relationships could form on the mission field. She was only on Rooke Island for 4-5 days.)

September 24, 1960

My dear Miss E. Redeker,

Grace, peace and love from our Lord Jesus Christ be with you and me. Amen.

Well, I want to write a letter to you now, because when we went down to the Gizarum wharf and we decided that we shall write letters to each other. So I can't break my promise I have to write to you so that wherever things happen here at Gelem I am willing to tell you. I was so sad when we brought you to the Karapo to the Umboi to go back to Wabag, while you are still on board we came ashore and all of us did not get home quickly we came so late, we left Gizarum at 10:45 in the night and our Teacher has hurried us to get home we wanted to wait for a while but he said no otherwise Misi will gets angry so we hurried to get home so quick as possible as we can.

When we arrived here the light has gone and we came near our Teacher's house we brought him in and we went down to our dormitory to sleep. We did not go to bed early we went to bed so late, while the day's breaking those girls who worked with me washing the clothes, we saw the Umboi and standing near the tank and watching it while she went.

On the 20th & 22 Sept we have got our Bible & Catechism's Exams and all of us boys and girls in the class have passed & some had failed. In Std. III all the boys & girls have passed their Exams except Stephan from Menyamya and Mesehai from Twam have failed. We had finished the Gospel of Luke and now we have started the Acts & Epistles of Luke and we are not going to read just write on the board and learn it from the board, because our Teacher has said that to us. So in 3rd term we have lots and lots to do in school and also out of school.

Also I have a piece of news to tell that we girls & boys in Standard VI are going to Dregenhafen for our Std. VI Exams. We shall leave Rooke Is. on the 12th of September we shall go to Dregerhafen for the Government Examination there. We shall have that exams on the 20 & 21st Oct. We shall go with our Teacher, because the shore at Lae will be closed at this time.

Are you happy while you are on board and also your voyage to Lae? You sick sometimes on the boat or not? Perhaps you did not get sick. I am hoping to see you some time later on Rooke Is. I cannot think of anything to write because it is time for playing "Basket Ball."

So far in love I shall close my letter now with many thanks and Best Wishes to you.

I am, Yours Affectionately,
R. Rcety. Samaritio

September 26, 1960

Dear Wilma, Willard & Darrell,

Hi! How are you? Was good to hear your voice on the tape, Wilma. Why didn't Darrell and Willard say something? Bet Darrell is really growing. Send me a picture of you all sometime.

I just got back from vacation. Was out at an island, Siassi. Sure had a good time besides visiting schools. Had fun canoeing, swimming, hiking, etc. Darrell would have gotten a thrill seeing some of the big fish we caught in the ocean behind the "Umboi," the boat which travels from the New Guinea mainland to this island.

Very rainy here these days. Seems like we're in the rainy season again but it's not really supposed to be yet.

Mom mentioned Rev. Mappes left. Hope you get another pastor soon. Ferrin was blessed in getting another one so soon.

Wilma I'm enclosing two checks. The one from Montgomery Ward would you please deposit in my account. I ordered some things from them and they didn't have them so they sent me back my money-so would you please deposit it? Also finally the money I owe you. I owe you $350.00 but I want you to have the $10.00 I added to it-so the check is $360.00. But Wilma don't cash it until about the end of November as I just deposited $450.00 in the bank through the Mission Board in St. Louis. And it may take a month or so before it is transacted.

I'll send you a list of my accounts. I also will add the 4 bills of $33.75 each which you'll have paid out of my Life Insurance.

Wilma, I don't know why they sent that book I told you about directly to me, but they did, so I took care of it. Thankx for asking about it.

Well, I'll close for now. Hoping you are all fine. Guess winter will be with you soon. Hope mom & dad's house gets finished. Write to me soon. God's blessings be with you! A hug for Darrell!

Love, Eunice

Banking sheet attached:

Eunice Account September 26, 1960

I'll start with November 1959
I'm still a member at Hope Church, Levittown, that's why the contributions there.

November Balance			$314.80
Check 18	Hope Church	$30.00	
Check 19	Richard Redeker Sr.	3.00	
Check 20	Elvin Simshauser	25.00	
Check 21	Concordia Publ House	2.85	
Check 22	Mrs. Richard Redeker Sr.	6.00	
Check 23	Lutheran Education Assn.	6.00	
Check 24	Betty Redeker	6.00	
Check 25	Concordia Publ House	3.77	
Check 26	Colliers Encyclopedia	3.95	
Check 27	Rosalie Ann Redeker	3.00	
Check 28	Hope Church	25.00	
Check 29	Montgomery Ward	64.67	
Check 30	Herbert H. Emde	41.00	
Check 31	Wilma Maschoff	360.00	
Deposited February '60			112.50
Deposited September '60			450.00
Wilma paid for insurance		101.25	
	Totals	$681.49	$877.30
			-681.49
			$195.81
Montgomery Ward Check Deposit			25.15
	Balance		$220.96

(With Birthday card)

October 1960

Dear, Florence, Richard, and Charles,

Hi! Was so good to hear your voices on the tapes. The tapes are a wonderful invention. How's everything? Hoping Charles is still happy in school. Send me a picture of you all sometime.

I've just gotten back from a trip to Siassi-an island off the coast of New Guinea where our Australian Lutheran Mission is. Was most relaxing and enjoyable. Island life is quite different and the coastal natives are culturally much more advanced.

School is coming along fine-not without problems though. Much more of a challenge teaching these "kiddoes." They're cuties though. Well, hoping you are all fine. Write some time. God's blessings be with you!

Love, Eunice

(Form Letter)

October 1960

Greetings from New Guinea,

As I am writing this letter, we are enjoying a most beautiful afternoon. The sun shining brightly on the beautiful hues of green on the mountains and valleys around us. This is normally the dry season, but we've had a lot of rain and so everything is at its height of beauty. So many beautiful flowers are also in bloom. Many times when we become discouraged and things seem to depress us, stopping to look at and enjoy God's wonderful creation around us, quickly revives our drooping spirits.

Now that almost a year of school work is completed, we look back and wonder where it has gone so quickly. It has been most enjoyable working among the boys and girls here, but also many times challenging and discouraging. Lack of textbooks, materials, and a real purpose for learning amongst the students, challenges us greatly. All of our school buildings were completed in June. These certainly help our program. Our little campus now includes a large two-room school, workshop, two boys' dormitories, one girls' dormitory, cookhouse, and three teachers' residences. My little house was also completed in June and has been a blessing to me. It's a big help to have all my things unpacked and at my disposal when I need them. Our thirteen girls have worked into our co-educational program very well. Academically they are also keeping up with the boys. Even their shyness and feeling of insecurity is wearing off more and more. It's a blessing, too, to see the boys holding an air of respect for them, whereas before they treated them more as animals. It is especially a thrill to see them come to class every morning with clean shiny skins, lap-laps and blouses.

We're looking forward to next year, when we will have twenty boys from our sister synod, the Australian Lutheran Mission, Rooke Island, join us. (They had extra teachers also that Eunice's mission needed). *The coastal natives are culturally much more advanced than our highland natives, also they are ahead educationally, so these boys should be an asset to our school. I just returned from a three-week holiday at Rooke Island. It is an island 65 miles long, and 35 miles wide at its widest point, and about 37 miles off the northeast coast of New Guinea. Around it are also many smaller islands. Island life is much different and I enjoyed the change. Canoeing, fishing, and traveling around to smaller islands was adventurous and exciting. One island was only 10 acres, but had 450 natives on it. This little island is noted for its beautiful shells, and I got a nice little collection. There was a coconut and cocoa plantation on this island. I watched the drying processes of both products. The cocoa beans are dried in large trays in the sun. The copra* (dried coconut) *is dried in a copra kiln, on wire racks with a hot fire below. The natives love to drink the milk from the green coconut as well as eat its meat. The only time I appreciated it was when we're on a long hike and was hot and thirsty. After the hot-humid climate there, I'm quite thankful to be back here in the highlands.*

We are very thankful to have added to our staff now a pastor, the Reverend Kopitzky; a doctor, Dr. Connor; and two teachers, David Schaus and Ralph Bleeke. All arrived here the middle of September. Since two new areas are being opened by the government, we hope to move two missionaries in there very soon. And so we are always in need of more men as some missionaries are also away on furlough. The added teachers will boost the education programs at our various stations. We hope eventually to have Grades 1-6 at our stations and we here at Pausa will have only Grades 7, 8, and 9, and Teacher Training. It'll be a great help once we have some trained native teachers, but that will take several years, yet. You can see the education here is still in its early stages.

Once again this month we rejoice over the baptism of about 600 adults at one of our newer stations, Papayuk. This is where the Reverend and Mrs. E. Spruth have been working since they arrived here in 1954. We request your prayers in behalf of these new fellow Christians, that they might always remain strong in faith in our Savior, Jesus Christ.

I extend to you my deepest thanks for the many letters, gifts, and messages, which have been sent to me again during the past months. It's always a boost to us to hear from you. And since we see a store only once a year, when on holiday in Madang, the packages are such a thrill.

We ask you to continue to remember us in your prayers, that God would bless His Word upon the hearts of these people, so that more and more might hear and believe in Jesus Christ, as their Savior from sin. The power of God, the Holy Spirit, at work is indeed beyond our comprehension. But once you see a person changed from his former heathen practices, beliefs, pain and torture, to a person filled with the peace and joy that beams forth after he knows Jesus as his Savior, you would never doubt for a minute but that God the Father, Son, and Holy Ghost, Trinity in Unity, is the true God. He lives and works through us today even as He did the Apostles and Evangelists in Bible times. May the Holy Spirit strengthen us all in the true faith in Christ, that we might aid in bringing souls to Him, through our personal witnessing, as well as our prayers and support to those who are carry-

ing the Gospel message throughout the world. We do not know how long the Lord is giving us to spread His Gospel, so may we work with zeal now while we have the opportunity. Remember our school here at Pausa in your prayers, asking God that He would give us wisdom and understanding as we, under the guidance of the Holy Spirit, lead these boys and girls to Him and prepare them for service in His kingdom here; that the boys and girls might be filled with a zeal and love for Him which will spur them on to greater service.

Wishing you all a very Blessed Christmas, a prosperous and joyous New Year, 1961!

In the Name of Our New-Born King!
Eunice A. Redeker

December 3, 1960

Dear Florence, Richard & Charles,

Greetings to you all! And how are you? Seems like ages since I've heard from you! Mom mentions you in her letters though.

Well, a whole year of school here is almost completed for me. And what a year it's been! So many unusual experiences, challenges, and decisions. But now that I'm getting use to everything it's much more enjoyable. With our school building program now completed all should continue to run much more smoothly. Next year we'll have an increase of about 40 students so the load will be heavier. Classes will range at 50 students. Too many to do an effective job!

Was good to hear your voices on the tapes and I'm hoping to get them back to you soon.

I'm working on a pageant with some of our students at present. It's most unusual to see Joseph, Mary, the angels, and all the characters as dark skinned people, but effective as Jesus loves them too.

How's school coming, Charles? And now you must be getting well along with your Christmas Program. You'll have to tell me all about it. Hope "Santa Claus" is good to you this Christmas. What are you hoping for?

Well, must close for now. Hoping you are all fine. God bless you at this blessed Christmas season, and all through the New Year!

Much love, Eunice

P.S. Write sometime!

Wabag, New Guinea

March 1961

Dear Friends in Christ,

Greetings once again from the "Isle of Rain". These past two months have certainly brought us an abundance of it. This is our rainy season and we get an average of about 3 to 5 inches of rain a day. Our mornings are beautiful and sunny, but by noon the clouds are thick overhead and it soon pours for most of the afternoon and evening.

Since my last letter many experiences have again been enjoyed. In December, our students gave a Christmas Pageant in simple English. To them this was a new experience. They had never visualized what it must have been like that night in Bethlehem, when Christ was born. So, this made the Christmas message more real to them. They especially enjoyed wearing the costumes and making the stage scenery. (They then "took their show on the road," so to speak, to the mission stations at Sirunki, Irelaya, Yaibos, Raiakama, and Mambisanda).

We enjoyed a relaxing school holiday for five weeks after December 22. Christmas Day was very impressive since we traveled the valley to our highest station at Sirunki, 8,700 feet. We stopped at another station, Irelya, on the way up to witness a baptism of about 600 people. All in all the jeep ride was 65 miles and we were tired and dirty by the time we arrived at the home of Rev. and Mrs. Stotik. They had a delicious turkey dinner waiting for us so we were soon revived. Being too weary to travel back that evening, we stayed overnight.

In January, we had our Annual Missionaries Conference. One of the important decisions made was to move into three new areas just west of us as soon as the government opens the territory. These are primitive areas where white man has not been. Some of these people are supposedly still cannibals. Pray for God's protection upon the missionaries entering these areas, also that God will mightily bless the preaching of His Word to these people, that they will accept the Gospel message and receive the blessings of forgiveness of sins, life and eternal salvation.

On January 31, our new school term began here at Pausa Lutheran School. So far things have been running very smoothly. Our students seem to show a greater interest in their studies and greater desire to serve their Savior. We pray that it will continue. I've been teaching our girls some simple cooking this quarter. We've done things like fry banana cakes, steam vegetables, pot roast and make stew. I always have to make sure that anything we do can be done later at their homes. They can buy iron pots, made in Hong Kong, cheaply, at their little trade stores now, so they enjoy cooking in them immensely. Today they baked some green vegetables in banana leaves. Two batches burned to a crisp, but so we learn! They cook on an open fire, using the upper half of a 40 gallon kerosene drum over the fire.

The past two Sundays have been spent going out to outstations with our Sunday School Teachers. Both stations were about eight miles and some pretty rugged climbing. The scenery, however, is so beautiful and the hike refreshing as well as bringing you a little closer to the natives and their way of life. During this past year, I've been teaching the Bible Story for each Sunday to about thirty of our schoolboys and the teachers (older men) *from the Yaramanda Congregation each week. Then they go out to the various outstations to tell the story in the native language on Sunday morning. Most of these outstations are quite a distance. I go with them occasionally to sort of check their teaching, attendance, as well as encourage the teachers. Yesterday we were at the most beautiful place I've been at yet. The congregation gathered in a little spot, valley like, between two very high mountains, along one side ran a stream of water. It was so peaceful and quiet. The children gather a little farther off so both the church service and Sunday School service could go on at the same time. The native evangelist standing in front of the group seated on the ground was a sight to behold. It reminded me so much of how Jesus used to preach to the people gathered on the mountainside. It's a great inspiration and blessing to see the Word of God being brought to these people and to know our Savior loves them too. Especially do we think of this during this Lenten Season, when we meditate on all that Jesus did for us by suffering and dying for our sins. That we, who believe in Him, might enjoy the blessings He has purchased for us with His blood. Our great joy lies in that our Savior lives and is preparing our heavenly home so that we might one day live forever with Him.*

Once again, we extend to you our sincere thanks for all the messages and articles received in the past months. The letters and encouragements as well as a reminder that you are praying for us, gives us ever greater zeal to do the Lord's work, with His help, here.

May you all enjoy a very Blessed Easter. "Because I live, ye shall live, also," Jesus tells us in John 14:19.

In the name of our Risen Savior!
Miss Eunice A. Redeker Teacher
Pausa, New Guinea

(The writer, Wilmer, followed Eunice as Principal at Hope, Levittown. His wife Bessie was in class with Eunice at RF and was the second teacher, after Eunice came to Hope. Wilmer was the third teacher, then Bessie and Wilmer married.)

June 26, 1961

Dear Eunice,

I would like to play ostrich right now and hide my head in the sand. Believe it or not, Eunice, last year at district Convention, I wrote a letter to you and I know you never received it. Before going to convention this year, I looked for information in last year's handbook and there I found the stamped letter to you. Was I ashamed when I showed it to Bessie.

The people of Hope speak very highly of you and are still admiring your consecrated work for the Lord's Kingdom. We are all remembering you and your work in our prayers and have much concern for you. By the Grace of God you had accomplished much here at Hope, as I had mentioned in my other letter.

We are certainly blessed with a very wonderful pastor to replace Pastor Maier. Pastor Maier was a great inspiration to me and my work and I am grateful to him for his past labors here. Our church is continuing to make great strides forward. We will make up our current deficit I believe, because we will discontinue our past custodial payments and, in the Fall, when school resumes the pastor and I will begin driving the school bus.

My past two years were extremely busy years here at Hope, but ones of joy because I can serve the Lord as I have not had opportunity to before.

Bessie and I are very happy in the home we purchased and she has been a big help to me in my work. For the coming year Bess will have grade one; Miss Mary Mummert of RF, grade two; Mr. Richard Poppe of Seward, grade 3 & 4; and I will have grades 5, 6, & 7.

I am serving as secretary for the moment to begin a Lutheran Junior High School in the Fall of 1962, beginning with Grade 7. We will not have definite info until our Sept. meeting. This school could greatly relieve our financial stress & "building pains" at Hope.

A word of appreciation, Eunice, for the letters and films sent to Hope, which the children greatly appreciated. The school enrollment will be approx. 160 next school year, with perhaps 8 in grade 7.

Evelyn Fettes enjoyed her year at RF immensely. Next year Janet Daley will attend Bronxville, Concordia.

I am writing this letter above the convention hall while sitting on the bed. Hope you can read it O.K.!

I promise, so help me, Eunice, to write like a faithful scout from now on.

The Lord's richest blessings to you Eunice and may His gracious Word be a comfort to you in lonely moments. I shall never forget you in my prayers. Will look forward to seeing you.

Yours in Christ's Kingdom,
Wilmer G. Kuske
P.S. Love from Bessie.

(We have extant at this time, 3 letters from Eunice's mother. While having little formal schooling and being raised speaking only the German language, Anna Twenhafel Redeker taught herself English. Hence not all the grammar is as you and I might speak or spell, however, considering being self-taught, we think it admirable.)

July 23, 1961

Dear Eunice,

I am sorry I did'n write last Sunday. we had company Aunt Helen and Onkel Paul were here. Wilma and Willard came too. In week we was so busy. Luther left to Minnesota was with National Guard for two week. He don't like that. He got his oats combine Wed. and Thursday he left. It sure sounds no good yet with the war. We have to pray to the Lord. If his will He can make peace. We find Tuesday night on TV if they call them boys to go. May be Luther be in to. It is worry to see the boys going.

Paul and Erna was here helping build our house all week. Another week or two, the old house be down. Erna help Paul. She went on the roof and take shingle off. It worry me she went up their you shut see how bad it looks now.

We have nice shower rain this last week everything look good, corn and beans. We have tomatoes to eat now. Erna gave me pickles to can. Now plum getting ripe. Erna, Paul got Betty from airport. She was this last week to Roger folks. She enjoyed when she was in Florida. She had nice time last week to. We got you letter last week. It help us if you can come next year, I can wait till then. When Edith leave from there. I look for them to come over here.

The people always ask about you. How you been. Next Sunday Ferrin give dinner for teacher Brandt, a fair well dinner. We havend no teacher yet. They call two already. They did'n accepted. Thursday they want call a different one. We havend enough kids for 4 grades. If they wood call all the grades maybe they come then. Their only 27 children in school. For our part they can do what they want. We don't know what the best is. Pastor want the 4 lowest grades to Hoffman. That cost so much. I want send you a package for you Birthday. I hate you didn't get on your Birth-day. But I can help it. We so busy.

God be with you and keep you.

With love,
Dad Mom Betty Luther

Wabag, New Guinea (Form Letter)

October 23, 1961

Greetings from the home of the Bird of Paradise!

Since I saw a Bird of Paradise for the first time several weeks ago, I had to mention it, as it was strikingly beautiful. New Guinea is the only place where they can be found. The richly bright coloured feathers were particularly beautiful on this one, red neck, hues of blue and green on its back and wings, bright black on the rest of its body. Some of them, however, are not particularly beautiful according to others who have seen them.

Since my last letter the Lord's work here has been moving along and especially here at Pausa Lutheran School we have great cause for thanks to God for His grace and blessings of this school term. Indeed there have been many failures on our part and many moments of discouragement (these discouragements could take various forms: a lack of interest in learning; the children getting discouraged easily;

them seeing no future in learning; while some did, many did not; some wanted to just go home and raise pigs or dig up gardens for the women; some wanted just to eat sweet potato; and some just wanted to make bows/arrows for times of war with another tribe) *but when one looks over the whole term and sees the progress, we can only praise God. There lies before our students also tremendous hurdles to conquer, the chief of which is the study of English and working in it, a foreign language for them. Next week our Standard six boys will be taking a government examination. If they pass it, they will be qualified to teach the lower Standards one and two. They will also be able to go on to Standard Nine and Teacher Training if they so desire. The ones who will go out to teach will be a tremendous help as teachers are very much needed. So many little ones do not have the opportunity to go to school at all.*

Several weeks ago it was discovered that eight of our students had active T.B. It was most likely brought to the Highlands by some coastal natives and since these people have never been exposed they are highly susceptible. These eight boys were sent to the coast to a sanatorium for treatment. It is quite a loss for us, but we can only be thankful no more have it.

This week we are having a change in staff here. Kenneth Bauer, who has been here at Pausa since 1957, and started this school, is being transferred to another station, Wakemare. He will be in charge of all our mission schools. He will play a big part in giving in-service training to the native teachers who are teaching at present, all of who have not had above a Standard One and Two education. Joe Neubacher is coming here to replace him. This change is possible since we have just added to our staff three teachers, Mr. and Mrs. Don Yarroll, Mr. and Mrs. Gary Cook, (both are teaching native children), and Mr. and Mrs. David Lorenz, who will be teaching at Highland Lutheran School where the children of our missionaries attend. Also added to our staff are two pastors, Rev. and Mrs. Stanley Padgette, and Rev. and Mrs. Dwight Wenger. We are very thankful that the Lord has sent these workers. Through their coming it has been possible for the Lord's work to proceed and the four new areas opened in June by the government have been able to be moved into. Rev. and Mrs. Heinicke have just moved into the Kandepe and as soon as a bush home is completed in the Maramuni, Rev. and Mrs. Padgette will move in there. Both of these places are very isolated. The Kandepe has a small airstrip, so a small Cessna plane can fly in there but the Maramuni can only be gotten to by walking approximately ten miles, over some rugged native paths. A challenging task awaits both of these families and they need our prayers. In the other two areas a missionary will not be moving into as yet, but a missionary from one of our present stations will go in regularly to check on the native evangelists stationed there who are carrying on the work.

September 23 and 24th, the Western Highlands had a native cultural and agricultural show, at Mt. Hagen about 45 miles from here. We can drive there by jeep since a road has just been completed. The road is quite adventurous a climb, at one place to 9,000 feet. The show was similar to a miniature State Fair at home (I'm thinking of Illinois). It was very interesting. Many different native tribes from various parts of the Highlands were there and it was interesting to observe the different dress of each tribe as well as their different types of dances. Also on display were many native artifacts, foods, animals of New Guinea (wallabies being most prevalent), and food introduced by Europeans, but which the natives are growing successfully as corn, potatoes, tomatoes, cabbage, lettuce, etc. In fact some of the booths looked like grocery stores. On display also was coffee from different areas of the Highlands. Coffee is the main export of the Highlands, and coffee, cacao, and copra (dried coconut) the chief exports of New Guinea. A representative from the staff of National Geographic *was there so you may see it featured in it.*

On October 8th, several of us single people on the staff here began a youth group with the native youth of our Yaramanda congregation, aged 12-20. A need for something like this has been felt for a long time by our pastors, to keep these young people interested in the church and also to afford them with an opportunity for further instruction in God's Word. It also provides an opportunity for Christian fellowship, which is foreign to them. So far, we have had two meetings and they have proven successful. If it continues we'll be starting them at each congregation. It's quite enjoyable to be with them, they are so thrilled at everything. They enjoy the simplest games tremendously.

Our students are once again beginning to practice on a Christmas Pageant. We hope to expand and improve it very much over last years performance. We plan to give it at the Yaramanda church, which holds over 700 people. This will give a larger number of people an opportunity to witness it and we pray it will help them to visualize our Savior's birth and make it more meaningful to them. Most of all we pray it will make their faith in Him much stronger.

Since this letter will be reaching you very near to the Christmas Season we pray that you too, will enjoy a "Blessed Christmas". May the news and deep joy of our Savior's birth fill your hearts with peace. I'm adding a little poem which I hope you will enjoy and that it will help you to see a little clearer the true meaning of Christmas. It was written by one of our nurses, Miss Anita Simonson.

God bless you all and grant you a "Happy and Joyous, 1962".

In the service of our Savior,
Miss Eunice Redeker

P.S. Many thanks also for all the letters, cards, etc., with which you have once again remembered me. They help to make our stay and work here possible.

What is Christmas---

In a land that never saw snow?
Where no stores out-do each other
in an effort to beautify the hearts of men—
Where Christmas trees
don't smell like Christmas trees should—
And Christmas choirs
Are found only on discs

Where Christmas shopping
Is practically non-existent

And Christmas cards
Often arrive in June---
Where at present there is no term for "Merry Christmas"
used by the "local folks"
And the Christmas meal
is sweet potatoes, just like any other day.
Where giving gifts is something new
And just now beginning to be learned
And even mistletoe is considered a weed
And can't be bought "down South"
And would you believe it?
They've never heard of Santa Claus!

So what is left---
Without these things so known and loved by us?

Why the Christ Child!

The Christmas Message!

The Savior come to earth!

The shepherds, the wise men,
They've not been lost!

A joy–filled present
A future filled with hope.
The smiling Christians
adoring their new found King.

And though the hymns are strangely non-melodious to our ears
Yet praises to our God ring out
And our bright red poinsettias bloom all year round
reminding us that Christmas is not meant only for December.
We seem to get along so well
without the other "things"

And with the thousands of "local folk"
We have Christmas.

(While we do not have copies of every Annual Report, we have included all those we have been able to access {both from Eunice's records and from CHI}. These reports went to both the executives on the mission field, as well as The Board for World Missions, The LCMS, St. Louis, Missouri).

Annual Report – Eunice Redeker – 1961

STATION WORK – By the grace of God we have again completed another school year here at Pausa. We began our school year January 31, 1961, with 96 students. During this year, I again taught English, mainly, and one class of Religion and Art. Also, Home Economics to our six girls. Discipline in the classroom is still a problem for me. *(Absorbing the teaching could be difficult for the older children, so they could lose enthusiasm and drop out).* Each year seems to show a little more progress amongst our students academically. I was advisor to our Christian Growth Committee and it has sponsored several activities – as weekly chapel services with Missionary or Enga Elder as speaker – An all Pausa Sport's Day to build school spirit – A volleyball and checker tournament – visited students who were sick at Mambisanda and carried food to them – conducted evening devotions – brought spiritual comfort and aid to students with problems, difficulties, etc. (we need to do much more of this and plan to in the coming year) – gave a Christmas Pageant at Yaramanda Church on December 8, which was attended by approximately 2,000 Enga people. Many parents and friends of our students from other stations came. In November we had a change in staff, Kenneth Bauer became Mission Education Officer, and Joe Neubacher came here to replace him. During the coming year, 1962, my teaching responsibilities will be similar to last year. I pray that with the experience gained in the past two years, the classes I will teach will be filled with more applicable, interesting and helpful material.

OTHER WORK – Teaching Pausa students who are Sunday School Teachers teaching at outstations in the Yaramanda Circuit. Teaching the Sunday School Teachers from the Yaramanda Congregation. Visited some of the outstations with our students while Rev. Hintze was on furlough. Helped work with the young people of the Yaramanda congregation since September starting a youth group. This is a project of our Wabag Luther Society.

HEALTH – Good except for a number of malaria attacks.

VACATION: No vacation as such was taken this year, however, I spent a week in Madang both in June and September for dental work.

PLANS: -- To return to the U.S. in July, 1962.

ALL PRAISE AND THANKS TO GOD for the countless blessings He has granted us again this year spiritually and physically. We ask forgiveness for the many times our weakness and failings kept us from doing His work with greater zeal. We pray His forgiveness for all our wrongs and ask His continued blessings, wisdom, strength and guidance in the coming year.

Respectfully submitted,
Eunice Redeker

(Form Letter)

March 24, 1962

Dear Friends,

Greetings once again from the Isle of Eternal Spring. As we hear over the news (Voice of America) *about the weather getting warmer and the first day of spring in the United States, it reminds us of the constantly beautiful spring weather we have. The grass and trees are always refreshing hues of green.*

Since I have a large amount of correspondence piling up on me to be answered, I've decided to write a Newsletter to answer you in this way. With the heavy school schedule plus trying to get a lot of things done before leaving here, I find little extra time.

I'm planning to return to the States sometime this September or October. The terms for single workers have been shortened to three years out here. We're very thankful the Board for World Missions has made this decision, as the lack of contact with civilization makes a break after three years very welcome. God-willing and if plans work out, one of the nurses and I plan to travel home by boat via Europe. It should be very interesting and educational. We will be calling in at various ports along the way in Asia, the Middle East and the Mediterranean. Then we hope to tour the Holy Land and Europe, catching a boat in London back to the U.S.

We are very happy to report that the Lord's Word here is moving forward. Five new areas have been opened by the government since my last letter. Native evangelists have been sent into all of those areas. Plans are being made to send a Missionary into some of the areas. We're hoping and praying it will be possible for the thirteen staff members our Mission is calling this year to come out so that the work can be carried on. We ask you to remember these people and the work here in your prayers. Especially also pray that God will bless His Word on the hearts of the people so they will believe and one day be with us in heaven. Also, remember the native evangelists in your prayers. Many of them have very little training, but God can and is using them in a very wonderful way to spread His Word. Sometimes they are able to work much more effectively than we as they understand their own people and the language much better.

Pausa School year got under way February 5, with one hundred students, brought in from various of our Mission Stations. The Standard Six students of last year are now at Rooke Island, taking Standard seven. After Standard Seven they will take teacher training for one year and we hope come back here to the Highlands to teach. We also had a lot of drop outs, which is a problem here. Some just can't make it intellectually, while others lose enthusiasm and interest. As long as education isn't compulsory this will most likely be a problem. I've also been working on a few booklets and outlines for our Girl's Program. This is turning out to be quite a job.

In closing, a sincere thanks to all of you for the messages which have come my way, especially also all the Christmas letters, cards, etc. It certainly is a joy hearing from you. We pray God's rich blessings on you all and may you all enjoy a "Blessed Easter" in our Lord who lives.

With Christian greetings,
Miss Eunice Redeker

(The following was added by Hope Lutheran, Levittown, PA:)

NOTE FROM THE PASTOR: Miss Eunice Redeker formerly was a teacher at Hope School. She in 1959 accepted a call to be a Missionary Day school teacher in New Guinea. Her correspondence keeps Hope's members informed as to the Lord's work in the New Guinea Mission field. The Board for Parish Education of Hope has tentatively set the month of August 1962 as 'Operation Eunice' in which the New Guinea mission field will be emphasized. We sincerely pray that Miss Redeker may be in our midst sometime in the fall of '62 to speak with us. Our prayers are requested for the Lord's work in the foreign mission field.

(Pastor Walter A. Maier Jr., Pastor at Hope when Eunice served there accepted a call to another congregation. This letter is from the Pastor at Hope, Levittown, PA, serving in 1962)

September 12, 1962

Dear Sister in Christ:

I sincerely pray that this letter finds you in the best of health, and that the Lord has showered His continual blessing upon you. We here at

Hope constantly remember you in our prayers, and are eagerly looking forward to seeing you.

With your approval, this is the tentative schedule that has been drawn up by the Board of Parish Education in conjunction with "Operation Eunice," with which a mission drive will be proposed.

I sincerely pray that the following dates will meet with your approval, and naturally subject to your arrival: Wednesday, November 14, an open house for all the Philadelphia Circuit area churches of the Atlantic, English and Eastern Districts are invited to Hope for the presentation and program (I am the evangelism representative for the Philadelphia Circuit); Saturday, November 17, the Board has denoted as Family Night at Hope with a fellowship supper; Sunday, the 18th, I thought in place of my sermon, if you are willing, you can give your heart-rending experiences under the Word of God for approximately 20 minutes, which I believe would be most inspiring for our people and for myself as well.

Vice-president Clarence Roth of the Eastern District has written a letter to me requesting, if you can possibly, tell of your experiences to his parish in Easton on Friday the 16th, during the week that you will, God-willing, be in Levittown. I told him that I would write to you and let him know of your answer.

I know, Eunice, that this is more or less a personal visit to the congregation, and yet it can be a real nourishing for Christ's sheep through His words from you. On the other hand, if you do not feel that you are "up to it," please do not hesitate to let me know.

Wishing you God's blessings, I remain,

Yours in Christ,
Santo L. Puglia, Pastor

October 7, 1962

(Postcard mailed from Zurich)

Dear Richard, Florence and Charles,

Hi! Happy Birthday Richard! God bless you and grant you many more. We're in Switzerland and it's so beautiful we'd just like to stay. Are going to walk up a mtn. peak just now but thought I'd get a few cards off first. Every bit of our trip has been wonderful. Glad we're use to walking from New Guinea.

Love to all, Eunice

(During all of Eunice's furloughs, an expectation of the LCMS Board of Missions {and herself}, was that she would travel to numerous congregations {throughout the Midwestern US and beyond}, particularly those who had and were supporting her through their tithes and offerings, to present slide shows and information on the work being conducted on their behalf in spreading the Word of God in New Guinea. The following two entries are excerpts from her home congregation, Bethlehem Lutheran Church, Ferrin, Illinois.)

December 2, 1962

Bethlehem Lutheran Sunday bulletin

Men's Club will meet Mon., Dec. 3, 7:30 p.m.

Walther League will meet Mon., Dec. 10, instead of Tues., Dec. 11. Miss Eunice Redeker will show slides at both of these meetings, which she took while in New Guinea, as teacher. She showed these slides at school *(Bethlehem had a Lutheran Day School at this time)* this last week. The slides are not only extremely interesting but also heartwarming when we see how the Lord has blessed the efforts of these faithful workers in this mission field.

December 9, 1962

Bethlehem Lutheran Sunday bulletin

Ladies Aid Christmas party, Thurs., Dec. 13. Potluck dinner but the meat and potatoes will be furnished by the committee. Bring 50 cent gift for exchange, children 25 cent gift...Miss Eunice Redeker will speak and show slides of her work in New Guinea.

Christmas 1962

Shattuc, Illinois
Greetings at Christmas!

....And with this message we pray you all will enjoy a truly blessed Christmas, and that the great joy of our Savior's birth will fill you and remain with you in the coming New Year!

With a heart filled with praise, I greet you from Illinois! The past months are once again a wonderful testimony to the protection and mercy of our God. Reta Wiebe, a nurse from New Guinea, and I traveled home to the States via the Philippines, Hong Kong, Singapore, Colombo, Bombay, Karachi, Aden, Egypt, Europe, England. It was a most enjoyable trip, a tremendous experience, and an opportunity to see what is being done to bring the Gospel into all the world.

A brief overview of our trip: I left New Guinea August 10, which was a close "call," since I didn't receive my passport until the evening I left, and the plane I was to take out of the Highlands couldn't land due to fog. Later that evening our mail plane was able to stop and pick me up. This made it possible for me to get the next plane at Goroka to Madang on the coast. The next morning I was off to Manila via Wewak, Hollandia, and Biak. At Hollandia we could not leave the airport since the natives were having a demonstration against the Indonesians. At Biak we transferred to a jet, the first I'd seen, and in it enjoyed a smooth, fast ride to Manila. At the airport Mrs. David Schneider, the wife of one of our missionaries in Manila, and Reta, who had been in Australia for a visit, met me. We spent a most interesting week in Manila and Baguio City area. We were also able to make a trip into the mountain areas with Rev. and Mrs. Herbert Kretzmann one day. This was especially interesting since it reminded us very much of New Guinea. It was a joy to meet many of our mission staff there and also our fellow-Christian Filipinos. Then on to Hong Kong on a DC-8 Cathay-Pacific flight. The deluxe service and comfortable accommodations are very much appreciated after New Guinea service. Hong Kong was an exciting and interesting place. We enjoyed the scenery, beaches, and visits with our missionaries there, as well as the opportunity to buy things cheaply. Quite a treat after not having seen a department store for three years. A tremendous mission challenge awaits us in Hong Kong—many souls remain to be reached. We left Hong Kong after one week, on the SS VICTORIA, an Italian ship. We had become acquainted with it through Rev. and Mrs. Hafner of Hong Kong, who had traveled on it the year before. We traveled from Hong Kong to Naples, stopping at Singapore, Colombo, Bombay, Karachi, Aden, Suez – including a day trip to Cairo – meeting the ship again in Port Said. During this time we had an opportunity to be among the Orientals—Chinese, Malayan, Indian, Pakistanian, and Egyptians—as well as Europeans. This was in itself an education. There were very few Christians among them, which reminds us "many do not know our Savior"—a great task awaits us. We enjoyed "Shish Kebab" in Singapore; looking at beautiful, precious stones and jewels in Colombo; the community washes, gate to India, curried foods, Hindu temple, Indian silks in Bombay; the hot and sand climate, veiled women in purdah, oxen, goat and camel driven carts and wagons, beautiful American embassy, and lovely Anglican church and service in Karachi. A hot, dry Aden (had to have a tooth pulled there and was fortunate to get treatment from the British Royal Air

Force free of charge). Aden, as Hong Kong, is also a duty free port and things can be bought very cheaply. Our day trip to Cairo was filled with experiences including the Egyptian Museum, old Cairo (in it is the church where Joseph, Mary and Jesus were to have hid), the pyramids, and camel ride. Then on to Naples, a very beautiful seaport, and with the arrival there we were beginning to feel the nearness of home. We also toured Pompei with its interesting excavations, and the isle of Capri. We went on to Rome, Florence, Pisa, Venice, Milan in Italy; to Luzerne and Zurich, Switzerland; Paris, France; Luxembourg; Heidelberg, Mainz, Bonn, Cologne, Germany; Amsterdam and the Hague in Holland; Brussels, Belgium. From Ostend, we took a ferry over to Dover and went by train on to London, Cardiff, Wales, and Southampton, where we boarded the SS QUEEN ELIZABETH and sailed for New York. The whole trip was so very interesting, each country has its beauties and attractions. The weather was grand all the way. Italy with its mild climate was lovely, and as we traveled north we enjoyed the fall season, which we had missed in New Guinea. As we were in London, it was quite cold. Prices also kept going up as we moved north. Reta and I stayed at youth Hostels in every instance. We really enjoyed them as it gave us a wonderful opportunity to meet a lot of young people, fellow-travelers, as well as being economical. We were glad we were used to walking, and wished we had had a pedometer! We enjoyed the London sights, architecture, scenery, cultures, as well as the people. We had stiff necks from looking up at the ceilings in the cathedrals, etc., throughout our travels, but they were too beautiful to miss. In London we were fortunate to see the Queen, Princess Margaret, and Princess Alexandra, even tho' only a glimpse, as they were in the "Opening of Parliament" parade. I was also able to make it out to Cardiff, Wales, where Rev. and Mrs. Marvin Brammeier are stationed. Since knowing them from our area in Illinois, we had a most wonderful visit. The new church there won the British Architectural Award this year.

The QUEEN ELIZABETH was luxurious and most beautiful. Being a very heavy ship the ride was very smooth except for the first day when we hit a tremendous storm. Arrival in New York was at 11:45 p.m., November 6. It was a crystal clear, moonlight night, and the New York skyline was simply astounding! We just marveled, and our hearts were filled with gratitude to God for the blessings we had known, and to see our own United States again. We were not allowed to disembark until 8:00 A.M. the next morning. We were up most of the night—too excited to sleep. We were off on the dot of 8:00, and there to meet us were eighteen friends from the congregation of Hope Lutheran Church, Levittown, Pennsylvania, where I had taught for three years before going to New Guinea. Also there to meet us were Rev. and Mrs. Kenneth Hoener, Centereach, Long Island, and Mr. and Mrs. Don Bickel and sons of Paramus, N.J. What an unforgettable thrill—and the bond of Christian friendship and fellowship we all felt, the oneness in Christ! I spent several days in Centereach, Paramus, Levittown, and the Philadelphia area. The days were very uplifting and faith-strengthening, as the zeal of fellow Christians shone forth in the people as we were able to share our experiences of the past three years.

On November 24th my brother and sister drove from Illinois to Levittown to pick me up and take me home to Illinois. We arrived in time for Thanksgiving. It was a tremendous thrill to see my parents, brothers, sisters, relatives, and friends here again. I'm just enjoying every minute while at home. I haven't decided definitely what I will be doing, but am praying the Lord for guidance. As our Pastor in one of the Advent services said, "Let us enter the New Year with these words on our hearts and lips, 'Take Thou our hands and lead us, Lord Jesus'."

In closing, I pray the Lord's rich blessing on us all. May He keep us in the true faith until life's end. And, as we kneel before the manger again this Christmas, may the love of God shine in our hearts as we see this Jesus as our Savior from sin, Satan, and hell, and may His love remain with us in the New Year, and give us the courage, wisdom and zeal to share Him with all whom we meet.

In our Savior's name,
Eunice A. Redeker

Annual Report – Eunice Redeker – Teacher – New Guinea – 1962

This past year again has been richly filled with blessing from our heavenly Father. In January I prepared for the beginning of our school term at Pausa Lutheran School. I also wrote a booklet on Ways of Cooking for our girl's program. February through June I was kept occupied at Pausa. I also worked with young people of the Yaramanda congregation and the Sunday School there. I taught the teachers from Pausa and Yaramanda. During the Easter holidays Reta Wiebe and I walked the eleven miles from Mambisanda to Pawari and spent Easter with "the Fehrmanns'".

On August 10, I left New Guinea, flying to Manila, via Hollandia and Biak. I met Reta Wiebe in Manila and we spent a week in the Manila-Baguio area. We met a lot of the Missionaries and got acquainted with the work being done there. I also had two lectures there. Then we spent one week in Hong Kong and again enjoyed the sights as well as visiting with the Missionaries. I had several lectures there. Then we travelled by boat, the S.S. Victoria, through the Orient stopping at Singapore, Colombo, Bombay, Karachi, Aden, Suez with a day trip to Cairo, Port Said, Naples. Then we travelled by train and hitch hiking across Europe for forty days. In England we met some of our pastors and visited churches in London and Cardiff, Wales. We arrived in New York, November 6. I spent three weeks on Long Island, Paramus, New Jersey, and the Philadelphia area, during which time my lecture schedule was very heavy. I arrived at my home in Shattuc, Illinois, November 25, and relaxed a bit as well as lecturing on various occasions.

I have been in good health.

In closing, we praise and thank God for His innumerable blessings, his guidance and protection. We pray that He would abide with me so that again this year I might serve Him in His kingdom in the way He leads.

Respectfully submitted,
Eunice Redeker
Teacher – New Guinea

(Over the course of the next several pages, you will read, sometimes interspersed between other letters, eight correspondences which Eunice continually sent throughout the years on the mission field to individuals and organizations within individual congregations, thanking them for their support of both her and the mission work being done in New Guinea.)

Holy Cross Ladies Aid, c/o Onida, South Dakota

January 6, 1963

Dear Friends in Christ,

Greetings from Shattuc, Illinois! It is indeed a joy to be home and, in the U.S., again. Although I found it took a little adjusting to get use to all the conveniences and pace of life in America. But God has granted us a wonderful country for which we ought daily thank and praise Him.

I want to extend to you my sincere thanks for the $5.00 you sent to me. It is especially very helpful at this time. I have been busy lecturing and just started teaching in a Lutheran School this past week. I will teach till June after which I plan to return to New Guinea about August. I will have to see how plans develop, but if possible, I will stop by next summer as I tour the west before returning to New Guinea. I have appreciated your many kindnesses and faithfulness in encouraging me in this work of our Lord.

We pray each of you will be richly blessed with joy and peace in our Lord and may your zeal to bring the Gospel to men everywhere be ever more fervent.

With Christian love,
Eunice A. Redeker

(Trenton, New Jersey)

January 7, 1963

Dear Pastor Leber,

Thank you for your letter of December 11. It was a joy hearing from you.

I was happy to hear your children at Bethany Lutheran School would be interested in supporting a native missionary in New Guinea. I know this will bring some vital interest to them, as well as giving them a real part in bringing Christ to those who don't know Him. I would suggest you write to Rev. William Wagner, Wabag, New Guinea. He is being placed in a new area and will be in direct contact with these native missionaries. You might mention that I suggested him to you and I'm sure he will give this immediate attention.

The blessings of our Lord be upon all of you in this New Year and always.

In our Savior's name, Eunice Redeker

(Aurora, Illinois)

January 7, 1963

Dear Mrs. Siefrid,

Your letter of December 31 was received and I shall try to be of as much help as possible to you in arranging a booth for your mission fair. I am enclosing several newsletters with general information on New Guinea. Then under separate cover I am sending you some native artifacts for display. I would appreciate if you could return them as soon as possible after your fair since I use them when I lecture. The following is a translation of the Bible verse you plan to put on your miniature Bibles – this is the Pidgin English, one of the main languages used in New Guinea – "Got, onepela tok bilong Yu, em I lait bilong lek bilong mipela, na lam bilong rot bilong mipela." (In English: The Word of God is the one talk that belongs to you, God is the light to our legs and is the lamp to light the road for us).

We are thankful for your interest in this work of our Lord. May this fair be a real inspiration to many and bring honour to our Lord. His blessings be with you. If I can be of further help, let me know.

Faithfully yours, Eunice Redeker

January 7, 1963

Dear Dr. Koppelmann:

In answer to your letter regarding a lady teacher coming to New Guinea to take my place, I will list some of the qualifications I feel necessary for anyone working in the girls' program and general education at Pausa: 1. Being acquainted with elementary education generally. 2. An acquaintance with the field of Home Economics – a course would be helpful. 3. Being able to do general housework. 4. Knowledge of mothercraft and childcare. 5. A good first aid course, in fact, experience at practical nursing would be very helpful. 6. Being able to put ideas and theories into actual practice, adapted to the situation. 7. Enjoying physical activity and physical education. 8. Some knowledge of music and playing an instrument. 9. Being able to live alone with little social life. A lot of interests help. 10. A course in linguistics would be advantageous and a course in English as a foreign language would be very helpful.

After reading the letter on your applicant, I feel she could qualify for the situation at Pausa, however, she should, if possible, get acquainted with Home Economics as a course and general knowledge. I'd also check thoroughly on her emotional stability, you're on your own in New Guinea to an extent. Since there isn't another single woman teacher in our mission you don't have anyone to share little things with. It takes a mature person.

These are just thoughts that come to my mind now so I wrote them down for you. I realize they're asking for a lot in one person, and I don't have it either, but it's just for your help. Had a letter from Otto Hintze today. They're getting ready to move to Irelya. I'm sure his work as full-time in language, will be a big help to the mission. I'm teaching at present at Bethesda Lutheran School, Pine Lawn. Have been booked for lectures every weekend and keep getting more requests.

The Lord bless and guide you in this New Year as you serve Him in this great task of bringing the Gospel to souls.

Very cordially yours, Eunice Redeker

January 7, 1963

Dear Dr. Koppelmann,

Would you kindly extend my sincere thanks to the Board for the bonus of $65.00 given to me? I appreciate your kindness to me very much.

The Lord grant to each of you a rich measure of His strength, encouragement, wisdom and zeal as you work toward the extending of His kingdom.

With cordial greetings,
Eunice Hausler
Teacher – New Guinea

January 9, 1963

Dear Eunice,

Thank you very much for the two letters of January 7 and the annual report. One of these letters asks for a report to the Board and we shall express to them your thanks. Your annual report of course brings us up to date on your situation now and I am happy to know that you are in the school in Pine Lawn. I am sure this will give you a lot of the background experience that you need. With it we shall be waiting for you also to give us word on your possible return to New Guinea later on.

Also, I very much appreciate your giving us the information on what you feel a teacher is going to need. This really is a big order and I just hope it doesn't scare too many people out but perhaps if it does scare out a few it will finally give us a better teacher to do the job.

Your letters indicate that they are coming from Shattuc, Illinois. I wonder if you have an address out in Pine Lawn or a phone number that we might fall back on once in a while. If we could have information like that it may just prove helpful on occasion.

May your days in the U.S. classroom prove a real joy and satisfaction to you.

Very cordially yours,
Herman H. Koppelmann
Executive Secretary

January 15, 1963

Dear Pastor, Leah, Walter & David, (Maier)

Greetings to you! I have been wanting to drop you a line for a long time but as usual I didn't get at it. Seems like the days have just flown since I've been in the U.S. I have enjoyed every minute though and it's wonderful to be here. I enjoyed a few days with the Bickles and in Levittown. This was a real joy as you can imagine. It was good to see the progress made at Hope. You, Pastor and Leah, were a real missing link, though. It just wasn't the same. I hope I can get to see you sometime soon. I'd really enjoy seeing and talking with you. I'm teaching at Bethesda Lutheran School, St. Louis, so if ever you are down this way, let me know.

I'm planning to return to New Guinea in August, the Lord-willing. The need there is great and I feel leaving now would not be making use of the experience and language I have acquired, which takes time, and I could go back this time and move ahead. So, I'm praying about it.

How are Walter and David? Is Walter still taking piano? Hope both of them are enjoying school. After seeing the children at Hope, I know they'll have grown a lot. I hardly recognized some of the children at Hope, they had changed so much.

I've been kept busy lecturing now on weekends. I enjoy it, an opportunity to witness for the Lord. You also meet many fellow Christians, eager to serve the Lord, which is a strength to us.

We pray this finds you all well and happy and the Lord's rich blessing be with you!

In our Savior's name, Eunice

P.S. Would enjoy hearing from you when you have a minute.

(New York, New York)

January 15, 1963

Dear Mrs. Rabeler,

Your letter to me was received upon my arrival in Levittown, Pennsylvania. However, I have not gotten to answer it due to many commitments and the holiday season.

You requested that, if possible, I might visit your Ladies Aid. I have decided to teach for six months here in the States before returning to New Guinea in August. I am planning a trip to Niagara Falls, Ontario, in June for my girlfriends wedding so maybe I could arrange to visit you at that time. If this would be agreeable to you, would you kindly let me know and we could work out the further details.

We pray you had a Blessed Christmas and may the blessings of the Christ Child be with you in this New Year.

With Christian greetings, Eunice Redeker

(LWML, North WS-Upper MI Dist.)

January 15, 1963

Dear Mrs. Brismaster,

Greetings to you. I have been meaning to write you since I arrived home December 1, but my time has been kept occupied with lecturing, meetings and visiting during the busy season just behind us. We pray you enjoyed a Blessed Christmas and that His blessings will attend you in this New Year.

In regards to speaking at your Zone Spring Rally, I would consider it a special privilege to do so. About what dates would be involved? I'm teaching school at present so I would have to make the arrangements so I could line things out here. So maybe if you could let me know approximately when, I would try to see if I could arrange to make it. I would also like to visit the Topaz Ladies. They have been some of my sturdy supporters.

I shall look forward to your reply.
In Christ, Eunice Redeker

(Winamac, Indiana)

January 15, 1963

Dear Mr. Kroft,

Many thanks for your letter. It was good to hear from you. We also hope you had a very Merry Christmas and wish you the Lord's richest blessings in this New Year. Did you get to Levittown for Christmas?

On coming to Winamac and then to Levittown: I would be able to keep the Winamac date most likely but not the one on the 17th of April. I am teaching from January through June here in St. Louis at Bethesda Lutheran School. I have to go to Niagara Falls, Canada, in June for a wedding so I plan to go to Levittown then from there. So,

I'll have to skip going in April. If the 17th date at St. Paul's could be changed to Saturday afternoon or evening of the 20th I could maybe make that. The Board has set up a policy that congregations give us $.07 a mile for travel. I'm not sure how far it is from here to Winamac. If it would be as well with you that I speak there in June on my way to Niagara Falls that may work out as well.

I've been enjoying my days here in the States so very much. I sure feel the cold but maybe by the time the winters over I'll be use to it! Hoping this finds you well and in best of spirits.

I will look forward to your reply.

Sincerely, Eunice Redeker

(Trinity Lutheran Church, Boone, Iowa)

February 23, 1963

Dear Friends in Christ,

Sincere greetings to all of you and many thanks for the most enjoyable few hours I was able to spend with you and share with you the work of our Lord in New Guinea. May you continue in this zeal of bringing Christ to people in all the world. Thanking you also for the money gift. The Lord continue His blessings upon you.

In Christ's name, Eunice A. Redeker

(Trinity Lutheran Church, Centralia, IL)

March 18, 1963

Dear Pastor Kolb,

In answer to you note of March 13, regarding the adoption of a Missionary in New Guinea: The Missionary-Pastor at our station is Rev.

Rothenbusch, who just arrived in New Guinea last August, and consequently I have not met him. The two fellow Missionary-Teachers are Mr. Ralph Bleeke and Mr. Arlo Lehmann. Mr. Bleeke, I know, but Mr. Lehmann also just arrived on the field last August. So this gives you a little choice.

We are very appreciative of your interest in keeping close to our Mission in such a direct way. May the Lord grant that this venture will be an inspiration to all of you at Trinity and I know such contacts mean very much when you are out in the Mission field.

Sincerely yours, Eunice Redeker

Bethesda Lutheran School
4111 Cedarwood
Pine Lawn 20, MO

March 29, 1963

Dear Eunice,

I want you to know that the Board is very happy to have your word that you intend to return to New Guinea this fall. It means so much to us to have staff return and carry on the work that it has already become pretty well acquainted with. We know that you also are able to render some very genuine services to the work that a new person just would not be able to give at all. So may the Lord really bless your decision and let you see even more fruits during the second term of service than you did in the first.

Very cordially yours,
Herman H. Koppelmann
Executive Secretary

Cross Reference Sheet July 5, 1963
Name or Subject
Eunice Redeker

Regarding: Excerpt in letter to Karl Stotik from Paul M. Heerboth

I met with Miss Eunice Redeker on Friday, June 28, when she stopped by the office. She reported her father's illness; he is hospitalized in Lutheran Hospital and is in need of major surgery. Nonetheless she reported that she is preparing to return to New Guinea, and her hope is to leave for the field by September 1. She is proceeding with packing and shipping plans, but will wait a number of weeks to determine her father's condition before actually confirming air departure date.

(This was a native student at Rooke Island. Eunice had him as a student for 2-3 years previously.)

August 9, 1963

Dear Miss Eunice,

I was very thankful for your kindness of sending the Holy Bible to me. I was very happy indeed. All the students who saw the Bible, wanted to buy it from me. I said that it's mine. I haven't two so that you can buy it from me.

I got the letter which you wrote it to me. I read the notes that you told me in the letter and it was very interested to me. I would like to tell you some things that happen on Rooke Is.

In 14th June we dedicated one of our new school building here at Gelem. All people from all villages came here to Gelem because we invited them. Pastor Nagle preach us the sermon. After he had finished the sermon we sang a hymn and he prayed. We close our devotion by singing another hymn. He then told the people to go and see inside of the room.

There are five rooms. The big room we use as the Luther League room. Four of them are class rooms. The people were interested to see the rooms. After this we told the people to go and sit in the old class room. There we brought some food to them. After the meal they all went to their villages.

On June 7 we Leaguers from Gelem went up to Awelkon to have our Zone Rally. The people from Awelkon invited all Luther Leaguers from every villages and us here at Gelem. We played at night and made some rules. On Saturday we had a meeting of the marriage of how the boys and girls are going to marry. After that we had a sport. The students from Gelem won the sport. The Leaguers from every villages gave us a new basket ball as our prize. We were very interested to play and laugh together. At night we had some games. After the games we all went to bed. The time was ½ past 11.

Early in the morning on Sunday we had our bath and the bell rang. We all dressed up and went to church. We had Holy Communion in the church. After our church we went back to our houses.

The bell rang again and we went to have our meeting. The President of the Luther League close our meeting.

After that we all sing the National Song, "God save the Queen." We came out and took our walk to Gelem. Our next Rally will be held in December. I will tell you about it latter.

May God Our Father grant you His blessing and may our Lord and Saviour Jesus Christ be with you always. Hope to hear from you.

Yours very sincerely,
Willard Wemalo

P.S. My new address is at the top of the first page. Pardon me for my writing.

August 14, 1963

TO WHOM IT MAY CONCERN:

This is to certify that Miss Eunice Redeker is a missionary under appointment to the Board for World Missions of the Lutheran Church – Missouri Synod for service in New Guinea. Miss Redeker previously taught under our Board in the Mission in New Guinea from September of 1959 until the latter part of August in 1962, at which time she returned to the States for furlough. Her plans are to return to New Guinea the first of September 1963 for the second three-year period.

Miss Redeker is an American citizen having been born in this country.

The Board for World Missions guarantees transportation costs both to and from New Guinea as well as her keep while she is on the field and any costs of any repatriation should that become necessary for some reason.

Any courtesy that might be extended in renewing Miss Redeker's visa will be greatly appreciated by us.

Very truly yours,
(On official LCMS stationery with embossed seal)

The Board for World Missions of
The Lutheran Church – Missouri Synod
A.G. Erdmann
Business Manager

(Blue Aerogramme)

October 7, 1963

Dear Richard, Florence & Charles,

"Happy Birthday" Richard! Sorry, I don't have a birthday card. Hope you have a Happy Day! And Happy Year ahead. God's blessings be with you!

Well, how's everything? Haven't heard from anyone, except one letter from Mom telling about her burn- so I've been concerned and wondering how things are.

Everything here is going real fine! Have been kept busy, teaching since I got here, so it didn't ever seem like I had been away. Ralph Bleeke and Arlo Lehman are real good to work with too. Everything seems rather quiet after the hustle and bustle at home. I was sorry I had to leave all that packing for you, Florence, but I sure appreciate your help.

One of the big adjustments again is to get use to waiting for everything you need. Will be glad when a few of the things I've ordered will get here. My 2 barrels I sent off Aug. 1 are also at the coast so that was good time. They should get here any day.

Charles, how's school coming? Hope you're enjoying every day.

Yesterday we dedicated the new hydroelectric plant which supplies electricity for the hospital and Pausa, here. I sure am happy we have it again. Sure hated lighting kerosene lanterns.

I'm writing this as I'm sitting with the St. (Standard) *5's during their study period. They're such "cuties" and "sweeties" when they're busy.*

Must close. Hope you are all fine. Really getting wear out of the dress from Gert. Must write her soon. God's blessings be with you.

Much love, Eunice

New Guinea Lutheran Missions—Missouri Synod, Wabag, New Guinea

November 15, 1963

Dear Relatives and Friends,

Greetings once again from New Guinea! After a very enjoyable and busy furlough year, I have again safely arrived here to continue serving the Lord among His people in this part of the world. It is a joy to be back, although it was hard to leave family and friends in the United States.

Just to give a brief overview of my furlough…After arriving home on November 25, 1962, I enjoyed a month and blessed Christmas season with relatives and friends at home in Shattuc, Illinois. Then January thru June, I taught grades three, four, and five at Bethesda Lutheran School in St. Louis. It was good to be in an American classroom again and catch up on a few of the new ideas and methods in elementary education. Working with Principal Herbert Schollmeyer was also an enriching experience. We worked under rather trying conditions in the two basement rooms of the City Hall, next door to the police department office, but we were thankful to have this space during this time while they were building a new school. I saw the new school just before leaving the U.S., and it is a very modern and beautiful set up now.

My weekends and some evenings were spent travelling on speaking engagements. I found these very spiritually uplifting and inspiring as I was able to share the Lord's work with fellow Christians. The warmth and bond of Christian love I felt was such a wonderful experience and it was one way the Lord builds us and encourages us to continue His work. It's amazing what the Lord can accomplish through His people! How gracious and merciful He is to use us weak and feeble creatures to do His tremendous tasks! We can only pray that He will help us to ever be grateful and thankful for the opportunities He gives us to serve Him.

After school was out June 9, I began packing for New Guinea, and it was in the midst of this that my father became seriously ill and was hospitalized for seven weeks. We were kept busy visiting him, as well as keeping necessary things done at home. We were very happy when he could return home in early August. We were grateful for all of your prayers, as you wrote and told us how you were praying for him. The Lord heard and answered in His own way.

During August I travelled most of the time. First, east through Pennsylvania, across New York state, ending up in Niagara Falls, Canada, on August 10th for the wedding of my friend who travelled home with me via Europe last August, September and October 1962.

The wedding was beautiful, and Niagara Falls was a lovely setting for it.

Because of teaching full time in St. Louis, for the following speaking engagements, I flew to Kansas for the Kansas District Convention in Wichita, which was certainly very inspiring. I also got to the Kansas District Walther League Convention in Oakley, and it was a thrill to see so many young people active in, as well as being inspired to carry forward, the Lord's work. Then I flew to Cedar Rapids, Iowa, to a Lutheran Women's Missionary Retreat. Once again, a wonderful and inspiring Spirit-filled three days in the out-of-doors to share and be built up in the strength of the Lord. The wonderful memories of all these experiences are a strength in moments of discouragement and disappointment at times out here. I was not able to do all the travelling I had planned, but time and circumstances just didn't allow it. I regret that I didn't get to areas of the U.S., especially where some of you have done so much to help spread the Gospel in New Guinea in my contacts with you. But we pray you will continue to be filled with zeal to help carry the Gospel message to others.

One thought stands out, however, when I think of the many fellow Christians I met everywhere throughout the part of the world I saw in the past year, and that is the words in the hymn, "<u>Onward Christian Soldiers</u>" – "Like a mighty army moves the church of God" – "we are not divided, all one body we" – "Blend with ours your voices, in the triumph song: Glory, laud and honor, Unto Christ, the King!"

After spending a week and a half at home, it was a little sad leaving on September 5, but the Lord supplied the strength and courage. I then spent four wonderful days with friends at St. Thomas Lutheran Church, San Bruno, California. They gave me a royal send off, assuring me of their prayers and help. I was also happy I had the opportunity to attend the California-Nevada Sunday School Teachers' Convention while there. Then a beautiful morning flight to Hawaii on September 9th, where I met four couples who were going to New Guinea for their first time. We enjoyed a day in "beautiful Hawaii." We left Honolulu at 12:00 midnight and had a most enjoyable and safe overnight trip to Sydney, Australia. It was fast, only six hours—jets speed you around the world in a hurry! We spent a day in Sydney, and then flew on to Port Moresby that night. On this flight, however, one of the plane engines stopped so we had to spend a day in Townsville, Australia, to get it fixed. This was a wonderful opportunity to see a bit of that part of Australia. Then it was wonderful to be back on the island of New Guinea again. After spending a night in Port Moresby, we flew in to Wabag, making five stops on the way, so it took us seven hours to fly 400 miles – so you can see things really slow down once you get to New Guinea! But it did give the new people a chance to see a bit of the country on the way to Wabag. We arrived at Pausa, Friday p.m., September 13th. I received a warm welcome from students and staff. Even my house was all ready for me, beautifully decorated with flowers by the students. I started teaching the following Monday, since they had been short a teacher after Joe Neubacher left in July. This way I quickly got back into the swing of things, and it hardly seemed that I had ever been away, except that the school has added two new classrooms, two dormitories, a large dining room, and two new staff members, Ralph Bleeke and Arlo Lehmann, since last year! This is the amazing thing in the Mission generally, the growth, which has been fantastic! How richly the Lord has blessed His work here! Many new stations have been opened, many baptisms has increased the number of souls to almost 18,000, and 30 staff members have been added. Many new areas will be opened soon and we pray we will have the manpower to enter them. The Wabag Lutheran Church has over 250 evangelists (these are natives) *in new areas, these men too are missionaries and need our prayers. New Guinea is a field white for harvest. The need for more workers in the next couple of years is great. As the political situation stands, we never know how much longer the Lord will allow us to do His work here, so it's a matter of working now. Your prayers are needed for the progress of the work, for protection, strengthened faith, and the zeal of His laborers here, for daily reaching many more people with His Word, and for the preservation of faith of those who now believe in the Triune God. The Christians here in New Guinea also remember these things in their prayers for you, and all peoples of the world. Our oneness in Christ and Christian love is a tremendous blessing and treasure.*

Now that the Blessed Christmas Season draws near, may we all worship our Savior in spirit and in truth, and ever praise Him for coming to save us sinful men, so that now we have hope and joy in Him eternally.

A Blessed Christmas and Joyous New Year to you all!

Sincerely yours,
Eunice Redeker

Board for World Missions
The Lutheran Church – Missouri Synod

December 5, 1963

Dear Eunice,

Thank you kindly for your letter of November 15. It was a very interesting newsletter, summarizing your furlough activities and describing your fascinating trip back to New Guinea.

We could feel with you the touch of sadness you must have experienced as you left on September 5 – especially after the anxious days you experienced with the illness of your father. It was good to note, however, that your sorrow was very brief and that your fellow Christians along the way shared with you Christian joy and encouragement with their many kindnesses and assurance of continued prayer. This is shown too by the fact that you arrived safely in your place of work, where your people received you so warmly. You are living and working among bountiful blessings from the Lord with great opportunities still before you. We pray that the Lord will continue to bless your efforts in His service.

Keep us on your newsletter mailing list; it will be good to hear from you again.

Sincerely yours,
Paul M. Heerboth
Assistant Executive Secretary

(Blue Aerogramme)

December, 1963

Dear Richard, Florence & Charles,

"For God so loved the world, that He gave His only begotten Son, that whosoever believeth in Him should not perish, but have everlasting life" John 3:16

(This is followed by a 6" high ink print of the nativity).

"Glory to God in the Highest and on earth Peace, good-will to men"

Hi! How are you? Have been waiting for a note from you.

Our school was out Friday. Sure is wonderful to have a breather. I've certainly let things pile up, hardly know where to start. But it's good to have the pressure off.

Guess what? I drove the motorbike for the first time yesterday. Didn't think I'd ever get enough courage, but it isn't so difficult. Fortunately I didn't even have a spill. Arlo Lehmann and Ralph have both been wanting to show me so yesterday Arlo comes driving up and says "Here, Eunice give it a try" so I did.

How's school Charles" Getting any use out of the encyclopedias? etc.

Florence if you see your folks and Gert and family over Christmas please give them my warmest greetings. I hope I can get a note to them soon. Wishing you all a very Merry Christmas & Happy New Year.

Love, Eunice

ANNUAL REPORT – EUNICE REDEKER
St. Paul's Lutheran School, Pausa
Jan. 1, 1963 – Dec. 9, 1963

CHRONOLOGY OF IMPORTANT HAPPENINGS

1. Taught school at Bethesda Lutheran School, Pine Lawn, Missouri, January – June 15, 1963

2. Lectured most weekends January through June in Illinois and surrounding states.
3. July much time was spent travelling from Shattuc to St. Louis visiting my father in Lutheran Hospital.
4. July 21 – 26, attending Furloughing Missionary's Conference, Concordia Seminary, St. Louis.
5. August-toured the East, - Ohio, Pennsylvania, New York, and Niagara Falls, Ontario (was beautiful setting for the Wiebe-Thiele wedding).
6. On to Kansas for the Kansas Dist. Convention, Wichita, and Kansas Dist. Walther League Convention, Oakley, plus five congregations in Kansas, the Iowa District East LWML Women's Retreat, Cedar Rapids.
7. Ten "hectic" days at home getting ready to leave for New Guinea.
8. Departure for New Guinea, September 5. Spent five wonderful days in San Bruno, Cal., during which I attended and spoke to the Cal.-Nev. Sunday School Teacher's Convention.
9. Sept. 9, departed to Hawaii where I met the Rivers, Hartwigs, Lehmanns, and Housers in Honolulu.
10. Enjoyable overnight flight to Sydney, crowded plane! Spent the next day in Sydney, shopping and sleeping.
11. P.M. flight to New Guinea during which an engine on the T.A.A. DC-6 stopped and our course was reversed to spend a day in Townsville, Australia, getting it repaired.
12. On to N.G. landing at Port Moresby for an overnight stay, and the next day, A.M., Friday the 13th of Sept., on to Lae and the Highlands, taking seven hours.
13. Arrived at Pausa Sept. 13, began teaching Sept. 16, in St. 4, which was minus a teacher after Joe Neubacher left. Have enjoyed teaching, noticed much improvement in quality and ability of students at St. Paul's Lutheran School.
14. Traveled to Sirunki with the students in our Christmas Pageant to present it there Dec. 6. Presented it to a packed church.

HEALTH – Good, except for a few colds and periods of physical exhaustion.

OFFICIAL POSITION

1. Teacher at St. Paul's Lutheran School
2. Teacher/mother to girls at St. Paul's

ACTIVITIES

Teaching, lecturing, weekly faculty meetings, counseling youth group, Bible Study every Tues. P.M., taking short walks, trying to keep up with correspondence, reading, enjoying music.

VACATION – furlough in the U.S.

APPRAISAL OF ACTIVITIES OF PAST YEAR

Thanks to God for the many opportunities to witness for Him. Pray forgiveness for the many times I failed in doing this to the fullest.

It was an exciting, interesting year filled with innumerable unusual experiences. Marvelous protection by guardian angels.

PLANS AND PROSPECTS FOR THE COMING YEAR

1. Teach St. 5 at St. Paul's Lutheran School.
2. Work on the girl's program, revising the textbooks I have compiled for same, and investigating where and how the girl's program should be included in our changing school system.
3. Looking forward to working with Ralph Bleeke, Arlo Lehmann, and our new staff member.
4. Keep an interest in the Forms and Teacher Training Program as they are being developed here.
5. Give more time to daily study of the Word and prayer.
6. Assist in various extra-curricular activities as much as possible at St. Paul's to help make our program as effective as possible.

7. With the Lord's help to be more understanding and of greater help to our students in their many problems and daily frustrating encounters, encourage them spiritually, and pray for them.
8. Continue to work with the Yaramanda/Mambisanda Youth Group.
9. Learn to ride a motorbike.
10. Climb Mt. Hagen in May.

Respectfully submitted,
Eunice Redeker

Dr. Koppelmann, Executive Secretary
The Board of World Missions, LCMS

February 15, 1964

Dear Dr. Koppelmann,

Greetings to you, and many thanks for the Christmas message you sent. We also wish you and your family God's continued blessings and peace in this year, and especially may this Lenten season prove a real blessing to you as you contemplate on our Savior's willingness to suffer and give His all for us that we might be His eternally.

Would you kindly extend my sincere thanks to the Board for World Missions for the gift of $34.34, which was given me as a Christmas bonus? It is very much appreciated. And also to the Board may the Lord grant His guidance and grace in the important task He has place upon them.

Very cordially yours, Eunice Redeker

Rev. Paul Heerboth, Assistant Executive Secretary
The Board of World Missions, LCMS

February 15, 1964

Dear Rev. Heerboth,

Greetings from the beautiful highlands of New Guinea, and sincere thanks for your letter of December 5, as well as the Christmas message a little later. As you know, it is an added pleasure and spirit lifter to receive mail out here (Rev. Heerboth served in the mission field in Japan). *I'm thankful I had the opportunity to meet you last summer, as it means much more when one receives messages and hears your name mentioned often here on the field.*

Our school term for 1964, began January 27, with 127 students. So far everything has gone real well. I have a real good faculty to work with and we were thankful our two new classrooms were finished the week before school started. When I think back to four years ago when I first came here it's almost unbelievable the way the school has grown and ability of the students reached a much higher quality and standard. We can only thank and praise God for His immeasurable blessings.

We pray all is well with you and your family, and that the move to St. Louis has been possible and you are enjoying your home there. The Lord grant you His grace and guidance as you serve Him.

Sincerely yours, Eunice Redeker

(Form Letter)

April 24, 1964

Dear Relatives and Friends,

In these days following the Lenten and Easter meditations, I hope your hearts and lives, too, are filled with the peace and joy which our Lord has made possible, through His willingness to come down and live among us, and then suffer greatly—even death by crucifixion—for us and our sins. But then He also showed Himself the Victor over it all when He so gloriously arose three days later. And so we rejoice, and our lives can be filled with joy, as we hear His Words, "Because I live, ye shall live also!" John 14:19. This hope and joy of knowing that He lives should fill us with great joy even in the midst of sadness and trial. Because, "they which live should not henceforth live unto themselves, but unto Him which died for them and rose again." II Corinthians 5:15. May God grant us such a clear vision of Him and closeness to Him that our lives will glorify and serve Him here until this is fully possible when we enter our real home eternally, and can with the angels join in His praises more beautifully than we've ever heard or experienced here.

In New Guinea things continue to move forward—it seems too quickly many times. Many plans are made but lie unfulfilled since time just wasn't long enough. Since my last letter much has happened here. First of all there was the glorious Christmas celebration. Once again the joy of seeing the native Christians worshiping the Lord, fills us with joy indescribable. Most of the congregations have a Christmas pageant on Christmas Eve by students from the schools on their station. This is usually acted out. They also decorate their churches with a Christmas tree *(the casuarina, a type of pine-like tree that grows here), and other greens. They also use old Christmas cards with pictures of the Christmas story very often (supplied by the missionary) to hang on the tree and around the church walls. They too look forward to this celebration. Christmas morning they also have a service and some congregations have services Christmas night and the day after Christmas. This is their Christmas and sometimes I feel is really wonderful since they don't have the many distractions that we have, which often take our thoughts from the real meaning of Christmas. One of the thrills for me this year was that our students here at St. Paul's Lutheran school—who, since they are advanced in their studies—put on quite an elaborate Christmas pageant—were able to travel to various other congregations and present their pageant. This was a tremendous experience for them and a wonderful opportunity for them to witness for their Savior. Another real joy was the many cards and letters from all of you. These are truly a joy and very uplifting. One of my regrets is that it is impossible to answer them personally, but I am thankful through this letter I am able to share with you some of our experiences and blessings.*

During December I was able to make a quick five day trip to the coast to check on the curriculum for Girl's Education (since I was to present a paper on this for our General Mission Conference in January), and also checked on the curriculum of the Secondary School System, since this year St. Paul's Lutheran School has become a secondary school. The children come here after grade or standard six and enter Forms I, II, and III. This year is our first experience with Form I, and in the next two years, God-willing, we will add the other two Forms. Also next year we plan to start a teacher-training program. The Government has set up an A-Course Teacher Training Course for students who have passed Form I; this qualifies them to teach Standard I, II, and III. Then they also have a B-Course Teacher Training Course for students after Form III. Both of these courses last one year. The B-Course qualifies them to teach Standards I-IV. With these additions our station will continue to grow in numbers of students, staff, and buildings. But the need for trained teachers is great, and so we will be grateful to get some more native trained help. Until now we've been sending our students to the coast, but with the number of students increasing, it is advantageous cost-wise to set up a training program here.

For New Year a group of us single staff flew out to one of the new areas, Kandepe. This area has quite a few lakes and a river on which boat travel is possible to get to various mission stations, on the way by-passing several of the lakes. The Government also has a boat there, and we had planned to have a regatta, but since we could never get both motors working properly at the same time, we had to cancel the idea. Duck hunting is good there, the only place in the Western Highlands. Since this area was only opened about a year ago the natives are still uninfluenced by civilization. Their dress and weapons are a bit different from the people here, and so it was quite interesting. We enjoyed every minute of the one and a half days we were there until the last morning when five of us took the boat out for a last ride and the motor stopped, so we had to paddle our way back and barely made the Cessna that was to fly us back to our station.

Our January conference again was very inspiring and informative. The guest lecturer was Professor Pahl of Concordia College, Adelaide, Australia. Many helpful papers and book reports were given. Also much business was transacted in regards to our present work, and possibilities of expanding into new areas, as well as planning to make best use of our present staff, facilities, etc. The thought of starting a vocational school to train the natives in manual arts keeps coming up. A thought-provoking paper was delivered by Dr. Burce on our Mission in relation to the Wabag Lutheran church (the name of the organized New Guinea Christians). *We constantly have to keep ourselves aware of the fact that we are not here to stay, but as these people grow in the Gospel and advance in knowledge, they must take over the work and carry on. The Wabag Lutheran Church has made a good beginning. They have approximately 250 evangelists working in new areas and have five trained teachers, and eight doctor boy graduates* (male nurses).

Also of note during February and March were the first General Elections in the Territory of PNG. The Australian Government is trying to set up a democratic form of government here under the auspices of the United Nations. Getting men nominated from all the districts in the territory, and then getting all the people to vote entailed much patience and work, since (especially in the Highlands) few people are educated and have had any contact with civilization. Many Australian people were enlisted to help with the elections. The patrol officers spent many weeks before the elections visiting all the back area and telling the people what was happening. It seems that most people came in to vote and the government officials were pleased with the results. Now for the first time a majority of the men in the House of Assembly at Port Moresby will be native men. We hope and pray that by the time these people get their independence, they will be able to think clearly for the welfare of their people, as well as be informed in the procedures of democratic government, and spared the chaos and rebellion so many countries are experiencing.

The school year here at St. Paul's began January 27, and has gone along very smoothly thus far. I continue to be thankful and amazed at the advanced standard and quality of work of our students. Having trained teachers in the lower standards certainly shows through in every way when we get them here. We finished our first quarter and so have a week break. It's good to have a bit of time to get caught up on a few things. When school is in session it fills up the time since lesson planning and paper grading are endless jobs. Also being at a boarding school leaves us to care for the students after school hours, but it's amazing how well they know how to care for themselves. Besides catching up on correspondence and working on school materials, I hope I can get out into the yard around the house and girl's dormitory and work on some of the flower beds, and levelling the lawn. The school children cut all the grass on the station every week with sarifs, so much ground disappears as they "hack." There are many little native children around who love to dig in the dirt, and it's fun to work with them, so maybe we can get some dahlias and gladiolas planted—a change from the cannas and daisies that have been there since I've been back. The poinsettias I planted three years ago really are getting bushy and lovely. It takes them a long time to get started, but once they do, they really fill out, grow very tall, and are just beautiful.

This is getting rather lengthy, so will close with the prayer that the Lord will grant to all of you a rich measure of His Spirit, and keep you steadfast in His Word and in faith.

Sincerely yours, Eunice Redeker

(Mr. Paul Maroney, P.O. Wapenamanda)

June 19, 1964

Dear Sir,

Anita Simonson, Althea Weier, and I are planning to climb Mt. Hagen tomorrow. We are not sure where to go to in order to get to the path that leads up. If you could supply us with information as to the approximate place from the road that it is best to go up from, we'd appreciate.

Thanking you,
Sincerely yours, Eunice Redeker, Pausa

Dear Eunice,

Have asked all the policemen and none know of a decent track into Mt. Hagen range. However, Naningi of Yaramanda claims he knows of a track. As the Mountain is only used by the locals to hunt game there are no tracks as such. Naningi claims it would take you a couple of days. What I suggest you do if you want a walk is take the LR to the road camp and ask some of the roadworkers if they know of any tracks towards Mt. Hagen – at least you may be able to get reasonably close for walking up. I think you're probably a bit ambitious if you want to climb the mountain in a day – be best to take it easy tomorrow and see what you're up against for a later walk.

Best of luck, Paul M.

July 11, 1964

Dear Florence,

Well, again I'm getting this off much too late but anyway the thoughts and wishes are just as sincere. I thought of you on your birthday and wanted to send a card then but just couldn't without getting a bit of a note in it. Know you too have been very busy and burdened with all the illness this past spring. Do hope you are all well now and not kept too busy, as I know these are your busy months. I think of you all often and am so glad we got to see each other as often as we did when I was home. Can't forget this time last year.

I received a letter from your mother last week and it was just so good to hear from her. She has been so good to me and her encouragements and faith are a strength to me.

All here is coming along very well, can't ever thank the Lord sufficiently for the tremendous blessings we witness of the growth of His kingdom here. I never would have believed four years ago our students would be able to reach the standards they are at today. One of my St. 5 boys wrote a play in May and we presented it to the rest of the classes. (The program was included in the letter and is printed below). *They listen and obey so much better and even do their assignments.*

Two weeks ago I flew out to the Pogera to visit the Busses' for three days. It was so good to see them. They really seemed glad to have company. They are in a new area and very isolated, a 3 ½ hour walk from the airstrip. Danny & Craig took me for a walk every morning. I think they miss having people around, and children to play with, after all the excitement of furlough. Dale loves his work – really has to do a lot of hiking. Of course, many problems and difficulties always when starting in a new place.

Three of us also made it to the top of Mt. Hagen, alt. 14,000 ft. It was quite a climb but worth it. The scenery was so beautiful. Will send some pictures one of these days.

I've also finally mastered the motorbike. We got our little BSA back last week after a year in the workshop. I won't ride a Honda, they're just too heavy. Took my first long ride yesterday to Birip, to work on a paper Elinor Burce and I have to do on the Muslims for Women's Retreat, July 25-26. It's going to be wonderful to be able to get to places without having to depend on someone always.

Florence, I also received a bill from Collier's Encyclopedia for my 1964 Yearbook. I'm paying the bill, assuming that the book arrived at home. Will you please check if it did? If so, Charles can just add it to the rest of the set.

Also, Florence sometime when you're at the folks, would you check the piano and bench and maybe my trunk to see if I left my music books: Liturgical Organist, & Chorales and Preludes by Albert Beck. They didn't come with my things and I was sure I had taken them to Dreimeyers. I'd really appreciate if you'd check. Thanks so much.

One of these days I'll get some pkgs. mailed to you. I still want to get you a wood tray, as I felt badly that you got the broken one that last night.

Hoping you are all fine! Always remember you all in my prayers. Our Lord bless, guide and protect you!

With much love, Eunice

The Standard V Play Program

<u>ISAAC'S FAMILY</u>
A PLAY
WRITTEN BY
RAENE II

PRESENTED BY:
STANDARD V-B
ST. PAUL'S LUTHERAN SCHOOL
PAUSA, NEW GUINEA
June 10, 1964 7:00 P.M.

(Page 1)

<u>CAST</u>

ISAAC........................ Thomas, Sirunki
REBEKAH .... Ratame, Irelya
VOICE OF GOD..... Romane, Irelya
JACOB .... Raenell, Irelya
ESAU........................ Taryo, Yaramanda
RACHEL.................. Rachel, Sirunki
LABAN..................... Ratii, Irelya

ANGELS .... Sirione, Rasii, Sukuri, Sodo

CHOIR: Pipae, Yakapao, Ranyatta, Raene I,
Reme, Riame, Romasa, Rupen, Sabarane, Takapona, Timone, Torata, Wai, Yada, Yapata

(Page 2)

THE PLAY

The play tells about Isaac and Rebekah and their sons, Esau and Jacob. Isaac and Rebekah feared God and God blessed them richly. Their son, Esau, was a hunter and a man of the field. Their son, Jacob, was a gardener and quiet man.

(Page 3)

EVENTS

1. Isaac and Rebekah pray for children.
2. God promises them children.
3. They have twins.
4. Esau sells his birthright.
5. Rebekah helps Jacob trick their father and get the blessing of promise.
6. Esau wants the blessing and is angry because Jacob stole it.
7. Jacob is sent to Laban, Rebekah's brother, for protection and getting a wife.
8. Jacob meets Rachel.
9. Jacob meets his uncle Laban.

(Page 4)

STAGE MANAGERS: Tome, Reto, Tipttapi
PUBLICITY: Timone, Ratii, Rasii, Tabarane, Yada
COSTUMES: Riame, Pipae, Takapona, Torata
PROPERTY: Romasa,
Tabarane, Raene I,
Yapata, Tipitapi, Sodo, Rachel,
Sukuri, Ranyatta, Sirione, Rasii, Wai

(Page 5)

OUR THANKS

We thank all of you for coming to see our play, and we pray it has been a blessing to you in understanding this part of God's Word more clearly.
Miss Redeker &
Standard V-B

(Page 6)

(Kerala, South India)

August 15, 1964

Dear Eunice,

Greetings from rain-soaked Kerala! As always it was a delight to receive your letter last week! Your letters are real day brighteners and during this rather dreary season they are especially appreciated. Not long ago, I also enjoyed hearing from Anita S. Your women's retreat sounded inspiring and enjoyable. Would loved to have heard your paper on Islam. Do we have Muslims here? Wow, do we! In the area there is a pocket of Muslims- Malappuram is about 70%+ Muslim so actually our mission work here is directed toward this group. As you realize from your paper, to leave Islam and follow Christ is indeed a great test and sacrifice, especially here in India where the Muslim community is an intimate group and zealous in their efforts to keep anyone from leaving the "fold." The Muslim history in this area has an interesting beginning- (Mopilla Rebellion 1921) and there are peculiar traits to this populace. Most of the women are poorly educated and lead secluded and restricted social lives. The women's quarters are located at the rear of the house and that is where they are expected to spend their time. These "Mopilla" women have a peculiar dress and do not strictly keep Purdah. Instead of a veil over their face, they have a head covering and always carry an umbrella to shield them from glances of men. It is with these women, that most of my public health work will be. Generally, they are not clean people – compared to the Hindus who bathe religiously.

Spent last weekend in Wynand visiting a missionary family. Wynand is a small mountain range about 60 miles from here and a lovely place. Despite the weather we had an enjoyable time. While there we visited a coffee estate – the British owner was an interesting chap. He also has 3 beautiful race horses, pet birds and goats. We visited an elephant farm where they catch and train wild "annas" to work in the forests. There are 30 there now. Daily at 5 p.m. the annas are brought in from the forests, bathed and fed, then returned to the forest. Unfortunately, that day they were an hour ahead of schedule so we missed seeing them – next time! Actually, we see them rather often on the roadsides working or being bathed in the rivers. What monstrous creatures but how unbelievably graceful!

Haven't any earth shaking news – saw "The Big Fisherman" in Calcutta a couple weeks ago. Some of the English movies shown here are hopeless. No wonder they question our sanity! 'Tis good that an occasional decent film is shown.

Next week my teacher is taking a 10 day holiday so I am planning to spend the time visiting Hedy Gronback – remember her? Want to see what public health she is doing and how, etc. The only thing I dread is the train trip over – the trains are crowded and not very clean.

Hope your camera turns up – safe and sound from the post. Lost post is so irritating. We have our share of that here. Will really enjoy having a picture or two of you sent. I wish to send you some too as soon as my folks send the prints back.

Merle left for Germany June 30 as he is assisting Dr. Roensch – the pastor of congregations in Heidelberg and Mannheim. He will assist him and begin at the University when the winter semester begins in October. He sounds so enthusiastic about his work and studies and has preached and even played the organ for services! He has written 3 times since arriving there and I can hardly believe it! What a rare treat!

Remember Donna Livingston at 6636 San Bonita. She and her Dan are getting married this month! They make such a sweet couple and I am so happy for them. Suppose we will be granted the blessing of a Christian marriage?

Have done some sewing lately – seems clothing wears out so quickly here. Can't get quite such nice material here but I guess we're not really trying to steal any fashion ratings! What do you think of the topless bathing suit and dresses? Good grief, how indecent can western "civilized" women get?

Will close for now, my dear friend, hoping this finds you in good health and spirits. You are often in my thoughts and prayers, Eunice. How comforting to know He will never leave His children and promises to uphold us through life and its problems.

Love, Lois Kitzmann, Kerala, S. India

October 3, 1964

Dear Richard, (with birthday card)

Hi! Well, "Happy Birthday"! Thought you might forget your birthday so here's a little reminder. Ha! How's all? How about dropping me a line sometime. Sure hope Dad doesn't get sick again. My heart really aches when I think of them. Have been kept very busy with a lot of visitors the past month. Next month school ends so this is a busy time, finalizing everything. Guess you've been real busy too – Hope the summer and all the work went well. No more sickness after the mumps I hope. Hope you are all fine. Love to Florence and Charles.

Love, Eunice

P.S. Just a little gift – because I really appreciate you helping the folks so much! (Check uncashed!)

(Form Letter) (In the heading area above the greeting were 5 stars above "Southern Cross")

November, 1964

Dear Relatives and Friends,

Greetings from the beautiful isle of New Guinea, which lies in a position to clearly view the Southern Cross! This beautiful position of stars seen in the sky of the Southern Hemisphere also serves as a reminder of the love of our Savior, Jesus Christ, who gave His life for us on Calvary's cross, that we might be His own and live in His kingdom.

As once again we near the joyous Christmas season, may God shower on you all a greater realization and appreciation of His great love, in that He sent us the greatest gift, His Son. Because He was willing to do this, we now can know the peace and joy that passes all understanding. May this peace and joy fill your hearts this Christmas time, and throughout the New Year. May you also be filled with an ever greater love for Him, and a real zeal to do what you can, wherever you are, to help others know their Savior. Then life will ever hold a real purpose.

As I am writing this we are nearing the end of another school year. Our term is from February through November. It has been one of the most gratifying years I have had teaching in New Guinea, since the students are reaching an ever higher academic standard. One of the students is good at writing plays, so he wrote two which were presented to the rest of the student body here at St. Paul's. One was Biblical entitled "Isaac's Family," and the other about two merchants in Arabia. They, as all children, are natural actors, and love it. At present they are working up a puppet show, making their own hand puppets. An added asset is that it helps their English so very much.

Since mountain climbing in this beautiful area is one of the favorite pleasures of some of us, Anita Simonson, R.N.; Althea Weier, secretary; and I decided to climb Mt. Hagen (altitude, 14,000 feet) in June. Seven of our schoolboys accompanied us. The visibility and scenes from the top were worth all the effort. We stayed at the top one night in a tent made of water-proof paper. Fortunately it was a bright, moonlight night, so we had no worries of rain.

I had an opportunity to visit the Dale Busses', who are in one of the new areas first occupied in July 1963. The Pogera station is a hectic, three-mile hike from the air strip. Much of the work there is just beginning, and many difficulties arise in reaching the people since their language is of another dialect, and the topography is very rugged. This is one of the areas where some gold has been found, but not enough to be profitable commercially. It was interesting to see the New Guineans sitting in the Pogera River, however, actually panning gold. Some of them have found a nice little amount.

Reverend William Wagner and several of our evangelists were able to move into the last restricted area of New Guinea in July, the

Kopiago. We are thankful these people, too, are now being reached with the Gospel, and pray that those who hear the Word will also believe.

Special thanks to God was possible in September when the new staff assigned to New Guinea arrived: three pastors, two teachers, two doctors, and six nurses! All are in language school now studying the Enga language under Reverend Otto Hintze until December. After this, they will be assigned to their places of work.

At this time our Mission is in need of a printer. For over a year now we have been without one, and it is a hindrance not to have someone to take care of printing the evangelistic and educational materials which have been translated into the Enga language. Our Evangelism Committee just finished translating the Book of I Peter recently; Matthew, Mark, Luke, and John have already been done.

In closing, a special "thank you" for all your prayers for the work, and for us, here in this mission field! Also, a sincere thanks for your letters and gifts; these are always a source of encouragement to us as we realize they are given out of love for our Savior. Indeed, you are a real part of the Lord's work here, as you make it possible for us to be in the "harvest field" of New Guinea!

I pray this finds you all well, and in good spirits. May you enjoy a Blessed Christmas, and rich blessings in the New Year!

Sincerely in Christ, Eunice Redeker

ANNUAL REPORT – EUNICE REDEKER
St. Paul's Lutheran School, Pausa
Jan. 1964–January 1965

CHRONOLOGY OF IMPORTANT HAPPENINGS

1. Jan. 25, 1964 – began teaching St. 5 at St. Paul's Lutheran School, Pausa.
2. May – St. 5 presented a play "Isaac's Family", written by one of the students

3. June – during 2-week school holidays, climbed Mt. Hagen and walked to the Pogera.
4. Nov – completed another school year, due to God's grace and benediction. The higher academic standard of our students has made it a special reason to be thankful.
5. Dec – returned to the U.S. to visit my ill father, for six weeks.

<u>HEALTH</u> – Good, except for several malaria attacks.

<u>OFFICIAL POSITION</u>

1. Teacher at St. Paul's Lutheran School
2. Supervisor of the Girl's Program at St. Paul's Lutheran School.

<u>ACTIVITIES</u>

Teaching, weekly faculty meetings, Bible Study every Tues. P.M., hiking, correspondence, reading, enjoying music, sewing.

<u>VACATION</u> – trip to the U.S.A. to visit my parents.

<u>APPRAISAL OF ACTIVITIES OF PAST YEAR:</u> It has been one of my most enjoyable teaching years – since it was so clear to see tremendous progress in the academic standards and capabilities of our students. Much more creativity and self-expression is possible by the students. This is a result of early training and instruction under capable teachers.

Again due to human weakness and temptations, I was many times not as faithful, efficient and enthusiastic in my work as I should have been. For this I am sorry and pray for strength and help to improve.

<u>PLANS AND PROSPECTS FOR THE COMING YEAR</u>

1. Teaching St. 6 – at St. Paul's Lutheran School. I again look forward to working with Ralph Bleeke, Arlo Lehmann, Ron and Marlene Rivers, for whose cooperation and help in sharing in the Lord's work this past year, I am grateful.

2. Work with the girls' at Pausa and work on a program for girls in Form I, II and III.
3. Do more counseling with the students in my class.
4. Continue daily in the study of the Word and prayer. I plan to study books written by the minor prophets.
5. Continue correspondence to students away from their homes in New Guinea and the U.S. as well as try to keep up more efficiently on correspondence generally.
6. Take an educational correspondence course from CTC, RF.

Respectfully submitted,
Eunice Redeker

(From Standard Travel Service, STL, MO)

January 7, 1965

Dear Miss Redeker,

Enclosed herewith please find your air-tickets validated for your return flights to New Guinea, as well as your V.S. Passport (visaed for transit through Australia) and Permit to re-enter the Territory of Papua and New Guinea.

Due to your lay-over of longer than 6 hours in San Francisco there will be a charge of $5.07 for U.S. Transportation Tax which should be collected from you at the airport.

For your return to New Guinea we wish you the very best, and remain.

Yours very truly, Fritz Weidhaas

AIRSCHEDULE
For
Miss Eunice Redeker

January 16, 1965 – Leave St. Louis at 7:00 PM on TWA Jet Tourist flight #161
Arrive San Francisco at 8:50 PM

January 18 - Leave San Francisco at 8:00 PM on Quantas Economy Jet flight #531
January 20 - Arrive Sydney at 7:00 AM.
-Leave Sydney at 9:45 PM on Ansett Ana flight #902.

January 21 -Arrive Lae at 8:00 AM
-Leave Lae at 9:00 AM on Trans-Australian Airlines flight #44.
-Arrive Wapenamunda at 1:30 PM.

All flights are as currently scheduled and subject to change at the option of the airlines concerned. All times are local.

cc.: Board for World Missions

Bethlehem Lutheran Church Sunday Bulletin January 10, 1965

Ferrin, Illinois

"Miss Eunice Redeker will be leaving Sat., Jan. 16, for New Guinea where she will resume her duties as teacher. May the Lord be with her on her long journey, as well as in the blessed work of bringing the saving Gospel to the people of New Guinea."

(To Eunice Redeker, Wapenamanda, New Guinea)

January 8, 1965

Dear fellow missionary,

When we attended the 1964 Texas District Convention, Dr. Roland Wiederaenders made the presentation of the Synodical President's report. In that report, as he gave a picture, among other things, of our church's mission in the world, he indicated that it is a shame that our people can give names of sport heroes and world leaders and know much about them, but can name few, if any, of our missionaries.

We here in Orange are making a small effort to change that picture just a bit. Since it involves you, we want you to know about it. Each week we publish in our Sunday bulletin the names of 5 or 6 of our missionaries. We include these BY NAME in our prayers in the service that day. We encourage the members to do the same in their private and family devotions during that week. You and your work were the subject of our prayers in recent weeks. That is why we are addressing this letter to you at this time.

We feel this has several values. Certainly, it brings you and your work before our people here and helps them to see their place as part of a world-wide mission of the Church. It also helps them to bring you and your needs and problems before the throne of God in prayer. Such prayer can do much to aid you and strengthen you in your work. Rest assured that at least in this one little spot in the world, you and your work are much in our minds and in our prayers.

If you have the time, the congregation would appreciate hearing of your work, your needs, your problems, your joys. About once or twice a month we read letters from missionaries and talk about the work of these missionaries in our regular Sunday service. If you let us hear from you, we will bring your message to our people.

As we are thus concerned about one another – you about us and we about you – and do all in our power to build up and strengthen one another, even over the distance of many miles, we will each become more effective in our work of bringing the Gospel to all the people of this world. It is our prayer and the prayer of all the members of this congregation that God would richly bless you, your family, and your work, so that you will be a blessing to many.

Sincerely, Eugene Heckmann, Pastor
Grace Lutheran Church, Orange, Texas

March 27, 1965

Dear Florence, Richard, and Charles-

Just received your letter and will write you a line right away or I'll put it off and not get at it. Thanks so much for writing. I really appreciate. It's so much easier to take when you know. I must say I was quite shocked as I never realized Dad's prostate would give him anymore trouble. Hope this operation is successful. So my prayers and thoughts are with you all often - and our Almighty Lord always provides the needs, courage and strength for any situation we may have to face in life. He is good and His mercy never failing - on us undeserving sinners. Especially during this Lententide - we again more fully realize His great love for us as we meditate on His Passion.

Sorry to hear Charles has still been bothered with head colds, etc. Hope it clears with the warm spring weather. I have a doll (2) from Hawaii for Charles and Violet and an elephant (carved) *from Fiji for Charles. One of these days I'll get around to sending them. And I just* <u>*must*</u> *write to Gert. I've never answered her letter she sent just before I left.*

How is your Dad, Florence? And your Mother? She's just so sweet and thoughtful.

Do hope you get a pastor from the Sem(inary) class. I know the congregation lags without a full-time leader. I didn't think, when I heard them mention Pastor Buls-that he would accept.

Well, all is fine here. Kept very busy - which is good - but at times I could stand a bit of a breather. Have lost the weight plus more that

I put on while home, without even trying. It's good - can move faster - but I'll probably put it on again when things are back at a normal pace. The kiddoes are making puppets (hand) at present. They're so excited. We hope to do a show when they finish.

I'll miss Howard's confirmation. Alvira was planning quite a day. We'll be thinking of you all. On Bibles, the Holman, World and Oxford are all good. Also Harper Holman has a nice Devotional guide which I've thought a good feature. World has the 24 page Reader's Aids which is a feature I like in it. Any of these you get will be good.

I should see the dentist today – he flew in from Lae. I lost a piece of a filling. He'll be here till Monday. I hope to spend this P.M. with the secretaries at Kumbas – just to get away for a little while. You kinda need to get away for a little while each weekend – but I don't always. The weeks just go smoother – and things don't get you down as easily.

Well, your busy time will be here again with the field work beginning. Hope the weather is good so you can get all your crops in. Don't work too hard. Our Heavenly Father bless and keep you! A Blessed Easter!

Love, Eunice

(around) *May 1965*

Dear Charles,

So sorry this is late for your birthday, the date just slipped upon me. Hope you had a happy day! Grandma mentioned you had the measles and before that mumps. So, you've had quite a siege. Hope you're all well again and enjoy the warm weather.

God bless you! Love, Eunice

Territory of Papua and New Guinea TELEGRAM May 15, 1965
Office of Origin-CD Centralia, Ill. Words-21 Time-2.55
Eunice Redeker LT
Wapenamanda TNG

Our Heavenly Father called Dad to rest Friday 3-40 pm funeral Monday 2 pm Mother alright.
Luke *(Eunice's brother Luther)*

May 19 (1965)-Wed. eve.

Dear Richard, Florence and Charles,

Just received the news of Dad leaving us today. As you can guess my heart aches with sorrow and yet deeply I cannot but rejoice. I know he believed and we pray that during those last days as his mind wavered – that the Holy Spirit sustained his faith, and now the joy and bliss of heaven he knows. How wonderful it will be when we can all join him there. May the Lord strengthen us all in faith and love for Him, that already we might know His peace and joy as we serve Him. I have been thinking of Mom. I hope all is O.K. and the family situation has been peaceful. Please write and tell me about the last days, moments and funeral. I'm anxious to hear. In a letter from Alvira today she mentioned they had taken Dad home May 9 – so that seems a bit strange.

I hear you have to move. I hope and pray something good turns up for you. May the Lord guide, direct and help you as you make these important decisions. How the Lord works! It seems He let you stay there as long as the folks were there. Especially has this been a blessing for Mom as she bore much with Dad and your nearness was a real comfort to her. For all you have done for the folks – I shall be forever grateful. The Lord has seen and He will care for you! How I wish I could see you all but this is not the Lord's will at this time. My thoughts and prayers are daily with you all! Your loving sister, Eunice

P.S. I wish you could read the comforting cards and letters from my students this afternoon. A real comfort and joy! I couldn't teach this afternoon.

(around) May 1965

Dear Eunice,

Well how are you by now? We are all O.K. I bet you were surprised to get the sad news of Dad. Let's hope he is better off. He sure is out of misery. That same Friday afternoon Wilbert went to see him. He still knew Wilbert. Wilbert again asked him about Jesus. He shook his head and said yes. So that does make a person feel a little better. Wilbert wasn't home ½ hour when a call came they said he passed away. Wilbert had asked the nurses how he was getting along. All they said was; "He's doing just fine, there is nothing wrong with him. He is just laying there." So ½ hour later when Wilbert was home, Dad was dead. So that don't make sense.

I'm sending you some pictures from Dad's funeral which we took ourselves. I think they had the undertaker have some pictures made which they might send to you. The service went on tape recording. Eileen sort of mentioned it.

Well Eunice, Howard received the hymn book just like you had said. Your name was with it too. We found out now that the New Testament came from Roger and Betty. Howard wants to "Thank You" for it. So "Many, many thanks." Well I guess I'll close for tonight. Friday is the last day of school. Saturday there will be school picnic. Monday night the 31st is 8th grade graduation. Howard has a little job for the summer. He will be helping Rufus Hoffman out in the store. I don't know how long he'll like it. This is a good experience for him. Well so long and be good.

Well Good night and the Good Lord Bless you and us all.

Wilbert, Alvira & the kids

(Enclosed: 4 pictures from the mortuary, one from the cemetery, one of the current batch of Redeker puppies with Henry and Wilbert, and a list detailing the floral tributes).

(Form Letter)

May 29, 1965-Ascension Day

Dear Relatives and Friends,

Greetings to you in the name of our ascended Lord! It is a special joy to greet you on this Day as we remember our Lord's return to heaven and rejoice that He is preparing a place for us and will again return one day to receive us into our eternal home.

Have you ever been tempted to ask, "Is it worth it all?" I have! And the answer each time has been, "Yes, it is very definitely worth it all!" This has been my experience again this past week as I received news last Wednesday via telegram, that my father is no longer with us here but our Heavenly Father has taken him to our heavenly home. As I was filled with sorrow Wednesday afternoon, the thought went through my mind, "Why couldn't I have been with my family at this time, is it really worth it to be here?" The Lord very wonderfully showed me why at 3:30 P.M. that afternoon, as the children came to my door with cards and notes they had written when they also heard the news. The cards were so beautifully done and the scripture texts and personal notes so inspiring and uplifting that tears were soon gone and replaced with an inward joy that is indescribable. The joy and hope they now share with us in Christ is indeed a blessing the Lord has granted since he has granted us the privilege to come here and bring the Gospel to the New Guineans'. So indeed it is very definitely worth it all to be here!

Another privilege the Lord granted is that I was able to spend my school vacation from Dec. 5, '64 – Jan. 15, '65 with my parents in Illinois. I am very thankful I was able to be with them such a short time ago.

After returning here January 21, I had three days to prepare for the beginning of our new schoolyear. It was not nearly enough time and so the first quarter was "hectic", trying to keep up with daily classes, grading papers, making visual aids, as well as other activities connected with a Boarding School. We have added an evening study hall period which fills our days, but is a help to the students. On Tuesdays I have lunch duty (seeing that the children sit down while eating and not too many sweet potatoes skins get thrown at each other). So Tuesday's schedule runs something like this:

6:45-7:15 a.m. – lunch hall
8:00-12:00 noon –classes
12:00-12:30 --lunch hall
1:00-4:00 p.m. –classes
5:30-6:00 p.m. –lunch hall
7:00-9:00 p.m. –study hall & devotions

We are always glad we have five staff members, including our New Guinea evangelist, so this routine falls only one day a week.

The Enga language study program has been in effect since January 1963. All new staff and old staff, who do not know Enga, have been going to school at Irelya for a period of three months to study the language. Rev. Otto Hintze has been in charge. He came out as one of the first missionaries in 1948 and is gifted linguistically. He has been teaching the language school until this last January when Rev. James Larson took over while the Hintzes' are on furlough. The Wycliffe Bible translators have been of much help to us in learning the language.

Now that the last restricted area, the Kopiago, has been entered, work there is progressing also. Last week two of our former students, Kee and Wakere, volunteered to go to the Kopiago as evangelists. This makes us very happy and they will need our prayers. Rev. and Mrs.

William Wagner and family are there and are very isolated. Their living conditions are rugged and primitive, yet they write to us with enthusiasm that shows the joy they are experiencing in reaching the natives with the Gospel. An excerpt from Mrs. Wagner's last letter to us reads as follows: "Dear City-slickers, Our bush house is very cozy. Our pitsawn floors have many arches and cracks between each piece which allows for easy cleaning, the dirt falls right through. The ants and insects need constant attention and spray. Our seismograph paper room divisions have to be watched lest one of the children decide to poke a hole through to explore what's beyond. The clay around the house needs landscaping and as of now much of it is lifted in the house with the traffic of little and big feet. I need to bake bread today but our bread tins were left in the box that didn't get on the plane with us. So we hope it comes on this week's plane." (A Cessna flies in once a week with supplies.)

The Mission Aviation Fellowship, which does a lot of flying for our Mission now has a Cessna stationed here at Wapenamanda. This is a big help in getting supplies transported to our Mission stations, especially those not accessible by road.

The mission work in New Guinea is taking on a new aspect. Soon we are no longer going to be reaching people who have never heard the Gospel, but as in the rest of the world, we will be concentrating on teaching and building on the foundation that has been laid. Reapers will be needed, rather than sowers. May God bless His Word on the hearts of all who hear and as we see the whole world being reached by the Gospel, we are reminded of our Lord's Words, "And this Gospel of the Kingdom shall be preached in all the world for a witness unto all nations; and then shall the end come." Matthew 24: 14.

I want to thank all of you for the many Christmas and Easter letters, cards, and remembrances. I'm sorry I have not written sooner. They were deeply appreciated and of much comfort these past few months. Over and over, I am reminded of your interest, and love and praise God for you! May He continue to bless you and make you a blessing to many!

Rejoicing in His love, Eunice Redeker

June 1, 1965

Dear Florence, (typed letter)

Happy Birthday! Do hope it is a happy day for you and if I were there, I'd bake a cake! Sorry I didn't get this in the mail much sooner. I've been so very busy as ever, and Dad's leaving leaves one feeling emotionally not as strong as otherwise. Really the kiddoes, our staff and friends have been just wonderful during this time. I'm still getting many wonderful, strengthening, and uplifting letters and cards. We pray the Lord has also comforted your hearts, as He alone can. What a joy that death is a glorious step to being with our Lord, and we too can say "Come Blessed death." For loving us so, that He was willing to suffer and die for us and make our resurrection hope possible, we can never thank the Lord enough. How I would have appreciated a long talk with you too during this time, but the Lord knew it was best for me not to be there and He knows best. Well the good Lord gave Dad a better place with complete peace and joy. Giving up your parents is very difficult but the Lord does not fail us at this time. How is your Father, Florence? I want to write them soon. You're Mother has been such a jewel and her notes and letters have meant much to me. I do hope and pray they are getting along well. --- I know you are very busy now. Don't work too hard though. I heard the Hanke boys bought your place, is this true, and does it mean you will have to move? -- Charles, I bet is enjoying the vacation. Bet you really appreciate his help, too, at this time. I was amazed how well he could drive the truck when I was home. (Would have been 12 years old). *Did he get Reinhold's pony? ---Edith Schild mentioned they had spent a Sunday afternoon with you and really enjoyed the visit. They had sent me a tape at Christmas and I had just gotten around to returning it. She said she had sent it on to you.* (Edith was a nurse friend from New Guinea who returned to the States and brought a tape recorder to a Redeker family event to record greetings from the family which were then sent to Eunice in New Guinea) – *With deep appreciation, I want to thank you for the Christianity Today, 4 Translation version of the Bible. I can't tell you how useful it has been, and such a help and time-saver. So thanks a million. It got here fast compared to a lot of things. – Tomorrow Gaye Weier and her parents are coming to spend the day with me. Her parents are up from South Australia, and I know the visit will be interesting and enjoyable. Jan Haby, one of the secretaries from Adelaide, South Australia, is planning to come to the U.S. next year with me. She's a sweet girl. – (I'm baking rolls by the way and just had to run in to put more wood on the fire. I always get busy doing something and forget, and it doesn't help the baking situation. Ha!) – Last weekend I spent with Dr. & Mrs. McArthur and family. I've gotten to know them real well and Mary Ellen and I just seem to enjoy each other's company so much. We got put on the Women's Retreat Committee for 1966 and so will give us a few more chances to get together. They're from Salinas, California. – Well, I must close for this time. Do hope and pray this finds you all well and in best of spirits. Now may His peace and joy fill your hearts and His loving presence sustain you.*

Much love from your sis, Eunice

P.S. Oh yes, I have a tray for you Florence, as you got the broken one, and this one is quite nice, as you'll notice, the workmanship is really improving. I hope to get it in the mail real soon.

August 15, 1965

Bethlehem Lutheran Church Sunday Bulletin

"A letter has been received from Eunice Redeker reporting on her work in New Guinea. It has been posted on the bulletin board for all to read. Let us remember our sister and her work in our prayers and in our mission offerings."

October 10, 1965

Dear Richard,
(Written in Birthday card)

Hi! Well sorry I'm getting this off so late – but do hope you have a very "Happy Birthday." Will be thinking of you. How have you been? Write sometime.

Have you decided what you are going to do? Do pray you find a good place and work.

Tell Florence I sure have been thrilled with all the dried fruits she had in that pkg. last Christmas! She sure knows the things to pick.

I'm moving to a station school next year, I asked for this since I prefer the little children and the Executive Comm. granted my wish. It'll be isolated and primitive but good experience for a year. So hope you are all fine. God bless and keep you.

Love, Eunice

P.S. Did Charles get the pkg? There's another one on the way.

(Form Letter)

November 15, 1965

Dear Relatives and Friends,

Sincere wishes for a "Merry Christmas" and a "Blessed and Happy New Year" to you all from New Guinea! May the joy of our Savior's wondrous birth fill you with new zeal to go forward for Him, serve

Him, and make Him known to all people through the many avenues of communication which God has granted us today, that people might hear, believe, and have eternal life. Also, that all people might be a "praise in the earth" as Isaiah tells us: "You, who put the Lord in remembrance, take no rest, and give Him no rest, until He establishes Jerusalem and makes it a praise in the earth." (Isaiah 62: 6,7)

Life and mission work in New Guinea continues, but at an ever rapid and changing pace. The wonders of fast transportation and communication make the spread of the Gospel, as well as the development of this island, proceed quickly. Problems are also great when things move so fast, one of the main ones being getting the people to accept and handle the changes and the technicalities connected with them. It takes centuries to change former ways of life and culture, but here it is happening overnight, so to say. So many times one wishes he could preach the Gospel and leave things at that without bringing in all the other influences of Western culture, but when you see suffering and physical need on every side due to lack of knowledge of health measures, medicines, etc., which we have in such abundance, we cannot help but want to bring these helps to the people also. Our Lord Jesus gave us a good example—He was always helping the physical as well as the spiritual needs.

At present a lot of strides are being made toward Lutheran Church unity here in New Guinea. Two Australian churches have united, which also unites them in New Guinea. Our Missouri Synod is also meeting with them, discussing doctrines, etc. Just what will come of it all is hard to say at present. It would be a real boost, strength-wise, for the church if it becomes possible to unite. We are at present carrying on a joint effort in our teacher training program, and will also in our seminary training program which will begin February 1967 at Mt. Hagen, a town 45 miles east of us.

Things here at St. Paul's Lutheran School also are moving on. Much building is being done as we prepare for our high school program and influx of approximately 600 students which will descend upon us in 1968. At present classrooms and faculty houses are under construction; dormitories, dining hall, more classrooms and houses will continue to be built. I will be leaving St. Paul's this year and moving to a station school. Our Executive Committee granted this request, since I do prefer teaching smaller children. Then, too, the disciplining of the older boys is a problem for me. My interests will always be strong in St. Paul's, however, after five years in the classrooms, I will move to Sirunki (8,000 foot elevation), our highest station, which is colder and more isolated, but I'm looking forward to the experience and opportunity to work on a station. Mr. and Mrs. Richard Adler will be my co-workers in the Standard II and V classrooms on the station. My home will be a bush house and I will be teaching in a bush school. They really are quite nice, and I'm looking forward to the move about mid-December. The station is 75 miles up the valley from my present location. It is from these station schools that the children come here to St. Paul's, after finishing Standard VI. My address will be:

Miss Eunice A. Redeker
New Guinea Lutheran Mission
Western Highlands District
WABAG, NEW GUINEA

Our Standard VI classes finished their government examinations on October 27, 28, and 29. They were really quite difficult, considering the background of the children, and the lack of educational influence these children have outside of school. We hope they did well, as not passing means no further schooling for them. I am working in our school office this month of November, getting records in order, etc. – an enjoyable change from school routine.

In closing I do want to sincerely thank you for the many cards, letters, and help you have sent in the past months, especially also all the uplifting and consoling messages received after my father was called to our eternal home. We need your prayers always!

May God bless you and make you a blessing!
Rejoicing in Christ, Eunice Redeker

(Centered in the blue Aerogramme, a mimeographed picture of children bowing and praying around a manger with the Baby Jesus in it)

November 29, 1965

Dearest Richard, Florence and Charles,

Greetings and Merry Christmas! Can't believe it's been a year since I saw you - but time flies so! Was so pleased to get your "co-operative effort" last week. So good to hear! (Tape recording from the Redeker family). *Glad you got the dolls, Charles and I hope you get the other pkg. before Christmas, it has a few other things for you – and no money. You paid me for the dolls when I was home and this is a little gift from me. OK? All the prizes you been getting sounds just terrific! You and your Mother will hit the "Jackpot" yet! Will you be confirmed next year Charles on Apr. 3 or May 29? I would sure love to be there but I won't be able to leave here until Oct. or Nov. '66. I'll sure be with you in prayer and thoughts though! -Well Richard I'm sure that's the first note I've gotten from you!!!! And Gee whiz, it was good to hear! You ought to pick that pencil up more often – that's all it takes – you know. Hope the crops were real good this year! Are you going to be moving? -You asked about Garry Wolff – well, he's fine but Grandma Wolff – remember? – passed away on Nov. 7. The oldest brother and his girlfriend who were there that evening – are engaged. Saw Garry a lot as he's always riding around on his bike – while here at Pausa – but I'm moving up the valley 75 miles next week – I asked to be changed as the workload was getting me down here at Pausa. With a bit of hesitation, the Exec. Committee did grant my request. I'll be teaching part of Standard 2 and 5 at Sirunki with Dick Adler. His wife is from St. Louis. Aunt Augusta knows her folks. It won't be a boarding school so I'll be free in the evenings and won't have the children around day and night. Didn't know you had a fall Richard? How'd that happen? Sure glad it wasn't more serious. We'll have to get a "frame" to hold you up!! Ha, Ha! Florence, you're busy as ever! Wish I could get in on a few things like the Cake Dec. Dem., etc. Could sure use it out here. You sure did marvelously well at the Fair! You have so many talents,*

Gal! Will think of you and the Xmas tree, etc., this Christmas! Sure was beautiful! (Chrismon tree).

I'm getting my correspondence a bit caught up so I can start packing by the weekend and get ready for moving next week. Think 2 of the 109 jeeps will do the job. The Adlers are going to help me – they're a tremendous couple! I've been working in the school office this month. Listen the Bleekes – he was principal here this year are on furlough – they are real good friends and have been wonderful to me – they're going to visit Mom – would like you to meet them too. Her father was pastor in Decatur – remember I went there to lecture once. He's in Springfield now. Well, Bye for now. Much love, Eunice

P.S. Oh yes, must tell you I made a fruit cake from all the fruit you gave me, last week. We sampled it last night – after I had soaked it in a Brandy cloth a week. The station people say it's delicious – but I don't know. The fruit was just delicious! Can't beat our American products. I have enough to make another one and think I will as they're handy to have and seems always somebody is dropping in on me!

(From Eunice's mother)

December 24, 1965

Dear Eunice,

Just a few lines. I am pretty good kind busy for Christmas. They all were here Thursday night for supper. Everything went O.K. Wilbert (oldest brother) *were to. Mrs. K* (Wilbert's mother-in-law) *pass away last week suddenly heart attack. Wilbert have a job I am glad. And Howard* (Wilbert's oldest son) *is working Hoffman store.*

I have to quit Mail man come soon. Well Eunice I don't care if he good guy. Only if you can come home no more that be hard for me. I hope they all be O.K.

I give all you children $25.00 but Eunice Sandoval bank had wrote Wilma note there is no money in St. Louis never send money so I give Wilma $100.00 put in bank. I keep $25 So you own $75.

Wilma want me to write you. I wish Merry Christmas and happy New Year. Wilma told me I should write you. The bank in St. Louis didn't send no money.

With love and God blessed you,
Mother

(From Eunice's mother)

December 30, 1965

Dear Eunice

How are you, hope fine.

I am pretty good. Christmas is over. We have here peace. How wonderful He come that we have peace for our sins.

Reinhold came and get me Christmas morning to their church and have to stay for supper to. Then Elwin take me home. Hoffman church have the Christmas have the trees fix like we have last year. (Chrismon tree). *Couple ladies came to Florence. She help them. Last Sunday Richard Florence took ride look at the tree. Christmas eve I didn't go the weather was bad. We had terrible wind rain.*

Eunice you have to know about you Boy friend. Could He come along over here and teach here that would be wonderful. I would like that very much. I won't say No. You have to know.

We may not see us again. We will see in heaven. I would like you have a boy friend. You not by your self you have some to talk. I know my self. You can talk to nobody. His is nice boy that means a lot.

We have to pray that God no wats the best.

God be with you
With love Mom

ANNUAL REPORT – EUNICE REDEKER
1965

<u>IMPORTANT EVENTS</u>

January – the first part of the month was spent in the U.S.A. with my parents. Arrived on the field again January 22, and got in on one and one-half days of Staff Conference.

-Jan. 25, school began at St. Paul's Lutheran School, where I taught St. 6 this year.
Ralph Bleeke and I departmentalized in a class of sixty-four students.

February- Kept busy with our schedule at St. Paul's and general class preparation. Since St. 6 is the year of government exams, we were conscious of preparing the students for this the entire year.

April -Continued reports of my father's weakening and seriously ill health.

May -a one week vacation with Mrs. Ralph Bleeke in Lae.
-May 18, received a telegram stating my father's death on May 14th.

Sept.-government oral exam given to our St. 6 students.

Oct. -government written exams given to our St. 6 students. To date the results of these have not been returned.
-29th – school ended for St. 6
-Received word that the Committee of Schools had considered my request to work at a station school in 1966, and that I was assigned to Sirunki.
-30-31 the Bleeke family was with me before departing for furlough in the U.S.

Dec. -moved to Sirunki. Am looking forward to working with Mr. Richard Adler. I will be teaching St. 2.
-Flew to Maramuni for Christmas with the Luther Leaguers.

HEALTH:

Several malaria attacks, and general weakened condition due to the strain of the schedule at St. Paul's. Otherwise, I enjoyed good health.

OFFICIAL POSITION:

Missionary-teacher at St. Paul's Lutheran School, Pausa, and now transferred to Sirunki Lutheran School.

VACATION:

Three weeks in January spent in Illinois with my parents. One week spent in Lae, New Guinea.

ACTIVITIES:

-Taught St. 6 and Girl's Home Economics classes.
-Supervised the Christian Growth Committee at St. Paul's Lutheran School.
-Once a month – Sat. P.M. – party with the students at St. Paul's.
-Served on Idupa Committee. *(Idupa is the Enga word for "now." "Things we have to do now")*
-Attended weekly Bible Study.
-Attended Luther League Meetings.
-Tried to keep up with correspondence.
-Reading.

APPRAISAL OF ACTIVITIES:

Teaching our sixty-four students in St. 6 was filled with many challenges. My prayer remains that the moments spent in teaching God's Word to the students will by the Holy Spirit's blessings be fruitful unto life eternal for these students. The feelings of inadequacy one feels when teaching these children of another society and culture remain high. One constantly realizes by God's grace and power alone can anything be accomplished. The preparations for government exams added more concern to daily class presentations. The strain of the heavy schedule at a Boarding School and disciplining of the older students had their effects on me, and I felt a need to ask to be placed at a station school and work with smaller children.

Much joy and satisfaction came from working with our Christian Growth Committee. We did various projects to make our chapel services more worshipful, visited and corresponded with sick students, and planned activities for Christian fellowship.

Soli Deo Gloria!
Respectfully submitted,
Eunice Redeker

(By this time, Ray and Eunice had met and were dating. Given that we have constructed the entire narrative of the book to flow chronologically, we include Ray's Annual report, even though they were not married until later in 1966).

Annual Report – 1965
Ray Hausler

CHRONOLOGY OF EVENTS:
July 30 – Arrived on the field.
Aug. – Oct. 9 - Constructed 'Economy Home' – Yaibos.
Oct. 11 – Dec. 8-Plumbing at H.L.S. (Highland Lutheran School)
Dec. 9 -Moved to Sirunki. General maintenance.

OFFICIAL POSITION:
Builder.

HEALTH:
Good.

ACTIVITIES:

-Visited Madang Schools with Arlo Lehmann during November.
-Became a member of the Luther League.
-Attended Bible Study and Worship at Yaibos and Sirunki.

APPRAISAL OF ACTIVITIES:

My greatest satisfaction is working with the New Guineans, attempting to pass on to them the skills of carpentry.

The short period I have been on the field has been blessed and rewarding.

New Guinea (Form Letter)

January 13, 1966

Dear Friends in Christ,

Greetings and wishes for a Blessed New Year from New Guinea! Now that the Blessed Christmas Season has swiftly passed, it is a joy to go forth in the renewed knowledge that, "God so loved the world, that He gave His only begotten Son, that whosoever believeth in Him, should not perish, but have eternal life." John 3:16

The past weeks have been very busy, yet filled with joy and blessings. I moved to Sirunki, December 8, and although it is much colder and more isolated here, I'm enjoying the change. Our altitude is actually 8,700 feet, and the temperature is a constant 60 to 65 degrees during the day and can go down to 30 degrees at night, but not often. My little bush house, is quite cozy although I really missed running water, electricity, and our 20th century conveniences at first. It has a detached kitchen, with a long verandah connecting it to the rest of the house. This, too, took a bit of getting used to.

The past two weeks, Richard Adler and I have been working on school books, visual aids and he has been supervising some native men in the rebuilding of a bush classroom for me. I have had some of the children help me wash tins of all sizes so we can paint them. We will use them in our new "Dienes' Method", Modern Mathematics Program.

Jan. 16-22, will be our Annual Staff Conference. This year our guest lecturer will be Dr. Harmon, from Concordia Seminary, Adelaide, Australia. It will be refreshing to hear his stimulating lectures.

Christmas, I spent in Maramuni, one of our newest stations, accessible only by our small Cessna plane, or a five-day walk. Twelve of us single people went and we really enjoyed our three days with Rev. and Mrs. Merlyn Wagner and nurse, Margaret Davis. They were happy to have us since they seldom see other white people. We had turkey and all the trimmings for Christmas dinner. The turkey came from the stores at the coast. All was really a treat.

School starts Jan. 24. I'll be teaching Standard Two, and a few subjects in Standard Five. I know teaching the smaller children will be a real pleasure. Not being a Boarding School will also relieve my after-school heavy schedule. However, I am working with the Sunday School and Youth Group here at Sirunki Lutheran Church. This is a challenge and joy.

Hoping this finds you and yours in best of spirits and good health. Our Heavenly Father bless and keep you in His grace and care.

With love in Christ, Eunice Redeker

Wabag, New Guinea, (Form Letter)

March 10, 1966

Dear ________________,

Greetings from New Guinea! Now that our school year is well underway, it seems the time is flying by. I have thirty-five Standard II girls and boys. They are so enthusiastic and responsive, it's a joy after teaching some of the older boys and girls, who seem to lose a lot of this initial enthusiasm. This is only natural, though. Today we planted flowers around our school, trees in our school yard and put stones on the path, all part of our Social Studies Project. They spent an hour this afternoon in the school gardens. This is also part of the school curriculum. They grow celery, carrots, potatoes and most root vegetables very well. It's a bit cold for lettuce, tomatoes, and vegetables needing a warmer climate.

Mr. Richard Adler was made Literacy Director. He was to have been the other teacher here. He will, however serve a valuable place as he writes material to teach our adults to read. Mr. James Lillie has taken his place. He and his wife, Nola, just came out in January, from the states. Rev. William Wagner is now working in the Kopiago, a new area, but will be here April 1, to take over the evangelistic work here. Being the only person who can communicate with the natives at present on the station, I've been involved in a lot of school, local and other matters of business and problems. It's been very interesting and I have a chance to work much more closely with the native people. I am thankful to have this chance for a year.

The latest news personally is that I became engaged in January, to Mr. Ray Hausler, an Australian, at present teaching Manual Arts at St. Paul's Lutheran High School, Pausa. He came out last August from Brisbane, Australia, and we have really seen the Lord's hand leading us together since then. Our faith in Christ and the oneness we feel through this, is our greatest blessing. For this we will always thank God. We plan to be married in December, 1966, this way I can finish my school term and three-year commitment to the Board for World Missions. We will make our home in New Guinea and Australia, but hope to be able to visit the States in the not too distant future.

May you enjoy a truly Blessed Lenten Season as we contemplate the great love God had for us, and all He did for us, that we might have forgiveness of sins, life and salvation. Then may the joy and hope we know through His Resurrection be yours at Easter and always.

With love in Christ, Eunice Redeker

(On a blue Aerogramme with a partial copy of above letter and the following):

Same as above

Dear Richard, Florence and Charles,

Hi! Well, I messed up 2 Aerogrammes as I did this stencil so I sent one to Mom, and am sending one to you. You can read the messed up part and part left out on Moms! I didn't want to throw this away since it is $.10 and besides this leaves a little more space for a note to you. How was your sale? (Richard sold all cattle and farm equipment). *Sure hope you made out real well. Hope you like living in Hoyleton real well. Write soon and tell me all your latest happenings.*

Guess you will be surprised to hear from me but I have wanted to write you for a long time. Guess Mom has told you of my engagement. The thing I always said I'd never do, but what do you do when you really love the "guy" and the Lord just works everything so we can be together. He's really a tremendous person, a wonderful Christian, for which I am so very grateful. I'm having some pictures made so one of these days I'll send some.

Did you get the tray, coconut baskets, etc. I sent you last Aug?

I like it here at Sirunki real well. Quite a challenge, and lots of work but also a real joy. I'm so much closer to the people and using the language so much more. I'll be glad when Rev. Wagner gets here, things get pretty complicated sometimes.

Well, the Vietnam War sure is continuing to "brew." Do hope and pray some kind of peaceful agreement can be reached soon. It's not far from us, only about 1000 miles

Enjoying my bush house. Wish you could visit me! Save your pennies, as I'd sure be thrilled to have you visit us some day! Take care! More soon. God bless you and kisses.

Much love, Eunice

P.S. Did you work on the Chrismons this year Florence? Saw a nice article in This Day on them. (Florence "introduced" them to several churches in Southern Illinois).

(This lady and her deceased husband were missionaries in China and had to leave when the communists took over, thus going to Hong Kong where he died. Eunice was in class with the son in River Forest and knew his parents were in China. Later, on her furlough, Eunice met this lady. On that furlough, Eunice and her traveling friend had dresses made in Hong Kong, which they had no room to then take with them on the remainder of the trip. Eunice is fairly certain this woman then mailed the clothes to her).

(Kowloon, Hong Kong)

May 24, 1966

Dear Eunice,

Thank you for thinking of me. Today is a holiday—Commonwealth Day—I am trying to write as many letters as possible.

First of all, I must congratulate you. I wish you and Mr. Hausler the Lord's richest blessings. May you have many blessed years together.

The pastor who performed the ceremony at our marriage in 1930, is now in the States. When he heard that Deth had left this vale of tears to be with his Saviour he referred me to Isaiah 57: 1 & 2 and this verse has given me much comfort. "The righteous is taken from the evil to come. He shall enter into peace." Surely that is true. There is much grief which one is spared by being with the Lord in heaven. I am assured that he has been praising his Savior for six months; together with those who have gone before him. The Chinese were just wonderful. Both old and young brought me much real Christian comfort. About a month ago six women travelled a long distance to call on me.

They brought hymn sheets and first sang, "What a friend we have in Jesus." Then one gave a prayer in which she asked God to comfort me, thanked Him for having allowed me to stay on and asking Him to bless my work. Then they sang, "Take my Life and Let it be." Wasn't that wonderful? I doubt very much whether I would have experienced anything like that in the States. I still can't believe that Deth is no longer here. The Chinese woman who works for me and I went to the cemetery to put flowers on the grave on Ascension Day. The grave is in such a nice place-a Christian cemetery not too far from here. We sat on the bench and read appropriate Bible verses. It was just six weeks since he had gone to the hospital.

I was going home in March. (The Mission Board treated me very, very well.) Then both the Seminary Board of Control and the Education Committee asked me to stay on. It took several months before I was officially employed. Now I teach English in the pre-seminary—also hymn-singing and each student has a weekly piano lesson. We hope that they will be able to play hymns by the time they graduate. Then I go down to Concordia School to do tutoring in English and for more piano lessons. I am thankful that I am busy. I am still living in the same apartment. It is so near to all of my work. I can afford to keep on the Chinese woman full-time. She is wonderful to have around.

We usually don't have a spring but this year it has been lovely. According to the Chinese calendar this year has two third months. Wouldn't the picture on this stationary make a good honeymoon cottage?

Much love to you,
Yours in Christ, Frieda Thode

(This is from the wife of a Pastor {who married Eunice and Ray}, placed at a remote Outstation, reached by aircraft. Due to the remoteness, their children attended a boarding school, so family time occurred very infrequently).

May 26 (Year unknown)

Dear Eunice,

Your May 12 note arrived yesterday, so sometimes it takes quite a while to exchange thoughts. And since our mail won't leave here until June 3 it will be almost a month. However we have had almost weekly flights so have nothing about which to complain. Someone forgot to put our mail on the flight last week and it was sent to Wewak and then to here. Rather unusual.

Anything I need? Just write me once in awhile like you just did and that makes my day a bright one. Inter-mission mail means more to me now than Stateside mail, except from my mom and dad. After 10 years, friendships narrow down to a very few and these have stayed staunch throughout that time.

It was so good to hear about the children and to know they are all right. They are to come home next Thursday and I think I'll be a weepy old mother when I do see them. We do miss them very much.

I've asked several people to write to me about the wedding. It must have been quite different from the kind I'm accustomed to. I hope Althea and John will be happy. (An Australian secretary who married an American Med. Student). *If the reception was at Pausa you women must have been terribly busy.*

There doesn't seem to be any definite weather pattern out here. Pete and Bev Wilson were here Sunday afternoon and Pete says the rainfall figures are about the same all year round except for Oct. and Nov. when it is very dry. Otherwise, it rains a lot.

We get our freezer weekly from Wewak via MAF so Burns Phelps takes good care of us there. In fact I didn't want any meat yesterday because Bill is gone all week on a walkabout and deliberately didn't send in an order. But they sent me meat anyway. Very considerate of them.

I'm planning to come in for Women's Retreat on the 10th and stay with Laverne. We'll have to have some "hashing" to do that night in preparation for our part on Friday night. I'm surely looking forward to seeing everyone. I'll probably get a sore throat from talking too much.

I thoroughly enjoy it here. The only difficult part is not having the children home. Healthwise this hot and humid climate is ideal for my sinuses and hay fever. I was having a terrible time before I left again at Mambisanda. The Committee on Evangelism is to decide where we shall be placed after furlough. Karl had a talk with Bill about his preference, but Bill said he wanted to leave it up to the committee. They know where he is needed most and as you said in your note "The Lord never fails." If God wants us here then He will bless our family even though we are separated. If we can serve Him better elsewhere then we shall do our best there. Our lives are in His hands and may we always be ready to follow His guidance.

Thank you for your note. Today is a gloomy old day, rainy and cloudy and quite unusual. Maybe it will clear up this afternoon.

Love, Ruth Wagner

Wabag, New Guinea (Form Letter)

June 25, 1966

Dear Relatives and Friends,

Greeting and best wishes to you from a cold, damp and wet, Sirunki, New Guinea. We pray this finds you all strong in faith, physically well and in best of spirits.

It's been a long while since I've been able to share with you via this newsletter, but it seems the past months have been filled with so many happenings and my time for correspondence has been cut very short. The school year is going very well. I enjoy working with the smaller Standard II children here at Sirunki and their joy and enthusiasm in learning is a special joy for me also. Since my co-worker returned to the U.S. on June 1, I am the only teacher on the station. This has increased my administrative responsibilities as well as adding to my list of duties the supervision of our 17 outstation schools. These schools are taught by native teachers, who have had only very limited schooling and training. (Eunice would visit each one of these out-station schools, at least once per school term or more frequently if needed. These communications with the teachers were in Enga and Pidgin English. These visits continued after she was married and no longer serving as a teacher). *They teach Class I, II, III, and IV. This is a program established to reach some of the many children who do not have the opportunity to attend the Standard schools, due to lack of Staff and facilities. The main emphasis is to make the children literate in the Enga and Pidgin English languages, teaching them Bible Stories and simple number work. We can be grateful for the faithfulness of our 17 teachers this year, as they have come in every other Saturday for their instructions and lessons.*

The Rev. and Mrs. Gerald Arndt and family left for furlough in February, and we were without a pastor for two months, when Rev. and Mrs. William Wagner and their 5 daughters were assigned here in April. It was good to have them arrive as many problems come up, and many times it was hard to know just how best to handle them. Our road into Sirunki station was also impassable during the rainy season, even jeeps were getting stuck. Rev. Wagner did a good job grading it and getting it back into good condition.

This past week the Wabag Lutheran Church had their Annual Conference. It was well attended and a tremendous joy to see this young church move forward as a mighty force for the Lord. Some of the expressions of deep faith in God were inspiring. One of the big decisions was to move our school for training evangelists from Birip, to Papayuk, 60 miles up the valley. This is only 12 miles from Sirunki. Many problems face this church, shortage of staff, and poor stewardship on the part of many congregations, being uppermost. The devil and forces of evil are at work here just as diligently as in other parts of the world.

The latest personal happening is my engagement to Mr. Ray Hausler, of Brisbane, Australia, at Easter. He came up to work at our Mission in August, 1965, and is teaching Manual Arts at St. Paul's High School, as well as, supervising the building expansion program there. We plan to be married November 26, 1966. We plan to continue to serve our Lord, here in New Guinea for the next few years.

As ever your prayers are our needs. For daily strength, increased faith and wisdom, for the upbuilding of God's kingdom here, for protection as we travel by air and over mountainous roads, and for making all people a praise in the earth to the glory of God's name, we seek your prayers.

It has been a real joy hearing from you, through your cards and letters. Our Lord bless and keep each of you in His protection and care, make your faith strong and prosper your life for Him.

Rejoicing in Christ, Eunice Redeker

(We are uncertain all these years later why there were two different letters with the same date.)

Wabag, New Guinea (Form Letter)

June 25, 1966

Dear ______________,

Greetings and best wishes to you from New Guinea. As most of you enjoy the warmer summer weather, we have the same cool climate here at Sirunki. It has gotten down into the 30 degree area lately and feels pretty cold, especially with no heating but my little wood stove. I'll be glad to move down valley again next November, it's so pleasant and wonderful at a lower altitude. I am thankful for being here this year, though. Teaching the small children is such a joy and their enthusiasm is so heartwarming.

I am the only teacher on the station at present as the other teacher returned to the U.S. after only three months in New Guinea. I'm kept busy with all the administrative work, supervising the 17 outstation schools and teaching my 34 little Standard Twos'. We have 691 students in the outstation schools, Classes I to IV. We're thankful to have native teachers working in them, although their training is meager, and leaves much to be desired.

Even though Sirunki is far out, 65 miles from Pausa, and the roads are bumpy and muddy, we still get a lot of visitors, since the Kandepe, Papyuk and Muritaka stations are further out west of here. So, we don't feel very isolated.

Next weekend our Luther League, consisting of the single staff working for our Mission will be coming up for the weekend. There are 23 coming up, so it will be a nice group and should be fun, as all of them have plenty energy. I'll be kept busy getting enough stuff baked this week, especially bread. Sometimes one wishes a grocery store were just around the corner!!

Our Wabag Lutheran Church had their Annual Conference this past week. It was well run and each year one sees the growth and progress of this young church in greater measure. There are many conflicts, trials and signs of growing pains, but by God's grace there is progress—more workers are constantly being trained, more souls reached by the Gospel and won for Christ, more souls built up in the Word, as it continues to be preached daily. The total membership today numbers approximately 36,000 members.

Personally, all is well. Ray had a serious accident a month ago when he, on his motorbike, collided with a jeep. Through God's marvelous protection he escaped with only bruises and no broken bones. The roads here are narrow, up and down the mountains, and many blind corners, so they are quite dangerous.

Praying this finds you all in best of health and spirits. The grace of God and His rich blessings to us in our Lord Jesus, be yours now and always.

With love in Christ, Eunice Redeker

(Personal note added to the above letter to Richard, Florence and Charles)

Hi! How are you? Sorry, I have to send a duplicated letter but I'm just not able to keep up with correspondence any other way. My load of duties is so heavy at present. I'll be glad come Dec., and I can <u>just keep</u>

house, Ha! Ha! Already they have me scheduled to teach music and Social Studies at Pausa next year, but I haven't said "Yes." With the shortage of teaching staff, guess I will.

How's your new home? Hope you like it real well and Richard you like your new work. Charles, will you go to Nashville High School? They were our bitter rivals when I was at CHS (Carlyle High School). *Did you ever get the books I asked CPH to send you for your Confirmation?*

What's the situation with Mom? She writes so seldom that I'm a bit worried about her. No one writes and tells me her real condition, so I wonder. Ray has been telling me lately, guess because I keep talking about her, that if I feel I should, I should go and see her before we get married. What do you think?? Please write me and let me know, tell me the honest facts, you know I understand.

Well, Ray and I plan to be married Nov. 26, unless something else comes up. The ladies at Hope made my wedding dress of white brocade. The pictures of it look beautiful. So much wish you all could be here. Sure will think of you! Take care. God be with you.

Much love from your sis, Eunice

Wabag, New Guinea (Form Letter)

Sept. 13, 1966

Dear ____________,

Since it seems I have no other way to answer your most welcome letters lately, due to so many things that demand my time these days, I will resort to this way of at least getting a line to you. I hope after December I will have more time and be able to write more faithfully. At present I'm drawing to the end of the school year, which is always a busy time, bringing everything to a close, final tests, grades, meeting with parents, etc. Our outstation schools and teachers need assistance also with these things. Then in between it all we're trying to plan our wedding, which will be November 26. Here in New Guinea, you have to think ahead and order, which always takes several months. We will be married at Highland Lutheran School. We will invite our Mission Staff and close native friends to the wedding and reception. My thirty-four little ones will sing. They are very excited about it. Loving Christian friends at Hope Congregation, Levittown, Pa., made my wedding dress of white brocade. We'll be looking forward to its arrival in a couple of weeks.

Ray will continue to teach at St. Paul's next year, and because of shortage of staff they've asked me to help out too. Ray is also helping along with the building program there, which is quite extensive at present, as they prepare for an influx of approximately three-hundred students, February 1968.

We had our Intermission Sport's Day several weeks ago and my children enjoyed it immensely. The jeep ride down was a thrill, as most of them had not been away from Sirunki. They also won several prizes in the races, high jumping, and bow and arrow shooting, which added to the joy of all.

As ever, we need your prayers, that God's Word may be effective unto life eternal, upon the hearts and lives of these, His people. For the blessings He has showered upon us all and the privilege to know and work for Him, we can never be sufficiently thankful. May He help us ever to glorify and honor Him, until we can forever do so fully in the bliss of heaven. His blessings and peace be with you.

In His name, Eunice Redeker

October 28, 1966

Cover-Chi-Rho-

"The symbol stands for marriage in Christ. Marriage is represented by intertwined rings. Christ by the Christogram, an ancient symbol made up of Christ's name in Greek XP, and formed into a cross."

Mrs. Richard G. Redeker
requests your prayers
for the Nuptial ceremony
joining her daughter
Eunice Anna
And
Mr. Ray Walter Hausler
on Saturday, the twenty-sixth of November
Nineteen Hundred and sixty-six
Highland Lutheran School
Amapyaka, New Guinea

November 2, 1966

Mrs. Richard Redeker
RR #1
Shattuc, Illinois

Dear Mrs. Redeker:

Thank you so much for the beautiful announcement of the marriage of your daughter Eunice Anna to Mr. Ray Walter Hausler in New Guinea on Saturday the 26th of November, 1966.

I know how much you would enjoy being there if that were possible.

About a year ago it was my privilege to visit the New Guinea field and also to spend some time with Eunice. I had to admire her for her courage and patience in working as a teacher under difficult circumstances. The Lord certainly blessed her work. We join you in the prayer and confidence that the Lord will also bless this marriage, and we wish for them many years of happiness together in His name.

I have a feeling that the wedding will really be a happy occasion. I had opportunity to attend such a wedding in India. The missionaries and their families certainly make up for absent relatives in a most wonderful manner. The setting at Highland Lutheran School is also a beautiful place.

Once again thank you for the announcement, and we pray that the Lord will continue to be with you as well as with them.

Sincerely,
Paul M. Heerboth
Asst. Exec. Sec. for Personnel
Board for World Missions, LCMS

The Wedding Service Cover- (Cross with interwoven rings) "Lord, who at Cana's wedding feast didst as a Guest appear, Thou dearer far than earthly guest, vouchsafe Thy presence here."

The Marriage Service
Of
Eunice Anna Redeker
And
Ray Walter Hausler
Saturday, November 26, 1966
9:30 a.m.
Highland Lutheran School
Amapyaka – New Guinea

Wedding Preludes
Chorale Preludes.............Bach
Sheep May Safely Graze.....Bach
My Spirit Be Joyful..........Bach

The Wedding Processionals

Goodness and mercy, all my life,
Shall surely follow me;
And in God's house forevermore
My dwelling-place shall be. Amen.

The Nuptial Eucharist
The Words of Institution
Pax Domini
Distribution

The Benediction

The Hymn
Let us ever walk with Jesus,
Follow His example pure,
Flee the world, which would

Solemn Processional......Handel

Take Thou My Hands and Lead Me...R. Wienhorst

The Invocation

The Psalmody

The Gloria Patri

Glory be to the Father and to the Son and to the
Holy Ghost; As it was in the beginning, is now, and
ever shall be, world without end. Amen.

The Wedding Address...........Isaiah 21:10

Fear thou not; for I am with thee: be not dismayed;
for I am thy God: I will strengthen thee; yea, I will
help thee; yea, I will uphold thee with the right
hand of my righteousness.

Choir....."Children of the Heavenly Father"...C. Berg

(Sung by Eunice's children-Sirunki Lutheran School)

The Marriage Rite

The Teaching of the Word

deceive us.
And to sin our soul's allure.

Ever in His footsteps treading,
Body here, yet soul above,
Full of faith and hope and love,
Let us do the Father's bidding.
Faithful Lord, abide with me;
Savior, lead, I follow Thee.

Let us suffer here with Jesus,
To His image e'er conform;
Heaven's glory soon will please us,
Sunshine follow on the storm
Tho' we sow in tears of sorrow,
We shall reap in heav'ly joy;
And the fears that now annoy
Shall be laughter on the morrow.
Christ, I suffer here with Thee;
There, o, share Thy joy with me.

Let us gladly live with Jesus;
Since He's risen from the dead,

The Expression of Mutual Consent

The Exchange of Marriage Vows and Rings.

The Marriage Pronouncement

The Lord's Prayer

The Hymn: The Lord's my Shepherd, I'll not want;
He makes me down to lie
In pastures green' He leadeth me,
The quiet waters by.

My soul He doth restore again,
And me to walk doth make
Within the paths of righteousness;
E'en for His own name's sake.

Yea, tho' I walk in death's dark vale,
Yet will I fear no ill;
For Thou art with me, and Thy rod
And staff me comfort still.

My Table Thou hast furnished
In presence of my foes;
My head Thou dost with oil anoint,

Death and grave must soon

release us

Jesus, Thou art now our Head,
We are truly Thine own members;
Where Thou Liv'st there live we
Take and own us constantly,
Faithful Friend, as Thy brethren.

Jesus, here I live to Thee.
Also there eternally. Amen.

The Recessional
Trumpet Voluntary……Purcell

In Christian marriage Christ Himself unites the bride and groom to each other. In the Sacrament He supplies them with His presence that their

Faith in Him and their love for each other may grow. Your participation in Holy Communion with them can

testify to the Christian faith that you share with them. It can also be regarded as an expression of thanks-

And my cup overflows.
(Continued top right column
p 172)

giving and praise to God for both the gifts He is giving to them today and to you.

The Wedding Sermon: Rev. James Herzog

Isaiah 41: 10—"Fear not, for I am with you, be not dismayed, for I am your God; I will strengthen you, I will help you, I will uphold you with My victorious right hand."

When two select servants of the Lord decide to marry it is quite a different thing than what the rest of the world usually imagines. They imagine any new couple will establish a home and settle-down to a life of comparative security and conformity, as everyone else does. And for that reason, they aren't afraid of marriage (in spite of the usual jokes to the contrary). They think anyone can do it.

Little do they realize that when two devout Christians marry and settle down in their midst…a mission station has been established and is going to be working day and night in the energy of the Lord to bring the living Word of God to bear on the lives of all the neighbors.

It is true, at times Christians themselves, in the excitement of establishing their homes, forget what they are about to do. They forget that they are forming a unit, a most basic unit, of the Lord's far-flung mission forces. They forget that they, in addition to establishing a normal home and all that goes with it, are going to carry on extensive mission work as a smoothly running team.

However, such is not the case with you. You know and you remember; and today we say it again in the presence of God, of this assembly, and of all the invisible guests: this marriage is a marriage of kindred spirits, not just of bodies; and today more than a new home is being established in our midst, a new mission station is opening before our eyes.

A MARRIAGE IS A MISSION ORGANIZATION

Your marriage is a mission organization as surely as is N.G.L.M. *(New Guinea Lutheran Mission)*. And your home will be a mission station from now on as surely as is Sirunki or Pausa itself. It is not your only station here in New Guinea, of course, but it is the most basic, more basic than even your staff assignments, and should always be your first consideration as missionaries of Jesus Christ. The command of Jesus to leave one's loved ones and to follow Him gives no one even the slightest indication that it is right to neglect his own household in favor of the larger organization. If a man so interprets this word, he stands in danger of becoming "worse than an unbeliever" (I Tim. 5:8). But, if a man does all he can in the strength of the Lord to make his family cooperate with, instead of hindering, the Lord's mission, then he has interpreted this word of Christ correctly.

When you think of the responsibility and the challenge of leading your household as a mission organization, and the house and property as a mission station, then we find it difficult to say lightly: anyone can do it. Then we really have cause to fear marriage. We stand awed at the prospect of overseeing a mission which includes among other things: business, economic, health, education, and spiritual responsibilities. In view of this awesome task draw near and hear the Lord say: FEAR NOT, FOR I AM WITH YOU.

THE FEAR OF LEADERSHIP

Of course, if you think being a leader means to do everything yourself, or worse, to plan everybody else's job for them and then to force them, one way or another, to carry out your "projections", then you will have real cause for fear...for then you are not walking with God, nor are you leading your staff to walk with God. You are teaching them to pay lip-service to the ever present and leading Lord while attempting to serve Him in unconsecrated willpower.

But there is no fear if you entrust the leadership to God who personally and exactly guides your every step. And when you are unable to detect this route at times and you find yourself in error, He will even more marvelously reroute your way to include even your failures as a vital part of His marvelous will for you. Thru Jesus' righteousness this is not only possible but is the very gospel with which we are entrusted to evangelize the world.

And when you are called up to administer discipline you will be sure that its ultimate aim is to point out the danger of disobedience to God's personal leading…not just of disobedience to the commandments of men. If God is Himself with you in the leadership then what need is there of fear? Then you become a true leader, that is, a leader who himself is the finest example of a follower.

THE FEAR OF YOUR WILL

But be careful that the enemy doesn't take you to the other extreme and cause you to be so self-conscious of your "own" will (as opposed to God's will) that you become afraid to have a will at all. God doesn't extinguish your will, He sanctifies it. Your will, which you daily subject to Him for correction and direction, then, becomes one of the very means by which He moves you to carry out His commands…"for God is at work in you, both to will and to work for His good pleasure." (Phil. 2:13). If you never exert your will and power which you have received of the Lord (after faithful and searching prayer) then you are as disobedient to God as if you rushed ahead without seeking His counsel in the first place. So, don't fear your will, but daily consecrate it by the Word of God and prayer, and then exert it in love as the Lord provides the power.

THE FEAR OF YOUR CIRCUMSTANCES

And finally, don't be afraid of your daily circumstances. Some days it will seem that the nearer you draw to the Lord for guidance the further He removes Himself from you and you stand, as it were, in darkness. At times it may seem that the terrible sharp sword of God's Word is aimed at you for destruction. At times when you cry for His strength most urgently, it will seem that you are left utterly weak and helpless, a victim for the scavengers of hell. At times your hopes in the promises of victory will seem to mock you with impious cruelty. At times like that, with the eyes of faith, look inside that dark cloud and see that God dwells in the midst of it, and, with His uplifted sword in His hand, He says to you:

Fear not, for though it seems that I am against you, I am really with you all the way. Be not dismayed, for though it may appear that I am doing you evil, I am really your God. Though it may seem that I am out only to weaken you and leave you utterly helpless, I will strengthen you, I will help you. I will uphold you with my victorious right hand…and for that reason I must first gain the victory over you.

Let God lead your marriage, direct your will, and win every dispute. Enter into such a marriage without fear. Amen.

(Form Letter)
(Above and to the left was a Wedding pic of Ray/Eunice)

December 1966

Dear Relatives and Friends,

Greetings to you from Ray and Eunice! As we together are now able to share with you the wonders, joys, blessings, trials and tribulations of the tremendous task of bringing the Gospel to New Guineans, we are especially grateful that God is letting us do this. For leading us together, and showering our lives with His abundant blessing thus far, we thank and praise God!

As this is our first letter to you since we are "united as one," we will keep it to a letter of rejoicing and happiness in Christ. What a wonderful time to do that as we celebrate the birthday of our Savior, whose coming has made all our joys and gladnesses possible. As we hear the glorious Christmas message may it fill us with an abundant measure of joy and peace this Christmastide. We'd like you to share this message with us now from Luke 2:1-20:

"And it came to pass in those days, that there went out a decree from Caesar Augustus, that all the world should be taxed. And this

taxing was first made when Cyrenius was governor of Syria. And all went to be taxed, everyone into his own city. And Joseph also went up from Galilee, out of the city of David, which is called Bethlehem; because he was of the house and lineage of David; to be taxed with Mary his espoused wife, being great with child. And so it was, that, while they were there, the days were accomplished that she should be delivered. And she brought forth her firstborn son, and wrapped him in swaddling clothes, and laid Him in a manger; because there was no room for them in the inn.

And there were in the same country shepherds abiding in the fields, keeping watch over their flock by night. And, lo, the angel of the Lord came upon them, and the glory of the Lord shone round about them; and they were sore afraid. And the angel said unto them, "Fear not; for, behold, I bring you good tidings of great joy, which shall be to all people. For unto you is born this day in the city of David, a Savior, which is Christ the Lord. And this shall be a sign unto you; Ye shall find the babe wrapped in swaddling clothes, lying in a manger. And suddenly there was with the angel a multitude of the heavenly host praising God, and saying, 'Glory to God in the highest, and on earth, peace, good will toward men.' And it came to pass, as the angels were gone away from them into heaven, the shepherds said one to another, 'Let us go even unto Bethlehem, and see this thing which is come to pass, which the Lord hath made known unto us.' And they came with haste, and found Mary, Joseph and the Babe lying in a manger. And when they had seen it, they made known abroad the saying which was told them concerning this child. And all they that heard it wondered at those things which were told them by the shepherds. But Mary kept all these things, and pondered them in her heart. And the shepherds returned, glorifying and praising God for all the things they had heard and seen, as it was told unto them."

What a message! What love God had for us! What joy and peace this message contains! What glory it will bring to those who believe it! It is a message beyond human comprehension, but dear friends, may God send His Holy Spirit in ever greater measure into your hearts, that you might believe and receive the glory which God has waiting for you!

May this Jesus live and abide in you and may His presence cheer you, sustain you, and shine through you to all whom you meet, that you might be a light to lead others to their Savior, and life eternal!

God grant these blessings to you in 1967!

With love in Christ,
Ray and Eunice Hausler

(Form Letter)

January 3, 1966

Dear _______________,

Greetings to you! And wishes for a truly Blessed and Joyous 1967. May the "Good News" – "For Unto You is born this day in the City of David, a Savior," Luke 2:11, be your strength, joy and hope, each day of this New Year.

Now to catch up on all of our excitement and activities of the past two months: First of all the last two weeks of November were quite busy for us both. Eunice finished the school year on November 18,1966. The Sirunki people gave her a very warm farewell. They had a muum and about twenty pigs were killed for this. Ray also finished school at St. Paul's High School on November 18, and after final tests and paper grading he felt relieved. Then there was the week before our wedding. No need to say, we were both kept very busy. Eunice moved to Pausa, where we are living, on the weekend, then stayed at Amapyaka, where our wedding was held. Eunice finished last minute things, like making sure everything was there, pressing and putting everything together. Ray put up a tent for the reception and did a lot of riding around getting needed things and other details. Then Friday after school, we set up the chapel for the wedding in a large double classroom at Highland Lutheran School. Eunice had made white curtains for the altar background.

That evening we had rehearsal and a delicious Rehearsal Dinner served by Mr. and Mrs. Richard Adler. They are teachers and Richard Adler was the best man and Loretta Adler the matron of honour at our wedding. Garry Wolff (teacher) *was groomsman, and Janice Haby* (Secretary), *was bridesmaid. Lisa Wagner, daughter of Rev. and Mrs. William Wagner of Sirunki was flower girl.*

Then came Saturday morning. It was really a wonderful morning. We had a relaxed wedding breakfast with the Adlers'. Then Ray and his attendants dressed at Green's, (the houseparents' at Highland Lutheran School). Mrs. James McArthur helped Eunice get dressed at Adlers'. Eunice's gown was white brocade, simply designed with a round neckline, empire waist, straight-floor-length skirt, long sleeves coming to a point over the hands, and a long train attached at the empire waistline in the back. It was a gift as well as made by the ladies of Hope Lutheran Church, Levittown, Pennsylvania. Eunice carried a prayer book, topped with white gardenias. The attendants wore dresses floor length, fashioned like Eunice's in a Christmas green and carried yellow frangipani bouquets. Lisa wore a floor length white gown of par de soi and carried a white basket filled with rose petals. Rev. William Wagner married us and Rev. James Herzog delivered the address. Mrs. Chris Cooper, an accomplished organist, played the reed-pump organ. The Standard II children of Sirunki sang, "Children of the Heavenly Father". In their little white gowns and green bow ties, they looked very special and precious.

All went well and the service started on time and went off as scheduled and planned. We had many of our New Guinea friends and students, and our Mission family present, which thrilled us, also that they could commune at the Lord's Table with us. The reception was held outdoors. A simple lunch, punch and wedding cake were served by Mr. and Mrs. Richard Brandon. The wedding cake had four tiers, and was beautifully-meaningfully decorated by Mrs. Willard Burce. Tier one was covered with bells for "Joys of Christian Living". Tier two had "Flowers of the Field" for "Don't worry or care for your heavenly Father cares for you". Tier three had grapes and vines for "I am the Vine, you are the branches". Tier four had a Chi-Rho for

"Marriage in Christ." All was beautiful and our wedding day remains a wonderful memory.

At 2:00 P.M. we flew via M.A.F. Cessna to Goroka, on the first leg of our honeymoon. Then we spent a week at a cottage in Bulolo, then several days in Lae with the Busses', our missionary friends at Balob Teacher's College and then a week in Menyamya with Rev. and Mrs. Russell Weier, working for the Australian Lutheran Mission. Mrs. Weier is Ray's sister. We had a relaxing and enjoyable three weeks and it was a joy to see so much of New Guinea.

Then we got home a week before Christmas and were busy getting our bush house in order and preparing for Christmas. The Richard Adlers' spent Christmas with us. The Pausa station staff all got together Christmas Day for a Christmas dinner. We had a large Christmas tree, which Ray got by climbing half-way up the mountain near our house. It was a type of spruce tree. The week after Christmas was busy with getting more settled and visiting friends who had invited us. New Year's Eve and Day, we spent 85 miles up valley at Papyuk with the Daniel Kunerts'. Four teacher's families got together and it was most enjoyable: included in the activities were our worship services, a Chinese dinner, shooting firecrackers, hike, and making fondue.

Now we are back at work. Ray is busy helping set up the new sawmill at Walyia, 10 miles from here. Eunice is busy doing the usual homemaking duties and typing a book for the Committee on Schools. Next week the Busses' will be with us from Lae. Then our Annual Staff Conference the following week, and then the new schoolyear begins. Ray will again be teaching Technical Drawing and Woodworking, and Eunice will be teaching one sewing class.

We pray this finds you and yours in best of health and spirits. Our Lord grant His grace upon you!

With Christian love,
Ray & Eunice Hausler

February 2, 1967

MEMO TO: The Rev. Mr. Paul M. Heerboth

I wish to recommend Mr. Ray Hausler for appointment for five years for work in the New Guinea Lutheran Mission.

I make this recommendation on the basis of the field Executive Committee resolution of September 20-21, 1966 and – on the basis of some rather extensive personal consultations with the Executive Committee and the Hauslers.

You are aware of the fact that Mr. Hausler is the husband of Eunice Redeker, formerly teacher at Pausa. Mr. Hausler's contract finishes as of February 1, 1967. That contract was for 18 months.

Eunice completed three years of her second term of service in September, 1966.

The mission chairman and myself have agreed that the mission owes Eunice her return travel to the States. We have also agreed that in the event that the Board would agree to appointment for five years, we would pay Eunice's trip from the States to New Guinea and Ray's trip from Australia to New Guinea.

Mr. Hausler is to receive an appointment as a builder and building instructor. He works half-time under the Construction and Equipment Committee and half-time as industrial arts teacher at Pausa.

There are not intentions of continuing his appointment beyond five years. The Hauslers themselves are planning to locate in Australia at the end of their term.

The Hauslers have agreed to stay on the field until November, 1967. (The field is extending his initial 18-month contract to enable this.) If the Board grants an appointment, he should be appointed as of January 15, 1968. Salary under that appointment would begin in January, 1968, and the Hauslers (who will have come to America between November 15 and February 15) plan to be back on the field at the opening of Pausa, on or about February 15, 1968.

Kindly observe that this involves us in travel across the Pacific to the United States for Eunice. Her travel to the States we already owe her; we would hereby commit ourselves to travel to New Guinea from the States. In the case of Mr. Hausler, an Australian, we commit ourselves to nothing beyond Australia.

Yours in Christ, Jim Mayer

April 5, 1967

Dear Florence, Richard and Charles,

Hi! Well, where do I start? I have been writing this letter to you for a long time in my mind, but just didn't get it on paper. You sure been in our thoughts, conversation and prayers often. I'm sorry I didn't get this wedding info to you sooner and you've most likely seen it all at Mom's, but I thought you might appreciate a copy of your own. For the marvelous blessing God has showered upon us and our marriage we are truly grateful. We feel very undeserving, but pray that we might always be faith-filled and zeal-filled servants for our Lord, esp. as we again rejoice that "Our Savior lives" during this Easter season, we are filled with joy, hope and anticipation for the day when we can live with Him, as He has promised.

How do you like your new home and living in Hoyleton? We're looking forward to seeing you all the end of this year. We only pray, God-willing, Mom will still be with us. How is she, really?? She never says much about herself.

How is High School, Charles? You're in Jr. High yet or is it Senior High? Time flies so quickly, one sometimes loses track. Bet you have grown many inches since I saw you. Have you any plans of what you'd like to do after High School?

Florence, many thanks for all you did to help pack my things to be sent out here. Mom, mentioned you worked hard at it! Just a million thanks! We're thankful to have all the things, and have been putting them to good use. Everything got here safely, for which we are very grateful. Florence, if anything should happen to Mom, before Dec., would you check for my wooden shoes from Holland, my boxes of slides

9" x 11" boxes of New Guinea-there should be 2 of them and my travel books of the various countries I saw. I'd appreciate having those. As I say, we are truly thankful and grateful for all you've done for us.

Ray is looking forward to meeting you all also. He's kept busy on construction in the A.M. and teaching in the P.M. I keep busy with teaching in the P.M. and other jobs as typing books, etc. Just housework is enough to keep me busy fulltime, but I sorta hustle it along. Ray did our yard last Sat. P.M. He got all the grass in shape, flower beds made, etc. It looks nice. I'm glad he likes doing that, as I just don't find time to get out there.

Well, must close for this time. Will write soon again as I should have more time. Hope you are all fine. Greetings to your parents and Gert and her family and Ralph and his family, Florence.

God bless, keep and protect you.

Love from us, Ray & Eunice

(Mailing included wedding service and pictures)

Wapenamanda, New Guinea (Form Letter)

May 31, 1967

Dear ________________,

Since it seems we cannot find the time to get a personal note to each of you without doing it via form letter, we shall do so, as we think of you all often and you are in our prayers. We pray this finds you and yours in our Lord Jesus and healthy in body. May His peace ever be with you.

Here at St. Paul's High School, things are running along smoothly. Ray is busy in the mornings on construction. They are building new classroom blocks, more dormitories, and houses for staff. At present, three staff houses, four dormitories and toilet block, and one classroom building are under construction. The staff houses are of bush materials and tin roof. The classrooms and dormitories are of Masonite siding and tin roofs.

In the afternoon Ray teaches Woodworking and Technical Drawing and Eunice teaches Music four days a week and sewing on Friday. We're kept busy and we like it this way.

We have also been very busy with overnight guests and visitors. Most of these are fellow-staff members, who have come down valley for medical and business reasons and stay over as the trip would be a bit too much to make in one day, although it can be and is done when necessary.

June 19-23, will be our Wabag Lutheran Church Conference. It will be held here at Yaramanda, a mile up the hill. The four women, here at Pausa, will help the two Yaramanda women and so it'll be a week of cooking for us. Each of us will house five or six pastors and teachers overnight, and at noon will be feeding about 60 at Yaramanda. The Christians at Yaramanda will be housing and feeding the New Guinean delegates in their homes. Since their diet is mostly sweet potato and they sleep on mats on the ground in their houses, their duties will be considerably less than ours. We however, pray God's blessings upon this Conference, that the men might be filled and guided by His Spirit and all decisions fruitful to the upbuilding of His kingdom here. Please remember these people in your prayers.

We are beginning to think of our furlough. We will have three months, Nov., Dec., '67, and Jan., '68, God-willing, we plan to visit the U.S. for two months, and about two weeks in Australia, the rest will be taken up in travel time. It will be a new exciting experience for Ray, as he has never travelled outside of Australia and New Guinea. Eunice is getting very excited too, to see friends and loved ones again, and to show off her homeland to Ray.

Will sign off this part of the letter so, we have room for a personal note. God bless and keep each of you in His care, and love.

With love in Christ, Ray and Eunice

P.S. (personal note to Richard, Florence and Charles). *Hi! Well a line to you – seems the time flies so is so full, I don't get at writing like I'd like to.*

Hope you are all fine and enjoying your "new" home. I gathered from Mom's letters that you have moved into another house there in

Hoyleton. Where about is it? We're looking forward to seeing you all and catch up on all the happenings and events there. I know the time will fly by much too quickly but will make the most of it!

We have some lovely dahlias, carnations and salvia blooming at present. Ray enjoys doing the yard and flower beds. That's his Sat. afternoon hobby. I sure appreciate and help when I have time. Otherwise, it seems our work keeps us very busy.

We had our Women's Retreat last weekend. It was very inspiring and refreshing. Bible Studies were on the Holy Spirit. Other items were a Banquet and talk on Women's Work (New Guinean), *Flower Arrangement demonstration, Music Concert, and Fun Night.*

Well, hope you are all fine. Hope Richard likes his work real well and all is going … God grant you His nearness, and abiding peace and blessings.

Much love, Ray & Eunice

Dear Rev. Mayer,
LCMS
St. Louis, Missouri

August 22, 1967

It is with praise and thanks to God that I accept the Appointment as a Builder and Craft Instructor, here in New Guinea, for a period of five years, extended to me by the Board of World Missions. I shall try to serve our Lord and Master to the best of my ability and shall seek His guidance at all times.

Both Eunice and I appreciated your letter, included with the Appointment. After three months of furlough, October 30, through January 30, 1968, in the U.S. and Australia, we look forward to our further stay here beginning February 1, 1968, among these people. We pray that we may be useful instruments in God's plan to bring many more of these people to the saving knowledge of Jesus Christ, our Savior.

We pray God's guidance and blessings always upon you, The Board for World Missions, and our fellow Christians there. His abiding strength and peace sustain you.

Cc: Rev. Paul Heerboth

Rev. Karl Stotik

Yours in Christ,
Ray Hausler

August 29, 1967

Dear Paul,

Received a copy of the letter sent you by Mr. Ray Hausler.

He writes that he accepts an appointment as a Builder and Craft Instructor.

There is a conflict of opinion between a couple of the mission committees as to where Mr. Hausler is needed.

Therefore would appreciate receiving details re: his appointment in order to be prepared for possible discussion arising from conflict of interest.

Sincerely, Karl (Stotik)

(In October of 1967, both Ray and Eunice were to submit "Personnel Information" for the Board of Missions of the LCMS. We are including excerpts from Ray's here, and a few tidbits of Eunice's because even though the reader is already quite aware of Eunice's background from both her first book {Thank You Lord for the Privilege} and the information included thus far in this, her second book, there are a few additional points in regard to prior service.)

Ray was born, baptized and confirmed in Toowoomba, Queensland, Australia. Subsequently he had moved with his family to Redcliffe, Queensland. Both of his parents were also born in Australia. Ray had always held membership in the Australian Lutheran Church.

Ray's church activities included:

-Sunday School Teacher 1954-1960
-Luther League President 1957-1960
-Sunday School teacher 1960-1964
-Builder at Yaibos - 1965, Builder/manual arts teacher – 1966-1967

Ray's schooling included:

-Grades 1-6 in Toowoomba
-Grades 7-8 in Redcliffe
-Grades 9-12 at Concordia Memorial College, Toowoomba
-Brisbane Technical College, 1954-1959, With a degree in Carpentry and Joinery

Ray's occupational history (beginning at present and working back) including assignments that could have had a special bearing on his proposed mission work:

- (See final bullet above under "Church activities" for the most recent)
-1960-1964—Employed as a builder in Toowoomba
-1955-1959—Employed as an Apprentice and builder in Redcliffe

-What made me join the Mission was the fact we have very little time left to bring these people to Christ, here in New Guinea.

Eunice's church activities:

-Hope Lutheran Church, Westcliffe, CO:

-In addition to serving as the day school teacher (and principal), she was Sunday School teacher, Youth Counselor, and organist, in addition to weekly being responsible for publishing the Sunday Bulletin. (The congregation had no pastor during the year of Eunice's teaching there).

-Hope Lutheran Church, Levittown, PA:

-In addition to being teacher/organizer of Hope Lutheran School, she served as Principal, youth leader, Sunday School teacher and part-time organist. She also served as a youth counselor at the Eastern District Walther League Camp.

-In New Guinea:

-Teacher at St. Paul's Lutheran—1959-1965
-Teacher at Sirunki Lutheran—1966 in Wabag
-Youth Counselor in Yaramanda for 2 years.

Eunice's education: In addition to the grade school, high school and colleges attendance, she took two summers of graduate classes at Temple University, in school administration.

Eunice's occupational history, including assignments that could have had a special bearing on her proposed mission work:

-I think the assignment to open a school in Levittown, and the evangelistic work involved in working in that congregation and school inspired me to go further to bring the Gospel to souls. Hope Cong. was a Mission Field in itself, with many converts, and much opportunity in the neighborhood to witness to the unchurched.

-Many incidents in my work at CTC., RF, where I served as a S.S. teacher, and youth counselor to a mission congregation, as well as teaching at Hope, Westcliffe, CO, gave me many opportunities to witness for Christ to those who had never heard.

-Since I am now a wife, my prayer is that I will continue to witness for my Savior, in every possible way with His continued help and guidance.

February 14, 1968

Dear Relatives and Friends,

Greetings and love to you from New Guinea! May the grace, peace and love of God, our Father, Jesus, our Redeemer, and the Holy Spirit, our Sanctifier, ever be and abide with you.

Yes, we are safely back in New Guinea. We can truly say our trip around the world was a miraculous witness to God's Almighty and all-wise guidance and protection. We travelled without any mishaps and all our travel arrangements went off very smoothly. We never even lost any of our luggage at any time. If we sound boastful, well we don't mean to, but we are thankful and happy in the Lord, because He alone could make this possible. It was a most wonderful trip because it helped make us both much closer and understanding of each other. Now that we have met each other's families, and lived around the world together, we share so much more.

We left a cold, nearly 0 degree St. Louis, January 5, 1968, and it was very difficult to bid good-bye to our Dear Mother, brothers and sisters, relatives, and friends, who bid us farewell. But we had to look forward, as the Lord was calling us to tasks He wanted us to do. Then we flew to Wichita, Kansas. Rev. Martin Pullmann, Student Recruitment Director, for Concordia College, Winfield, Kansas, met us. We enjoyed our visit at the College, speaking to the students, and a thrill was to see some very interested and showing a desire to go into Foreign Mission work. We enjoyed visiting with the Pullmanns' and others of the Concordia College family that evening.

On a very cold, snowy Saturday A.M., Rev. and Mrs. Pullmann, saw us off at Wichita and we flew on to San Antonio, Texas; Albuquerque, New Mexico (which was lovely and warm); and on to Los Angeles. We spent Saturday evening and Sunday seeing the sights around L.A. We especially enjoyed seeing Disneyland. Eunice was even captured by the Big Bad Wolf for a few minutes, while Ray got a picture.

Then on to San Francisco, where we spent a most enjoyable four days with dear friends in San Bruno, California. We stayed with Betty and David Raff and their four children, whom Eunice had met via the L.W.M.L. Committee on her first trip to New Guinea in 1959. She has spent a few days with them each time she went through California on her way to and from the U.S. and New Guinea. The Ladies of Tabitha at St. Thomas Lutheran Church had adopted Eunice since 1959 and she had become very close to this congregation. During this trip, we also enjoyed fellowship with many from First Lutheran Church, South San Francisco. Betty Raff showed us the sights of San Francisco by day, which we both thoroughly enjoyed.

On to Honolulu for a day. We enjoyed the lovely warm sunshine and sights of this enchanted island.

On to Brisbane, Australia, - on the way we lost a whole day and arrived there on the eve of Jan. 12. Ray's family was there to meet us and what a thrill to meet them! We had two wonderful weeks with them in Redcliffe, a seaside resort, 37 miles north of Brisbane. We enjoyed one day at the clean, wide, lovely beach of Bribie Island, the rest of the time we were busy visiting and getting ready for our trip back to New Guinea. One weekend, we spent in Toowoomba, 70 miles inland. This is a lovely spot, rolling hills, rich farmland, lovely scenery. It reminded Eunice of the Blue Grass country in Kentucky, scenery-wise. Ray's sister, Thora, is manageress of the Lutheran Bookstore in Toowoomba. Ray was born there. It was the midst of summer and very hot in Australia.

Then Jan. 25, we returned to New Guinea. School started on Jan. 29. We hustled to get settled and ready for school. In the midst of it all Eunice managed to get very sick with a virus for a week. We also have found out we can look forward to the arrival of our first little one in early September, God-willing. We are both very happy and excited and look forward to this blessed event.

150 students are enrolled in school. There are eight staff members. All are kept very busy, this being a Boarding-High School. Ray enjoys teaching and is teaching Religion, Health, Physical Education, Manual Arts and Technical Drawing. He has Study Hall every evening this week, so I see very little of him. He comes home for meals and after 10:00 P.M.

Well, must close for now. Our Lord Jesus in Whom we live and move and have our being, keep you strong in faith, and safe in His protection and care.

In Christian love, Ray & Eunice Hausler

(Added to the above-He was Eunice's 7th & 8th grade teacher at Bethlehem Lutheran School, Ferrin, IL.)

Dear Mr. and Mrs. Harnagel,

Greetings and love to you from us! We hope this finds you happy and well and rejoicing always in the Lord. We're sorry we missed seeing you Mr. Harnagel, while home, but we certainly enjoyed the chats and visit with you Mrs. Harnagel. How thankful we are to God that He has preserved you in such good health, strength and spirits.

We thank you deeply for the gift of $10.00. That was so much. We certainly do appreciate it. Isn't the bond of love in Christ, marvelous? That love is so strong, one can't comprehend it. How wonderful when we can enjoy it fully in God's presence.

God bless you richly, now, and always,

Much love, Ray & Eunice

(Form Letter)

March 22, 1968

Dear Relatives and Friends in Jesus,

Greetings to you from New Guinea. Yes, we are still here, even though you haven't heard from us for a while. We pray this finds all of you in good health and spirits.

Christ is Risen! As this glorious message sounds in our ears again during this blessed Easter Season, may it fill you with exceeding joy and peace. "For if Christ be not risen our faith is in vain." I Cor. 15:17, "but now is Christ risen and become the first fruits of them that slept." I Cor. 15:20. "Because He lives, we shall live also." John 14:19. May the joy of His resurrection so live and abide in us that through His power we might ever abide and live in Him and witness for Him daily in our words and actions to all we meet.

Since our last letter, we have passed through a very busy and filled year. We were both very busy teaching here at St. Paul's Lutheran High School last year, Ray in Woodworking and Technical Drawing Dept. and Eunice in the Music and English Dept. Ray was also doing building and plumbing in the expansion program here at St. Paul's. A new Science-Library building, four new dormitories, shower-toilet block, and four staff homes were built. At present, a girl's dormitory, toilet-shower block, staff house and new classroom are under construction. According to our builder, Clem Janetzki, this is all we can build this year, as with the budget cut these are the only funds at our disposal.

School started this year on January 27, 1968. We have 117 boys and girls in Form I, the first students to have finished Standard Six at the station schools and entering Form I (High School) *here at Pausa. This is a big step forward, as before those in school here had also been trained in their Primary education here. There are sixteen boys in Form III. The schoolyear is progressing well, and the new students have fit into the school system very well. Ray is teaching manual Arts, Religion, Health, and Physical Education. Each year the students seem to be of a higher caliber and have greater learning ability. For this blessing we can only thank and praise God.*

The work of New Guinea Lutheran Mission has really expanded and become diversified. The main theme, if we could choose one, of our Mission is "Training Programs", - educating and preparing these people in all phases to take over and help themselves. It would take a volume to tell you about the expansion in each phase of our work, Evangelism, Education, Business and Economic Development, Youth Work, Printing and Literature Production, Literacy, Medical Work, etc. So, we'll just hit a few highlights for you.

Our English Seminary, Martin Luther Seminary, is at present at Lae, where we have joined our efforts with the American Lutheran

Church and Australian Lutheran Church. We have eight students enrolled from our area there. Dr. Burce, one of the first missionaries to the New Guinea Highlands in 1948 is on the staff there.

At Lae, also, is Balob Teacher's College, and it is also a joint effort with the American Lutheran Church and Australian Lutheran Church. It is a two and three year training program thus far, training Primary Education Instructors. We already have four teachers training in our Standards schools who graduated from Balob. It really is a joy and mark of progress to see these people take over the work done by us before.

Our vernacular Seminary, which trains Evangelists in the local language, Enga, is still at Birip; it is in the process of being moved to Pyakain, a new station 60 miles up valley near Papayuke. It has been a blessing in supplying men to take over the many congregations that have been started until we can have more fully trained pastors. Seeing these men in action really reveals God's Almighty power and shows the Holy Spirit in action. God uses men who are willing to give themselves and He uses them mightily. Sometimes one feels God can almost do more through these humble men, as they don't have the obstacles of intellectualism, and reasoning, so much, to hinder God.

Educationally – St. Paul's High School is growing and has its largest enrollment this year. Also our station schools, eight at present, will be feeders to the High School. We are thankful for seven more teachers which were added to our Mission Staff this past year. They were sorely needed and most of them served as replacements for the staff that have left or are on furlough.

Youth Work – too is moving forward as we have two staff members, lay evangelists, working on this full time. They are at present setting up a Youth Camp and Youth Leadership Training Program as well as having regularly scheduled meetings with the youth in several congregations. This is an age where the Wabag Lutheran Church also loses a lot of its members.

Medical work – is expanding in that more native medical orderlies are being trained and filling outstation clinics. The infant Welfare Clinics are a tremendous force in cutting down on infant mortality. Most of these are run by European nurses. This March, two of Eunice's former girl students will graduate as full-fledged New Guinean nurses from the Government Medical Program in Lae. Eunice is very proud of them as they've had a hard row to hoe and many obstacles but as they say, which is certainly true, "God helped us." One will be here working at Immanuel Hospital, Mambisanda soon. We have only Dr. McArthur at Mambisanda at the moment as our other Doctor, Dr. Dan Kleinig is in Scotland for a year of further study.

Business and Economic Development – our Waso Company is growing. Many of the local people have bought shares in the Company. So far it has come out ahead each year and been able to pay dividends. The people continue to grow a lot of vegetables for export to the coast. Pyrethreum, used for insecticides, is also a profitable crop produced here in the Highlands. Coffee is also a moderate export from the Highlands. (The Waso Company is the business center for the mission. They are in charge of the exporting of: vegetables, coffee, tea and products grown locally, then sent to the coast, thus giving natives in the Highlands, a way to earn money).

In Adult Literacy, we have materials written to help the adults learn to read and write. Most congregations have classes in Literacy and many adults have and are learning to read and write in the Enga language. A big problem after they learn to read is that so little is written in the Enga language to read.

March 29 – April 2, 1968 is our Cultural Conference at Amapyaka. We have been fortunate to have an anthropologist, Rev. Ted Westermann, in our midst for three years. He will conduct this Conference and we're sure we will all gain from his findings and insights. He leaves April 8, 1968 and will be teaching at the Senior College, Fort Wayne, Indiana.

In our personal lives God has richly blessed us. We have a comfortable wood-frame home with Masonite walls. We also have electricity twenty-four hours a day since we are connected to the Mambisanda Hydroelectric plant. We are one of the few stations who do have power full time. We have a wood-burning stove, which we like because it gives us heat in the cool evenings and mornings. Eunice has learned to cook and bake with it quite well. Eunice isn't teaching this year since we are "expecting a new arrival" in early September, and she has not been too well. She will be kept busy with her household duties, typing for Ray and also materials for the outstation schools. Every Monday morning at 7:30 A.M. to 9:00 A.M. her time is pretty well taken up with buying our weekly supply of vegetables from our fellow New Guineans, who bring them in to sell. We have almost all the vegetables that we are accustomed to having in the States growing here now, and the New Guineans have learned how to grow them quite well. Our laundry is done with a gasoline-run Maytag machine which we bought from a fellow Missionary who went back to the States; Eunice is especially thankful to have it. We are kept busy with showing hospitality as fellow staff members come down the valley for business or medical purposes, and they need food and lodging. This we enjoy a lot as we otherwise would not get to see the people from further out very much.

Our treasured memories at the moment are our trip to the United States and Australia, October 25, 1967 to January 25, 1968. We left New Guinea for Manila, Hong Kong, Bangkok, New Delhi, Athens, Rome, Frankfurt, Paris, London (spending about twenty-four to forty-eight hours in each place), then New York, where it was such a thrill to have beloved fellow-Christians from Hope Lutheran Church, Levittown, Pennsylvania, meet us. We spent two wonderful weeks in Levittown and the spiritual upbuilding there was wonderful as we shared in Christ. We were able to see New York and Washington, D.C. during this time. Then, Thanksgiving Day, flew on to St. Louis and the reunion with Eunice's mother and family. We spent eight wonderful weeks there with relatives and friends. During that time we were able to make a lecture tour to Topeka and Great Bend, Kansas. This also included a reunion with dear friends in Christ. After sad farewells to our family January 5, we flew to Winfield, Kansas, for a speaking engagement at Concordia College; then on to Los Angeles for two days, and the highlight there was Disneyland. On to San Francisco for a reunion with dear friends in Christ, and a wonderful five days of visiting and sightseeing; thence to Honolulu, and the sights of that glorious island for one and one-half days. The last leg of our trip was to Brisbane, Australia where Ray's parents and family met us. Again a wonderful two weeks with family and friends and seeing the sights along the eastern coast of Australia and inland toward Toowoomba, Queensland. We got in a day at the beach near Redcliffe, Ray's hometown. It was a cold snowy 0 degrees and below in St. Louis when we left, then middle of summer in the 90 degrees in Australia, so you see we hit extremes of temperature. The final leg of our trip was to New Guinea and back to work. So for blessings innumerable, rejoice and praise God with us!

We want to thank you all for the many cards, letters and remembrances of this past year. It's always such a thrill to receive these. We promise to keep you more informed in the months ahead.

God bless you all richly, keep you strong in faith and grant you a truly Happy and Blessed Easter in our Risen Lord!

With love in Christ, Ray & Eunice

(Blue Aerogramme-Birth Announcement for Paula Ann)

October 16, 1968

Dear Mr. and Mrs. Harnagel,

Just a line while I'm waiting for Paula to wake up. Seems I have to make use of the spare moments these days as it seems the days are so filled and time slips away, and I just don't get around to writing. I do want to get a note to you though as we enjoyed hearing from you so much in August and then the other day a wonderful package with all kinds of useful things for Paula came. We sure appreciated all so much, she's already wearing the little jacket and booties. The cup will sure be a blessing when she is ready to drink from it. We are very thankful I've been able to nurse her so far. This is a very healthy, strong girl and for this we are so thankful. Your love, goodness and thoughtfulness is so much appreciated. God bless you!

All is fine here and school is coming along real well here. Ray has the boys busy making all kinds of things, like ladders, book cases, letter holders, trays, etc. They do enjoy it.

We were happy to hear you are both well and to think you are 85 Mr. Harnagel. That's really a wonderful blessing and may God richly strengthen and keep you both in His grace in the days ahead. May the joy and thankfulness of the blessings God has granted you in the years past sustain you through anything you may face in the future.

We were so sorry to hear about (...) but know he is much better off being with our Savior. One day we'll see him there. May God strengthen (...). Give our love and greetings to Gertrude, Bob and family. We think of you all often. Would just love to pop in for a visit, but we'll have to wait a bit for that. Our Lord be with you and fill you with Himself.

Much love, Ray, Eunice & Paula

(Birth Announcement for Paula Ann)

October 18, 1968

Dearest Richard, Florence and Charles,

Well, have meant to write you all year and here it is Oct. and I've missed all your birthdays so I'll just send greetings to all three of you! Hope you had a Happy Birthday in May, Charles and Florence in July and now Richard in October. God keep you and bless you in your lives. We wish we could see more of you, but such is not possible just now.

Hope you've had a good year. Richard in your work, Florence in the home and Charles in school. What did you do this summer, Charles?

Well, our little Paula Ann is just a bouncing, alert, and active little girl. She's growing like a weed and hit the scale yesterday at 12 lbs. I'm breast feeding her, so it seems it must be agreeing with her. We're especially thankful for her good health. She has just started to smile and "coo", so of course, that makes us just more excited about her. She looks like Winston Churchill at the moment, Ha!, with a very fat little face and a ridge of hair around her head, and has lost all on top of her head! We just pray she'll grow up to love her Savior and stay close to Him. The world situation is such, one wonders what they might have to face. Just looking at Czechoslovakia, you hope and pray Communism will never take over here.

Our school year has gone real well. The Form III's have their final exams this week and Ray will be busy grading papers and sending in reports to the government. The Form I's go until Nov. 25. They've enjoyed building ladders, coffee tables, book ends, benches, etc. this year. They do enjoy it.

We were so pleased to hear from your Mother, Florence. She sounds as chipper and busy as ever. To think your Dad had his 85th birthday. Really a marvel as he was so sick in '62. So sorry to hear little (...) left us, but for him it's a blessing. He suffered so much and went through so much. Hope (...) found strength and consolation in the Lord!

Mom, seems to be hanging in there. Just hope and pray her mind doesn't fail her too much. So thankful for Mrs. Lederbrand. Well, must close for this time. Hope you are all fine. God bless you and keep you.

Our love, Ray, Eunice & Paula

(Picture of Ray, Eunice and infant Paula in upper left corner)

November 28 1968

Dear Relatives and Friends,

Greetings and love to you all from New Guinea! Once again the Blessed Christmas Season is with us, and we wish you all a very Blessed and Merry Season! The peace, joy and love eternal our Savior brought, be yours now and always! Again the wonderous message of John 3:16 comes to us to fill us with God's peace, "God so loved the world that He gave His only begotten Son, that whosoever believeth in Him should have everlasting life." This is the real joy of Christmas, to know we are, through Christ, partakers of eternal life!

A lot has happened since our last letter to you. The biggest happening is the birth of our little girl, Paula Ann, 7 lb., 4 oz., on August 19, 1968. She is growing and developing rapidly and a real blessing and pleasure to us. She now weighs 14 lbs., 4 oz. I suppose, as all parents feel about their children, so we feel proud and happy and can hardly thank God enough for her.

As we look at our desk and see still many unanswered letters on it, we feel badly. But we pray you understand how it is when one has a little one and still the same amount of other work. It's hard to find enough time for all. But little by little, we'll get to all of them as we think of you often and need your continued prayers and letters.

The work here continues to move forward. Probably not with the same "gusto" and force that it did when Eunice first arrived here in 1959, but with more solidity and of a "building on what has been laid" nature. The Mission celebrated its 20th anniversary on October 6, 1968. We were honored with the presence of Dr. and Mrs. Oliver Harms, president of The LCMS. Approximately 5,000 to 7,000 New Guineans attended the anniversary service. The St. Paul's students did a pageant showing life before, then the arrival of the missionary, and then life after. They enjoyed doing it as acting is especially enjoyable entertainment for them. There were guest speakers, a special service and a muum (native cooked meal in the ground). *It was a day of rejoicing, indeed, and the words, "The Lord has Led Us Hitherto" rang out in our hearts and minds.*

For Ray another school year will be completed on December 6. It has been a very good year filled with much joy in serving these students. They have completed many projects in their manual arts classes and are proud of them. The most profitable project was making step ladders (4 foot type), which they sold for $4.00 each and made $75.00. With this money they will buy more materials for their classes. Ray is especially pleased now that a power saw, bought by the congregation in Claflin, Kansas is here and they can do so much more in the way of making things. Ray will be busy during the holidays with the on-going building program here at Pausa. One of his projects will be remodeling the old dining hall into a Manual Arts classroom. He also has taken over the Photo Club since Ron Rivers left on furlough. He has learned *to develop film and print pictures and will work with the students on this as an extra-curricular activity. Some of the students own little Kodak Starlite cameras.*

Eunice is kept busy with the daily household chores, caring for Paula, keeping up on correspondence, being Ray's secretary, providing for our many guests and trying to get a little piano practice in on the piano we just received from Ray's friend in Redcliffe, Australia. We do enjoy it a lot as it gives us moments together of pleasure and relaxation.

Ray's parents and sister, Thora, will be coming up from Redcliffe and Toowoomba, Queensland, Australia, to visit us for Christmas. We certainly are looking forward to their stay and visit. His father is 80 years old, so we hope he stands the trip okay.

Eunice's mother is still living at her home near Centralia, Illinois. She has a fine Christian lady caring for her which we are very thankful for, and five of her children are nearby to look after and care for her also. Her health is not good so she is in our thoughts and prayers so much. One does wish to be able to just visit and phone her occasionally. The Lord in His wisdom provides and cares, as ever.

Ray was out buying firewood today. He buys it from the New Guineans for about 2 or 3 cents a stick. We use it for our wood stoves and heating water in the copper boiler for washing clothes. Ray buys it for the school as well as for fellow staff members here at Pausa.

We have had Dr. and Mrs. Repp with us from Concordia Seminary, St. Louis, since August. He is on sabbatical leave and has been teaching at our Seminary at Lae during this time. He was up here in the Highlands several times and we enjoyed their visits. Mrs. Repp was a good grandmother to many of the missionary children up here, which is something the children do miss.

Monday evening Ray was up until 1:15 a.m. as one of our New Guinea neighbors, a fellow Christian, came and got him at 10:30 p.m. to help him settle a problem. Another tribe was accusing him of having sexual relations with a woman from their tribe. These kinds of things become tribal affairs. Ray spent yesterday morning at the Wapenamanda courthouse, where the white man's law *(as the New Guineans call it) is used. Anyway, the hearing is to be Friday. Ray thinks the fellow is innocent; it's just that the other tribe is" pulling a fast one," thinking they can get a few extra pigs or money out of it. When this kind of thing happened before, the government came in, the fellow accused either paid off or there was a tribal war, which usually ended up in several men killed and many wounded. Now the government has things fairly well under control, although there are still tribal wars. As you see, sin still lives out here and the work of bringing Jesus as the Lover of Souls and the Helper of the sin-sick and needy must go on. We always need your love, prayers, and understanding.*

As we bring this to a close for this time, our love, prayers and thoughts of you all are ever before our Heavenly Father. May His blessings, and especially strong faith in His Son, Jesus, be yours this Christmas and forever, until you are with Him in eternity!

Rejoicing with you in Christ,
Ray, Eunice, and Paula Hausler

July 30, 1969

Dear Relatives and friends,

Kotaka! (The Enga way of saying Good-day or Greeting!) As we send these greetings to you we are especially thoughtful of the fantastic jumps between our primitive way of life here in New Guinea, and the great advances in civilization you know. Especially with the advances in scientific knowledge and expeditions you are experiencing and witnessing it is just unbelievable! The students here at St. Paul's High School were very interested in the Moon Flight and walk on the moon, they just laughed as if to say "You sure are telling me a big story now, who'd ever believe that?" Television would have been wonderful to have here, but we're thankful for the detailed coverage by radio. Both Voice of America and the Australian Broadcasting System were excellent in reporting. We thank God for letting men explore His wonders of creation and pray it will strengthen faith in Him and make men see His great power, wisdom and majesty.

Things here are moving along and it seems almost too quickly. We meant to get this letter to you much sooner, but so much time has crept from us. Our family has enjoyed good health and a happy year, thus far, - very busy however, in the Lord's work for us here. By God's grace, our second child will be joining us in early September. Paula has been a tremendous joy and blessing to us. She is a very active little girl and these days climbs up on low things and walks around anything available. So, we suspect she'll soon take those first steps. We look forward to her first birthday, August 19.

Ray has been very busy in school. His days are filled from 8:00 A.M. to 4:00 P.M. with classes. Then there are the extra-curricular activities after school on Tuesday, Wednesday and Thursday. The students especially enjoy the "Fix-It" Club, as they can get their bicycles and other items repaired then, and doing it themselves means more to them. The Photo Club members are taking better pictures (in focus) and with more thought. In class they just finished small looms for weaving, which they will use in Art Class. Last Friday they had a Sport's Day and thoroughly enjoyed themselves in Intra-mural volleyball and baseball competition. They are eagerly listening to the radio: for the progress of the finalizations for the South Pacific Games to be held in Port Moresby, August 20 to 24, '69. These are like the Olympics for the islands of the South Pacific with most of the islands sending competitors. There will be entries in almost every event possible. Two of our students are being sent as observers. This is the first time PNG has been host for the games.

Eunice has kept busy with the home, keeping up with Paula and showing hospitality to many visitors. Highlights of our visits thus far this year were Ray's parents, two sisters, a niece and nephew in January. They were here two weeks and we had a wonderful time together (you do miss your families up here). His 82 year old father amazed us with his zeal, alertness and keeping up with activity. Then at Easter, we had Dr. and Mrs. John Klotz with us for five days. Dr. Klotz was on Sabbatical leave from our Senior College, Fort Wayne, Indiana, and was studying the fauna and flora of the South Pacific Islands, Australia, and New Zealand. Ray especially enjoyed two days of interesting field trips with them. Also, over Easter Dr. Oswald Hoffmann and his wife were here. We thoroughly enjoyed them. We thoroughly enjoyed his inspired being and Bible Study. In June, we had 9 high school students from California here at Pausa for three days. They were sponsored by their hometown Rotary Club. They had a marvelous time, with so much life and enthusiasm and did some real sharing with our students. It is reviving for us to have visitors like this from the U.S. and Australia.

Our Scripture Translation Committee has made great strides in translating the New Testament. They have completed Mark, I Timothy, I Thessalonians, I Peter, James, Epistles of John, Philippians, II Peter, and Acts. The drafts for Galatians, Ephesians, Philippians, Colossians, Romans, Luke, Matthew and John will be completed this year. The work is very difficult, takes long hours and meticulous discerning. The Good News for Modern Man has been a great help. The orthography of the Enga language is still undergoing reconstruction, so this adds to the complication. Our Committee, after it draws up the final draft, meets with the consultants of other Missions, discussing interpretation, language style and usage. The people having the Word of God in their own language is a marvelous help and your prayers are needed for this area of work also. The powers of Satan are hard at work trying to destroy what has been sown in the hearts of these people, so in your prayers, please remember to ask God to use His Word mightily to strengthen the faith of these people and draw them closer to Him, that they might be able to withstand every temptation and in the end gain eternal life.

Our Martin Luther Seminary in Lae will soon be under construction. Mr. Clem Janetzki, our builder from here, will do the building. It will be a joint effort with the American Lutheran Church, Australian Lutheran Church, the German Missions and Missouri Synod. Up until now, the Seminary has used the facilities of Balob Teacher's College and, as you can imagine, has been very crowded and inconvenient. We'll miss Mr. Janetzki up here in the Highlands; he has been our chief builder since 1957. He's from near Ray's home.

We miss the William Wagners', who left us in May. They have been here since 1954. Rev. Wagner married us. He is now studying at Concordia Seminary, St. Louis, and will take a pastorate in the States after that. We are happy about the arrival of Dr. Groh and his family, who will be with us for one year. He is a General Practitioner from Indiana. Two doctors are really needed and Dr. Kleinig is especially pleased as this will give him more time for surgery. Also added to our staff are Mr. and Mrs. Woodburn and their six children. He is a graduate of our Lay Training Institute in Milwaukee last year and will be the Business Manager of Christian Press, another joint effort of our Lutheran Churches in New Guinea. They print books and other religious materials, in our various major dialects. In September, two teachers will be added to our staff and we will be grateful to have them join us.

Well, we could go on and on but must sign off for this time. We hope to have a Christmas Letter for you and the news of our second little arrival in it. We pray you are in good health and spirits. Our Lord fill you with Himself; His blessings of joy, faith, and peace.

With joy in Christ, Ray, Eunice and Paula

(Form Letter)
(Birth announcement of Charla and pic of Paula across the top of the letter)

September 20, 1969

Dear Ones in Christ:

Greetings to you from us Hauslers'. Yes, we are very happy and thankful for our little Charla Lynn. She is a good girl and not a lot of colic like Paula had, which is good for Mother, who seems to always be tired. All is fine here and we are also thankful at this time that Ray's x-rays, on what was thought to be a kidney infection, or something of that nature, have shown nothing, so that concern is over. Paula is a bouncing, bubbling one year old. She doesn't walk on her own yet but around everything. She crawls so quickly that it seems to be faster to crawl than try that walking.

School is continuing to progress nicely, and only eleven weeks to go in this school year. Ray's new classroom is now completed and we are now able to be in it this term. It is so nice and roomy and allows the boys so much more working space and places to keep their projects, etc. It's truly a joy to have this new building. The boys are at the moment working on pews for the chapel, magazine racks and atlas stand for the library, saw stools, and game tables for their recreation room. They are pleased to be making things that they feel a need for and will be using in their classroom.

We just had two teachers and one pastor added to our staff this month. We are thankful to have them safely in our midst. It may interest you to know that our staff is being cut 6% each year, due to financial difficulties. Staff going on furlough are reviewed and if possible to do without them, they are asked not to return.

We'll keep this letter short and fill you in on more news in our Christmas letter. We pray this finds you all well and in best of spirits – in continuous communion with our Lord and rejoicing in Him!

In Christ, Ray, Eunice, Paula and Charla

(Pictures of male graduating class and Ray/Eunice each holding one of the girls across top of letter)

(Form Letter)

December 1969

Dear Relatives and Friends in Christ,

Greetings to you at this Blessed Christmas Season! We hope this finds all of you enjoying the true peace and joy of this Season as we contemplate on the mysteries of God's love in sending His only Son to save us sinful human beings. God's wonderful message comes as a soothing and healing balm to a sin-sick and war-torn world. Trusting Him, we know He loves us and will never leave us or forsake us.

Here at our home all is well and we continue to be thankful for the opportunity to be here and be able to bring the message of salvation to these people. As the talk for independence here gets stronger, we never know how soon that day may come. Therefore, we are working more and more on training the natives to be able to take over our work. The Board for Missions is also pushing this angle as they are cutting our staff and this forces us to put New Guineans into jobs we hold. This is basically good but "trying" and calls for much patience.

On December 5, twelve students graduated from Form IV. This is the first time we've had Form IV here at St. Paul's. They would be equivalent to 4th year high school students in the States. These boys plan to go into various advanced schools of learning: three to agricultural school, four to University of PNG at Port Moresby, one to Secondary Teacher's Training, one to Martin Luther Seminary, and three to Balob Teacher's College. We hope all goes well for them and they will be able to serve their people in these various capacities. We are enclosing a picture of these boys.

We are at present hoping and praying that our doctor, Dr. Daniel Kleinig, will stay at Immanuel Lutheran Hospital. He is an excellent doctor and surgeon and his leaving would be a great loss to all of us staff members, as well as the New Guineans. He has a good offer to be a full-time surgeon in Port Moresby. Surgery is his special field and he seems inclined to go there.

Several teachers have just returned from Balob Teacher's College. They have completed their training for Primary School teachers. They will be a welcome addition and great help to our Primary schools. All are former St. Paul's students. All these activities take place here at this time of year because the school year ends in December in this part of the world and the new school term begins the first of February.

The other morning one of our former students who is in the Pacific Island's Regiment (New Guinean Army), *stopped by to see us. He has been all over the Territory and to South Australia and Victoria. He sounded very informed and well disciplined. They change a lot once they get out into the world and away from tribal life here in the Highlands.*

We had a sad experience on Thanksgiving Day. Mrs. Gruenhagen of Crown Point, Indiana, was visiting her son and family here, along with her husband. She died suddenly that day at 4:30 in the afternoon of a heart attack. Her body was flown back to the United States, and the American Consulate was so good at helping with all the arrangements. How quickly and wonderfully the Lord took her to heaven, but it's always hard for those who are left.

Our family is fine. Paula continues to become more active every day and keeps her mother busy just keeping up with her. She says more words each day, and has even learned some words from the Enga language from our houseboy. She loves her bath in the evening as that is her special time with her Daddy. Daddy seems to be their big joy after being with minding-conscious Mommy all day! Paula's activity keeps her sister, Charla, busy for long periods just watching her. Charla is also doing very well. She's alert and active. She talks such a lot in her own sound language. We continue to be very thankful for our lovely daughters; they bring us much joy.

In closing, may God's peace and love be yours and His abiding presence remain with you in this New Year 1970! Again, many, many thanks for all your letters and support in prayer and other means this past year. It is all very deeply appreciated.

With joy in Christ,
Ray, Eunice, Paula & Charla Hausler

ANNUAL REPORT – 1969
RAY HAUSLER

Chronology of Significant Events:
January - the visit of my parents and two sisters.
April - the visit of Dr. and Mrs. John Klotz
August - the blessing – Charla Lynn, arrived.
December – Form IV Graduation.

Health:

We were all blessed with good health, apart from the regular ailments. The Lord has been good to us. We spent an enjoyable week's vacation in Madang during January.

Evaluation of 1969:

When I look back, there are many things undone, such as completing the Trade Practice Programmes for the Four Forms. As the subject expands, however, much work will have to go into these programmes. Enjoyed working with the students on some practical projects during the third term, making table tennis tables, game tables, - things which the students use in the school.

Bible study was held rather regularly, but we found it nearly impossible for both of us to attend with the two little ones. Regular Sunday Worship services were held with the students, these fairly well satisfied our public worship needs.

We have our regular family devotions. We are now reading: Spurgeon's "Morning and Evening Devotions from the Bible", and find these to be very edifying.

Goals and Expectations for 1970:

Am looking forward to introducing metalwork as a part of Trade Practice here at St. Paul's. With the return of Jerry Schmeling, I'm looking forward to an enjoyable and exciting year working with the students, teaching them what a wonderful gift hands are, wonderful gifts from the Lord.

Respectfully submitted, Ray Hausler

Chapter 3

The 1970's

October 12, 1970

Dearest Florence and Richard, (with birthday card)

Well, just can't send this card without at least a few lines, even though the hour is late. We think of you often but to get a letter written is something else. It seems the girls just don't give me a chance to write during the day, and at night I'm usually so tired, or busy with some activity. Hope this finds you all well and everything going well for you. How's Charles? Believe Eileen mentioned he's at Concordia, Missouri. That's a lovely spot. I can say too I'm glad he's there, rather than at RF. The big city, and drugs, etc., etc. these days doesn't sound like a good place to be. The world is sure in a turmoil.

We're all fine. The girls are growing so quickly. Charla started walking 2 weeks ago. She and Paula are really good pals and play together very well. Paula is quite a talker, and does well speaking in sentences already. Charla is at the making animal sounds stage. Wish you could see them just now, it's a precious stage. Ray's busy with classes always and in free moments he is often developing B & W pictures. He enjoys that, so he does it for the students & some for fellow staff.

We almost were sent home. The Mission Board cut our budget so drastically that we had to send 18 staff members home. It all came as quite a shock and surprise. Those of us staying take an 11% salary cut. We don't know the details behind all this, one wonders if the money is really that short and if so – why? Seems the bickering, etc., in our church at present is at a high point.

How are your folks, Florence? Is your father still with us here? Give them love and greetings from us, Gert, Bob & family too, Ruth, Ralph & family too.

Well, it's so hard to see Mom in a home, etc., but I do realize it's all you could do. Just pray she doesn't have to suffer too much in anyway. It sure would be nice to be nearer, but this is not meant to be yet. I guess this will be our last term in New Guinea, then we'll have to decide where to settle. The money shortage won't allow us to come back most likely.

Four of our staff members from St. Paul's are leaving in the next 4 weeks, so we have a round of farewells ahead. You do get very close to fellow staff out here.

Well, I must close and get to bed so I'll be able to navigate tomorrow. Take care and God bless you richly.

Much love from us "Four"!

(Another letter with same content dated Christmas 1970 contained pic of the four in upper left.)

October 26, 1970

Our Dear Relatives and Friends,

Greetings and love to you and wishes for a very Blessed Christmas and Joyous New Year! As time marches on, we rejoice ever more greatly in this glorious joy of our Savior's birth and the hope, peace, joys and life eternal it brings. God grant each of you also these blessings.

It has been a while since we've gotten a letter on its way to you. There have been many reasons and much has happened in the past year. Here at St. Paul's, we are nearing the end of another school year. It has been a good year for the students without any unusual 'ups' and 'downs'. One hundred ninety-five students are enrolled, and we're thankful to God for their general Christian character and wholesomeness. As a whole they continue to show real interest in their education. It's still too much of a privilege to be taken for granted.

In July, the National Teaching Service went into effect and the Government took over control of all of our schools. Our staff here at St. Paul's, were very much against it and we tried to stop our Mission Schools from joining it, but our voice was not heard. The leaders of our Mission here, and our Area Secretary of the Board for World Missions, felt it was the thing to do, to join. For the next couple of years things may still stay Christian here in our Mission Schools as we have them staffed with Christian teachers, but as the Government gets more and more in control and assigns teachers of any source to our Mission Schools, what will happen, remains to be seen. This along with the fact that we must take in any student that wants to come here, will do much to hinder the Christian tone and atmosphere we now have, and always have had here at St. Paul's. We did all we could to oppose it but to no avail, so now we are working under this system and must make the best of it. God for some reason permitted it to happen. One of the reasons may well be the shortage of money which is now facing our church. If the money situation is as bad as proposed, our schools would have had to close anyway. So we trust the Lord to guide and direct us, and He, who has helped in the past, will not let us down in the future.

That brings us to the happenings here this past August, which most of you have heard about, and many of you have written to us about with great concern. This is the cutting of twenty of our staff members, and the eleven percent cut in salary the rest of us, who are staying, are taking. Well, the news was a shock to us when we were called on the eve of Aug. 18, and told we were on the list to be sent home. We were told funds were so short, sending staff home was the only other resort to meet our Mission Budget, with the amount of money being allowed us. Then our name was not on the final list of those who were actually being sent home. We are thankful our service here in New Guinea was not brought to such an abrupt end. Especially for Eunice, after eleven years here, this would have been heartbreaking. We both find our service here a joy and privilege, but we also realize now more than ever that our time left here may be short. So we pray we will be able to, with God's help, make the most of the time we still have here. Anyway, what all is involved in the shortage of the money and the results of this here on the field, remain a big question mark in our minds. One thing we say with deep hurt and honesty, that if the so called, "Wheels" of our Church would cut down on their flash expenditures like flying trips to various places, expensive meetings in the most expensive places, (hotels, etc.) with the finest accommodations, plus all the other mis-spending that one witnesses being done in many places, there may not be a shortage of money. Each person, however, is a steward, and must account to God one day for the way he uses God's gift of money, and so this is not a judgment, but we hope and pray a call to conscientious stewardship. God grant that all of you may not withhold your support from the Lord's work. Souls are being won; the work of the Kingdom is moving forward. God will not judge you by what happened to your support, but by how you gave. He looks at the heart. The widow in Mark 12:43, gave her mite with a grateful heart and without thinking of the consequences, she gave all she had, and she was taken care of. The same will hold true for us all, God will not leave us or forsake us if we put Him first in our lives and giving.

Many of you have asked, "How will the cut-back effect the work in New Guinea?" We don't feel it will hinder it too much, as we tried not to cut the major programs and evangelistic outlets. It will force us to depend on more and more New Guineans, which is in itself good. We feel the cut-back came prematurely, but maybe this is the only way it could come.

Family-wise all is fine. Our little girls are growing up quickly. Charla started walking, September 23, and so is very independent too, now. They have a way of keeping Mother very busy and needing a lot of attention at this age. Paula's little friend, Denise Schaus, left for the States last week with her parents, so she's been lonely. Both girls love books and music, and we hope these interests continue. They also love the outdoors and any animal that may appear on the scene. The mumps and chicken-pox have been around here, but so far, our girls haven't gotten them. Paula had malaria a month ago, but has recovered after the course of anti-malarials. Eunice continues to be busy with the many household tasks, hosting many guests, and taking part in school activities as much as possible. Ray keeps busy with school classes and activities. The latest projects class wise have been suitcases for the boys leaving school, candlesticks, and plaques of New Guinea. The plaques were made as farewell gifts for the Missionaries leaving the field. Hauling sweet potato from about ten miles up the road and firewood for the students is also an added job lately.

In closing, we pray on all of you a rich measure of the Holy Spirit and a real zeal for serving the Lord! Only one life will soon be past, only what's done for Christ will last! We need your prayers too, as you see, many problems and discouragements also face us

A Blessed Christmas! A Joyous New Year!

Rejoicing in Christ,
Ray, Eunice, Paula & Charla Hausler

(Blue Aerogramme)

October 28, 1970

Dear Florence, Richard and Charles

Greeting and love to you! I will write a little general Newsletter and then add a few lines personally. Seems we've gotten so far behind on our correspondence Time has a way of slipping by so quickly. We hope this finds all well your way and your lives filled with many goodnesses.

All is fine here. Ray is kept busy in school. Now that there is only one month left, it makes for a busy time with closing activities, parties, final exams and grades. The students are having a Fine Arts Festival on November 19. It will be an evening of playing musical instruments some have learned to play, a few one act dramas, a few choir selections, reading of original poems, and speeches, and a debate. The students look forward to this. Last Friday P.M., they saw the movie the "Littlest Cowboy", a Walt Disney production. They certainly enjoyed it and in

Woodworking they've made candle holders, suitcases and plaques of New Guinea as their latest projects. We have no Form IV this year, so no graduation. This is because our Mission Schools took in students only alternate years in earlier years.

(Two paragraphs follow on the cuts, similar in tone to the above letter, but with this line included: *"By doing this, we can at least keep most of our evangelistic programs moving forward."*)

Three of our St. Paul's staff members are leaving this month, the Schauses, Coopers, and Connie Pucci. Connie is the only one returning. Schauses will be in Saginaw, Michigan; Coopers in Adelaide, Australia. We especially miss the Schauses as Paula and Denise were such good play mates.

Ray's parents are celebrating their Golden Wedding Anniversary today in Redcliffe, Australia. We all especially would love to be there. His Father is 83, and his Mother, 70. They still do wonderfully well for their age, still taking care of their home, garden, and themselves.

Eunice's Mother is still living, but has failed a lot, this just goes with hardening of the arteries. We think of her often.

P.S. Just as we were getting ready to run this off, we got the sad news that David Schaus died on his way home from New Guinea in Hong Kong. He leaves his wife and four young children. This news is a shock for us all. The Lord's will be done. (End Form Letter.)

Hi! Will just add a line to this and that way you'll get a bit of news as we wish you a Merry and Blessed Christmas! Know it'll be special as Charles is with you during this season! We're going to Australia to visit Ray's folks for a month, we'll be there to celebrate his folks Golden Anniversary Christmas Day. Government pays Ray's fare and Ray's sister sent the money for my fare, so it's all a miracle really. We're thankful though! Hope this finds you all well. We are all fine – the girls growing up quickly - it seems they are such good companions. Write sometime! God keep you in His loving care!

Much, much love,
Ray, Eunice, Paula & Charla

ANNUAL REPORT – 1970
RAY W. HAUSLER

Chronology of Significant Events:

Jan. - Vacation in Madang for two weeks.

New school year begins.

Feb. - A small "Products Club" begun.

Mar. - Spent Easter with the Gruenhagens at Kundis.

April - Bleekes leave for furlough.

June - Reluctantly made a member of National Teaching Service.

Aug. - Told we were on the list of those possibly to be asked to leave the field.

Sept. - Secondary Inspector visits Pausa.

Oct. - Our dear friend, Dave Schaus, called to his Eternal Home.

My folks Golden Wedding Anniversary.

Nov. - Coopers and Connie Pucci leave.

"Open Day" was a success.

Form III's leave.

Dec. - School Closes.

Begin Preparation for 1971 School year.

Health

The girls suffered with ear infections spasmodically the first half of the year.
Paula had a malaria attack in Sept.
Otherwise, Eunice and I have enjoyed good health.

Official Position

Trade Practice Master at St. Paul's Lutheran High School, Pausa.
Member of Construction and Equipment Committee.

Study Programme

Read several books on Woodworking and Metalwork.

Evaluation of Year's Work

I was generally pleased with the overall results of the students. Many thanks to Jerry Schmeling for his help and advice in all areas of Trade Practice, especially in Metalwork. Still have a hard time trying to get the idea of neatness and of accuracy across to the students. Several students began operating the lathe and have turned some candlesticks.

I was alarmed to learn that some of the NGLM staff do not hold to the confessions as put down in the Book of Concord. If one cannot stand by the Lutheran Confessions then one should not call oneself a Lutheran, because one cannot live a lie.

Goals for 1971

Revise work programmes for Form I – III, and draw up a new programme for Form IV.

We pray that the work in Christ's Church in this country may go forward and that our differences within the NGLM be overcome and that we be guided by the Holy Spirit in all things.

Respectfully submitted,
Ray Hausler

(This letter was written by one of the first students Eunice had in PNG. Ray was the best man at the wedding and Paula the flower girl, dropping petal by petal down the aisle, getting to the front of the sanctuary, realizing there was still a full basket of petals, and promptly dumping them all out! Ray and Eunice hosted the dinner for them. Note that the letter came from Waso Ltd. For Ray and Eunice, this is such a representation of how much the natives learned and absorbed. Ray and Eunice did this type of thing for several of those first students.)

July 8, 1971

Dear Eunice, Ray, Paula and Charla Hausler

It's almost four weeks now since Lean and I were married but we haven't forgot to write and thank those who were involved and came along.

Firstly, Lean and self would like to say thank you both very, very much for your co-operation and the arrangements you've made which went very well for our wedding, and we'll never forget your participation and you've been so very great to us. Our word of thanks especially to Eunice, particularly for arranging the Reception and this will be never forgotten.

We also thank you Euni for making Paula available as a sweet flower girl even though it was a good fun watching her throwing the flower only on one side and the all at the end.

We also thank you Euni on behalve of Abby for making her petticoat which of course she appreciated at the last minute.

On Ray's part I especially thank you for being my best man and giving a spectacular speech during the Reception.

We also thank you both for your gift cheque. You shouldn't have given us a thing because everything that was concerned of the wedding came from you.

We really appreciated every bit of your assistance and we'll never forget it in years to come. We just can't think of a word to express our thanks toward your very kind attitude toward us but just a word of thanks will do you we hope.

Once again, thank you very much for everything you've done to us.

With kindest regards,
Love, Lean and Dian

(Form Letter) (Picture of the girls in upper left of letter)

October 5, 1971

Our Dear Friends in Christ,

Greetings to you all! The grace, peace, and love from our Heavenly Father be with you all.

Again, a while has gone by since we've gotten a letter written to you all. As always, we have deeply appreciated your concerns, letters and support. You are the Lord's means by which He sustains and keeps us here.

The Lord's work here has taken on different tones and directions in the past year. Under the National Education System, we have thus far been able to continue almost as we were, except that some students don't attend religion classes or attend religious services. We are not permitted to do much in this direction. As we get more and more non-Christian teachers the atmosphere of the school will not be so pleasant. Thus far our staff has worked together well and the Government has been amazed at the co-operation and dedication of staff, they admit that the Government High Schools have most of their problems with staff. As Christians we do have our differences, etc., but with God's Spirit and in the light of His Word we have a common bond and through God's forgiveness and by His grace this forgiveness working through us, we do have a friendly and working relationship. A Christian school is a gold mine for souls for eternity.

The Wabag Lutheran Church (WLC) had one of their most controversial Conferences in June. It had to do with the leaders, who were selfishly inclined, the president of the WLC also wanted to run for the House of Assembly and try to carry out both jobs – (House of Assembly is the Government House of Legislation in Port Moresby). This would have meant no leadership for the WLC as the President would be in Moresby most of the time. Fortunately, at the middle of the Convention several resolutions were brought up to stop the declining moral standards, as well as resolutions to address the high living standards we should expect of our church leaders. When some of the unruly behavior started, they stopped the meeting and an inspiring talk by several missionaries brought the meeting back to order. The President resigned and decided to run for the House of Assembly. The new Pres. was elected this past month and things seem to be working upward. So this new church is struggling but may God continue to fill them and lead them. A lot they do is not the way we Missionaries would do it, but they must learn to think for themselves and learn from their own doings and mistakes. God grant that they might emerge a strong Spirit-filled people and Church.

We have problems also in the spiritual oneness amongst staff at St. Paul's Lutheran School. Ray and I find this very disturbing and we will leave at the end of the school year as our term comes to an end then.

Our Mission President, Rev. Victor Heinicke, had a heart attack in August and had to resign from his position, Mr. Elwyn Ewald, has filled his position. Mr. Ewald was working on Community Development, and that work has just been dropped.

As the cry for Independence gets louder in the Territory, it reminds us that our days here are numbered. The anti-white feeling is getting stronger. A white District Commissioner was recently murdered in Rabaul. The white man has not always done the best for these people and so the resentments have built up over the years.

Here at St. Paul's our work among the students remains a joy. The eagerness for learning remains high generally. We only pray that many God-filled and God-fearing leaders will emerge from this school. We have already seen a core of our students go forth as real leaders and Christian examples in various phases of work in the Territory. We both see many of our former students as a real salt, influencing the future of the Territory. This is joy indeed. Of course, we also have some students, who have not done well and some even have ended up in jail, but for them we pray that they will return from their mistakes, and make good again.

Our students have been getting together with other High School's at Mt. Hagen and Goroka for Sport's Competition. This has really been good for the students and helped them find out how other people live and operate.

The Hagen Show held in August was not as successful as before. They were all prepared for tribal fights which they expected, but for-

tunately did not happen. Again, many tribesmen from all over the Highlands were there and it was very colorful. Rain interfered and hindered many of the usual activities. Hundreds of visitors from all over the world still came.

For us the loss of many dedicated staff members who have left us the past two years has been a sad note. You get very close to fellow workers out here and miss them. We are due for furlough, December, 1972. Whether we will get to the States or not remains to be seen. Since Ray is Australian, the Board for Missions will most likely not pay our way to the States, although, they have done it for some. We would appreciate being able to share with you, our loved ones in America also the joys of service in God's kingdom. So if the Lord wants us to do this, He will make a way possible. The Lord has been very good to us and so abundantly blessed us. We can truly say, that if you give your life to the Lord, trust and abide in Him, your life will be richly blessed. The closeness to Him, we enjoy, continues to sustain us, in spite of disappointments which come our way, too. But with you, we are running the race as St. Paul says, and look forward to the victory in Christ Jesus our Lord!

Our family is fine. We had a wonderful stay in Australia with Ray's family last Christmas for four weeks. The ocean and beaches at Ray's parents' home in Redcliffe were wonderfully relaxing. His 82 year old father is at present in failing health. Ray had hepatitis in May and was very sick. He was in bed for 4 weeks and it took almost 3 months for him to feel back to normal. Our girls are fine. Paula is now three and Charla two. They are such good playmates and so far have been healthy, thanks to God. They are bubbling over with energy, which we try to channel into constructive activity as we can. They love art activities, puzzles, books, music and Paula is a lover of insects and animals.

In closing we pray this finds you all in good health, filled with faith and joy in Christ. As the Blessed Christmas Season arrives may the rich blessing our Savior brought us be yours. God loves us so much that He gave His only Son! John 3:16. May we let our lights and love shine for Him!

Rejoicing with you in Him,
Ray, Eunice, Paula and Charla

(In the process of combining the multiple documents required to complete this book, a story that further helps to illustrate Eunice's life of faith, came to light. Though we do not recall the exact date of the occurrence, we know the girls were very young, hence it is included at this point).

Madang Vacations

Every year the Mission gave us a week of vacation in Madang. It was a fun and restful place. The mission had a house we could stay at. It was on the coast and had a small beach. There were Chinese stores and our Mission supply store-Lutmis.

While there, we visited the native villages and saw them making pottery, and also carving out canoes. It was always a fun and relaxing week.

One of our vacations, Eunice got very ill, we think it was from drinking bad water. Paula and Charla were little, so Ray had to take care of them alone. I was delirious and went into a coma-like state. I had a "dream" during this time and in it there was a ladder going to heaven. Angels were going up and down and Jesus was standing at the top. I kept pulling back and felt like I was saying, "I can't go up yet, I need to take care of Paula and Charla." When I woke up, I felt like I had had a wonderful step into heaven and I was reassured that Jesus was always at my side.

Whatever I had, it left me very sick for three or four days and when I got to feeling better, I could only thank and praise God for letting me get a glimpse of heaven. I was assured that He is always at my side. It was an experience that made me want to spread the message more and more and with great assurance.

It is still a very vivid experience for me today. And so, repeat a portion of one of my daily prayers: "Remind me daily that I am a pilgrim without a home here, and help me to assist my fellow travelers by sharing their burdens and showing them the glory of the life in You."

(Form Letter)

May 23, 1972

Dear Friends in Christ,

Greetings and love to you from New Guinea. We pray this finds all well your way and your faith and joy in the Lord strong.

As we write this it is almost mid-year calendar-wise, and also school-wise for us. Time flies by so quickly, it seems like the year just started. School is moving along and although there have been many changes due to our new leadership, we can say we still find a lot of joy in working with these students. They show a lot of enthusiasm in their work. A new double classroom was completed in February and our new spacious library should be finished by August. These were much needed with our increase in students. We have 298 students this year. We could have had twice that many but just no room. Many Standard Six students just didn't get to go on for further education (because the mission just didn't have the number of teaching staff to accommodate more students). *This creates a lot of problems.*

This year was also election year for the New Guinea people. A Coalition Government of two coastal parties won the election. This has created a lot of hard feelings amongst the United Party, which was composed of mostly Highlanders. So it will be interesting to watch how this all works out. A new developing country also is filled with problems.

Most of our teachers in our Primary Schools here in the Western Highlands are our former students. Amongst them we have some fine dedicated leaders, and for this we rejoice and thank God. This also is one of our real joys in many phases of life here, some of our former students are leaders in Government, Education, Church, Economic Development, Police Force, Pacific Islands Regiment, Kristen Press (the Christian publishing company for materials printed for the churches in PNG), *Agriculture and other fields. We just thank God that He has marvelously guided these precious lives which were in our care for a short time. We only pray they will be real bulwarks, and stabilizing influences as this new country develops toward Independence. It sounds like that day is not far off.*

The Church as such, has a long way to go. The Word continues to be preached but the production of fruits in people's lives is not as evident as we would like to see it. God works through His Word, however, and it will not return void. More and more the leadership and responsibilities of the organization of the church here is being put in the hands of our New Guinean leaders. This changeover is difficult but necessary.

Two weeks ago, we attended a wedding of two of our former students. It was a very Europeanized wedding, and we are not so keen that they leave completely their former customs. The bride had made her own white gown and veil, and Eunice was very proud of her as she is one of the girls who did well in her sewing classes. They had about seventy guests and served rice with a meat stew, rolls, Jello salad, wedding cake and punch. These occasions make for much rejoicing. Last Saturday we also attended a baptism feast for the little girl of one of Eunice's former students. They had a native muum, and we always enjoy their foods cooked this way too.

Our family is in the midst of many decisions at the moment. We have decided not to return to New Guinea after this term, which ends December 1972. As of now it looks like we will be in the States for at least a year while Ray works on getting a Teaching Degree in Industrial Arts. He is a qualified builder, but has taken a real liking to teaching since in New Guinea and would like to pursue this field. As the Lord leads, we shall see what He wants us to do in the future. The Mission Board is paying our way to the States in December, and this is an answer to prayer. We are thankful that we will have this chance to be with Eunice's family as well as, all of you in the States. We will probably find the adjustment to living there hard at first as we've become so accustomed to life out here. Rev. Mayer did tell us that the Board for Missions in St. Louis needs money especially for Missionary fares and salaries, and if any of you would like a special project you could designate funds for a certain Missionary and send it to them in St. Louis, and it would be used for that purpose.

Paula and Charla both attend Pre-school two days a week now, which three of us mothers are teaching. They love it and the contact with other children is very helpful. They've learned so many wonderful things, as well as, a few bad behavioral traits, but such is life and this is where our training must come in. We admit it's hard to bring up children and it takes a lot of prayer, patience, consistency, common sense and understanding. They are very precious, though, and we thank God for giving us two little precious lives to love and care for, for Him.

As we have just celebrated the Ascension of our Lord and His sitting at the Right Hand of God in glory, may it fill us with the faith, hope and joy that He promised to take us to Himself in the Heavenly Mansions of bliss and glory.

With joy in Christ,
Ray, Eunice, Paula, Charla Hausler

(Birthday card for all 3)

October 13, 1972

Dear Florence, Richard and Charles,

Hi! And Happy Birthday to you all! Hope all is well your way. Is Charles still at RF? (Nope, Seward, NE!) *We're pleased he's going into the Lord's service and remember him in prayers. We also are looking forward to seeing you real soon, we'll be there sometime the end of December or so. Things should be a bit less hectic this time, since we won't be rushing back to New Guinea.*

It's so dry here and we've had cold nights and frosts. This is really unusual. The sweet potato has frozen so that people have no food. They've called a state of Emergency and are feeding 1 lb. of rice, 1 Vit. C tablet a day and 1 tin of fish a week per person. It's costing a fortune so the Gov't is asking Relief Agencies and Missions to help. These people have never known hunger so it's something for them.

We're busy getting things ready for leaving. There is so much to do. We did get our crates off so that's a big job done. Ray has to teach full time till we leave so we do the things he has to help with in the P.M.

Paula and Charla are getting so big. They have a lot of little friends here on the station, so it makes for a lot of fun for them. They'll miss this but will soon be ready for school so it probably won't be too bad.

Bet we'll notice a lot of changes. It'll take a bit to readjust to life in the States. One reads so much about the drug problem. Is it prevalent around there?

Well, must close for now and we'll have big chats when we see you. Hope your parents, Gert and Ralph's families are all fine Florence.

God bless and keep you all!
Much love, Ray, Eunice, Paula & Charla

November 1, 1972

Dear Relatives and Friends:

As the time draws near for us to leave New Guinea, we think of you, who have so graciously, lovingly and abundantly helped and supported us in the years we have served here. We thank God very deeply for you all, and through you our years in New Guinea were more pleasant and uplifted. We hope we will be able to see many of you and convey our feelings personally.

We plan to leave here November 24, 1972. We will spend a month in Australia with Ray's family and then arrive in the States early in January. Plans after we arrive there are not definite yet. We have mixed feelings about leaving here. We will miss the many New Guinean friends we have learned to love dearly. We also will miss the climate and slower pace of life. However, we are also looking forward to the challenges and adventures awaiting us as we go back home.

We hope and pray we will be able to effectively witness for our Savior there also.

Things are in pretty bad circumstances here in the Western Highlands and also the Southern Highlands at present. We have had very dry weather and frosts (something these people can't remember having had since before yet, some older people, think the early 1940's). Anyway, it has frozen their sweet potato and this being their main food, it has left many people starving. The Government has called this an Emergency Relief Area and is sending in rice and tinned fish to keep the people from starving. One pound of rice per day per person and one tin of mackerel per week per person is the ration. This will have to go on for at least four to six months, till their sweet potato, which they have replanted, have matured. Our school is busy on a re-planting venture. The students have planted about 60 acres of sweet potato, white potato, and cabbage. Then when the seedlings are several weeks old, they will be sent to the stricken areas. It's quite an experience for the students, as well as staff. We are all praying more for real needs as we hear of individuals we know in much distress.

Next week are the Form IV Government Examinations, so there is a lot of excitement and studying amongst that class at present. We hope a good number will pass and go on to further training for a useful occupation.

We have been getting our shots (typhoid, smallpox, tetanus, and cholera) in preparation for travel the past several weeks. The cholera and typhoid left us feeling sick for a day or two. Paula and Charla took the shots well this time, they shed no tears.

We have amongst our staff here some who are very involved with the Charismatic Movement, Spiritual Renewal, etc. We are having Mission Staff meeting this month to discuss all this. Seems these are troubled times for our church everywhere.

Eunice is writing a history of St. Paul's High School at present. Since she helped start this school, they don't want to leave her go without doing a history. It's taking time and research, especially on the early years when few records were kept. Fortunately, her Photo Albums, newsletters, keen memories of those first students, and her diary have been of much help.

We are looking forward to seeing many of you soon. We hope it will be all of you somehow. We pray our moments of meeting will be a spiritual boost for us, as well as you. May our Lord, whose coming we will soon celebrate, fill you with all grace and peace in believing. As we have seen through the years in New Guinea, God's promises are sure: "Lo, I am with you always, even unto the end of the world." Matthew 28:20. And "I will never leave you nor forsake you." Hebrews 13:5

Again, a million thanks to all of you, who have helped us so much, we remain deeply grateful.

With joy in Christ,
Ray, Eunice, Paula & Charla Hausler

(Then followed their addresses in Australia & the USA)

With the Hauslers' leaving New Guinea, headed for Australia, before getting to the U.S.A., it was decided that Eunice needed to have a Driver's License for Australia, thus the following:

Reference No. ______________ License No.__________________

PAPUA NEW GUINEA

Motor Traffic Ordinance 1950-1967

LICENSE TO DRIVE A MOTOR VEHICLE CLASS ONE

Name in full: Mrs. Eunice A. Hausler c/o St. Paul's High Sch. Wapenamada

Description---Age: Height: Ft. in.

Eyes (without spectacles) ________

Hair:__________Complexion:__________ is hereby licensed as a Driver of a Motor Vehicle Class ONE

within Papua New Guinea for one year from the 22nd day of November 1972. (Sealed with dated Stamp)

(Postcard)

December 7, 1972

Dear Richard, Florence and Charles,

Hi! How are you? Hope all is well. Anxiously awaiting to see you soon. Hope to arrive in St. Louis, Dec. 29. Having fun here in Redcliffe with Ray's family. The girls love the beach, TV and stores. Have a Merry Christmas and rich blessings in 1973.

Much love,
Ray, Eunice, Paula, Charla

Carbondale, Illinois (Form Letter)

January 1973

Dear Relatives and Friends,

Greetings to you from Southern Illinois this time. We've seen and done a lot since we left New Guinea, Nov. 25, and our hearts and minds are filled with many wonders, joys and mixed emotions, but as time moves along and we become adjusted to life here in the States, things will most likely fall into a routine and pattern again. It was hard to leave New Guinea, after so many years there a bit of yourself is there. We do miss the life and work there, but we know God is working in many people there and that He will use them mightily to accomplish His work there. Our prayers are daily needed for the Lord's work there. After leaving New Guinea, we spent a month with Ray's parents in Australia. We helped his father celebrate his 86th birthday. He is doing well, but is frail. During this time we were busy getting all the things for Ray's Immigration Visa, to be able to work and go to school in the United States. We even had to make a trip to Sydney, Australia, which took three days, for a personal interview with the American Consulate General. Then we left a hot 98 degrees, Brisbane, Australia, 2:00 P.M. on December 20, and got to Hong Kong, 11:00 P.M. We stayed there overnight on the Airlines and flew on to Tokyo the next morning at 8:00 A.M. We arrived in Tokyo at 2:00 P.M. and my girlfriend, Phyllis Chamberlain, with the Evangelical Alliance Mission, met us. She showed us Tokyo the two days we were there, and we certainly enjoyed our stay there. Phyllis had been there twenty-two years, so she gave us many interesting insights and highlights. While there, we also met Barbara and John Knoble and their two children. Barbara and Phyllis had travelled with Reta Wiebe and me, from Hong Kong to Naples, Italy, in 1962. They are wonderful Christians and good witnesses for the Lord, and we shared precious moments of Christian fellowship. Our two little girls were quite the attractions as we walked the streets of Tokyo with their blond hair. Tokyo is like any modern city, only we were surprised when Phyllis took us walking two evenings and we went down dark and out of the way streets with no fear of crime. We had two Japanese meals of tempera, clam soup, and Japanese pickles. We enjoyed the food.

Then we flew on to San Francisco, Saturday, December 23, 2:30 P.M., and arrived in S.F., 8:30 A.M. December 23, seven hours later. This was a tiring day for us to live over, as we had missed our sleep. The Raffs and MacArthurs met us in San Francisco. It was so good to see both families. MacArthurs had been with us five years in New Guinea and we spent Christmas with them. It was so good seeing them. Also the Raffs, they have met Eunice every time she's gone through San Francisco, which has been quite a few in thirteen years. Betty is now chairman of the Southern California L.W.M.L. Committee, who meet missionaries going overseas or returning from there. While with the Raffs, we got to have dinner one day with the Ken Bauers', who were in New Guinea during Eunice's first years there. That was a happy reunion. Then December 26-29, we spent in Park Rapids, Minnesota, with the Lennord Pitneys, who are wonderful friends from Eunice's Levittown days. It was very cold there but the Hope Lutheran Sunday School, Congregation, and many of you had sent money, so we could buy warm clothing and coats, and that was really a blessing. Thank you all deeply, we are very grateful. We enjoyed the snow while there and it was so good to find the Pitney's happy in their nice home in retirement. Then we left Park Rapids in a blizzard, by bus back to Minneapolis, Dec. 29, and flew on to St. Louis. We arrive there 5:00

P.M. The weather was bad and it was a complete instrument landing. Eunice's brother Luther and wife Eileen, were there to meet us. Then the drive to Shattuc and reunion with Eunice's family. We had a lovely New Year weekend and the weather was much milder in Illinois.

On January 3, we drove to Carbondale, Illinois, where Ray is enrolled in Southern Illinois University. All that week was spent getting enrolled, finding housing and buying a car. We got a '71 Pinto (Ford), reasonably and are thankful it is very economical to run. We moved to Carbondale, Sunday January 7, and classes started January 8. We have a furnished two-bedroom apartment. It is small but adequate. We were fortunate to find an apartment right away. The Lord has been so good in so many ways. We have received so much help in gifts of food, clothing, money and physical help. The Lord keeps His promise and they that serve Him can be sure He will provide and take care. Another wonderful blessing was that Ray has been accepted as an Illinois resident since Eunice is one, and this cuts the tuition in half. This will really mean a lot when the Board of Missions will not be helping us after May 1973. Ray is taking Physics, Psychology, Health and English Composition this quarter. He's kept busy with his studies and just getting accustomed to studying and school routine. He finds the students quite amiable, sincere and concerned. Eunice is getting adjusted to keeping house in the United States, keeping two little active girls happy in a small apartment, and trying to catch up on a lot of correspondence. We also have some lectures coming up, also our physical examinations on February 8, with the Board for Missions, this is general routine for terminating missionaries. We also are to take Paula and Charla to Rochester, Minnesota for check-ups on their feet.

This covers a bit of our news of the past two months. We just are very thankful to the Lord and you, our many wonderful Christian friends, relatives and others, who have made life so happy for us. We thank you deeply for all your concern, prayers, love, financial and physical help. We only pray we can continue to use our lives fully for the Lord always. His peace, joy and blessing be yours in 1973.

With Christian love and joy in Christ,
Ray, Eunice, Paula & Charla Hausler

March 1, 1973

Dear Florence and Richard,

Hi! It was good hearing from you today and Florence I really would like to go to the sale at CPH Saturday, but we are scheduled to go up to the Paul Walther's at Charleston, Illinois, so we can't make it. I really would love to go as children's books, cards, and books for us are certainly things I'd love to get.

All is fine here. We had good news on the girls' feet in St. Louis at Barnes on Tues. They have no deformity and need to just be made conscious of walking with their toes pointed straight ahead.

By the way, I did enjoy the Vitamin article. We had a little girl in New Guinea die from an overdose of anti-malarial's, so we're conscious of keeping them out of reach.

Ray's really busy now as the end of the quarter draws near and papers are due and final exams soon. I think once he gets through this quarter he'll be better adjusted and more confident.

Well, I must close as it's supper time, but wanted to answer your letter right away, sure appreciate you letting me know and if I could, I'd go.

Take care now and God bless.

Much love,
Eunice, Ray and girls

Installation-Induction Service
Trinity Lutheran Church, Hoffman, IL

September 9, 1973

(For Eunice and two other staff for the school, with biographies on each. No order of service extant.)

September 28, 1973

Dear Ray,

This letter brings the official word that the Board for Missions at its September 20-22, 1973 meeting granted you a peaceful release from service in New Guinea. Your Board for Missions termination date was identified as May 24, 1973.

Each member of our Board as well as each staff member expresses sincerest thanks for the meaningful service which you rendered in New Guinea since 1965. We recognize the personal dedication to our Lord which you brought as you performed your daily tasks in His name.

We also express a word of special appreciation to Eunice and your children for the important role they play in God's mission.

We hope that things are going well for you as you continue your studies at Southern Illinois University. We wish you well.

We pray that our Lord will keep you in good health and give you and your family strength and courage to meet the challenges which He brings to you each day.

Please drop us a note, especially if you feel there are occasions when we might have an opportunity to serve you.

The best to you and your family in our Lord!

Edgar Fritz
Assistant Secretary for Personnel, LCMS

(Form Letter)

November '73

Dear ________________,

Greetings to you! It seems a long time since we've had a chance to write to you all, but we do think of you and remember you in prayer. We hope this past year has been a blessed one and filled with many joys!

The Lord has been good to us and we met many changes and adjustments this past year, but He helped us through them all. After our arrival in the U.S. the end of December, we lived in Carbondale on the campus of Southern Illinois University for three months, which helped Ray to get settled into school. Then Eunice and the girls moved to Hoyleton, Illinois, into a vacated farmhouse belonging to her sister and husband. It took a lot of work to get it cleaned and fixed up, but we've all enjoyed the country living. Paula and Charla really didn't adjust until we were settled and they could have pets, swing set, etc. Ray lived in a trailer at Carbondale until June and came home on weekends. He enjoys his classes and has done well. During this time, we had a lot of lectures, and Eunice made one trip to New York. We both enjoyed a weekend in Levittown, Pa., in May. Eunice started work as a Nurse's Aide in April at Friendship Manor Nursing Home where her mother lives. She worked there until August when her work started at Trinity Lutheran School in Hoffman, Illinois. She teaches fifteen First and Second Graders, and loves it. Paula and Charla have been fortunate to have their Aunt Wilma and Uncle Willard take care of them when Eunice is at school – this is a marvelous blessing!

In July we had Mildred Schulz, who had been in New Guinea with us, and her sister visit us from St. Louis. In August we had the Dave Gruenhagen's who had also been with us in N.G., and also the Len Pitney's (who've been like parents to us) from Park Rapids, Minnesota. It was wonderful having them with us. We do enjoy visiting, but with our busy schedules we haven't done as much as we'd like. Since we are in the States now we'd like to see more of our relatives and friends. On November eleventh and twelfth we are looking forward to having Rev. and Mrs. Harry Fruend with us from New Guinea. They are on a round-the-world trip via ship and bus, and have been in New Guinea for 40 years or more. Our joy at Christmas will be having Ray's sister and cousin from Toowoomba, Queensland, Australia, with us.

Ray will finish school in December '74; his studies will be completed in May then student teaching from September to December. Paula loves Kindergarten and her first report was very good, for which we thank God. Charla is having the most difficult time as she wants so much to go to school, and also misses her mother during the day. We all have enjoyed the seasons so much this past year after not having them for so many years. Ray planted a garden and we had an abundance of fruits and vegetables. We froze and canned a good portion of these.

We find our opportunities for witnessing for Christ to many here in the U.S. also, and pray we will use each opportunity that comes our way even more.

In closing, we pray this finds you all well and in the best of spirits. May the joy of our Savior's birth fill you with peace, love, and hope unto eternal life. The joys of serving Him and making Him known to others are the greatest!

Love in Christ,
Ray, Eunice, Paula, & Charla Hausler

Except from The Nashville News (IL), Hoyleton section

January 1974

On Sunday evening (the third Sunday evening fellowship meeting January 20, at 7:00 o'clock) guest speakers at the United Methodist Church here, will be Mr. and Mrs. Ray Hausler, nee Eunice Redeker, who will lecture and show slides of their life and work in the Western Highlands of New Guinea, before coming to this area to live. Mrs. Hausler was born near Shattuc and received her grade school education at Bethlehem School, Ferrin, graduated from the Carlyle High School and then attended Concordia Teacher's College, River Forest, where she graduated with a Bachelor of Arts degree in 1956. After teaching in this country a few years she accepted a call from the Board of World Missions to begin a school for girls in New Guinea. This materialized and continued through the high school years, thence establishing St. Paul's Lutheran High School there. In 1965 she met Ray Hausler from Brisbane, Australia; they were married in 1966. They have two daughters, Paula and Charla. While Mrs.

Hausler lived in New Guinea, she was fortunate to be able to travel back to this country three times, in each case she went around the world. Her husband came to New Guinea as a builder and taught Vocational Education, helping the natives build houses and other carpentry for themselves. He now attends SIU, Carbondale, and is working on his degree in Vocational Education. Mrs. Hausler is teaching the lower grades in the Hoffman Parochial School. These people are vitally alive, interesting people and just listening to their enthusiastic accounts of life and its possibilities in the country they served is an education in itself. Following their lecture, an hour of fellowship will be enjoyed in the church basement. Members are asked to bring sandwiches; drinks will be furnished.

Hoyleton, Illinois (Form Letter)

June 14, 1974

Dear _____________,

Greetings to you! Once again time has flown by and we have many letters to answer so will write our news this way and then add a personal note. We pray this finds you all well and in good health and spirits.

Since Christmas we've been busy with school activities as usual. Eunice finished a good year on May 31. The children were sad to leave, you get attached to them always. It seems the time flew as there were Lenten services to attend and sing at, a Mother-Daughter Banquet we performed for, our visits to various companies around Centralia, closing school and graduation exercises. We had two nephews graduating also, one from High School and the other from Concordia Teacher's College, Seward, Nebraska. He'll be teaching in Glendale, California next year. He's being married July 7, and Paula will be flower girl in this wedding. Eunice made her a long dress this week and Charla will have to have one too. Much competition goes on between two girls close in age.

Ray finished school, June 7. He finished in good standing and received honors at the Honor's Convocation, May 25. He is now student teaching at Belleville, Illinois. He finished, July 26, and will graduate in August. So far, he doesn't have a job for next September, but we're praying something will turn up. The Southern Illinois University Placement Board handles that.

Paula finished Kindergarten with flying colors and is looking forward to first grade with her mother. Charla is very anxious to go to Kindergarten and September seems too far away for her. They both will take swimming lessons starting next week. They love being home too and are so busy with their animals (two peacocks, 2 ducks, dog, cat, plus a daily catch of frogs, turtles, and bugs of all sorts), and their toys and school activities.

We have a lovely garden, due to Ray's efforts. We are eating lettuce, radishes and rhubarb at present and the cabbage, beans, peas, beets, peppers, onions, carrots and potatoes will soon be ready too. We freeze a lot of the vegetables in our freezer. It helps the budget a great deal. We picked 24 quarts of strawberries and they are good to have.

Our problems in our church and country continue to give us much concern and we daily pray that things will work out to a God-pleasing and uplifting conclusion.

The Lord richly bless, guide, and keep you in His Word and faith.

Love in Christ,
Ray, Eunice, Paula & Charla

(An example of the speaking engagements Ray and Eunice continued to engage in even once back in the USA after completing their term of service in New Guinea:)

Immanuel Lutheran Church Sunday Bulletin September 29, 1974
Festus, Missouri

<u>Guests:</u> We have as our guests this morning, Mr. and Mrs. Ray Hausler, missionaries from New Guinea. Mr. Hausler is to speak to the Adult

Bible Class this morning and Mrs. Hausler is to speak to us after the potluck dinner this afternoon. We hope to begin about 12:00 and encourage all of you to come or stay for this event this afternoon.

Hoyleton, IL

December 1974

Dear Relatives and Friends,

As once again the Joyous Christmas time is here, we pause once again to marvel at God's grace and goodness in sending His only Son to save the human race from eternal destruction. What praise, obedience and thanks our lives should daily send out to Him. Having Jesus, we have all.

We hope this finds you all fine and in good health. We hope the year, 1974, has been filled with good for you and 1975, will bring even richer blessings from our Heavenly Father.

We had many happenings for which we are grateful this past year, and then some sad notes too. Eunice taught at Trinity Lutheran School, Hoffman, Illinois, and enjoyed teaching Grades One and Two. Paula was in her class from September on. Eunice's mother went to her heavenly home on March 21, which was a blessing too, as we knew she couldn't get well. Ray graduated with a degree in Occupational Education, August 9, 1974. His father also was called to eternal rest on July 24, 1974, at Redcliffe, Australia. Ray went there for three weeks to be with his family. He was happy to be there during that time. Then he got a job the end of August, teaching at Delavan High School, about 150 miles north of here. So, he has been living up there and Paula, Charla and Eunice in Hoyleton. They will move up with Ray after Christmas, and are looking forward to being together as a family again.

Paula loves Grade 1 and is doing well. She has grown so much and is tall for her age. Charla is in Kindergarten and is fairly happy. She could stand a more challenging program, however. Both of them are not keen on the idea of moving, having to make new friends, and leave the farm with all their pets. They also have enjoyed all the attention from Eunice's family. Our address after Christmas will be c/o Delavan High School, Delavan, Illinois 61734

We wish you all a very Merry Christmas and a Blessed Year, 1975.

Love in Christ,
Ray, Eunice, Paula & Charla

Delavan, Illinois (Form Letter)

June 5, 1975

Dear Relatives and Friends,

Greetings to you all. Once again we greet you via a Newsletter as much mail has accumulated and time is limited and we do want to get a line to you all, as we so appreciate hearing from you. We pray your life has been filled with much joy and happiness and that the Lord continues to fill your life. In Him alone is fullness and certainty for this life and the life to come. Again this past Easter, came the wondrous message of how Jesus lived and died for us then sealed it with His Resurrection. Great joy is ours because Christ was willing to do this for us. Billy Graham was on TV from Albuquerque, New Mexico, this P.M. and this tremendous message, always so firmly based on the Bible, was most inspiring and faith strengthening. May God raise up mighty evangelists and workers for His kingdom's sake that this county might be spared the doom it seems to be headed for.

All of us have been busy in school. Ray taught Industrial Arts, Eunice was a substitute – which turned out to be full time, and Paula and Charla successfully completed Grade 1 and Kindergarten. Both girls loved school and did well. Ray has signed the contact to teach here another year. Eunice hopes to get a job in a Christian Day School, teaching in a public school just doesn't have the same joy and satisfaction.

Paula is a tall slim blonde. She is looking forward to nature experiences, swimming, and piano lessons this summer. Charla is enthusiastic, and tries to do everything her sister does. She reads well for a Kindergarten child. She is also tall, slim and blonde. She also looks forward to living at Hoyleton this summer and swimming and music lessons.

Ray will be going back to Southern Illinois University this summer for six weeks to work on his Master's Degree. We will all live at Hoyleton, near Eunice's family during this time. Hoyleton is 150 miles south of Delavan. We put in a garden there and it was doing very well last week. We both took the Kennedy Evangelism Course the past three months and gained a great deal from it. We have been blessed with a good church home and Pastor here in Delavan, we also have the same in Hoyleton, so feel especially blessed.

Eunice will be busy keeping the family happy this summer, as well as, canning, freezing, etc. She loves the times when she doesn't have to have a daily work schedule away from home.

We had a lovely spring this year. (Unfortunately, the rest of this letter has been lost).

Lincoln, Illinois,

July 1976

Dear Relatives and Friends,

Greetings from Central Illinois, in this beautiful summertime. I guess the New Guinea in us still makes us enjoy summer more than winter. But God's creation is wonderful and always amazes us. The blessings of God are with us each day and his abiding presence gives us constant joy, peace, and guidance.

We hope this finds you all filled with joy in our Lord and healthy in body and spirit.

Ray had a successful year at Delavan High School again and continues to enjoy teaching Industrial Arts there. He is now at Southern

Illinois University, Carbondale, Illinois, working on his masters. One more summer after this and he'll have that completed.

Paula and Charla completed a successful school year. Both are good students for which we are thankful. Paula enjoys writing and has written some interesting stories for a second grader. Charla also likes to write; she learns very quickly. Both enjoy swimming, they had six weeks of lessons in April and will have two weeks again in July. Both are at Hoyleton with their Daddy while Mother had to stay behind in Lincoln finishing school orders, meetings, etc.

(The following has been inserted into the original letter so that the reader has background for the concluding paragraph of the letter: Ray and Eunice were concerned as they lived in Delavan that Paula and Charla weren't going to a Lutheran School, so they prayed about this so much. One Sunday afternoon they went to Lincoln, IL, for a seminar. The speaker was Pastor Pflug from the LCMS, Springfield, IL seminary. When they got to Zion, Lincoln, they saw the beautiful church and the large building next to it which had a gym on the upper floor with a stage and 8 Sunday School rooms on the lower floor. They walked through it before the seminar and said to each other that it would make a wonderful Lutheran school. Pastor Plug gave a wonderful inspiring Bible talk. After that was over, Eunice went up to the front to talk to the Zion Pastor, Rev. Goldberger, and Pastor Pflug was standing next to him. Eunice said, "You have a wonderful building here for a Lutheran School, many classrooms and a gym. Pastor Goldberger was a little taken aback, but Pastor Plfug said, "Yes, Pastor Goldberger that would be a good addition here. When I started my church in North Dakota, I started a school right away. It builds the church." Pastor Goldberger invited Eunice to a Board of Christian Education meeting the next evening, Monday. She spoke to the group about a Christian Day School and its value and how their building was so well set up for a school. They were receptive. Afterward they had a prayer, and Eunice began it saying that they all had to say a prayer, which they did. Then one of the persons was very concerned about a little boy in the congregation who had a severe illness {Rhys disease} and was not expected to live through the night, so Eunice led them in prayer for him, and again had each person add to the prayer. She told them to pray with faith: when one prays and believes that God can heal: God can do that! They all said another prayer. Then they invited her to their next Board of Education meeting. The next morning a lady from the meeting, Helen Hasely, called Eunice to say that the little boy had taken a turn for the better in the night and was expected to live. And he did! When God wants work to move forward, He always makes a way. At the next congregational meeting they concluded that if Eunice could get 12 students, they would start a school. She called on many families in June and July and could only get 9 students. She was worried when she went to the meeting July 20. Praise God, they said they would start the school with the nine students. Now she had her work cut out for her! Getting the classroom ready: they knocked out a wall to make a room bigger. They did the same to start the Kindergarten. {They already had a pre-school.} She had a lot of administrative work to do as well. A school was closing in Shobonier, IL and they got their desks, shelves, etc. So, by August 19, they were ready to start school. Eunice's background of starting a school in Levittown, came in very handy. This whole adventure was a miracle and Ray and Eunice praised and thanked God for His great love and mercy and…they had a Christian school for their girls! Now to continue the letter…)

That brings us to Eunice, who is very thankful to the Lord for health and strength as she completed a taxing school year. Getting a school started took a lot of extra time, anxiety and patience but the Lord has richly blessed all efforts, far beyond our thinking. We will have 57 students in our school next year, quite an influx over the 20 we had this year. We are thankful so many more boys and girls will have the opportunity to learn God's Word along with their other subjects next year. We called a male teacher, who is coming and will teach Grades 3 and 4 next year, and work into being Principal. Eunice is anxious to get out of that position as it takes a lot of extra time and since our girls are still small it would be nice to have that time with them. Ray, Paula and Charla are wonderful helpers at home. -- We've had visitors from various places the past weeks and it is a real joy, bringing in first hand news from other countries and other States is always most interesting. Having a large house makes it easy to have visitors.

May the Lord bless and keep you in His grace and power. In Him is fullness and eternal peace.

Love in Christ,
Ray, Eunice, Paula & Charla Hausler

Lincoln, Illinois

December 1976

Dear Relatives and Friends,

Greetings to you! It is good to be able to greet you all as we again rejoice over and celebrate our Savior's birth. Each year, as we more and more realize our sinfulness, that amazing birthday 2000 years ago becomes more and more precious. On that Babe in Bethlehem depends our hope, faith, joy, and life now and eternally.

Our life, as usual, has been busy and filled with opportunities to serve our Savior. Ray has been busy teaching at Delavan High School in the Industrial Arts Department. He worked on ten more hours towards his Master's Degree in Occupational Education this past summer. He has been busy in the activities here at Zion Lutheran Church and was appointed an elder last month. Singing in the choir is also a joy for him.

Eunice rejoices over the growth of the Christian Day School we started by God's grace here at Zion last year. It grew from 20 students last year to 60 students this year. We thank the Lord. Eunice is principal and also teacher of Grades 1 and 2. We have Pre-Kindergarten, Kindergarten, and Grades 3 and 4 also. We plan to add Grade 5 next year. We see a new spark in many families as they grow in the Lord and the Holy Spirit enlivens them. So with being a wife and mother, it keeps her pretty busy.

Paula is a little lady at 8 years. She enjoys life. She likes school and had her first experience this year with a male teacher. She does well and is also enjoying piano lessons and swimming. The girls have a cat, Goldie, who is a very real part of our family. He favors a miniature lion!

Charla is a competitive little girl, keeping up with her sister is a challenge which she meets! She thinks it will be good not to have her Mother for a teacher next year! She is one to whom learning comes easy. She started piano lessons this year and loves it. She loves swimming too.

Our family is planning to go to Australia to visit Ray's family from Dec. 18, '76 – Jan. 4, '77. Ray's Mother has been quite ill so we were going to send Ray and the girls, but since then, the Zion congregation here has decided to collect money so Eunice can go too. Christian love does wonderful things.

We still enjoy going to our sister's farm home at Hoyleton, Illinois, which we claim, when we have a chance. It's always a refreshing and relaxing break.

We hope this finds you and yours well and happy. May the Lord's guidance and protection be yours in 1977. In Him is fullness of joy.

Love in Christ,
Ray, Eunice, Paula, & Charla Hausler

From the Zion Lutheran Church Sunday Bulletin
Lincoln, Illinois

December 19, 1976

My Dear Friends in Christ,

You will never realize what great joy you have brought to me personally, and to our family also this Christmas. It's hard to find the words to express the deep feelings of joy and thanks which I feel. It is really a miracle that after knowing me for only 16 months, you would do such a thing as pay for a trip for me to Australia. Anyway, this is real love in Christ in action, I've seen a lot of it while here at Zion and I praise God for it. I pray it will grow & grow and become a living symbol in this congregation. God loves each one of you and He was born for you, lived for you, died for you. Give your all for Him, believe in Him, love one another, and you will reap peace, joy and happiness, such as nothing in this world could ever give – and it will just go on and on when you die throughout all eternity.

Be assured that during this week as I prepare to go to Australia, as we fly across half the world and as we enjoy the beauties of Australia, I will think of you and thank God for you often. I wish you could all get a glimpse of it all with us. The vastness and beauty of this universe is breath-taking and faith strengthening.

We leave St. Louis, 4:15 pm Saturday, Dec. 18, and arrive in Australia 12:10 pm Monday, Dec. 20. Since we will cross the International Date Line, we will have no Sunday Dec. 19. Paula calls it our "none day." We return to St. Louis 6:45 pm Jan. 4. We will have two Jan. 4 ths, as we cross the International Date Line the other way coming back. Friends will be meeting us at all our stops which also makes it exciting.

We will be thinking of you especially during the Christmas Day School Program Dec. 22, and your Christmas Eve and Christmas Day services. May they all be a great blessing to you and draw you close to Jesus.

I have one request to make of all of you and that is that you would pray the Lord to give us many opportunities to tell many people of Him on this trip. If just one soul could be brought to Him, it would be our greatest joy.

Ray, Paula, Charla and I wish you a very Happy and Blessed Christmas and richest blessings in 1977 as we serve our Lord together. Again, a very deep thanks from all four of us.

In Christ, Eunice Hausler

Western Union Telegram
From Redcliffe, Queensland, Australia
To Zion Lutheran Congregation, Lincoln, IL

December 23, 1976

Wishing you a Blessed Christmas from warm sunny Australia

Ray, Eunice, Paula, Charla

January 16, 1977

Dear Florence and Richard,

Hi! Just a line to tell you we all got home safely. Had a safe and very good trip. Ray's mom is not real good but she did enjoy our visit, was really thrilled to see the girls and all. Australia means a lot to them now.

We called Charles and Linda from L.A. as we had a 30 min. lay over there which turned out to be a 3 hr. one as they had to fix the plane, but it was from 12:00 A.M. to 3:00 A.M. Anyway, Charles and Linda seemed fine and in good spirits.

Well, we plan to come to Hoyleton soon as Ray has to make a trip to Carbondale.

The weather is dreadfully cold, can't ever remember such a cold winter.

Well, take care. God bless and keep you. Keep warm!

Our love,
Eunice, Ray, Paula, Charla

Christmas 1977

Dear Relatives and Friends,

Once again it is that time of year when the joys of our Savior's birth fill us with feelings of sharing and love. We continue to be deeply grateful that Jesus was willing to come down for us, to be poor, so we might be rich and have the hope of heaven.

The past year has been filled with much goodness. We will forever be grateful that we could spend last Christmas with Ray's Mother in Australia, since the Lord called her to her eternal home on October 16, of this year. Even though we miss her, we know she is safely in our Lord's care. Without suffering, the Lord took her quickly and quietly with a heart attack.

Ray continues to teach at Delavan High School in the Industrial Arts Dept. Last May we were privileged to take the Seniors on their Senior trip to the Lake of the Ozarks in Missouri. It was a very memorable and enjoyable trip. Ray went back to school this past summer and got his Master's Degree on August 5. We are thankful for the Lord's guidance and blessings in all this. Ray will be going to Australia for two weeks again this Christmas on business, and seeing relatives and friends.

Eunice continues to teach here at Zion Lutheran School. She is teacher of Grade 1 only now, and happy to be relieved of the principalship. Our school now has 92 students, quite a jump from the 20 we started with two years ago. Eunice got to go back to Levittown, Pennsylvania in September for the 25th anniversary celebration at Hope Lutheran Church. It was a special thrill to be there for this momentous occasion and see our Christian friends again.

Paula is a busy 9 yr. old. She is in grade 4 and has Mr. Eggerstedt, our principal, as her teacher. She takes piano lessons, is in Girl Scouts, plays on the basketball team, is in choir, and takes acrobatics and tap dancing.

Charla is a busy 8 yr. old. She is in the third grade with Mrs. Donna Sauer, who was our Pre-Kindergarten teacher last year. She also takes piano lessons, choir, acrobatics, tap dancing, and is in

Brownies. She is very competitive. She just got glasses so this is something she has to adjust to. We continue to be very thankful to the Lord for our family.

Eunice's sister, Betty and family, of Annapolis, Maryland, spent some time with us in July. It was good having them with us. Some of Eunice's family came up for Thanksgiving and this was a thrill. The Saturday after Thanksgiving some of the members here at Zion gave us a surprise 11th anniversary party. It was a lot of fun.

We pray this finds you all happy and filled with joy and peace in the Lord. His closeness and abundant blessing be with you in 1978.

With love in Christ,
Ray, Eunice, Paula, Charla Hausler

October 11, 1978

Dear Florence and Richard,

Well, just a short line, as ever am kept too busy to do all the things I'd like too. We hope you have a very Happy Birthday. We are all fine. We enjoy our home, just don't get to spend enough time in it. Our Building Committee has had so many meetings lately as we make the final plans to have groundbreaking on Nov. 5 for the school we are building. We're pleased with all the plans. Also pleased we have a principal.

How's all at Hoyleton? We wanted to come down last weekend but just too much to do. Eileen invited us for this weekend as Rev. Otto Hintze is speaking at Ferrin, but we can't make it as Mildred and Bee Schulz are coming up from St. Louis. We haven't seen them for ages.

How do Charles and Linda like it in Wichita? Bet it's quite a change after California? Hope they have a good pastor to work with as well as faculty. We know Pastor Martin Pullmann at St. John's, Winfield real well.

Well, must close as it's past bedtime and have a day of school left this week. Don't know when we'll get down, but you can come up anytime!!

Take care and God bless you and keep you.

Much love, x x x x
Eunice, Ray, Paula & Charla

December, 1978

Dear Relatives and Friends,

Once again that wonderful time of year in which we celebrate our Savior's wondrous birth is here. How we must daily thank and praise our Lord for leaving His heavenly throne to come to this earth to save us. He certainly loved us with an everlasting love, more than words can ever express. So we say, "Thousand, Thousand, thanks shall be, Dearest Jesus unto Thee."

1978 has been a year filled with many and varied experiences for us! Ray is still teaching at Delavan High School and enjoys it, although there are the usual difficulties of working with High School students. He spent the summer building a garage for Uncle Lawrence at Hoyleton, Illinois. We all enjoyed being there, during July. He also is an elder at church and keeps busy with responsibilities and activities there.

Eunice continues to teach at Zion Lutheran School. She enjoys teaching Grades 1 and 2. We again had a change of principals in August as Kim Eggerstedt took a call to CTC, RF, IL. We were grateful to get David Gruenhagen as our new principal. We knew him from New Guinea. We outgrew our present educational building so broke ground on Sunday, Nov. 19th to build a new school ($1,000,000 by the way) on 7 acres of land the church owns west of town. The Lord has so richly blessed this whole school effort here at Zion. If any of you feel inclined to help our cause we would appreciate it as every bit *helps. – Otherwise, Eunice keeps busy as a wife, mother, and serving on the Evangelism Committee and School Building Committee, and belonging to several organizations.*

Paula is now 10 and a tall girl. She likes school and also started violin lessons this year. She enjoys that instrument. She also enjoys piano and swimming. She won several ribbons in Cat Care and Leather Craft in August – her 4-H entries.

Charla is a tall girl also at 9 years. She is a good student as well. She is taking flute lessons; it took a while to catch on to blowing but she has succeeded and does well now. She enjoys piano lessons and really enjoys swimming. She also did well in winning in her 4-H entries in Cat Care and Leather Craft.

Goldie, our cat, is now 3 years old and a fat contented roly-poly, who gets his share of attention.

Ray's trip to Australia last Christmas was busy, as he got the house ready to rent. Our plans are still not definite as to what we'll be doing in the future. We did buy a house here in Lincoln. It's much smaller than the large parsonage we were living in. It has 3 bedrooms and we like it. Rent is so high we figured it best to go this route for now.

We wish you all a very Merry Christmas and Happy and Blessed New Year. The Lord Who loves you all and came down to save us all from eternal death, strengthen you in faith, love and service to Him.

With love in Christ,
Ray, Eunice, Paula & Charla Hausler

(Form Letter)

December, 1979

Dear Relatives and Friends,

Well so quickly another year has gone by. We hope it has been a good year for you. We also pray the days and weeks ahead, as we prepare for our Savior's birth, will be filled with much joy, peace and strong faith in Him. Thanks be to God for sending us His Son to save and redeem us. Through His great love we have hope and confidence in this world filled with trials, and troubles.

This year has been filled with many happenings. Ray has been teaching at Delavan High School in the Industrial Arts Dept. again. Even though there are the usual discipline problems, as a whole it is a good school system. We all enjoyed being in Hoyleton, IL, again for the summer when he added a room to our Uncle Lawrence's house. It's nice being near the relatives for that 2 months.

Eunice has been teaching Grades 1 and 2 at Zion Lutheran School again. We are building a new $1,000,000.00 school and it is nearing completion. We should be in it after Christmas. God has richly blessed this whole endeavor. Eunice also got to attend most of the Lutheran Church – Missouri Synod convention in St. Louis in July which was a thrilling experience. She also had breast surgery in August, but it was benign so recovery was speedy.

Our big event was when Ray's brother Alva, and his wife, Noela were with us for 5 days, from Australia. We did a lot, and had a great time discussing our two countries, and catching up on family news.

Paula continues to be a busy girl in sixth grade. She is doing well besides keeping up with violin lessons, piano lessons, Junior choir and 4-H. She is almost as tall as her mother now.

Charla is also doing well in school. She loves her flute and plays it well. She also enjoys piano lessons. She is also busy in 4-H. They both won firsts on their leathercraft, at the County fair and Charla got to take hers to the State Fair where she got a second.

God-willing, we plan to spend next summer in Australia, June-August, 1980, as we need to take care of some things there. Most of our New Guinea possessions which we could never afford to bring to the U.S. are still there and need sorting.

We wish you all a very Happy and Blessed Christmas as you celebrate our Savior's birth and may rich blessings abound in 1980 for you and yours.

Lovingly in Christ,
Ray, Eunice, Paula, Charla Hausler

Chapter 4

The 1980's

To the Glory of God April 20,1980
Dedication of Zion Lutheran School, Lincoln, IL

The Rite of Opening the Doors

Opening Prayer: O eternal God, who dwellest in the high and holy place and with Him also, who is of a contrite and humble spirit, we beseech Thee, graciously look upon us, and let us enter this school built to Thy glory with Thy blessing, through Jesus Christ, Thy Son our Lord. (Cong: Amen).

The builder shall present the Key to the Architect, and say, "This building has been completed by our craftsmen according to the specifications, & in token of this we present this key."

The builder shall present the key to the Chairman of the Building Committee and say, "This building has been completed to our design. It is our sincere hope and prayer that the congregation and the community will find in this design, a school that is distinctively Christian as well as practical and efficient."

The First Principal shall cut the ribbon.

The Chairman of the Building committee shall present the key to the Chairman of the Congregation and say, "The Building Committee has completed the task given to it by Zion Lutheran congregation. In token of the completion of this work, we give this key to you as the chairman of the congregation. We feel that this school will be of full service to the congregation in its educational programs, giving honor to God, who has guided and directed our task."

The Chairman of the congregation shall then respond, "Whereas, by the grace of God, we are permitted this day to dedicate this building to the Glory of God, we hereby open the doors for the schooling of our children in a Christian manner and atmosphere."

The Door Unlocked by the Chairman of the Congregation.

The Door being unlocked, the Pastor responds, "Lift up your heads, oh ye gates, and be ye lifted up ye everlasting doors, and the King of Glory shall come in. Enter into His gates with thanksgiving and into His courts with praise. Glory be to the Father and to the Son, and to the Holy Ghost, as it was in the beginning is now, and ever shall be." (Cong: Amen)

The congregation will then enter the building in processional while singing the following hymns.

"WE PRAISE THEE, O GOD, OUR REDEEMER, CREATOR."

We praise Thee, O God, our Redeemer, Creator, In grateful devotion our tribute we bring;
We lay it before Thee, we kneel and adore Thee, We bless Thy holy name, glad praises we sing.

With voices united our praises we offer, To Thee, great Jehovah, glad anthems we raise.
Thy strong arm will guide us, our God is beside us. To Thee, our great Redeemer, fore'er be praise. Amen.

"BEAUTIFUL SAVIOR"

Beautiful Savior, King of Creation, Son of God and Son of Man!
Truly I'd love Thee, Truly I'd serve Thee, Light of my soul, my Joy, my Crown.

Fair are the meadows, fair are the woodlands, Robed in flow'rs of blooming spring;
Jesus is fairer, Jesus is purer; He makes our sorr'wing spirit sing.

Fair is the sunshine, Fair is the moonlight, Bright the sparkling stars on high;
Jesus shines brighter, Jesus shines purer; Than all the angels in the sky.

Beautiful Savior, Lord of the nations, son of God and Son of Man!
Glory and honor, Praise, adoration, Now and forevermore be Thine!
Amen.

IN THE NAME OF JESUS TO THE GLORY OF GOD

Invocation: Pastor Goldberger

Hymn by the congregation: "WITH THE LORD, BEGIN THY TASK"

With the Lord begin Thy task, Jesus will direct it. For His aid and counsel ask, Jesus will perfect it. Ev'ry morn with Jesus rise, And when day is ended In His name then close thine eyes, Be to Him commended.

Let each day begin with prayer, praise, and adoration; On the Lord cast ev'ry care, He is thy Salvation, Morning, evening, and at night, Jesus will be near thee: Save thee from the Tempter's might, With His presence cheer thee.

If thy task be thus begun, With the Savior's blessing, Safely then thy course will run, Naught thy soul distressing Good will follow everywhere, While thou here must wander Thou at last the joy wilt share, In the mansions yonder.

Thus, Lord Jesus, every task, Be to Thee commended; May Thy will be done, I ask until life is ended. Jesus, in Thy name begun, Be the day's endeavor; Grant that it may well be done, To Thy praise forever.

The Word of God: Deut. 6:1-9
The Prayer of Dedication

Song by school children: "WE ARE THE CHURCH" Grades Kindergarten – 3rd

Pastor: Thy wife shall be as a fruitful vine by the sides of thine house;
People: Thy children like olive plants round about thy table.

Pastor: Behold, that thus shall the man be blessed;
People: That feareth the Lord.

Pastor: The Lord shall bless thee out of Zion;
People: And thou shalt see the good of Jerusalem all the days of thy life.

Pastor: Yea, thou shalt see thy children's children;
People: And peace upon Israel.

Pastor: O Lord our Lord,
People: How excellent is thy name in all the earth.

Song by the Children: "HOW WONDROUS AND GREAT" Grades 4 – 7

Hymn by the Congregation: "GREAT IS THE LORD OUR GOD"

Great is the Lord, our God, And let His praise be great;
He makes His churches His abode, His most delightful seat.

In Zion God is known, A Refuge in distress;
How bright has His salvation shone, How fair His heav'nly grace!

Oft have our fathers told, Our eyes have often seen,
How well our God secures the fold Where His own sheep have been. Amen.

The Dedication Sermon: Dr. Walter A. Maier, Jr., Concordia Seminary, Ft. Wayne, Indiana
"WISDOM IS THE PRINCIPLE THING" Proverbs: 4:7-13

The Offering for the School Building Fund

The combined Choir of Zion Lutheran
"YE PARENTS HEAR WHAT JESUS TAUGHT"

The Prayers: Pastor Goldberger

The Lord's Prayer: (in unison)

Congregation: Amen.

The Closing Hymn: "PRAISE TO THE LORD, THE ALMIGHTY"

Praise to the Lord, the Almighty, the King of creation! O my soul, praise Him, for He is thy Health and Salvation!
Join the full throng; Wake harp and psalter and song; Sound forth in glad adoration!

Praise to the Lord, who doth prosper thy work & defend thee, Who from the heavens the streams of His mercy doth send thee.
Ponder anew, what the Almighty can do, Who with His love doth befriend thee.

Praise to the Lord! Oh, let all that is in me adore Him! All that hath life and breath, come now with praises before Him!
Let the Amen sound from His people again; Gladly for aye we adore Him.

The Announcements

Hymn by the Congregation: "FOUNDED ON THEE, OUR ONLY LORD"

Founded on Thee, our only Lord On Thee, the everlasting Rock,
Thy Church shall stand as stands Thy Word Nor fear the storm nor dread the shock.

For Thee our waiting spirits yearn, For Thee this house of praises rear,
To Thee with longing hearts we turn; Come, fix Thy glorious presence here.

Accept the work our hands have wrought; Accept, O God, this earthly shrine.
Be Thou our Rock, our Life, our Thought, And we, as living temples, Thine. Amen.

Pastor: O Lord, open Thou my lips.
People: And my mouth shall show forth Thy praise.

Pastor: Make haste, O God, to deliver me.
People: Make haste to help me, O Lord.

Pastor: Glory be to the Father and to the Son and to the Holy Ghost;
People: As it was in the beginning, is now, and ever shall be, world without end. Amen.
All: Hallelujah!

The Responsive Reading: Pastor Fjordbotten

Pastor: Except the Lord build the house
People: They labor in vain that build it.

Pastor: Blessed is every one that feareth the Lord;
People: That walketh in His ways.

Pastor: For thou shalt eat the labour of thine hands;
People: Happy shalt thou be, and it shall be well with thee.

This building is dedicated to the Glory of God by the congregation of Zion Lutheran. Our aim and Prayer is for each family as a total unit to live to worship the One True God, the Father, the Son and the Holy Ghost.

Eunice's speech upon the dedication of Zion Lutheran School

April 20, 1980

Dear Friends in Christ,

I stand before you today because I am excited! Today is a very special day for this congregation and the school it has established. I know it has taken a lot of faith, a lot of prayer, a lot of trusting God to turn hearts to Him, and today it all stands - a reality. When I stood before you 2 years ago, I saw with the eyes of faith what God can do. Today, 2 years later, I stand before you with the reality. I hope and pray this does for you, what it does for me. It assures me that God keeps His promises. My dear friends, when we asked God for spiritual blessings, and Zion Lutheran School is a spiritual blessing, we need never waver, just move forward, trusting and praying, God will do the blessing. Not one of you can deny this miracle as we sit here today. Each one of us should be filled with the words: "The Lord hath Blessed Us Hitherto and Hitherto Hath Helped Us."

But where do we go from here? We have a school, most of you are sending your children so that they will get that one thing needful, the Word of God. God says: "Heaven and earth will pass away but My Word will not pass away." (Matthew 24:35). The mission potential of Zion Lutheran School is fantastic, many children are being led to Jesus, as well as their parents and sisters and brothers. Thank and praise God for this. After all, this is why God is letting the world stand yet today so we Christians can be about our Father's business, teaching and preaching the Gospel to all men. These are some of Jesus last words to us: "Go ye in to all the world and preach the Gospel to every creature." (Matthew 28: 19-20). And this world of wickedness God is letting stand yet today because of the Christians in it. But for how long? The days of Lot and Noah are upon us, the wickedness is great, and how long the Lord will be patient and still let us work we don't know. So our job is to work while it is day, before the night comes when no man can work.

And so today is not the end for Zion Lutheran School – it is a marvelous beginning. With another leader-teacher in our school, the fourth in 2 years, this is fantastic. I know the angels in heaven are singing right now over the joy of more children being led closer to their Savior. How we ought to get on our knees and thank and praise God today. Then also remember your work is just beginning – as 80 children enter our building this year, we need your prayers more than ever, we need your financial support more than ever, we need those willing hands, arms and feet to work for Him more than ever. As we work together in the days and weeks ahead may it be a tremendous joy, a real strengthening of faith and seeing Jesus more clearly. The devil, world and our flesh are constantly trying to discourage us, to stop us, or else fill us with pride. All of these are deadly. The only way you can march forward as a Christian is to take Jesus by the hand each day. You have to have a clear view of Him, as you go about your work each day. You have to walk out the door with Him each morning, you have to keep Him before your eyes all day otherwise you will falter and fall. People, happenings, news items, etc, will all pull you away from Jesus, so you have to keep reading the Bible, believe every word, write it indelibly on your mind and heart. Then you will stay with Him and nothing will separate you from the love of God which we have in Christ Jesus. Do not become a lukewarm Christian as Revelations says because the Lord will spew you out of His way. Become an alive, working, joy filled Christian, enthusiastic Christian and life will become so filled, so happy, and it'll lead you, and through you, many others, to heaven.

God grant that you all see today as a milestone as well as a new beginning. Keep praying, for your school and its teachers – you have done well – and God has richly blessed you. Keep it up and I venture to say that in the next 2 years we will have an eight grade school with more dedicated teachers in your midst and the future holds for you a strong Zion Lutheran Church with solid leadership, many fine Christian pastors and teachers coming from your children who will lead our church tomorrow. It's beautiful, it's God's work and nothing can be more joyful or rewarding, I know. But remember don't become discouraged or proud, they are deadly sins, and the future is bright, it is filled with God in your midst, it is filled with building an earthly Zion which will be translated into a heavenly Zion one day and our petty grievances and shortcomings will be no more! We will know fully and be in God's beautiful heaven forever.

God grant it for Jesus sake.

And personally, I want to thank you for your prayers, support, and wonderful help the past 2 years. It has been great. Then I ask you to do the same for Mr. Eggerstedt. You've provided me a marvelous faith forward Board of Education to work with, they've been a marvelous blessing. I pray you'll continue to do this and pray for this group as they make many big decisions in the next year.

A New School
(from the LINCOLN COURIER, Lincoln, IL)

(A member of Zion Lutheran Church, Mr. Ed Richardson, served on the staff of the Lincoln Courier and ran the following article).

Congratulations to the members of the congregation of Zion Lutheran School. The dedication ceremonies, last Sunday, officially opened the new school, even though it has been in operation for a few weeks.

It was not long ago, that members of the congregation were wondering if the school should be built. Undoubtedly there are still some members who don't think it should have been built, but with the new facility, it should be put to use.

If you are for, or against the facility, now is not the time to raise your eyebrows. It has been built, now it must be put to good use.

The facility has been designed with the students in mind and should create a good learning atmosphere. Those sending their students to Zion Lutheran obviously have to have strong religious beliefs, because even if the student attends Zion, the parents are still paying taxes for public schools. The private schools, like Zion, are funded through the congregation and tuition.

The building of Zion School was started in March of 1976 when the committee on Christian Education authorized the chairman to approach the planning committee in regards to starting a building fund. It was in October of 1977 before the congregation decided to interview architects for the possible construction of the school on Route 10 west of Lincoln.

Ground was broken for the new school on Nov 19, 1978 and the cost of the facility was not to exceed $1 million. Construction started April 16, 1979 and the cornerstone was laid Sept. 30, 1979. Many members of the congregation helped with the building by donating several hours of their service for various projects, such as painting, installing ceilings, etc.

What started as a dream of Eunice Hausler, a member of the congregation, has become a reality. Now it is up to the members of the church to make the school prosper.

We certainly wish them all well in future endeavors.

November, 1980

Dear Relatives and Friends,

Once again, much too quickly, another year has passed and it's time to rejoice in the Wonderous Celebration of our Savior's birth. What a wonderful, loving God we have that He was willing to send His best, His only Son, to save us from our sins, and now in Him, Jesus Christ, our Lord, we have peace, joy and the assurance of eternal life forever in heaven. May this be your great joy this Blessed Christmas season and always.

This year 1980 has been one filled with great blessings, wonderful assurance of God's promises and a seeing of a great deal of His beautiful world He created. We all were busy in school until the 26th of May. Ray is still teaching Industrial Arts at Delavan High School, Eunice teaches Grades 1 and 2 at Zion Lutheran School where Paula and Charla are students in Grades 6 and 7. One of the highlights of the year was the dedication of our new school on April 12, 1980. It is truly a beautiful building and a great blessing has been bestowed on Zion Lutheran congregation through it the past five years. Many children and parents are being brought to the Lord by this means. We pray many workers for the Lord will be produced in it also.

Then we left Lincoln May 26, and drove to California via Iowa, North Dakota (Mt. Rushmore), Wyoming (Yellowstone), Idaho, Utah, Nevada, California. It was a beautiful relaxing drive. We left our car with the Raffs in California, then flew to Australia via Hawaii, and New Zealand. We were in Australia for 2 months till July 30. We stayed with our good friends George and Gladys Ost, who were most gracious and wonderful Christian friends. George helped us for five weeks sorting through our belongings from New Guinea, Ray's mother's things, and painting the house at Redcliffe. It was fun, as well as hard work. Fish and Chips on the beach every day was a highlight for Paula & Charla, who love Australia, as do all of us. We were also fortunate to have our own car while there gotten for us by Ray's wonderful cousins, Auburn & Ollie Mueller. This enhanced our stay. It was winter there but their winters in Queensland are beautiful, like Southern California. Then we took a 2 ½ week tour by car to Toowoomba, Queensland, - through the malee of New South Wales, to South Australia where we saw Ray's sister and husband, the Russell Weiers, the Borossa Valley was beautiful, on to Lobetbal and Adelaide, South Australia where we saw former New Guinea friends, the Clive Schubert's, the Henry Fruends, the Louis Heppners, Dean Russell, Ray's sister Thora, nephew John Weier at the Seminary, then on to Coonalpyn to see the Ian Kleinigs, and Clem Janetzkis, and then on to Victoria to see Don Weiers, Naomi, Haff, and the Philip Theiles'. Eunice was sponsor to Jonathon Thiele and what a thrill to be there in Barker's Ridge, Victoria, for his confirmation July 20 – truly a blessed day! Then on to the nation's capital, Canberra, New South Wales, also Sydney and the famous Opera House, and then on up the Pacific Highway back to Brisbane, Redcliffe and Petrie where the Osts live. We saw much Australian wildlife as kangaroos, emu, goulahs, etc. on our drive. In Brisbane we saw former New Guinea friends, the Bill Days and Walt Schmidts. We also had lovely visits with Ray's sister Joyce and brother Alva and their family, and friend June Wilson, plus many other good friends. Then we left Australia July 30, with our good friend George Ost and his son Jeffrey coming with us back to the U.S. We stopped 3 days in New Zealand, saw Auckland, Rotorua and the Bay of Islands via a van. Then flew on to Hawaii for 3 days and toured the island, then on to Los Angeles, seeing Disneyland and some of the city. Our good friend Dave Raff was there to meet us as he had brought our car down to Los Angeles. Betty and Dave are wonderful friends since Eunice started going to New Guinea since 1959. They have met us every trip through San Francisco, as well as have hosted many of our friends and relatives who have come through. We then drove via Las Vegas (Hoover Dam), Flagstaff, Arizona (Grand Canyon & Painted Desert), New Mexico, Texas pan-handle, Oklahoma, Missouri (seeing St. Louis) and on to Lincoln. It was all marvelous and a perfect trip, not one incident of sickness or car problems – so we just thank the Lord. Then we sent George and Jeffrey on to Philadelphia (after showing them Illinois) to our good friends the Werberigs, who showed them a marvelous time and took them to New York & Washington, D.C. Jeffrey left to go back to Australia Aug. 30, and George took in a few more things till Sept. 10. We missed them a lot after being together for almost 3 ½ months.

School started again August 25, and we're still trying to catch up with many things but we move one day at a time, just thankful to the Lord always for His guidance, love and care.

We look forward to hearing from you again this Christmas as it is always a great pleasure. We went to the Great Mission Convocation in St. Louis yesterday, we only got in one day, but it was inspiring, 6,000 attended from our Lutheran Churches in the U.S. and Canada. Approximately 15,000 attended the Rally last p.m. It was very inspiring and filled us with the desire to continue to do all in our power as the Lord provides strength, to spread the good news of the Gospel to everyone we meet wherever we may be.

God continue to bless you and yours richly in 1981 and make you a blessing.

Love in Christ,
Ray, Eunice, Paula, Charla Hausler

Christmas 1981

Dear Friends and Relatives,

Once again, the beautiful messages and sounds of Christmas are sounding all around us. Thanks to God for His great love in sending His only Son into this world of sin to save us. Now, we can enjoy a truly joyous and blessed Christmas as we rejoice in His birth. May the Lord keep us in true faith, and His joy and hope in the New Year ahead.

We are happy to be able to greet you via this letter, even though seeing you would be much better. We hope you and yours have had a good year and all is well your way. We look forward to hearing from you during this Christmas season.

We were in Lincoln until August. Ray finished teaching in April, and since he could not get his citizenship by then, he could no longer teach. They tell us he should be able to get it in eighteen months so hopefully he'll be back teaching by September 1982. In the meantime he is doing construction work here at Hoyleton and Eunice is teaching at Trinity Lutheran School, Hoffman, Illinois. We are enjoying being back here close to Eunice's family. Paula and Charla are enjoying school at Trinity Lutheran, Hoyleton. All of us have enjoyed good health this year, for which we thank God.

Some of the highlights of the year were a visit from our Australian friends, Jim and Esme Janetzki in April – our first eighth grade graduation at Zion Lutheran School, Lincoln, Illinois, in May – my nephew Darrell Maschhoff's wedding in July, during which time Eunice's sister Betty and Roger Thusius of Annapolis, Maryland, and their two children were with us for two weeks. It was good seeing them again after several years of not seeing them. - In June, Roy and Judy Schache and their two children and Judy's mother spend an overnight visit; it was really good seeing them after eight years. They were in New Guinea with us, and Roy is also an Australian. – October 8-12, we spent in Fargo, North Dakota, with our dear friends Ruth and

Lennord Pitney. Len was seriously ill with cancer and has since been called home to heaven.

Paula is a grown-up 13-year-old. She is 5'5" and if she grows more will leave her mother behind. She is still active in sports, basketball and baseball, and in piano and violin lessons. She sings in the school choir. Charla is a bubbling 12-year-old and is also busy in basketball and baseball. She also takes piano and flute lessons and sings in the school choir.

So far, we have had a rainy fall; in fact, a rainy year since May. Most of the farm crops have been harvested in between the rains. The yields were good this year. Last winter was very mild here.

We hope this finds you and yours well, strong in faith, and rejoicing in the Lord. His blessing and peace go with you in the New Year.

With our love,
Ray, Eunice, Paula, Charla Hausler

The Carlyle (IL) Banner & The Centralia (IL) Sentinel
Week preceding June 6, 1982

"Trinity teacher observing 25th anniversary" & "Open House for Hoffman Teacher" (under Eunice's pic)

Mrs. Ray (Eunice) Hausler of Hoyleton, a teacher at Trinity Lutheran School of Hoffman, will be honored Sunday, June 6th, for 25 years in the teaching ministry.

A service of praise and thanks will be held at 10:00 a.m. Sunday in the Trinity Lutheran Church of Hoyleton, where Mrs. Hausler is a member. Then at 12:30 p.m. an anniversary potluck dinner will be held at the Hoffman school.

Friends are invited to attend both events.

Mrs. Hausler teaches third and fourth grades at Trinity Lutheran School.

She received her early schooling at Flaherty School and Ferrin Lutheran School, then graduated from Carlyle High School in 1952. She graduated from Concordia Teachers College at River Forest in 1956 and began her teaching career at Levittown, PA.

She spent 13 years teaching in the western highlands of New Guinea. After her return in 1972, Mrs. Hausler taught at Hoffman, then at Lincoln, and now is at Hoffman again.

She and her husband Ray live near Hoyleton. They have two daughters, Paula and Charla.

Trinity Lutheran Church (Hoyleton, IL) Bulletin June 6, 1982

Today: On this Trinity Sunday/Mission Sunday, we give praise to Father, Son and Holy Ghost for the gift to the church of Mrs. Ray (Eunice) Hausler. For better than 25 years Eunice has been a highly dedicated worker in Christ's Kingdom, and our gracious God has accomplished great things through her. We pray that our Lord will continue to use Eunice to lead others to the Savior and to also strengthen those whom He has called by the Gospel... (then follows words about the potluck with this sentence) ...Following the meal we will honor Eunice with a special anniversary program.

Also in the above bulletin was the following:

Mission Sunday Story!

"Spread the Good News"
"...they (the laity) went everywhere preaching the Word." Acts 8:4

"It was just too good to keep to myself," said a friend to me one day long ago. He had discovered a certain "fishing hole," where the fishing was fantastically good; and he wanted me to enjoy it also. But how loath and slow we are to tell others about the Lord Jesus, which is the best news of all. Truly the joy of salvation is too good to keep to ourselves.

A party of missionaries were sitting at tea one afternoon, when suddenly an ant appeared on the white tablecloth, made its way to one of the tea plates, walked around it, and finding nothing to eat there, made straight for the sugar bowl. After eating some bits of sugar, it went off with a small piece. The party watched it go off the table, down the table leg, along the floor of the room, and disappear underneath the door. Not long afterwards, it returned with several of its relations, climbed up the leg of the table, and marched along the top. Led by the first ant, they all entered the sugar bowl. After they had eaten their fill of sugar, they all departed, each with a piece of sugar in its mouth. But that was not all—presently a swarm of ants arrived to partake of the same sweet food.

What a great lesson those ants teach us. The one who came first of all, went and told others the "good news"; they, in turn, went out and told the glad story to many more. Shall we let the ants put us to shame? Surely not. Like Isaiah, the Demoniac, the Woman of Samaria, and others, we must "go and tell" the glad story of God's redeeming love!

-M.R.D.

Worship Service June 6, 1982

The 25th Anniversary of Mrs. Ray (Eunice) Hausler
In the Teaching Ministry

"Fear not, for I am with you, be not dismayed, for I am your God;
I will strengthen you; I will help you, I will uphold you with My Victorious right hand." Isaiah 41: 10 (RSV)

Hymn- "Hark! The Voice of Jesus Crying"

1. Hark! the voice of Jesus crying, "Who will go and work today? Fields are white and harvests waiting, Who will bear the sheaves away?"
   Loud and long the Master calleth, Rich reward He offers thee;
   Who will answer, gladly saying, "Here am I, send me, send me?"

2. If you cannot speak like angels, If you cannot preach like Paul,
   You can tell the love of Jesus, You can say He died for all.
   If you cannot rouse the wicked With the Judgment's dread alarms,
   You can lead the little children To the Savior's waiting arms.

3. If you cannot be a watchman, Standing high on Zion's wall,
   Pointing out the path to heaven, Off'ring life and peace to all.
   With your prayers and with your bounties You can do what God demands;
   You can be like faithful Aaron, Holding up the prophet's hands.

4. Let none hear you idly saying, "There is nothing I can do,"
   While the souls of men are dying And the Master calls for you.
   Take the task He gives you gladly, Let His work your pleasure be;
   Answer quickly when He calleth, "Here am I, send me, send me!" Amen.

The Homily — The Reverend James Herzog

Children's Choir Selections — Grades 3-4, Hoffman
I am the Church & It's me O Lord

Guest Speaker — Dr. John W. Klotz

Congratulatory Messages &
Presentations

Master of Ceremonies	Mr. Ray Richert
Board of Education Chairmen	
Trinity, Hoffman	Mr. Ralph Twenhafel
Trinity, Hoyleton	Mr. Jerald Rixmann
Closing Prayer	Pastor Peter Kurowski

"The Lord hath Helped Me Hitherto"

1. The Lord hath helped me hitherto By His surpassing favor;
   His mercies ev'ry morn were new, his kindness did not waver.
   God hitherto hath been my Guide, Hath pleasures hitherto supplied,
   And hitherto hath helped me.

2. I praise and thank Thee, Lord, my God, For Thine abundant blessing
   Which heretofore Thou hast bestowed And I am still possessing.
   Inscribe this on my memory: The Lord hath done great things for me
   And graciously hath helped me.

3. Help me henceforth, O God of grace, help me on each occasion,
   Help me in each and ev'ry place, Help me thro' Jesus' Passion;
   Help me in life and death, O God, Help me thro' Jesus' dying blood;
   Help me as Thou hast helped me! Amen.

WORDS OF THANKS

A word of thanks is given to the Board of Education members and their wives for their work with the Anniversary Dinner, and to the members of the Anniversary committee for their work in organizing this special celebration.

A special thank-you is extended to all who have helped honor Mrs. Hausler's 25th anniversary of serving the Lord in the teaching ministry. Your presence is greatly appreciated, as well as your cards and gifts.

We thank our Lord and Savior, Jesus Christ, for all His blessings upon us and ask for His continued protection upon us all as we travel home this afternoon. May His Word continue to guide us as we serve the Lord together.

"Stand firm, then, my dear fellow Christians, and let nothing move you. Always keep on doing a great work for the Lord since you know in the Lord your hard work isn't wasted." I Corinthians 15:58 (Beck)

Christmas 1983

Dear Relatives and Friends,

Greetings to you at this Blessed Season. With great joy and excitement Christmas comes every year as we await the celebration of our Savior's birth, who so willingly left His heavenly home to come down here and save us so we can now look forward to heaven as well. May God grant you all strong faith in this Jesus this Christmastide and always.

The year 1983 has been filled with so much so it will be hard to cover it all. A few of our highlights were the arrival of George Orst, our good friend from Australia. He was here for Charla's Confirmation the end of March which made her very happy. Then we had a lot of relatives and friends for that solemn occasion in Charla's life on March 27.

The middle of April we made the move into our new home which Ray designed and built. We all love it even though it still needs finishing touches. May ended school for Paula, Charla, and Eunice. Charla also graduated from elementary school.

June was busy with Eunice getting more things moved and Paula and Charla started work, babysitting at a nursery. Ray kept busy all summer on various construction jobs. Still nothing has happened in regard to his citizenship. The end of June, our good friend, Ruth Pitney, from Minnesota spent a week with us. It was so good to have her. Her son and family also made it up during that time from Kentucky.

July and August were very hot months, and we had visitors from Lincoln, Illinois several weekends. August started out with Eunice spending two weeks caring for her brother Luther's and Eileen's two children while Eileen had surgery. Then it was time to be back at school for Eunice.

Paula went to the Lutheran Youth Gathering in San Antonio, Texas, August 11-17, and enjoyed it immensely. Then she and Charla were busy with High School band from August 15 on. They are both in High School now and are happy there. They are both taking violin, and Paula has just been accepted into the Community Orchestra. They had their Christmas Concert December 4.

During September we had visitors from Lincoln, Illinois, Australia, and San Francisco, California. It was such a wonderful renewing of friendships time. Our good friends Betty and Dave Raff from San Francisco, finally made it to Illinois after all the times we have spent with them.

The Rev. Ian Kleinigs, Gordon Egels, and Don Jeffers were with us five days the end of October. What a joy to reminisce about New Guinea days. It was their first trip to the U.S. Eunice had lived with the Kleinigs her first months in New Guinea, and they were wonderful.

Then the end of November we had Rev. and Mrs. Greg Lockwood and family with us. After 2 ½ years in the states at Concordia Seminary, Rev. Lockwood has gotten his Doctorate, and now they are returning to New Guinea for further service to the Lord.

So you see, it has been a filled year for us, and a blessed one. Our Heavenly Father cares and provides, to Him all praise and glory. We pray that Ray will find more permanent work in the New Year. Sometimes we aren't sure what the Lord has in store. In the meantime, we trust Him. We pray you have all had rich blessings in the past year and wish you much good and God's continued blessings in 1984.

Love in Christ,
Ray, Eunice, Paula, Charla Hausler

Christmas 1984

Dear Relatives and Friends,

Grace and peace from God our Father and our Lord and Savior Jesus Christ, be yours. Especially as the world situation seems to get more and more filled with turmoil and fear of war, we can thank God that we have peace in our Savior who came in Bethlehem's stable long ago and saved us from sin, death and condemnation. His peace and joy fill you this Christmas and always.

The past year seems to have gone much too quickly for us. We started out with a zero and below January – which was a little tough on the old bones. - - - In March Uncle Lawrence Redeker went to his heavenly home. We miss him - - - In May, Trinity Lutheran School gave a musical, Kid's Praise, which had some beautiful songs. Paula, Charla, and Eunice finished school the end of the month which is always welcome. - - - June, Eunice started work at a restaurant on the Interstate, as a cook. It was a good experience. In June also our dear friend Es Egel, was called home. She was a friend from New Guinea days. She helped us a lot when Paula and Charla were little. We were thankful we had seen her just a year ago.

Then in July, Eunice's sister Betty and family from Annapolis, Maryland were here for two weeks and their visit is always a welcome get together. Also in July, Paula and Charla went to music camp at SIU, Carbondale, Il. They had a grand time. - - - In August our good friends and Pastor of our Congregation, Peter and Jan Kurowski, left to start a parish in New Orleans, La. Also, in August our friend, Reta Thiele, was here from Australia for two days, and it was a thrill to see her again. Then school started again and we had to get back in the groove. Paula got her driver's license and is now keeping the car going. - - - Also in August, Eunice, Paula and Charla when to a Lutheran Youth Gathering in MaComb, IL. It was inspiring.

In October Ray and Eunice attended the Great Mission Convocation in St. Louis. It was very motivating. Eunice met her college friend, Charlotte Hoener, whom she hadn't seen for 23 years and that was a thrill. Her husband Ken was also there and Ray got to meet them for the first time. It was a thrill. - - - Now in November Ray hopes to get his citizenship. It is to happen Nov. 27. Then he can get back to teaching. He's been remodeling buildings and houses this past year. We're thankful he had work. Eunice is still teaching at Trinity, Hoffman, Paula is in the Centralia Symphony Orchestra and they will give their Christmas Concert, December 3, 1984.

Both girls play the violin, Paula also plays the saxophone and piano, Charla also the flute and piano. They are both good students for which we thank the Lord and we pray their lives will be useful in His kingdom. Paula is thinking seriously about the college she will be attending. Paula is a Junior, and Charla a Sophomore this year. - - - That covers a little of our past year. We look forward to hearing from all of you at this time of year. We hope you've all had a good year and pray God's richest blessings upon you. The peace and joy of Christmas fill you always.

Love in Christ,
Ray, Eunice, Paula, Charla Hausler

Christmas 1985

Dear Relatives and Friends,

Greetings to you all at this Joyous Season. The great joy of God's great love for us in sending His only Son to save us from our sins remains ever wonderful, ever amazing. We join the hymn writer in the words "Joy to the World the Lord is come!" May the people of the world all learn to know Him.

1985 has been a filled and fast year for us. In April, Ray got back into teaching. He is teaching Graphic Arts at the Centralia Correctional Center and enjoys this work a lot. He's happy to be back at teaching.

In February, Eunice was elected chairperson of the Board of Evangelism and Social Ministry of the Southern Illinois District, which automatically put her on the Board of Directors also. So, meetings plus teaching and homemaking keep her very busy.

In April, Paula and Charla were both inducted into the National Honor Society and Modern Music Masters. We are thankful for the abilities the Lord has given them. In April also, Kindergarten – Grade Four at Trinity Lutheran School, Hoffman, IL, where Eunice teaches, gave their musical "Noah's Ark." This is also enjoyable for the school families.

In May, Eunice, Paula and Charla were happy to say goodbye to the books for the summer. Paula got her first job as waitress at Ken's Pizza. She enjoyed the experience. In July, Eunice's sister, Betty and family were out from Annapolis, Maryland. This is always a joy and we then have a family reunion. In August, Charla got her driver's license which now makes the car situation a little hectic at times.

In September, it was back to school and work. Paula is now a senior at Nashville High School and Charla a junior. Paula is busy seeking out a college for her to attend September, 1986. She was a Queen candidate for the School's Homecoming and got to be Maid of Honor. Charla's class won the float competition so she was thrilled. Both girls are still busy in orchestra, band, chorus, violin lessons and piano lessons. So there is always a lot of activity going on around our house.

November 16, 17, 18, Eunice's brother Wilbert, had three heart attacks. He is at present in critical condition at Barnes hospital, St. Louis. We only pray the Lord's will be done for him.

We pray this finds all of you well and happy in your life. The Lord bless and keep you in 1986.

With our love,
Ray, Eunice, Paula, Charla Hausler

(While each year in the annual letters, we reported Ray and Eunice's employment, in order to cut the redundancy in reading these letters back-to-back, Ray was employed at the Centralia Correctional Center {CCC)} from 1984 to 2000 and Eunice continued at Trinity Lutheran School, Hoffman {TLS-H} from 1981 to 1996, as teacher and sometimes as principal as well. Subsequently, only specifics to these occupations will be related going forward.)

November, 1986

Dear Relatives and Friends,

Greetings once again from our house to yours! We hope this has been a good year for you and yours. Once again, our gracious and loving Lord has let us live in a land of freedom and plenty. We can never be grateful enough for His grace and love which gives us these. As we celebrate His birth and the greatest freedom of all which He bought for us with His precious blood and freedom from sin, we rejoice, praise and thank Him. May we always witness to others about Him so they too will believe in Him and enjoy heaven with us one day.

Life at our house has once again been very busy this year. Ray continues at CCC. He likes it and finds it challenging along with many opportunities to witness to the prisoners. He often does carpentry work on Saturday and evenings as people request his services. He is busy in church work and he and Eunice are now on the Evangelism Board at our church at Hoyleton.

Eunice is still at TLS-H teaching Grades I and II. She is still chairman of the District Evangelism and Social Ministry Board which takes a lot of time. So trying to keep up with the home front is often a challenge.

Paula is now a freshman at Eastern Illinois University at Charleston, IL. She likes it there very well but still has not decided on a par-

ticular field of study. She loves her Art courses, however. She is still involved in music, violin and piano. She ran for Washington County Queen this summer and came in second.

Charla is a senior at Nashville High School. She leans heavily toward academics and is doing well. She was very pleased to have been chosen Homecoming Queen of Nashville High School in October. She is still active in Band and Orchestra and accompanying the chorus on the piano. She plans to attend the University of Illinois next year, God-willing. She went to the Lutheran Youth Gathering in Washington, D.C. in August and thoroughly enjoyed every minute.

Our big event of the year was the arrival of Ray's sister, Thora, from Australia in May for Paula's graduation from High School. She met Eunice in Los Angeles as she was at an Evangelism Execs meeting, and they flew back to St. Louis together. We spent a wonderful month with her. We did some travelling and a lot of visiting. Time went too fast.

We wish you all a very Merry and Blessed Christmas in our Lord. The joy and peace of His coming to save us fill you! Rich blessings be yours in 1987. We look forward to hearing from you!

Our love in Christ,
Ray, Eunice, Paula, and Charla Hausler

Christmas 1987

Dear Relatives and Friends,

Greetings to you all once again at this Blessed Christmas Season.

What is the Reason for the Season? Why was it "the Word became flesh" (John 1:14)? Why the mystery "preached among the nations" (I Timothy 3:16)? Many can answer those questions. Fortunately, St. Paul said it well: "All have sinned…and are justified (forgiven) by His grace through the redemption that came by Christ Jesus." Romans 3:23-24.

We are the reason for His coming for we needed a Savior! We needed to know and to have the love of God, the new life only possible through Christ's coming into the world, into human hearts by faith. We are the reason He came, that He comes in Word and Sacraments, that He finally will come again in glory…ready or not! May the blessings of His coming be yours.

This year has been another one of God's grace richly shown to our family. Ray has continued at CCC and he has had many opportunities to witness for the Lord. He has attended various Seminars in Chicago and Springfield for continued education. The last one was in November, Graphics Expo '87. It was very enlightening on the latest in technology. Things are changing so quickly in that realm—who knows what the future holds.

Eunice is still working at TLS-H and on several Boards of the Southern Illinois District, LCMS. This will end February '88, as she has served two terms and is not eligible to serve again. This last May the Evangelism Conference was in Omaha, Nebraska, and was very uplifting. The training received was very helpful. She and Ray went to Nashville, Tennessee, for a week in August. It was relaxing and good to get away. Eunice's sister, Betty and family from Annapolis, Maryland, were also here in August and it was good seeing them.

Paula is a sophomore at Eastern Illinois University, Charleston, Illinois. She likes it and is doing well. She is still thinking of majoring in Interior Design or a related field.

Charla graduated the top of her class at Nashville High School in May. She is now attending the University of Illinois. She is adjusting – as it is a large school, 32,000 students. She is heavy into Math at present but still is thinking of Law or Engineering. Both girls will be home in two weeks which we are looking forward to. Charla will get her summer job back at J.C. Penney Co. and Paula at Little Nashville, Inc. The Hausler house has been unusually quiet with both girls away.

1988 will be exciting with the Presidential election taking place. At this point we would like to go to Brisbane, Australia, for the Expo '88, but with two girls in college that most likely will not be possible.

We hope this finds you all well and in good spirits. The Lord bless you and keep you in His loving care always.

With love in Christ,
Ray, Eunice, Paula, Charla Hausler

September 5, 1988

Dear Relatives and Friends,

Well, here it is a month already since we've been back from our most enjoyable trip to Australia. We really enjoyed our stay while there, and all the warm hospitality, good food, loving acts of goodness and kindness. We have wonderful remembrances of our visit and lots of pictures to help us remember the beauties of the country, and all of you.

We arrived home safely August 7, 8:30 A.M. Ray went back to work on Monday, August 8, and Eunice went back several days that week and full time the next week, for her it was getting ready for the opening of school on August 26.

After we left Australia, we flew to New Zealand and toured from Auckland to Rotorua, around Lake Taupo, up into the tablelands of Chateau Tongariro, over to Highway 4 and on up to Hamilton. In Hamilton we saw Rev. Alan Heppner and his family. (For those of you who read "Thank You Lord for the Privilege", Eunice's first book, Alan was the youngest son of Louis and Lorna Heppner, who's older son drowned shortly after Eunice arrived in PNG in 1959. Alan became a pastor and was placed in New Zealand. This incident is also referred to earlier in this book, in Eunice's second letter from PNG, dated February 1960 in Chapter 2.) *We had a good visit and were able to attend church there. Then back to Auckland. New Zealand is a beautiful country and it certainly has millions of sheep. Then we flew on to Fiji and had a beautiful stay there. We drove from Nadi to Suva and back. Fiji is not so commercialized yet so we enjoyed seeing the people, their customs, etc. It would be a good place to spend a vacation if you want to just relax. Prices are very reasonable too.*

Then on to Honolulu which is of course very commercialized, a busy hectic seaport. We did enjoy a tour around the island, seeing Pearl harbor, and spending a few hours at Waikiki beach.

Paula and Charla were both here to meet us when we got home. Of course, we were very thankful to God for all the protection and care He had given during the four weeks we were apart. They were home several days, then it was back to school for them too. They seem happy at the University of Illinois.

We'll add a little personal note to this but thought we'd do the general this way, otherwise we may not get a letter to each of you.

Christmas 1988

Dear Relatives and Friends,

Once again another year has swiftly passed by and it's time for that joyous time of year when we celebrate our Savior's birthday. We pray your faith in this baby Jesus, our Savior from sin and God's Son, will be strong and remain forever until you can see Him face to face in the glories of heaven one day. We're reminded of this as every year when we go over our Christmas list, we have to delete several dear friends who have departed and gone on to our heavenly home. The joy is we will see them again, however.

This year, 1988, has been filled with many rich blessings from the Lord. Ray continues to find his work interesting and filled with opportunities to witness for our Lord. He and Eunice are on the Evangelism Committee at Trinity Lutheran Church, Hoyleton, which allows many opportunities for witness and service. We have both joined the church choir since October and will be singing in their Christmas Concert, December 14.

Eunice still teaches and loves those little ones. She is happy to have a respite from serving on District Boards. She does serve on a Committee for the Elderly.

Paula is a Junior at University of Illinois, Champaign, she transferred there from Eastern Illinois University. She was just admitted to the School of Architecture so she is pleased. Just what her future occupation will be remains to be seen. She and Charla both work at Denny's restaurant as waitresses.

Charla is a sophomore at the University of Illinois. She and Paula live together in an apartment with two other girls. Charla is in the field of Mathematics and leans toward being a teacher. We pray daily that both girl's faith remain strong and that they be protected from the danger and evils that surround them.

Ray and Eunice were thrilled that they could make the trip to Australia in July. Orville and Vera Heseman, friends from here went with us. We had a wonderful and safe trip. The greatest thrill was being with all of Ray's family again. The first time all five had been together since 1961. They also had a reunion with cousins, nieces, nephews, etc. one Sunday. We were able to see and stay with some of the families we knew in New Guinea and this was a special joy too. We also got to see Expo '88, the Great Barrier Reef, Hopevale Mission, New Zealand, and Fiji. As we celebrate Thanksgiving this week in America, we have much to thank God for.

(Further explanations about the Australian sights mentioned above: Expo '88 was the World's Fair and was hosted in Brisbane. The Great Barrier Reef, is a large barrier reef off the coast of northeastern Australia and is visited by people from all over the world, due to its uniqueness. The Hopevale Mission is an aboriginal mission in Northeastern Australia, where missionaries are still sent. Aborigines were the people living in Australia before the white people arrived.)

We look forward to hearing from all of you again and hope this finds all good your way. The Lord's richest blessings be with you in 1989.

With love in Christ,
Ray, Eunice, Paula, Charla Hausler

P.S. Some other events from 1988 included: Ray's 50th birthday on May 18, celebrated with a dinner at the school basement in New Minden. Many came from Lincoln, as well as missionary friends. It was an exciting time of fellowship and fun. And during September, Herman Kanning and his wife Louise, Wilhelm and Marianne Suedemeyer, and William Kopper, all from Minden, Germany, visited and stayed with the Hausler's. Louise and Wilhelm were cousins of Eunice's father.

Christmas 1989

Dear Relatives and Friends,

Everywhere there is a lot of excitement as Christmas draws near. In school the children's eyes take on a special sparkle. In Europe there is great excitement as country after country opens the way to more freedom. All this draws us to get a glimpse into the real freedom we know in the Baby Jesus, our Savior, who took away the real bondage that confines us – our sins. As the doors open, let us proclaim this real message of freedom so that people everywhere, from our families onward, will be able to hear this glorious message. Only as the Holy Spirit works in our hearts through the Word of God can we know real peace, joy, and freedom. God grant it to all people everywhere!

It is always a thrill to hear from all of you and your happenings – so we shall highlight a few of ours from the past year. The time has flown by all too quickly.

Ray continues to enjoy his work. He bowls one evening a week on the Farmers State Bank team and enjoys that. He also still does carpentry work on Saturday for a local farmer.

Eunice took several seminars and a Manipulative Mathematics course this past summer to keep up with changes in education. She's always wishing there was more time to read. She and Ray are still in the church choir and serve on the Evangelism Committee.

Paula is an Architecture student at the University of Illinois. This is a five year course so she has one more year after this school year. She works as a waitress also and keeps very busy. Many late hours are spent in her studio, designing and building in miniature. She and Charla played their violins at many weddings during the year.

Charla is a Mathematics student at the University of Illinois. She will complete her Bachelor's degree next school year. She plans to teach in High School. She also works as a waitress and is kept very busy. She was in her good friend, Karen Bree's wedding last December and this was a highlight. She also went on a skiing trip to Nevada with classmates in January.

Some highlights of the year were: Paula and Charla attended the Foundation of Economic Education seminar in New York in April, and it was a helpful experience. While they were out that way they flew down and enjoyed a stay with their Aunt Betty, Uncle Roger and Ann Marie in Annapolis, Maryland. While there, they got to spend a day in Washington D.C. They also attended the Youth Gathering in Denver, Colorado, in August. It was an uplifting experience. 17,000 youth were there from the Lutheran Church-Mo. Synod in the US and other countries.

Ray and Eunice vacationed for a week in the next state, Missouri, in July. There is beautiful countryside down in the Ozarks. They attended the wedding of Joel and Lisa Rivers in June, in St. Louis. It was especially exciting since they had not seen the Rivers family since New Guinea days. Also in June the Gerry Schmeling family stopped in and stayed with us for a night. This was a thrill too since we had not seen them since we were back in the US. (Both the Rivers and Schmelings were on our staff at St. Paul's High School, PNG). We also attended a wedding of our Vietnamese friends, Mary and Peter Ngo in Houston, Texas in October. Mary's family was adopted from Viet Nam, by our congregation when we were in Lincoln, Illinois, and they have become very dear friends. We were treated royally while we were with them. The wedding was very beautiful combining the church ceremony at Beautiful Savior Lutheran Church and Vietnamese traditions.

May you all enjoy a really happy Christmas in Jesus, our Savior and a Blessed 1990.

With love in Christ,
Ray, Eunice, Paula & Charla Hausler

Chapter 5

The 1990's

Christmas 1990

Dear Relatives and Friends,

Greetings to you and wishes for a very Blessed and Happy Christmas! Once again we pray the joy and freedom from sin that came to us via the baby Jesus born in Bethlehem will be yours as you claim them by faith. With all the turmoil in this world it is good to know we have a loving and wonderful God who is in control and working it all out.

1990 has gone by so quickly. We all stayed well during the year. In addition to work, Ray teaches an adult Bible Class every Sunday and bowls on a Men's League every Friday P.M. We made many trips up to Champaign, Illinois, where our girls are in college this past year. We travelled to Detroit, Michigan, in April for our godchild's confirmation. It was a beautiful trip. Later in June, Matrina Hiler and her mother visited us. (Pastor Hiler was our pastor in Delavan, IL). We had such a good time and so happy to know her better. Also in June our good friend, Ruth Pitney, and her son and family visited us. We hadn't seen them for a long while. In June, Eunice's sister Wilma, had surgery for breast cancer so this took a lot of Eunice's time as she lives alone and needed someone to care for her. In early August, Eunice, Paula, and Aunt Wilma, flew to Phoenix, Arizona, for our nephew, Patrick Thusius's wedding. He's a navigator in the Air Force and stationed in Phoenix. While there we got to visit with our good friends

Gerry, Callie and Wendi Hauptli. We had gotten to know them when we lived in Delavan, Illinois. In September we attended the wedding of Anna Durdle in Delavan, Illinois and Beth Behm in Lincoln, Illinois. Besides enjoying the beautiful weddings, we had a reunion with friends whom we had not seen for several years.

Eunice has nineteen first graders and seven second graders this year, so keeps busy.

Paula is a fifth year student in Architecture at the University of Illinois. She plans to graduate May 1991. She works hard and puts in a lot of late nights designing and building models. She also still works as a waitress on weekends.

Charla is a 4th year student and studying Math. Eunice visited her classes one day and was completely lost. She works hard also and will be student teaching at Mohammed, Illinois next semester. If all goes well, she also will graduate in May.

We are looking forward to having them home for Thanksgiving and Christmas. We plan to take a trip south at Christmas, God-willing, possibly Louisiana or Texas.

We pray this finds all good your way and wish you God's blessings in 1991.

Love in Christ,
Ray, Eunice, Paula & Charla Hausler

1966 1991
Please join our family
On this joyous occasion
When our parents
Mr. and Mrs. Ray Hausler
Celebrate twenty-five years of marriage
At a Buffet Reception in their honor
On Sunday, the twenty-fourth of November
Nineteen hundred and ninety-one
At twelve-thirty in the afternoon

Trinity Lutheran Parish Hall
Hoffman, Illinois

Christmas 1991

Dear Relatives and Friends,

Greetings to you at this Blessed Season of the year. We rejoice that Jesus, our Savior from sin, death and the power of the devil was willing to come down to this earth of sorrow and pain and take our place, and save us. As we celebrate this joy this Christmas may our faith deepen in our Lord and Savior.

It was been a busy year and has flown by all too quickly. We are happy in our work and continue to be thankful for our jobs. Many opportunities for witnessing for our Lord are possible as we work. Eunice still keeps very busy on the District Evangelism Board as chair-person also. Ray ten pin bowls on Friday evenings and we have gotten a few evenings of square dancing in which we find good exercise. We also have been caring for Steve Dao, who is at Rose-Hullman University in Terre Haute, Indiana. He is the son of the family our church in Lincoln, IL., sponsored from Vietnam. He is a very good student.

Paula is still in Champaign, Il. She graduated in May with a Degree in Architecture. She is working for an architect, taking some graduate courses, and doing some waitress work. So, she is busy as ever. She was in two of her friends weddings this summer which she enjoyed.

Charla is still in Champaign also. She also graduated in May, but had to take a few courses to get her diploma. She has her Degree in Mathematics. She is doing waitress work at present but hopes to land a teaching job soon. She also was in a friend's wedding this summer and played her flute at another one. She is hoping to get back into music via an orchestra, etc.

Ray and Eunice celebrated their 25th wedding anniversary on November 24. It was a glorious day and much to praise and thank God for. We had Ray's sister, Thora, from Australia here, Janice Schubert our bridesmaid from Australia, and Kapa Yaka, a New Guinean student who sang at our wedding 25 years ago. He is now a representative from PNG to the United Nations in New York. Many other missionary friends and friends from congregations we've been with were here. It was so exciting! Our best man, Dick Adler, did a fabulous job as Master of Ceremonies. He and his wife Loretta had gotten many replies from our missionary friends who were in New Guinea with us when we were married. The book of memories is a treasure. Paula and Charla, with Aunt Thora, Scott Price, and Kristy Giffey (friends of the girls) did a skit on our lives. It was a lot of fun. With the help of many friends and students from Hoffman the day went very smoothly, a treasure of memories for the rest of our lives.

We pray this finds you and yours well and happy in Jesus. His rich blessings be with you always

In our Savior's name,
Ray, Eunice, Paula, Charla Hausler

Christmas 1992

Dear Relatives and Friends,

Greetings to you at this Blessed time of the Year! The joy of our Savior's birth, which was the beginning of His saving us from our sins and eternal death is always a very special time of year. We pray the real joy of Christmas will be with you and yours this Blessed Christmastime.

This year our greetings will be a little late as it has been a very busy yet happy time for us. Our daughter, Paula, was married to Scott Price on December 12. They were married here in New Minden so a lot of the arrangements were left to us to carry out. It was a Christmas wedding. The church was beautifully decorated and their colors were emerald green and ruby. They had a lovely day, filled with sun-

shine and the temperature near 50 degrees. Rev. James Herzog, who married us in New Guinea 26 years ago also had the message at their wedding. The wedding was at 5:30 P.M. in candlelight. We opened gifts the next day and then they left on their honeymoon to Aruba, an island in the Caribbean. Paula works as an architect for Matoocha Associates in Clarendon Hills, Illinois, and Scott is a photographer for the DuKane Company in St. Charles. Illinois. They will live in Oak Park, IL until April 1, and then in the St. Charles, Illinois area. This is just west of Chicago. Special guests at the wedding were Thora Hausler (Ray's sister), Kapaa and Levinia Yaka and son, Jordan, from New Guinea and now at the U. N., also the Cheng family from Houston, Texas, and our nephew, Patrick Thusius and his family from North Carolina. Patrick is in the Air Force.

Charla was maid of honor for her sister. She is still in Champaign, IL, and assistant manager of the Roundbarn, a nice restaurant. She wants to look for other work in the New Year.

Ray keeps very busy with outside activities as well. He still works on construction on Saturdays and bowls on a Men's League on Friday night. We also have taken up square-dancing which is good exercise. We're still learning. He's also busy at church and is the Bible Study teacher plus other jobs.

Eunice is still on the District Evangelism Board and Board of Directors – all of which take extra time.

We have done short trips to get away occasionally. We went to Branson, Missouri, and Greenspring, Wisconsin. Both interesting and fun places to visit. Greenspring, has the House on the Rock, and school and home of Frank Lloyd Wright. This interested us since Paula is in architecture.

Ray's sister, Thora, came out from Australia on November 9, 1992, and will stay until January 16. We enjoy her so much and she's been a great help during this time. We took her to Branson, Missouri, this weekend to see the Shoji Tabuchi Christmas Show. It was just beautiful and made Christmas so meaningful. If you ever get a chance to go to Branson, be sure to see this show. He mixes country music with a lot of other music. He's a superb violinist.

We pray this finds all good your way. God bless you all richly and keep you in His loving care in 1993. In Him alone is life, hope, peace, and joy.

With love in Christ,
Ray, Eunice & Charla Hausler

December 4, 1993

Dear Relatives and Friends,

Greetings to you all at this Blessed Christmastime! It is such a beautiful time of the year as we contemplate our Savior's wonderful birth – and to think He gave up His glorious home in heaven to come down and take our place so we could forever enjoy life with Him here on earth and hereafter in His beautiful home in heaven. As we keep Jesus before our eyes – life takes on real meaning and all our cares and trials become stepping stones to a closer life with Jesus. May this peace and joy Jesus brought us be yours and fill you in 1994 and always.

Ray and Eunice are still in Hoyleton. Ray continues to find his work challenging. He also still ten-pin bowls on Friday evenings. He's getting good at it. He and Eunice still enjoy square dancing when they can find an evening free.

Eunice has added the responsibility of being principal this year. It's kept days and evenings very busy. She is also still chairman of the District Board of Evangelism. This has added to responsibilities as we had a District Great Commission convocation, Witness Workshops and Dialog-Evangelism Clinics.

Scott and Paula live in St. Charles, IL near Chicago. It is about a 5 ½ hour drive from here. It's always very special when we can be with them. Scott still works for the DuKane company as a photographer. Paula finally is settled in with an architect firm in St. Charles. She was laid off at Matoocha Architects as they didn't have enough work. She worked as a retail person and also as chief cook for a while but was really glad to get back into architecture. Fozzy, their dog is still very much a part of their lives. They were with us for Thanksgiving.

Charla still lives in Champaign, IL. She worked as a manager of a restaurant this year and did substitute teaching. She decided to move to Australia in August and then had a physical and a lump was found in her throat. She finally had surgery in October and several lumps were found but all were benign so we thank and praise God for His mercy and blessings. She is still contemplating teaching in Australia or China this next year so we'll let the Lord lead her. She lives with a family who are avid hunters, so they taught her to shoot a gun and she shot her first deer, a 1 ½ year old buck during deer season four weeks ago. She was excited.

Our Vietnamese friends were with us in May. We still take special care of Steve, their son, who is at Rose-Hulman Institute of Technology at Terre Haute, Indiana. We enjoy the visits with this family.

We were happy to have Arthur and Wilma Schloss, from Australia, with us in August. God-willing Ray and Eunice with some of our friends plan to visit Australia next July 1994.

We wish you and yours a very Blessed Christmas and look forward to hearing from you again this Christmas. God bless and keep you.

Love in Christ,
Ray and Eunice Hausler

P.S. July went to Minnesota-to visit our friends the Raffs home on the lake, and then Ruth Pitney, and finally to the Schmelings in Minneapolis. Oct. went to Great Commission Convocation, Minneapolis, Minn.

(Postcard: Carins, Australia)

July 7, 1994

Dear Richard and Florence,

Hope all is good your way. We hear it's very hot there still. Has been cool at all the places we've been. We are in Cairns and go to Brisbane tomorrow, then will see Thora and Ray's family. Has been a wonderful trip, show you pictures later.

Love,
Ray and Eunice

Christmas 1994

Dear Relatives and Friends,

Greetings to you at this Blessed and Happy time of the year when we celebrate our Savior's coming to earth to save us from our sins so if we believe in Him we can have the peace and joy He came to bring us. We hear the angel chorus, "Glory to God in the highest and on earth peace, good will to men." Luke 2:14

As another year has swiftly gone by, we thank our wonderful God for endless blessings. The joy of daily food, clothing, health, good family and friends, a place to work are all wonderful blessings we thank God for.

Ray continues to have many challenges at work, but also opportunities to witness. Ray teaches Bible Class at church, is an elder, and still ten pin bowls every week.

Eunice still works as principal and teacher. This leaves very little time for other activities. Even socializing is at a minimum. The job is rewarding and working with 140 students and eleven staff, plus a congregation has its trials and rewards.

Paula and Scott live in Elburn, Illinois, near Chicago. Paula and Charla are in architecture, having started the Caddway Company. They seem challenged and enjoy their work. They both do side jobs to keep the cash flow alive. Paula also sells Mary Kay cosmetics. Scott works as a photographer at the DuKane Company in St. Charles, Illinois.

Charla lives about four blocks from Paula and Scott. The business is in her apartment. She works as a waitress part time and also sells

Mary Kay. Charla is hunting deer this weekend. Alice and Tom Jones, whom she lived with in Champaign, got her interested in hunting. They will all be home for Christmas.

Our big happening this year was our trip to Australia in July. Three couples from here went with us-Wayne & Marlene Maschhoff from Carlyle, IL and Dennis & Carol Knauer, and Dwain & Linda Franz both from Lincoln, IL. We had a wonderful trip. We visited New Zealand, Sydney, Adelaide, Ayers Rock, Alice Springs, Cairns, Brisbane and Toowoomba, Australia and the island of Fiji. We stayed with Ray's sister Thora, the last three weeks and seeing family and friends was wonderful. We also had a wonderful reunion with New Guinea missionaries-our friends-in Adelaide. We saw some of our New Guinea friends in Toowoomba and Brisbane. They are in school there. Our trip was a Brendan Tour and it was excellent. We were treated to the finest Australian hospitality.

Also a highlight was the visit of Eunice's sister, Betty, and her husband, Roger Thusius, after we got home August 1. We hadn't seen them for five years, so it was a good family reunion.

Occasionally we have ex New Guinea staff visit us and this is always a thrill, and we welcome any of you who come our way. Any of you who get near our area are always welcome in our home.

We pray this finds all good your way and we wish you the richness of God's love in Christ. His joy and peace be yours this Christmas and in the New Year – 1995.

Love in Christ,
Ray & Eunice Hausler

Christmas 1995

Dear Relatives and Friends,

This is such a special time of year to greet all of you! How much God loved us! - - so much that He sent His only Son, Jesus, to save us from our sins. If we believe in Him, we will be saved, and the joys of heaven await us. As I work with my little first and second graders for the last time on the Christmas program, their strong faith and beautiful voices are really precious. No wonder Jesus said, "unless you become as little children, you cannot enter the kingdom of heaven." God grant all of you and us a strong childlike faith in Jesus today and all your life long.

It seems again this year has gone by so quickly. Ray enjoys his work and has many opportunities to witness to the boys he works with. He continues to enjoy ten pin bowling on Friday evenings. He also is an elder at church and that keeps him busy with meetings. Next year our congregation will celebrate its 150th anniversary. This has taken a lot of extra meetings.

Eunice continues as principal and teacher. This takes all of her time. This is her last year however. After 40 years she feels it's time to quit. She is very thankful for the interesting and wonderful years the Lord has privileged her to serve Him. Last week the staff and students planted a ginko tree in her honor in front of her window. A beautiful stone plaque was placed under it. May it always be a memorial to praise our living Lord.

Paula and Scott have bought their own home in St. Charles, Illinois. They are happy in it as it is much larger and better set up for having animals. Fozzy is their dog. He looks like an Alaskan huskie. They also have two cats. Paula still works in architecture and has plenty of work. Scott is still working as a photographer for the DuKane Company. They and Charla were here last week for Thanksgiving and we enjoyed being together.

Charla left for Australia last Tuesday. She is visiting Ray's family until February. She was working with Paula but decided to do some traveling. She went deer hunting but no luck getting one this year.

A highlight of our year was visiting sister Betty and family in early July. They live in Annapolis, Maryland. There is a lot to see there and we had a day in Ocean City, on the Atlantic Ocean, also. We spent an evening eating Maryland crabs-and it does take an evening. We enjoyed seeing their son, Patric, and his family at Seymour-Johnson Air Force Base. Patric is a navigator on the F-16. Their daughter, Anne Marie, works for her father in investments.

We saw our good friends, Pastor and Ruth Budke, from New Guinea days, on our way to Maryland in Asheville, North Carolina. We had a great visit and Pastor was leaving for China the next day – teaching English for 6 weeks. Eunice and Ray are hoping to do this sometime soon.

So we wish all of you God's richest blessings in 1996. His peace and joy fill your heart and home!

With our love,
Ray and Eunice Hausler

A Service of Worship and Praise In Honor of
40 Years In The Teaching Ministry
1956-1996
Mrs. Eunice Hausler
Sunday May 19, 1996 9:00 A.M.
Trinity Lutheran Church, Hoffman, IL

"...You gave Your good Spirit to instruct them..." Nehemiah 9:20

In Faithfulness and Dedication to Jesus Christ-Forty Years of Equipping God's Children

The Processional: The First Class and Present Class, Hymn: "Alive In Christ"

We are alive in Christ! He came when we were dead; He broke the chains of Satan's power
And made us His instead; He set us free to serve, We'll serve Him then in love
Until that day when he returns to take us home above.

We are alive in Christ! And when we hear the cry of those abroad and those at home

Whose souls are doomed to die, we'll rally to the call, With willing hearts we'll give
Our gifts, our time, our pray'rs, ourselves, So dying souls might live.

We are alive in Christ, Our Teacher, who has said, "Go feed My lambs and feed My sheep
With richer food than bread;" We'll build and staff our schools and train a chosen band
To take the living Bread of Life Through ev'ry hungry land.

We are alive in Christ! Our numbers grow each hour, and arm in arm we'll march with Him
Protected by His power; We'll work while it is day, we'll turn the world around,
Our battle cry, "Alive in Christ," Will everywhere resound!

Invocation

P: This day we as members of God's Kingdom acknowledge the commitment, the faithfulness, and Service of Mrs. Eunice Hausler in the teaching ministry of equipping God's children. You have been blessed with His gifts and equipped with skills to carry out His work among His people. Yes, there were challenges, opportunities, but what a wonderful privilege! God has opened doors of mission for you through the Gospel and you have opened doors for others in the Spirit of Jesus.

C: We thank you, Eunice, for the gifts of faith, goodness, knowledge, self-control, perseverance, patience, godliness, kindness, and love. May we continue to faithfully encourage our children to read and study God's Word, to learn about His forgiveness, renewal, and redirection through the suffering, death, and resurrection of our Savior Jesus Christ. May the power of the Holy Spirit cause our children to desire always the pure, spiritual milk of the Bible, so that they may grow toward Salvation in Jesus Name.

P: God has supported you, strengthened you, blessed you. By His Holy Spirit you have been an example of faithful devotion to His Word and a blessing to many.

C: May the Lord keep you from all harm – He will watch over your life. The Lord will watch over your coming and going both now and forevermore. Amen.

Solo: "Seek Ye First"..Lisa Garland

Trinity Lutheran Children:
"The Butterfly Song"..K thru 4
"His Banner Over Me Is Love"................................K thru 4
"Celebrate"...K thru 8

Teaching and Wisdom

P: Hear, O Israel: The Lord our God, the Lord is one. Love the Lord your God with all your heart and with all your soul and with all your strength. These commandments that I give you today are to be upon your hearts. Impress them on your children. Talk about them when you sit at home and when you walk along the road, when you lie down and when you get up. Tie them as symbols on your hands and bind them on your foreheads. Deuteronomy 6:4-8

C: "Believe in the Lord Jesus, and you will be saved – you and your household." Acts 16: 31

P: Instruct a wise man and he will be wiser still; teach a righteous man and he will add to his learning. "The fear of the Lord is the beginning of wisdom, and knowledge of the Holy One is understanding." Proverbs 9: 9-10

C: "Get wisdom, get understanding; do not forget my words or swerve from them. Do not forsake wisdom, and she will protect you; love her, and she will watch over you. Wisdom is supreme;

therefore, get wisdom. Though it cost all you have, get understanding." Prov: 4:5-7

P: "He guides the humble in what is right and teaches them His way." Psalms 25: 9

C: "All the ways of the Lord are loving and faithful for those who keep the demands of His covenant." Psalm 25:10

P: When Jesus had finished saying these things, the crowds were amazed at His teaching, because He taught as one who had authority, and not as their teachers of the law. Matthew 7:28-29

C: "All this I have spoken while still with you. But the counselor, the Holy Spirit, whom the Father will send in my name, will teach you all things and will remind you of everything I have said to you." John 14: 25-26

P: "Peace I leave with you; My peace I give you. I do not give to you as the world gives. Do not let your hearts be troubled and do not be afraid." John 14: 27

C: So then, just as you received Christ Jesus as Lord, continue to live in Him, rooted and built up in Him, strengthened in the faith as you were taught, and overflowing with thankfulness. Colossians 2: 6-7

P: Teach me to do Your will, for You are my God; may Your good Spirit lead me on level ground. Psalm 143:10

C: All Scripture is God-breathed and is useful for teaching, rebuking, correcting, and training in righteousness, so that the man of God may be thoroughly equipped for every good work. 2 Timothy 3: 16-17

P: Show me your ways, O Lord, teach me Your paths; Psalm 25: 4

C: Guide me in Your truth and teach me, for You are God my Savior, and my hope is in You all day long. Psalm 25: 5

ALL: They replied, "Believe in the Lord Jesus, and you will be saved – you and your household. Acts 16: 31

Hymn of Praise: "Children of the Heavenly Father"

Children of the heav'nly Father Safely in His bosom gather'
Nestling bird nor star in heaven Such a refuge e'er was given.

God His own doth tend and nourish; In His holy courts they flourish.
From all evil things He spares them, In His mighty arms He bears them.

Neither life nor death shall ever, From the Lord His children sever,
Unto them His grace He showeth, and their sorrows all He knoweth.

Tho' He giveth or He taketh, God His children ne'er forsaketh,
His the loving purpose solely To preserve them pure and holy.

We Share God's Word
Romans 12: 4-8
I Peter 4: 8-11
John 21: 15-17

Congregation Hymn – "What a Friend We Have In Jesus"
The Sermon Message..............................Rev. James M. Herzog
(Including here, the text of the sermon he shared)

(LESSON PLAN for Sunday, May 19, 1996)

WHAT A BLESSED FRIEND WE HAVE IN EUNICE

(The Cause and Effect of true Happiness)

Matthew 5: 3-16

INTRODUCTION

Her friendship with Jesus, and what it really means. How it helped me in New Guinea, and still does.

The Beatitudes (Actually, "A" attitudes) of Jesus...see text.

What they mean to Eunice when she meditates on them:

How blessed you are because you have let Me humble you and keep you humbly dependent on Me all your life. The result is that the Holy Spirit is ruling more and more over every part of your life.

How blessed you are because you have let Me cause you to mourn and grieve and suffer the anguish of your soul. The result is that you are finding true comfort and satisfaction in the incredible amount of spiritual things you're accomplishing thereby.

How blessed you are because you have let Me keep you meek and lowly instead of become pushy and wealthy and endowed with lots of clout. The result is that now you are discovering that the whole world belongs to you and is eating out of your hand!

How blessed you are because you have let Me cause you to desire above all else to be fair and good like your Master. The result is that you are becoming more and more content, free of coveting anyone or anything.

How blessed you are because you have let Me make you be kind and merciful instead of harsh and vindictive. the result is that the people whose lives you touch are increasingly treating you far better than you feel you deserve.

How blessed you are because, in spite of your many sins and total unworthiness, you have let Me keep you from ever doubting the blood atonement I made on the cross for you and all mankind. The result is that you are able to experience My loving presence, and enjoy intimate communion and friendship with Me more and more each passing day.

How blessed you are because you let Me use you as one who always gets caught in between. The result is that you are becoming known more and more as a unifier, a settler of disputes and arguments, a mender of relationships, a daughter of the great Peacemaker above.

How blessed you are because you let Me teach you that being persecuted (and hated and hounded and accused for no reason except that you belong to Me) is all part of being a victorious and a successful Christian. The result is that you know what it means to reign with Me in the power of love.

Dear Eunice,

Let's examine a little more closely the cause and effects of true blessedness (happiness) according to Christ's sermon on the Mount:

The Cause

Jesus says:

"You have let Me conquer you. You have let Me have My own way with you. You have yielded and surrendered …

…to the way I am humbling you, the way I am tugging you to depend only on Me in spite of your sins and the awful waves that threaten to destroy you;

…to the way I acquaint you with bitter grief, and soul-wrenching anguish;

…to the way I mould and shape you through adversity to become meek and lowly and full of faith in the face of the impossible;

…to the way I starve you into a deep, ravenous hunger for becoming more and more like Me;

…to the way I chisel and sand away the rough edges of your personality;

…to the way I encourage you to trust only in the Atonement while facing your own judgment as a totally depraved and absolutely helpless sinner of the worst kind;

…to the way I often let you get caught in the middle between two warring factions;

…to the way I train you to make unjust punishment and persecution work for the more rapid and more effective spread of the Gospel."

The Effect

Jesus says:

"The effect of your surrender and yieldedness to Me is that

The people gathered here to honor you today see what you are really like even on days when
you yourself wonder if you're going backward instead of forward in your friendship and companionship with Me. They see that…

…the Holy Spirit is ruling more and more over every part of your life;

…you are satisfied and content with a life that included more than your share of suffering and agony, because of the things God accomplished by the anguish of your soul;

…the whole world belongs to you, and that, in spite of your frequent feelings to the contrary, more and more people, especially the children and parents whose lives you touched, are looking to you for inspiration and spiritual help;

…you have learned to be content in all circumstances;

…a deep sense of gratitude has replaced all bitter feeling of loss and of being treated unfairly;

…no matter how bad things get, you always act as if its never as bad as you really deserve;

…you are increasingly able to experience My loving presence, and to enjoy intimate communion and friendship with Me more and more each passing day;

…you are becoming more and more effective in bringing others into friendship with Me and with each other;

...and they are beginning to realize what it means to reign with Christ by the power of love, because they see you doing it!"

Conclusion

That's about everything our Friend, Jesus, promised us in this life – and you've got it, Eunice. And think of what all will still come to you in the life to come!

I know you are over-flowing with joy and happiness today because of the wonderful love and appreciation that is being shown you. But in the light of what still lies ahead (knowing what we know about your close friendship with the Lord), we already know you will be acting as if you are really blessed by God, even on those days when you will be tempted by Satan to be afraid of failure, or to feel sorry for yourself!

Remember, your life as a teacher for Jesus isn't over today – it has only just begun! And when it is finally over, and you have your next retirement party up in heaven, we'll all be there with you (and some of us will be there because of you). Jesus will be the guest speaker, and you'll hear Him say what all of us will be thinking:

"What a blessed friend I have in Eunice"

The Prayers of the Church

The Gathering of our Offering and Gifts

Offertory: (Trinity Lutheran School Children)
"We Are Brothers and Sisters in Christ"..............Grades 5 thru 8

-The Sacrament of Holy Communion -

"This is the Feast of Victory"

The Words of Institution and The Lord's Prayer

Distribution Hymns:
Duet: "Jesus Loves Me"
"I Love to Tell the Story"

I love to tell the story, Of unseen things above, Of Jesus and His glory, Of Jesus and His love.
I love to tell the story Because I know 'tis true; It satisfies my longings As nothing else can do.

Refrain: I love to tell the story, 'Twill be my theme in glory, To tell the old, old story of Jesus and His love.

I love to tell the story, More wonderful it seems Then all the golden fancies Of all our golden dreams.
I love to tell the story, It did so much for me; And that is just the reason I tell it now to thee.

Refrain

I love to tell the story, "Tis pleasant to repeat What seems, each time I tell it, More wonderfully sweet.
I love to tell the story, For some have never heard The message of salvation From God's own Holy Word.

Refrain

I love to tell the story, For those who know it best, Seen hungering and thirsting To hear it like the rest.
And when, in scenes of glory, I sing the new, new song, "Twill be the old, old story That I have loved so long.

Refrain

The Thanksgiving and the Blessing
Closing Hymn: "God Bless our Schools" (Tune of "God Bless Our Native Land")

Our Father tis to thee, We bring our earnest pleas;
God bless our school!

Thy saving Word is here, Fill us with holy fear, Make this a place most dear;
God bless our school!

Our Savior from above, Guide us with tender love, Our Lutheran School.
Help us Thy work to do, Teach us to e'er be true, Our number large or few,
God bless our school!

Spirit of God so dear, Our guide and comforter Rule in our school!
Here purify each heart, Faith, love, and hope impart, Our Sanctifier Thou art;
God bless our school!

Following the Worship Service, a Reception followed in the school gymnasium.

Agenda for the Retirement Dinner—Eunice Hausler

Directions for the Dinner

Table Prayer: Sung be everyone and led by Ruth Boehne. (Words were at each person's place setting).
Potluck Dinner
Recognition of Guests

- Family members
- Visiting Pastors
- Previous Faculty

- Anyone from Levittown, PA
- Anyone from Lincoln, IL
- Anyone knowing Eunice from PNG
- Anyone that has been a student of Eunice's-past or present

Music by the first and second grade class of 1973 (Eunice's first class at Hoffman)
Sharing Letters

- Rev. Kuhn, LCMS
- Dan Roth, Southern IL Dist. – LCMS
- Anyone who would like to say something (Pastor Herzog?)

Music by the Junior Choir
Special Presentations:

- President of Trinity Lutheran Congregation—Neal Michael
- Faculty—Steve Keiser
- Board of Christian Education—Keith Meier
- Class of 73—Lisa Garland
- On behalf of the students at Hoffman—Ruth Boehne
- PTL—Mike Luebbers
- Retirement committee presentation

Comments by Eunice
Closing prayer-Sung by all and led by Ruth Boehne

May 19, 1996

Dear Eunice,

It is with great joy that I and many others on this day give very special thanks to our loving God for you. I am reminded for St. Paul's letter to the Philippians where he writes in one of the early verses, I thank my

God for every remembrance of you. You indeed are one of those individuals about whom Caesar gave warning, Beware of him of whom everyone speaks well. You are and have been an example to the flock, the picture of Christian love and concern, one about whom almost everyone speaks well, and one for whom I give much thanks to God.

On this special day as the saints at Trinity gather together to celebrate 40 years of teaching ministry, I join with them in spirit, and in addition to giving thanks to God, I also give thanks to you for your life, your love and for your service given to various parts of the flock of The Lutheran Church—Missouri Synod. Your efforts have always been above and beyond the call of duty, the giving of that last bit of effort to make sure the task is done well, and the overriding determination that the whole matter be done to the glory of God. What an example! Again, many thanks to you for what you have done for Him and those in His kingdom.

As you begin a new chapter in your life, I pray that you and Ray will have the opportunity to do some of the things you have not had time to do before, and do those things at a pace that will be more restful and relaxing.

May our gracious God continue always to surround you with His love and care.

Your friend in Christ,
Robert T. Kuhn,
First Vice-President, The LCMS

June 26, 1996

Dear Pastor Kuhn,

Just a very sincere thank you for the very special letter you sent and which was read at my Retirement Dinner. I really appreciate your kind words.

We are indeed grateful that the Lord in His mercy has let us work in a special way for Him. He really did the work through us so to Him all praise and glory.

I'm sure you feel the same way – as the Lord has and is using you in so many special ways. Our prayers remember you daily as you lead our LCMS forward in difficult times.

God bless you and your family richly and keep you safe in His loving care.

Love in Christ,
Eunice and Ray Hausler

May 1, 1996

Dear Eunice,

It is with great pleasure that I take this opportunity to write you upon your retirement from the teaching ministry in The LCMS. I am sorry that I can't attend this celebration as I will be out of town.

Forty of anything is quite a bunch! Forty years was enough wilderness wander for Israel. Forty days was enough to put a shine on Moses' face. Forty years of ministry is also a large chunk of time. You and the church, have much reason for praise and celebration!

Your forty years has taken you to Colorado, Pennsylvania, New Guinea, and Illinois. During those forty years you have touched the lives of hundreds of children, their parents, Board of Education members, congregational members, and fellow teachers. You have planted many seeds and during these forty years I'm sure you have seen germination too. What a privilege that has been for you.

You have also served well at the District level. You have been a member of the District Board of Evangelism and the Board of Director's. I appreciate the effort and excellent work you have done on behalf of the Southern Illinois District.

For the future – well, that too is in God's hands. I pray it will be a future filled with rewarding experience, overflowing with divine blessings, and clearly charted by God's good and gracious will for you. Then the days ahead will also be days of praise and celebration.

God be with you and Ray!

Yours in Christ,
Daniel C. Roth, Executive Assistant
Southern Illinois District, LCMS

June 26, 1996

Dear Dan,

Just a special Thank You for the letter you sent on my Retirement Sunday. It was much appreciated. The Lord has indeed been good – and worked through me. To Him all praise and glory. It's been a privilege.

I also want to inform you that I will be teaching Grade 2 at Trinity-St. John, Nashville, IL next year for Mrs. Lange who wants a year off as she has a new baby. Only one grade and fourteen children – I thought I could still handle that. Have never taught just one grade. I haven't signed anything yet but it's all been verbal as they have their meeting in July. So it won't be official till August when I return from China – but I thought you should know.

Stephen Keiser is taking over the helm very well here at Hoffman. I know he'll do very well. God will supply his every need.

Thank you for all you have done to help me and our school over the years. I have really appreciated it – you were always so helpful. The Lord is using you also in many ways to extend His kingdom. His rich blessings continue to be with you and may He continue to give you His wisdom and strength.

In our Savior's service,
Eunice Hausler

May 7, 1996

My dear Eunice,

I'm so sorry I'm not going to be able to be with you for your special celebration of 40 years in Christian education. My goodness! What an accomplishment, and what a blessing you have been these 40 years for many, many souls, young and old! "Serve the Lord with gladness;" that you have surely done.

I think of you often and remember our first meeting at Hope, Levittown, Pa., in 1956. You were our first called teacher, and all we had to offer you was an empty basement and several little boys and girls waiting to learn about Jesus and His love. But you met the challenge and by opening day of school you were ready and waiting to begin the task.

We had many good times and bad times, fun times and sad times, but you were an inspiration to all of us by your sincere faith, dedication, energy and efficiency in serving the Lord at every opportunity.

And then came your Call to New Guinea; an undertaking that scared me half to death! But you weren't afraid; you were only concerned about getting your books over there! Again, the Lord blessed your efforts for 13 more years, and look what you brought back home with you: a wonderful Australian husband and two beautiful little girls! Amen!

Our sincere love and best wishes are yours as you now enter your retirement era of life. May the Lord bless you and Ray abundantly, and keep you in His love and care always!

Love,
Ruth Pitney

May 13, 1996

Dear Eunice,

Loretta and I send you our warmest greetings and heartfelt congratulations on this very special day. We wish we could be with you to share in this important event. Unfortunately, our eighth graders are being confirmed during the 10:30 worship service this morning.

We recall with fond memories the two years that we shared with you when we were teaching at Sirunki in the Enga Province of PNG back in the middle 60s. You impacted the lives of your Enga students with your Christ-centered life and your enthusiasm for learning. Your gifts of teaching and making music will long be remembered by all the students you have taught over the past 40 years.

God sends into our lives very special people who become lifelong friends and confidant's, who enlighten us with their outpouring of Christian love, and who are instruments in God's hands for shaping us into more useful vessels for the growth of His kingdom. We are forever grateful that our Lord brought you into our lives those many years ago. We shall always treasure your friendship and the warm hospitality which is a hallmark of your home.

God has blessed you in so many ways so that you might be a blessing to others. And we pray that He may now bless your retirement. May each of your days be filled with unlimited opportunities to continue sharing the wonderful message of salvation through faith in Jesus Christ as Lord and Savior.

Your sister and brother in Christ,
Loretta and Dick Adler
Holy Cross Lutheran School, St. Louis

To Eunice on May 19, 1996

Norma and I regret that we are unable to be with you for your retirement celebration. Previous plans were made for us which we were unable to cancel. Our thoughts and prayers are with you.

Although I attended CTC, RF during the time you also attended, I really became acquainted with you and your family in 1973 when we both came to Hoffman, Illinois, to serve as teachers at Trinity Lutheran School.

It was my pleasure to have you as a colleague for 14 years here at Trinity. Your cooperation to me as principal was wonderful, A+ style, you could say. Also, your untiring efforts on behalf of Christian Education at Trinity has been outstanding. You have guided and nourished the minds and hearts of many little ones in the lower grades of our school for many years. You have used your God-given talents and abilities as you have taught children the real meaning of life and of the love of Jesus for them. You have set an outstanding example and have been an inspiration to all of us. We have many pleasant memories of you and your service at Trinity Lutheran School, Hoffman.

We appreciate the friendship that we have had with you and Ray these many years. Pleasant memories fill our hearts when we think of the times that we have spent together. It has been our gain to have such friends as you and Ray, and we thank God for this. We hope that this friendship will be the same in the future.

And now, as you retire, may God our Gracious Heavenly Father continue to watch over you, and keep you in His loving care.

Sincerely in His service,
Ray and Norma Richert
Sorry! We couldn't make it today.

(Form Letter)
(Across the heading, picture of Jesus blessing the little children and two hearts—Jesus loves me! —Jesus loves you!)

Dear ______________

Sunday, May 19, 1996, was such a beautiful day. The beautiful A.M. service was so impressive and lots of praise to our God who made it all possible. Those who worked on putting the service together did a very thoughtful and uplifting job. As several people said, a taste of heaven.

The delicious potluck meal was scrumptious. So many people being there made me feel very humble but I loved seeing each one. Many of you could not be there – but I wish you could have; it was so beautiful. I know how it is, however, as we often have conflicts. The pictures, the program, and all the gifts were all more than I ever dreamt of. My heart overflows with deep thanks to each and everyone. May God bless you all richly.

I am very busy, finishing at school and getting ready to go to China, July 4, God-willing. Keep me in your prayers that God will open many opportunities to witness for Him. I'll be happy to share with you when I return.

I will add a personal note but had to do this much as a form letter in order to get a thank you to all of you.

Again, a million thanks for everything.

In our Savior's service

(Art-female on knees praying beside bed, with the words:" Thank You, Lord")

With love in Christ,
Eunice A. Hausler

Christmas 1996

Dear Relatives and Friends,

Greetings to you at this Blessed time of year as we celebrate our Savior's birthday. Praise God that He loved us so much that He sent His only Son, Jesus, to save us from our sins. Because Jesus was willing to die for us on the cross and save us from our sins, we are grateful. He died on the cross and rose again the third day and returned again to heaven. He is preparing a place for us and will come to take us home to the mansions above when His time has it planned. Each year brings us closer to that great reunion with Him in the skies. "Even so come quickly, Lord Jesus." Revelation 20:20

This has been another busy year for us. It has gone very quickly. Ray has been busy working at CCC . It saddens us to see the numbers there continue to grow. He has also been busy remodeling our basement. It will be very nice and will have a kitchen, store closets, and bookshelves. He worked on it a lot while Eunice was in China. He has also been very busy as Senior elder in our church. We celebrated our 150th anniversary this year and had many special services and occasions. He also does some carpentry work on Saturdays for a friend. Then he also does a lot of work for Eunice in her classroom at school. He also has done a lot of cooking as Eunice spent many hours at school while she was principal. It was a real joy when his good friend, Roy Weier and wife Shirley, visited us from Australia in May.

Eunice was principal and teacher until June 30, 1996. She then retired after 41 years of teaching/principalling at various times during those years in Lutheran Schools. The congregation at Hoffman had a wonderful retirement day for her May 19, 1996. Many surprises occurred on that day and many wonderful remembrances from many wonderful people. She praises the Lord for letting her serve Him all these years. Then July 4, 1996, she left for China for five weeks to teach English to teachers. This was a most exciting and adventurous experience. The people in China were wonderful to us. If you want the experience of your life this would be wonderful to do. Many teachers are needed again the summer of 1997, and also for two years and three years of service. There were 32 teachers from our church and altogether 90 teachers from other churches. We went out in teams of four. We were in Yongan, Fujian Province. It was beautiful there. The teachers were very excited about learning conversational English better so they can teach their students. We made wonderful friendships, and there were lots of hugs and tears when we had to leave. Then Eunice got home August 12, and on August 19 started teaching Grade 2, at Trinity-St. John Lutheran School, Nashville, Illinois. This was not planned but they needed a teacher for a year, as one of their teachers had a baby and wanted a year off. So she postponed retirement for a year. She does love teaching so this is a good unwinding year. Then the two of us are looking forward to a less hectic life style after June 1997.

Paul and Scott Price are doing fine. They live in St. Charles, Illinois. Scott works as a photographer at DuKane Company. He likes his work. Paula works as an architect for an engineer in Aurora, Illinois. She also does some work on her own. They are busy but we enjoy our visits when we can get together. Fozzy, their Samoyed, is still a great part of their life. They will come down Thanksgiving weekend and we are all travelling to Branson, Missouri, together. We will celebrate our 30th wedding anniversary. It will be good to all be together. Charla and her friend Russell Englebretsen, will also go with us.

Charla is living in Champaign, Illinois. She works for Time-Warner Company and also works for the University of Illinois as a computer analyst in the evening. She likes her work but is making plans to enter law school, September 1997. She had a wonderful trip to Australia last December, January and February. Ray's family and many of our friends were wonderful to her and she enjoyed every minute. She and Aunt Thora had a wonderful bus trip to Canberra, Melbourne, Adelaide and back to Toowoomba and Brisbane.

We hope you have all had a wonderful year and wish you all a very Happy and Blessed Year in our Savior, Jesus, in 1997.

With our love in Christ,
Ray and Eunice Hausler

January 18, 1997

Dear Eunice and Ray,

What a blessing it is to be such an integral part of your lives in spite of the fact that we have been living in widely separated parts of the country much of our lives. Such bonds of fellowship in Christ is one of the most portent proofs that Christ really is alive in us and that we share in His one and only Holy Spirit.

My surgery went fine, but the recuperation is going to take its own sweet time, I'm afraid. Chronic back pains plague me, and I have to work hard to make myself exercise and try to regain proper muscle tone. Unfortunately, my appetite is great and so I'm really fighting those spare pounds, too. Keep me in your prayers, that I will not give in to the desire to just vegetate on the couch all day and nurse my hurts.

This is the second time physical disability has forced me to retire from the full time parish ministry, only this time without disability benefits. I guess the closer one gets to the Lord, the bigger the challenge to our faith. I'm sure you are experiencing the same. The opposition never gets less, but the wings of faith get stronger and we can soar higher and higher precisely because of how high and deep the "peck peck" gets.

It reminds me of my high school days. I was not very big but was determined to play on the football team anyway. Because I was small and hated pain, I became one of the fastest running backs Killeen High School ever had (all because I hated being tackled.)

I'm really looking forward to Charla's wedding, and I want you to know that I will not take any money for it. It's my wedding gift to her and her husband, to perform the ceremony without charge. I wonder how many pastors are fortunate enough to have joined two generations of the same family in matrimony – all of them. Reckon I can hang on long enough to marry your grandchildren, too? It's possible if they don't wait till they're in their thirties to get married…(like <u>some</u> people I know!).

Well, it's time I got myself out to the park and take my daily constitutional walk. Just wanted to take a moment this morning to let you know how much I appreciate having you two as my friends and spiritual partners. May the Lord keep giving you power and strength, especially when you feel tired, worn out, and weak. When your natural strength and resolve wanes, may your patient trust and constant communion with God renew your strength and cause you to mount up with wings of faith like eagles. May you run the particular race He gives you without becoming weary, and may you walk in His steps without fainting.

One in Christ,
Jim (Rev. Herzog)

(Enclosed with the above letter, Rev. Herzog included his newsletter, a portion of it follows:)

Dear Prayer Partner,

Many of us have proven under fire that our God-given faith in the grace of Christ Jesus is so sure and strong that nothing and no one is able to keep us from practicing communion with God. We have demonstrated through many painful trials that disasters, persecution, poverty, imminent danger, crushing losses, threats of death, allurements of the world, lies and accusations of the spiritual underworld, anxieties about the future, our own guilt-inflamed conscience, sinful deeds and desires – none of these, or anything or anyone yet to come, will ever be able to separate us from loving fellowship and life-changing companionship with the Lord in this world, and perfect communion and ruling partnership with Him in the world to come. In the language of the Bible (Rom. 8:31-39), <u>we are conquerors.</u> Our faith in God's incredible unconditional grace and love has triumphed over every attempt to separate us from intimate friendship with Him, and we are certain that it will continue to do so no matter what happens, not only because it has already kept us thriving in our communion with God against incredible odds of every conceivable kind, but also because it is <u>Christ's</u> faith at work within us. (Eph. 2:8)….

April 21, 1997

Dear Ray and Eunice,

Things are fine here. Betty keeps busy with the ranch apartments, Sam is graduating in August and hopes to get a job with law enforcement, Minne loves her apartment and continues to get better, Jim and Heather (in S. Carolina) are fine, so are the grandkids. The weather has been incredible. The ranch is in full leaf and bloom now. I spend a lot of time out there.

We go to church in Temple (Immanuel) but have not gotten involved in anything else yet because I will soon be on my way up to the Appalachian Mountains. Hope to go by first of May.

My surgery is coming along fine, too. Am regaining a little bit of feeling in my legs, but I still walk wobbly and feel as if I'm going to fall. And two weeks ago, my upper back and neck became so painful I had to go to the doctor with it. Am currently seeing him four times a week for four weeks of special therapy. So far only pain pills have made it bearable. They told me in Houston that I would have to have surgery on that part of the spine, too. Guess they were right.

But, the greater the troubles, the greater and sweeter is the sound of praise from my heart. Many of us hurt more than people ever know. We just mix it with faith and make something good come of it, right?

Betty and I are looking forward to the wedding. Haven't heard from Charla yet, but I'm sure she will get in touch in plenty of time. I will probably be in Kentucky at that time, so I will have to let you know how to contact me there.

I'm including my two latest prayer newsletters. They will bring you up to date on my doings since December when I resigned from Bay City.

Hope this finds you in good health and in fine spirits. I'm praying for you that you will keep on witnessing to what you have yourself actually experienced of Christ's living presence and power at work within you, so that others around you, though they scoff at first, will share the fellowship and joys we have with the Lord.

Love in Christ,
Jim (Rev. Herzog)

(Enclosed with the above letter, Rev. Herzog included two of his newsletters, a portion of each follows:)

OUR GOD REIGNS BY THE POWER OF FORGIVING LOVE

March 1997

Dear Prayer Partner,

Although I have given up my parish ministry in Bay City, my intercessory ministry to God's great congregation at large goes on. Presently I am working from the ranch in Killeen. But soon I'll be looking for new headquarters in the mountains of Appalachia.

In addition to the intercessory work, which involves a great deal of writing and mailing, I hope to be involved in two other enterprises as well, writing the four books I've begun years ago but never finished, and doing volunteer work in reaching out to the poor mountain people in the wilderness of Appalachia.

As my prayer partners, I appeal to you to keep this in your intercessions.

My health is continuing to improve following back surgery in December. But I am still unsteady on my feet, and the numbness has not begun to subside yet. Doctors say it will take months before we know if any of the previous damage can be reversed at all. At least, they say, we caught it in time to avert the wheelchair.

Intercession is the most basic of all kingdom work. Every other form of ministry is dependent on the effectiveness of our prayer relationship with God and with each other. Thank God that HIS partnership with us is in no way disrupted by our sins (because of Christ's universal atonement on the cross). It is my prayer that YOUR and MY prayer partnership with God and each other will also remain intact in spite of our sins and unworthiness (because of our faith in the atonement). It is only when we approach Him with this exclusive trust in His grace that our prayer relationship with the Lord will be effective. The more completely we trust in His blood sacrifice alone, without one shred of reliance on our good works, or one bit of reluctance because of our sins, the more effective our prayer life will be. And when our prayers are flowing daily as they should, all the rest of our kingdom activities will fall into place by the power of the Spirit.

I want to take this opportunity to thank you for being my prayer partner even though I am not physically there with you and your prayer fellowship. My prayer support for you will go on as long the Lord keeps me alive. Of that I can assure you.

Today I am praying in the spirit of Christ to the Father that His name will be honored, His reign extended, and His will be done by everything you do and say, and that even your sins will be made to work for His glory and for our good by the power that raised Him from the dead.

I pray He will give you everything you need for the body and for the soul as the need arises, not so much that you will rely on those gifts, nor so little that you will lose faith in the Giver.

Most of all I pray that forgiveness of yourself and of others will flow from your heart like an ever-flowing spring, making you victorious over every temptation and sin, immune to the full consequences of sins, and fully yielded to the Spirit's leading and guiding in every part of your life.

I will continue to be your prayer partner, daily asking, seeking, and knocking that you may daily receive, find, and enter into the power of walking with God and doing as He would do, proving to the world that our God reigns!

Your partner in the ministry of intercession,
Jim Herzog

MY CUP RUNNETH OVER

April 1997

Dear Prayer partner,

Thanks for your prayerful concern about my health. I have a strong feeling that nutritional supplements are going to be a significant part of my better health. Correct me if I'm wrong, but it seems to me that the closer one gets to the heart and mind of the Lord, the more one respects the common sense approach to better health and healing, that is, a balanced combination of natural, spiritual, and pharmaceutical remedies.

Do you remember the book called "None of these diseases?" I don't recall the author, but it is about the best I've ever read on the subject of health and healing from a biblical point of view.

The fourth element in all this is fresh air and exercise in the great outdoors. Now that I'm home on the range again, I like to go hiking on the 1300 acres of scenic hills, creeks, meadows, and woodlands that make up our "back yard."

Yesterday, I went out for about four hours. I had to stop and rest often since I'm not fully recovered from my back surgery yet. The weather was just perfect. I hardly worked up a sweat.

As I was sitting next to the creek, watching it cascading over the rocky bottom and disappearing around the bend, the thought came to me that it is a good illustration of the way we each follow our particular course through life. The water follows the path of least resistance because it obeys the law of gravity. Eventually, it passes successfully through, over, and under every obstacle and runs into other streams, rivers, and finally the ocean.

We, as Christians, do the same. Whether it feels like it or not, we, too, follow the path of least resistance, that is, the particular race set before us by God, by obeying the leading and gentle tugging of the Holy Spirit. We successfully pass through every rough place and finally arrive in the promised land.

We may think that the Holy Spirit deliberately takes us along a path of greatest resistance in order to build up our faith. But the fact is that He really takes us the best and easiest possible way. Whatever happens to us, however rough and torturous some places are, it is still better than if we choose our own way.

As I sat there, meditating on this parable of the stream, it suddenly dawned on me that the cheerful, relaxing noise the running water makes is loudest in the roughest places. I knew what the Spirit was trying to tell me: that the noise the stream makes is its own way of praising God. And the rougher its pathway, the louder the praise. Then it came to me that the same is supposed to be true for us; the rougher and harder the path on which the Spirit is taking us, the greater our worship and praise to Him.

I felt great sitting there, having this conversation with the Lord in my heart. But suddenly, I became alarmed. A new thought came to mind: suppose that stream had a mind of its own and rebelled against the path that gravity chose for it, and it decided to go around some of those rough places and find its own way! It would simply stop flowing and just evaporate away.

Of course, a stream can't rebel. It has no mind of its own. It has to follow the law of gravity, and therefore, it will always reach its ultimate destination, the sea.

But WE can rebel against the path the Holy Spirit is taking us on. And when we do, and we try to avoid the rough and punishing places, we end up in disaster.

As I got up and continued on my way, leaving the cheerful, babbling brook behind, the thought came that too often I try to find my own way to "the sea." I don't always like the rough places through which the Spirit takes me, even though I know it is the best way, so I try to avoid it and find an easier route. And so often I've come to a dead end, and the water of life in my soul would begin to dry up.

Thank God He keeps on giving us other chances. I'm sure you've also been learning how to follow the Spirit by taking life as God dishes it out. That is the way the Spirit is leading us. And as long as we let our worship, praise, and thanksgiving sound out loud and clear when we hit those rough places, we're O.K. The rougher the path, the greater our praise, and we know we will eventually get to the goal: Eternal union and communion with God and His family, and the ecstasy of endless praise, worship, and adoration forevermore.

I didn't mean to "preach," I just wanted to share a little of my spiritual progress with you and reveal the nature lover within me. I am eager to get to the Appalachians in order to find maximum inspiration for my writing ministry. It seems that my spiritual senses are far more acute in the great outdoors. God's natural creation is full of parables to feed the weary soul. Nature and the Bible enable me to hear the enigmatic voice of the Lord better than anything else.

I hear Him calling: "Come talk with Me." And my heart responds: "Lord, I'm coming." I am certain it is a part of my God-appointed race, for I am drawn toward the mountains by a gentle but firm attraction, one I've come to recognize as the Holy Spirit. And I'll know it is of Him as all the wrong doors close and the right ones open.

Your prayer partner,

Jim Herzog

Then followed, written by Rev. Herzog:

Because He's my Shepherd I have all I need.
In green fields of Heaven I rest at His feet.
Beside the still waters of life He doth lead.
My cup runneth over with love, with love.

He heals me and helps me desire His will.
Thru deathly gray byways I'll fear neither ill.
Nor, will I fear emptiness, for He shall fill.
My cup runneth over with love, with love.

Hallelu, Halleu, Hallelujah I sign!
Hallelu, Hallelu, Hallelujah my King!

His goodness and mercy shall follow me home.
And with Him before me I never shall roam.
There Jesus shall make me forever His own.
My cup runneth over with love, with love.

Christmas 1997

Dear Relatives and Friends,

Once again, we greet you in the Name of our Lord Jesus, whose birth we celebrate. Thanks be to God that He loved us so much and was willing to send us His best to save us from our sins and eternal destruction. May the Lord in this season continue to fill your heart with strong faith, joy, and hope.

This has been another year of God's grace and many rich happenings in our lives. Ray continues at CCC and still enjoys his work. He runs the printing press – prints all forms, papers, etc. for the prison.

He teaches about 10-15 students while doing this. He was very happy to have his two sisters, Thora Hausler and Joyce Deuble, here for two months, June and July. He finished remodeling our basement just before the wedding and did a beautiful job.

Eunice officially retired May 30, 1997, from teaching. It was good as there was a wedding, June 28, 1997, (Charla and Russell) that needed a lot of last minute attention. Her sister, Erna, had a stroke two weeks before the wedding, so that took a lot of time, staying with her, etc. Taking care of older siblings who are failing in health has kept retirement time filled so far. I do like the less hectic pace but do miss the children. After 43 years of teaching, I guess that's to be expected.

Paula and Scott are doing fine. They live in St. Charles, Illinois. Paula still works as an architect for an Engineering firm and does some work with her own company. Scott is still with DuKane Co. as their photographer. They still have Fozzy, their Samoyed and two cats. Fozzy loves the big yard they now have. They are very excited as they will be in Australia this Christmas for three weeks.

Charla had a big year this year. She worked at Time-Warner the first half of the year. Then was married to Russell Englebretsen on June 28, 1997. Russell is a Parks and Recreation Administrator. They had a lovely outdoor wedding here on the prairie behind our church. Rev. James Herzog was here and gave the message, which he has done for all our marriages – very special. The pictures will give you a little glimpse of it all. Russell having grown up in Canada, brought a lot of friends from there for the wedding. They now live in Crown Point, Indiana. Charla is a law student at Valparaiso University and likes it. Russell works for the city of Tinley Park, Illinois.

After the wedding, Ray, Eunice, Joyce and Thora went on a sight-seeing tour. We went to Kenosha, Wisconsin, for Angela Herman's wedding, (which was beautiful), across to the badlands, Mt. Rushmore, down through Colorado to Westcliffe, where Eunice taught for one year while still in college and had always wanted to go back to. We saw such beautiful scenery, then on to Mesa Verde Park (cliffs where the early American Indians lived), on to the Grand Canyon, Painted Desert, Petrified Forest, and Oklahoma City – we saw the bombing site – so sad! (The bombing of the Alfred P. Murrah Federal Building in Oklahoma City on April 19, 1995 was the deadliest act of homegrown terrorism in U.S. history, resulting in the deaths of 168 people). *We also stopped at Grants, New Mexico, and saw the only 8th grade student Eunice had while teaching in Westcliffe. What a thrill! We had also seen her mother in Westcliffe, so double joy. Then on to Branson, Missouri, where we saw the Shoji Tabuchi show. Country western music has made Branson a big tourist town. Then back to Illinois and the sadness of saying "good-bye" to Ray's sisters as they returned to Australia. But we were thankful for the wonderful time we had together.*

I forgot to mention that at Charla's wedding and Angela Herman's wedding we had a reunion of a number of New Guinea missionaries, and this was great!

We hope this has been a good year for all of you and look forward to hearing from you. God's rich blessings be with you in 1998 and always.

Love in Christ,
Ray and Eunice Hausler

December 1998

Dear Relatives and Friends

Greetings to you all at this happy time of year as we celebrate God's great love for us in sending His only Son, Jesus, to save us from our sins. As we wonder at this miracle and the great and loving God we have, may our hearts and bodies bow in humble adoration and praise as the shepherds and wisemen did 2000 years ago. The hope and joy we have in our Savior, keeps us going each day until we can be with Him forever in the glories of heaven.

This has again been a varied and filled year for us. Ray is still working at CCC. As the prison becomes more overcrowded, his work becomes more tense. They had a big drug check last week and brought the "swat" team in to do it. Always some drugs are found in spite of them trying to keep it drug free.

Eunice is teaching again this year at Immanuel Lutheran, Okawville, IL. They needed a teacher for grades 5 & 6 at the last minute, and she needed a job to help our China trip for summer '99 along. She had varied experiences during the year, working for McDonald's for two months, then doing a survey for the WIC program (Women, Infants and Children), *then visitors, and finally teaching. Well, they say retirement is like that, busier than before!!*

Paula and Scott, St. Charles, IL, are doing fine. Paula still works for an engineer and likes it. Scott was laid off for a while but got a new job in photography for another company and also is happy there. They still have Fozzy, their Samoyed and two cats.

Charla and Russell, Crown Point, Indiana, are also fine. Charla is in her second year of law school at Valparaiso U., Valparaiso, Indiana. She's happy there, but it gets hectic at times. Russell is working at a big Recreation Complex as manager in Tinley Park, Il. They both have a 30-minute drive. They also have two healthy, well-fed cats.

In May we celebrated Ray's 60th birthday. We were happy many friends and relatives could make it. Special friends from Delavan, Il, now living in Phoenix, Arizona, Callie and Jerry Hauptli, came and it was such fun having them with us and renewing our friendship. We went with them on Sunday to Delavan for a wedding reception for their son and wife. A lot of reunion went on there also. Since Ray is always teasing, he got a few paybacks—a lot of fun. Paula celebrated her 30th birthday in August. We went up there and Scott had planned a lovely party for her. A little tricky to keep it secret. Many of their friends were there.

In July we had wonderful visits from our Australian (also New Guinea) friends, Janice and Lawrence Mirtschin and son Andrew. We enjoyed their visit so much. Also, Reta Thiele, she and Eunice traveled around the world together in '62, visited us and a lot of reminiscing went on. During this time, we had our 50-year New Guinea Lutheran Mission reunion in St. Louis. We had such a wonderful time seeing many of our New Guinea family and seeing pictures, videos, and children that had arrived and/or grown up.

In October, we were saddened by the sudden death of our good friends—Ray's good friend since he was young—George and Gladys Ost in Petrie, Australia. They were in a car accident. They were both such good witnesses for our Lord Jesus. Also in October Eunice's sister, Erna Tyberendt, was called to her eternal home. She had been battling cancer for about three years. We miss her.

Last week, over the Thanksgiving holidays, we took our children (Paula, Scott, Charla, Russell) to Nashville, Tennessee, for a few days. We had a fun time just being together. We enjoyed seeing the Omni Hotel, beautifully decorated; the Grand 'Ole Opry; and a dinner theatre.

We pray this finds you and yours in good health and filled with joy in our Lord Jesus. His peace be with you.

Love in Christ,
Ray and Eunice Hausler

(A word about the New Guinea Lutheran Mission reunions {mentioned above and in subsequent letters:} The Papua New Guinea Mission Society {PNGMS} Biennial Bung meets every two years in the USA {usually rotating around the USA}. These feature updates on mission work in the Enga Province, reports on the status of various PNGMS projects, opportunity to visit with friends and fellow missionaries and special events, as well as, usually, visitors from PNG, each gathering centered around a theme that will help the Gutnuis {Good News} Lutheran Church {GLC}).

Christmas 1999

Dear Relatives and Friends,

Greetings to you at this blessed time of year. Once again, we thank and praise God for sending His only Son, Jesus, to suffer and die for our sins—and the promise—whoever believes in Him will be saved. We pray the Holy Spirit to keep us all strong in the true faith unto life everlasting. The world with its cunning and crafty ways tries constantly to draw us away from our Lord. In Him and Him alone, however, is real peace, joy, and courage to live until He calls us home.

It has again been a busy year for us. Ray continues to teach at the CCC, he does, however, plan to retire in 2000.

Eunice taught at Immanuel Lutheran School, Grades 5 & 6, Okawville, Illinois, until May 30th. She has now fully retired—but that keeps her busier than ever it seems. She and Ray had planned to go to China to volunteer teach in July but that was postponed until July 2000, after Ray retires. We did get all our shots, one of them, the encephalitis shots cost $700 each, so we're hoping they're still good in 2000. Eunice also went to Alaska September 3-18, 1999, with sisters Wilma and Betty, Betty's husband Roger and brother Dennis. Betty and Roger's son Patric, is there in the Air Force. He was most gracious to let us all stay in his apartment. Brother Luther, son David, and friend Walter also came up so we had a wonderful time. Roger, Patric & Dennis went hunting for 10 days, they got a caribou and moose. The rest of us saw the sights around Anchorage, the glaciers at Whittier and the sights at Denali. The ride up to Denali in a dome train was so beautiful. Alaska is beautiful.

Paula is still working as an architect for an engineer, but is also getting her engineering degree. They lost Fozzy in July of a heart attack. It was a heartbreak but they soon got another Samoyed, a girl this time, Sadi.

Scott is still working as a photographer, in sales at present. He has an hour drive every morning and evening. He had his 30th birthday and we also surprised him June 6th with a party. He and Paula took a week trip to Bonaire in the Caribbean in September. They love scuba diving.

Charla is on her wind down in law school at Valparaiso University. She graduates May 2000. Last summer she worked in downtown Chicago at Barnes & Thornburg Law Firm, and they offered her a job beginning June 2000 so she has accepted that. She had her 30th birthday in August and we had a surprise party for her August 7th, a month early, so we could surprise her. We had it at Russell's mother's home in Champaign, IL. Both her and Scott's party were a lot of fun.

Russell continues to work at a big Recreation Complex in Tinley Park, IL., as a shift manager. He keeps very busy. He and Charla took a week trip to Canada in August with Russell's mother and sister and friends.

Some other happenings this year were the loss of loved ones, my aunt Ruth Redeker in May, Bea Schultz in June and Mildred Schultz in August. Mildred was in New Guinea with us as a nurse and we got to know her sister Bea, through her. Rev. Jim Herzog visited August 13-14th, and it was too short as we can never get everything talked about. He's such a spiritual help for our family. Lori and Kirk Clayton have fun staying with us often and this is fun. Lori was my student in Grades 1 & 2 in Lincoln, IL. She is now teaching at Immanuel, Okawville, and Kirk is a final year student at Concordia Seminary. We helped Wendi and Todd Garney, a little, get an older house in Belleville IL., remodeled. Then we helped them move in. Wendi is the daughter of our good friends from Delavan, IL, now in Phoenix, Arizona. They have a beautiful 7-month-old daughter, Callie Adell. November 13-15th, we were in Houston, Texas, for the wedding of Susan Cheng (our god-daughter) to Darrell Valentin. Susan came from Vietnam in 1979 with her family and they were sponsored by our congregation in Lincoln, IL. They are a beautiful, as well as, Christian family. Ray had the honor of giving away the bride.

We pray this finds you all well and happy in our Lord. The blessings of His coming be with you at Christmas and in 2000, the beginning of a new millennium!

Love in Christ,
Ray & Eunice Hausler

P.S. 25th Anniversary of Zion Lutheran School- April 1999; Rev. Adams 40th wedding and ministry anniversary June and Sept.; Paula and Scott went to CA for 7th anniversary Dec. 11-14, '99.

Chapter 6

The 2000's

The Millennium Christmas

Christmas 2000

Dear Relatives and Friends,

Greetings to you from us and wishes for a very blessed Christmas. As we are so privileged to still worship our Lord and Savior Jesus Christ openly and without persecution, we thank God. In our case also, we are wasting away outwardly, but inwardly we are being renewed. Our momentary troubles are achieving an eternal glory. What is seen is temporary, what is unseen is eternal. Such an outlook results from a confidence that comes from faith in God, who loves us in Christ, His Son, whose birth we now celebrate. May this faith and confidence be yours this Christmas and in the New Year and always.

As we look on the year just passed, we are thankful and grateful to God who made it a very blessed and eventful year.

Ray put in his last six months at the Centralia Correctional Center, retiring June 30th, amidst a lot of farewells, parties, etc. Even now he is being missed as materials are not being printed and as they have not found a replacement for him. Eunice and he left July 1, 2000, for seven weeks in China as volunteer teachers, teaching oral English to medical students. The people were so loving, kind, and wonderful. We were overwhelmed with their hospitality and pray we left a lot of loving memories also with them. Ray is now working part time with a friend doing carpentry work which he enjoys. He is finishing his last year as elder at church and that will relieve some of his duties. He continues to teach Bible Class every Sunday—we hope and pray for a helper so that he can get away once in a while.

Eunice is enjoying a more leisurely schedule. She does some substitute teaching. Keeping up with correspondence is a monumental task. E-mail is helping some. Our China trip was wonderful—Eunice for the second time. We just pray for God to raise up a Christian leader there so those people will realize some of the freedoms we in America take for granted. She teaches Bible Class at the nursing home two or three times a month.

Paula is working for another architect. She also does a lot of work on her own: nights and Saturdays. The engineer she was working with wasn't giving her enough lee-way to use her creative abilities. She's into building environmentally friendly houses. She also helps at her church-altar guild, etc.

Scott still works at Calumet in the photo sales division. He has gotten several promotions. He has to drive 1 ½ hours to work and back so that cuts into his at-home time. They are going to Belize for their 8th anniversary the week of December 12th.

Charla-this was Charla's big year. She graduated from Valparaiso University Law School—Summa cum laude—May 21st, 2000. She took the Illinois bar exam July 27-28. She started full-time work at Barnes & Thornburg, September 1st, downtown Chicago. She found out she passed the bar exam October 10th. She was sworn in as an attorney in the Illinois bar, November 9th. She is very happy in her work and has found the work she loves doing. They now live in Darien, Illinois, close to Russell's work and Charla takes the commuter train into Chicago each day.

Russell has been so supportive of Charla. He worked while she went to school. He loves hockey and plays on several teams. He still works at Odyssey World (recreation complex). He was moved to Naperville where they opened a new complex and is one of the managers. Naperville is very close to St. Charles where Paula and Scott live so they only live ½ hour apart now and get together often. Russell had appendicitis May 5, 2000, just as Charla was taking her final exams. Eunice was glad she was free to go up and help out. This helped us a lot also as one of our teammates got appendicitis in China this summer, and we knew a bit about helping her.

We were in Lanzhou, Gangu Province, China. After our five weeks of teaching we did a little tour to Zian where the Terra cotta warriors are being excavated, then to Beijing to see the palaces, Tiananmen Square and the Great Wall. Then down to Yongsan where Eunice taught in '96. What a thrill it was to see most of my students and laugh and party for three days! The students there become like your family.

For Thanksgiving our whole family plus sister, Wilma, brother Luther, and brother-in-law Paul, all flew out to sister Betty and husband, Roger, in Annapolis, Maryland. We had such fun being together. We also got to see Washington, D.C., Annapolis, (a very historic city), and Baltimore.

We pray this finds you and yours happy and well and wish you God's richest blessings in 2001.

Love in Christ,
Ray & Eunice Hausler

(The Hauslers and Chinese students/lifelong friends)

(Eunice first taught English as a second language in China in 1997. This was followed by both Ray and Eunice teaching there again {in different regions} in 2000 and 2004. What followed these trips were many email exchanges {as well as written letters, etc.} We have gleaned just two, to serve as examples of these exchanges and the loving care and concern flowing between Ray/Eunice and these students. Keeping in mind these students of Ray/Eunice were learning English, thus we have transcribed these letters as written.)

February 22, 2001

Dear Eunice and Ray,

Hello! How are you? I miss you very much.

Today is a very happy day for me, because I receive your two letters. One was written in December 2000, together with the photo of your family. The other was in February 2001. I should have received the former letter earlier, maybe our post office delayed it. Also I received your package with two dictionaries on December 27th, 2000. They are very helpful when I study English. Here I do want to say "Thanks a lot" to you.

I fell very happy and excited when I see the red heart you sent me on Valentine's Day. In recent years, some young people in China also have a celebration on February 14th, they send flowers, cards, or other gifts to friends of the opposite sex. All of these are maybe from western countries.

I often thick (think) *of the days with you in Lanzhou. At that time, you were our teachers, now you are our special friends. I improved my English level and learned much about your country from you.*

I am sorry I have not contacted with you until today. Now I am in the first year of my three-year's course of Dr. degree studying in Beijing, only in summer and winter holidays can I come back to Lanzhou to be with my family together. Another important thing I want to tell you is that on January 21st 2001, I have a baby, lovely boy. So these days I fell very happy and busy. Next week I will go back to Beijing to start a new term.

My new address in Beijing is: … Cellular Biology Department … My email address is: … My wife receives my letters for me and then posts to me.

I will close off now. Hope to contact with you often, and hope your health is good and your works are going well for you. Best wishes to every one in your family. Goodbye.

Much love, Yu Zuo Ren
(Colin)

March 01, 2001

Dear Mr. and Mrs. Hausler:

I'm Laura, Do you remember me? I'm sorroy that I haven't got in touch with you since I wrote a letter to you last August, really , I'm sorry. Belive me,my miss for you is deathless.Frequently, the memory of all the happy moments I have enjoyed with you come crowding over me, and I feel most deeply grateful to God and you that I have enjoyed them so long.

I'll graduate from the college of medicine in June, and then become a resident physician or work for CDC. For me, that will be a new start, a new life and a new road full of hope, happiness, of course, rough too. Anyhow, I'll try my best to take up the challenge.

I'm eager to tell you a news, which I am in love with Jack. We are happy, very happy, you know, how wonderful to be loved and to love. How I hope we could love each other like you, growing old slowly with ones own lover may be the most romantic thing in the world.

Learning English alread become an essential part of my life, day after day, I never stop trudging along the ro-ugh road, becouse I belive the pay-off will be worth the effort. Of course, my persistence ought to attribute your encouragement to me either. Do you remember that ad about Volkswagen showed by me? When I was aware that no one like it, my heart sank. It was you, Ray, that gave me a pat on the shoulder and said "You are the best.". Maybe you can not imagine how important your encouragement is for me. Thank you again!

I'm willing-perfectly willing-to see you again, in China or in U.S.A.

sincerely, Laura

(A word of explanation about the Volkswagen comment above: Part of an assignment in Ray's English class, was for the students to write a commercial about any product. Laura wrote one about the VW. After she shared her commercial, Ray asked the class who would buy a VW after that commercial. Not one person raised their hand. Ray quickly responded with words to the effect: "Well Laura, most likely the reason they wouldn't buy a VW is because they wouldn't have the money to do that." This helped to ameliorate and give a reasonable rationale for no one responding to Laura's "ad." Since Ray could see the hurt in her eyes, he further told her: "You did a good job" and with that, put his hand on her arm and reassured her of that good job. Several days later she gave Ray a gift of 4 beautiful glasses with the following note: "How wide and long and high and deep is the love of Christ. Always my teacher, now too, my friend. Best wishes from Laura.")

Obviously from Laura's response in the letter above, this meant so much to her.

Many other letters and emails have been exchanged between Eunice and the Chinese students, including Eunice sending them dictionaries {mentioned above} as well as expressions of Christian love, and the Chinese have responded, expressing very difficult life circumstances, in addition to also many heartfelt expressions of appreciation for bringing English more clearly to them.)

March 2002

Dear Relatives and Friends,

You are getting our Christmas letter as an Easter letter this year. But this is wonderful because the suffering, death and Resurrection of our Lord Jesus is a wonderful message to share. Since God loved us so much and sent His Son to save us from our sin and that He was willing to suffer and die for us—then believing in Him, we have forgiveness of our sins and because He rose from the dead the third day, we are assured of eternal life with Him in heaven. This is the hope and joy of all who believe in Jesus. God grant strong faith in Jesus to all of us all of our lives.

We were in Australia in December, 2001, and January 2002. The last week of January, Paula, Scott, Ray and I went to PNG. Charla is pregnant so she and Russell didn't go as the Doctor wouldn't prescribe anti-malarials for Charla. Ray and I had a wonderful time in Australia. We were with friends in Sydney, Melbourne, and Adelaide. Then on to Perth and Darwin where we were on our own. We had wonderful visits, reunions, etc. We saw many of our New Guinea co-workers and this was so wonderful. We have such a bond with them. We just carry on from where we left off the last time we saw each of them. Then December 23, we landed in Brisbane which is Ray's home area. We had Christmas with his three sisters and it was wonderful. It was very hot but that did not affect the festivities. We visited with many friends of Ray's, as well as family. It was so good having extra time. We stayed with Ray's sister, Thora, and it was close to the ocean so we took our early morning walks. Ray's good friend's son, Jeffrey Ost and family planned wonderful outings for us also. We had some wonderful seafood meals.

Paula, Scott, and Russell arrived, January 6 and 7, and then went up to Cairns for some diving around the Great Barrier Reef. Charla arrived the day they came back, so we all headed for the hills with the Ost family. It was a lodge in Binna Barra, and we had a wonderful time doing rainforest walks, eating together in the dining hall, and just doing fun things together.

Then our family went up to Maroochydore, along the coast. We were able to stay in a resort that belongs to Ray's cousins, Auburn and Ollie Mueller. It was a block from the beach so plenty of fun activities, and wonderful seafood. We were also able to have several get togethers with Ray's family and that was very special.

After this we were able to go to PNG for a week. We were in Madang and Paula and Scott got to dive in tropical waters. They said it was the most beautiful place they have ever dived. We visited places we remembered when we were working there, 1959-1973. Then we flew to the Highlands, Mt. Hagen. This was all possible through the help of our former student, Dian Roo, his wife, Lean, and their family, who live in Lae. We were met by Mark Reto, also a former student, and Wilson Dia, Dian's nephew, who Dian had sent up to accompany us on the ride to Wapenamanda. They drove us all the way from Mt Hagen to Wabag and we saw all the mission stations. We had wonderful memories. We stayed at Highland Lutheran School. It was wonderfully kept and many students are getting a good education there. Brent Kilbeck, from Canada, is doing a wonderful job as headmaster.

The next day we drove back to Mt. Hagen and flew on to Lae via Goroka. We had a wonderful stay in Lae. Dian and family showed us many happy times. We even saw a crocodile farm, Martin Luther Seminary and Balob Teacher's college. PNG is a wonderful country and has wonderful resources and scenery, as well as, people. They still need help from us former workers and others who want an adventurous experience.

Then we flew on to Brisbane, where Charla and Russell were waiting for us. We all flew back to the U.S. together. That was a great experience. We had a very bumpy stormy night but God's angels were watching over us. When we landed in L.A., we had much to thank God for and especially for safety during many miles of travel.

Then we were met by our good friends, Dave and Betty Raff. They had kept our car. We spent several days with them and got to see our friends from New Guinea, Ken and Viv Bauer. Ray and I drove home via Phoenix, Arizona, where we visited with our friends, Gerry and Callie Hauptli. Then back to Illinois and the catch-up game, which we are still on. I had to go back to work as I'm interim principal at Trinity Lutheran School, Hoffman, and Ray is still doing carpentry work for his friend, Herschel Kasten.

We had a snowstorm, Monday P.M., so we had no school for two days and this has been a help. Thanks for all your cards and letters. We love hearing from you. God bless you all and keep you in His loving care in the year ahead.

Love in Christ
Ray and Eunice Hausler

Christmas 2002

Dear Relatives and Friends,

Again, another year of life here on earth has passed by very quickly. It's another year that by God's grace we have remained in faith in our Lord Jesus. It's also a year that we as people in the U.S. and other countries remained free. We need to thank God daily for these blessings. As we celebrate our Savior's birth may we kneel at the manger and realize how God loved us so much that He gave His only Son that whoever believes in Him will be saved and have eternal life.

The past year has been a turbulent one but through it all God has showered His blessings. In December and January, we were in Australia. Our Christmas dinner was in the home of Mrs. Schulte by the Oceanside at a temperature of 96 degrees. It was hot but wonderful!

In PNG, we went to Pausa, Wapenamanda, Yaibos, Irelya, Wabag, and back to Amapyaka, where we stayed.-We were impressed by the work at Highland Lutheran School and Immanuel Lutheran Hospital. The church is still strong in spite of hardships. Scott and Paula bonded well with Dian's family.

Paula, Scott, Charla and Russell all had to get back to work after the trip. They are still in their same professions, Paula – architect, Scott – photography sales, Charla – lawyer for Barnes and Thornburg (downtown Chicago), Russell – manager at Odyssey World. They live in the Chicago area: St. Charles, and Westmont.

In June our Vietnamese friends from Houston, Texas, visited and we had a wonderful time. Also, Reta and Phillip Thiele from Australia visited and we had a wonderful time sightseeing and reminiscing. Then the last week in June was turbulent – both rejoicing and saddening. Our grandson, Aaron Ray, was born to Charla and Russell at 9 lbs. 2 oz. on June 27 – and my sister Betty, at the age of 63 yrs. had an aneurysm and died June 30. We miss her so much. Aaron is such a joy – Eunice goes up to Chicago by train and babysits two days a week.

Then Aug. 15, Eunice was relieved of her job by another retired principal. She really enjoyed the year and we (with wonderful help from so many people at Trinity) got through the State visit and were able to get our state recognition again.

In September our brother-in-law, Paul married again. He had been married to Eunice's sister, Erna, who passed into eternity in 1998. It was a family reunion. Brother-in-law, Roger and family from Annapolis, Maryland were also able to be here. At our age, reunions are getting very special.

Ray keeps busy in his new workshop that he built last year. He built a baby bed for Aaron and it is beautiful. He is still an elder at church and teaches Bible Class.

Eunice is still on the Board of the CHI and Christ our Rock Lutheran High School. We plan to open a new Lutheran High School, Sept. 2004. If you know anyone who would be a good principal for a new High School, let us know. Also, Ray and Eunice are both on the Board for South Africa for our Southern Illinois District.

For Thanksgiving our family and our adopted family, Wendi and Todd Gorney, Callie and Ashton were all together. The big news was that Paula and Scott are expecting a child in June 2003. This will make our second grandchild-a wonderful blessing-as most of you know.

We wish you all a very blessed New Year in 2003. The Lord be with you.

Love in Christ,
Ray and Eunice

Christmas 2003

Dear Relatives and Friends,

Greetings again in this blessed time of year when we think of Gods' great love to save us from our sins. Believing in Him, we have life in this world and also in the life to come, forever with Him in our heavenly home, which will be eternal joy and bliss. We especially feel this as we get older and many of our friends and loved ones are passing on to be with our Lord.

Our activities and happenings of the past year were:

January—May: Eunice still went to Chicago often to babysit Aaron, our grandson, son of Charla and Russell. Ray did a lot of work at home—he now has his workshop finished and does a lot of work in it.

March: we drove to Phoenix only to return after one day there because our sister-in-law, Florence Redeker, passed on.

April: we again went to Phoenix for a week (flew this time) to finish our vacation. Our friends, Callie and Gerry Hauptli, took us to many places, and we saw so much and had a wonderful time. We saw Sedona, Prescott, Tucson and Nogales, Mexico—and the sights in between. Later in April, our good friend, Dorothy Degnitz, nurse from New Guinea days, and now from Wisconsin, and her sister and brother-in-law stopped in for an enjoyable visit.

June: we had a baby shower for Paula early in the month. We, parents, were overjoyed at the thought of having a second grandchild. Later in the month we had a two-day New Guinea Missionaries reunion. Those days were so joyous and we had such a good time visiting and reminiscing. Also evident was that we are all getting older. June 22, 2003, our grandson, Evan James Price was born. He weighed 9 lb. 6 oz.—21 inches long. He's a miracle baby as there were two knots in his umbilical cord and he made it. He's a beautiful baby. He was baptized August 10, 2003.

June 22—August 6: Eunice was in Chicago helping care for Paula and the new baby. Ray was home making a crib and dressing table/dresser for Evan. After two weeks Paula was back at work as they had some pressing architectural work to complete. She could do a lot at home via computer. Paula has a nanny that comes to the house every day and Russell is now at home with Aaron, so Eunice hasn't gone up as often. Charla is still very busy at her law firm, Barnes and Thornburg, downtown Chicago. She likes her work but it demands too much time away from Aaron.

Sept.—Oct.: Ray repainted a lot of the interior of our house. Eunice started some major cleaning which never ends.

November: Ray finished a porch at the back of our house and then he had hernia surgery so he is still recuperating. All went very well. We are looking forward to his sister, Thora, arriving November 24, for six weeks. The grandsons are anxious to meet her and she them! We'll have some Happy Holidays.

We hope this finds you and your family in good health and strong in faith in Jesus. God bless you and keep you in 2004.

Love in Jesus,
Ray and Eunice Hausler

P.S. Went to godchild, Matrina Hiler and Bill Whitney wedding in Detroit; saw Bonner Christmas store in Frankenmuth.

Special Voters' Meeting May 22, 2004
St. John's Lutheran Church, New Minden, IL.

The voters were asked to become a "Sending Congregation" for Ray and Eunice Hausler's five-week mission trip to China beginning June 27th. No financial support is necessary, simply congregational prayers.

Motion was made, seconded, and approved to become said "Sending Congregation."

Christmas 2004

Dear Relatives and Friends,

Once again greetings at Christmas! Again, another year is quickly closing. How thankful we are that as it closes our hearts turn to our Lord and Savior, Jesus Christ's birth. Because God sent His only Son, Jesus, into this world to save us from our sins, we can live with joy, hope and peace. May the Holy Spirit constantly increase our faith in Jesus as we study and read His Word and grow closer to Him. We look forward to His second coming—we say with the Apostle John in Revelations 22:20, "Even so come quickly, Lord Jesus," so we can be with You forever in the joys of heaven.

Our year has been busy and gone so quickly. In January, we saw Thora Hausler, Ray's sister, off to Australia. She had visited us a month and we had Happy Holidays together and so it was sad to part.

In April, our brother-in-law from Maryland, Roger Thusius, visited us for a weekend. We had a good time and visit.

In May, our godchild, Paul Pitney, was married, and this was a very special occasion. This was in Madisonville, Kentucky. During this month we also helped our friend Andrew Mirtschin, get his property ready for sale so he could go back to Australia. He was living in Pacific, Missouri.

In June we celebrated our grandson's birthdays. Aaron Englebretsen was two and Evan Price was one. Both loved digging into their cakes. Ray made Evan a fish cake and Aaron a Nemo cake. They are so precious and lots of fun. We also had a visit from our niece, Ann Thusius, and her friend Steve. We are so thankful they come to see us as we miss our sister, Betty, very much. She died with an aneurysm two years ago. We also were preparing to leave for China. Yes, we were in Shan Yi, Hunan Province, teaching for four weeks and with travel were gone five and a half weeks. It's so rewarding to teach teachers and High School students. We also had good visits with the church and it was so wonderful to worship with the Christians. The churches are packed to overflowing—so heart-warming!

In August, we got use to being back in America. We helped Andrew Mirtschin with his final packing and got him on his way to Australia, August 26. We're missing him as we usually had holidays with him.

During September, we made trips to Chicago to visit our children and grandchildren. We also had a great nephew, Matthew Redeker, get married. It was precious and beautiful in Morton, Illinois. Morton is the pumpkin canning capital of the US. Fall is a beautiful time of year. Since Matthew had had some health problems during his life, we all praised God and had a wonderful celebration. He chose his father, Charles Redeker, as his best man. Charles is the son of Eunice's brother, Richard, who is in a nursing home. Wilma, Luther, and Eunice visit him regularly.

During this year Ray's brother, Alva, has been ill and is doing better again. His wife, Noela, celebrated her 80th birthday. It's always hard for us to be so far away at times like this.

During October, our godchild, Mark Payne, was married and we again praised God. He was adopted from Korea and his parents, Roger and Randy Payne, did a wonderful job raising him. He gave them a wonderful tribute at the wedding. He was married in Normal, Illinois.

Our children and grandchildren:

Paula—is still busy as an architect. Since she now runs her own company, she is kept very busy. She is expecting their second child next May.

Scott—is at the same job in photography at Calumet Co. He has an hour drive to and from work each day.

Evan—is growing quickly. He is a fast crawler and now walks. He's a beautiful and precious boy.

Charla—still a lawyer at Barnes and Thornburg in downtown Chicago. She also keeps very busy.

Russell—is still at home caring for Aaron. He also still likes to play hockey and plays on a team.

Aaron—is a bouncing two-year-old. He talks non-stop and is very active. Both boys are at a precious age. He and Evan keep Grandma and Grandpa hopping.

We pray this finds all of you in good health and enjoying the Christmas season with Jesus in the center. May 2005 be a very Blessed year for you!

Love in Christ,
Ray and Eunice Hausler

Christmas 2004

Dear Friends in China,

I'm sorry we haven't gotten a letter to you sooner. We arrived home safely, August 6, 2004. We just had such a wonderful time with you all and wonderful memories. We wish you lived closer so we could see you often. We hope you are all having a wonderful school year. Soon it will be half over.

We have been very busy since home again. We go to Chicago a lot to help our children and grandchildren. We have had several weddings—our great nephew, and also our godchild were married. Well, you know what that was like after we showed you an American wedding in our last cultural class. (For the readers of this book: When we taught at Shanyi, we performed a mock wedding with our class. We had volunteers for bride and groom, maid of honor and best man. Teacher Opper was the pastor. We got a long white dress and veil for the bride and a nice suit for the groom. We also made an altar. We did the wedding service, sang songs, and had a ring exchange. After the "service," we served a wedding cake and punch).

Now we are getting ready for Christmas. We celebrate the birth of Jesus Christ, God's Son, who came to earth to save us from our sins. We give gifts and eat many special kinds of food, especially candy, fruit cake and cookies.

We hope this finds you all well and having a happy life. We miss you and love you.

Love from,
Ray and Eunice Hausler

Christmas 2005

Dear Relatives and Friends,

Greetings once again at this Blessed time of year from Southern Illinois. As we grow older, each year becomes more precious and we are thankful our Lord and Savior, Jesus Christ, came to earth to save us from our sins, and believing in Him, we look forward to the life in heaven that He has secured for us by suffering and dying on the cross to take our sins away. God grant you all a strong faith in Jesus.

This letter will be a brief summary of activities this year as we want to include a couple of pictures of our grandchildren on the back.

2005 has been a very busy and blessed year for us. We praise God from Whom all blessings flow.

---March 10—April 17—we were in Australia visiting Ray's family and friends. Ray's brother, Alva, had his 80th birthday, a wonderful celebration with family and friends. Then great nephew, Paul Hausler, was married and another wonderful celebration. We have wonderful memories of special times spent with family and friends.

---May 18, 2005—on Ray's birthday, our granddaughter, Anna Rae Price, was born. She weighed 9 lbs. 6 ounces. She's a happy girl and watches brother, Evan, 2 ½ years old, with a keen eye. She was baptized June 26, 2005.

---July 23—August 2—we were in Portland, Oregon, Washington State and British Columbia. We enjoyed beautiful scenery. Our highlight was the PNG Missionaries Reunion at Concordia, Portland. Had a wonderful time reminiscing.

---August 13—our nephew, David Redeker, married Angie Hollenkamp. Our two grandsons were ringbearers. They were precious in their tuxedos.

---August 30—September 2—we made a fast trip to Levittown, Pennsylvania, for Neil Werberig's funeral. The Werberigs are dear friends from when Eunice taught in Levittown, 1956-59. We stayed with a dear friend, Carolyn Dufendach, and we had wonderful talks. She lost her husband last February, and since we were almost on our way to Australia, couldn't be with her and her family at that time.

---September 6—our grandson, Nathan George Englebretsen, was born. He weighed 8 lbs. 3 ounces. He had a beautiful head of black hair. He was baptized, October 2, 2005. He is dearly loved by his brother Aaron, 3 ½ years old.

---October 29—30—Our dear friend, Amanda Wolf, was married. Eunice had to miss it as she went to Levittown, Pennsylvania, for a Homecoming Reunion at Hope Lutheran School, the school she helped start in 1956. It was a wonderful and exciting reunion with many friends and former students.

---November 4-7—Eunice and Ray were in Annapolis, Maryland, to celebrate the wedding of our brother-in-law, Roger Thusius. It was a beautiful weekend as the leaves were at their peak in color.

Also, we were happy for Roger as he lost Betty, Eunice's sister, suddenly in 2002, due to an aneurysm.

---November 12—Eunice's great nephew, Curtis Meadows was married. Another beautiful wedding.

---November 20—our dear friend, Helen Poirot celebrated her 80th birthday and her husband, Robert will be 85 in February. A beautiful dinner was served at the Maschhoff Pork Farm Building.

---Ray and I are thankful for good health and God's love and protection. Ray still teaches Bible study every Sunday. Eunice is on the CHI Board and enjoys the challenges of that Board as we preserve the archival history of our church. She has spent a lot of time this year in Chicago taking care of grandchildren. Ray spends a lot of time in his workshop making things for grandchildren, children, and others.

---Paula is an architect and has her own business, Batir Architecture. She is kept very busy.

--Scott still works at Calumet, a photographic company.

---Charla is a lawyer with Barnes and Thornburg, downtown Chicago. She is also very busy. She enjoyed three months off this year when Nathan was born.

---Russell is a fulltime Dad, taking care of Aaron and Nathan. He enjoys it and does a good job.

We wish you all a very Blessed Christmas and God's richest blessings in 2006.

Love in Christ,
Ray and Eunice Hausler

Christmas 2007

Dear Relatives and Friends,

Greetings to you at this Joyous and Blessed time of the year, as we remember the wondrous birth of our Lord and Savior Jesus Christ. He came with the most glorious birth announcement ever – as the angel chorus sang it to the Shepherds. May we rejoice in this Savior who came to save us from our sins. He willingly came, willingly lived a life of service for us and willingly died for us. Certainly, unbelievable but certainly the most wonderful event our earth has experienced. May we all sing and rejoice with the angels this Christmas and always.

This has been another year filled with many blessings from our Heavenly Father. These are a few highlights.

January – we saw Ray's sister, Thora, leave again to Australia after an almost two-month wonderful visit.

April 22, 2007 – we dedicated our Christ Our Rock Lutheran High School, 17 miles from our home. God has richly blessed this venture and we now have 50 students receiving a Christ centered education in High School in our area. We started in 2002 and God has richly blessed all efforts.

April – July – Eunice spent a lot of time in Chicago taking care of grandchildren. Paula and Scott had lost their babysitter and they also were under much duress along with Russell and Charla as they had remodeled a house in Naperville, but with the housing slump, it wasn't selling. The mortgage was getting too much for them – but the Lord was good and sent a lady, who bought it July 3, 2007. How thankful we all were but feel for people who are in a similar situation and can't sell their houses.

May – we celebrated Ray and Anna's birthdays. Anna is two now and a bubbly little girl. Birthdays are greatly enjoyed by all the grandchildren – cake, candles, and balloons make their eyes sparkle.

June – Aaron and Evan celebrated birthdays. Aaron was 5 and Evan 4 years old. On June 30, 2007, it was a thrill to go to one of Eunice's former student's wedding. A lot of former students were there. Todd Simpson is a lawyer in New York City.

July – Ray and I got away for a few days to Branson, Missouri. Driving through the Ozarks is so beautiful and uplifting.

August – our great niece, Linda Maschhoff, was married to Steve Kleiboeker. The Kleiboeker family was well known to Eunice's family as they are from Shattuc, Illinois, where Eunice grew up. Aaron started Kindergarten at Zion Lutheran School, Hinsdale, Illinois. There is talk of closing this school because of finances. Pray with us that it doesn't close. Evan started pre-school at St. Mark's Lutheran Pre-school, St. Charles, Illinois. Both boys like school very much. We had a PNG Staff Reunion August 9 and 10. These are always wonderful and it's amazing how our fellow workers are like family and we carry on visiting as if we hadn't been apart for a while. Always a few have passed on into eternity and we miss them.

September – Nathan celebrated his second birthday. He's a happy – easygoing boy. Not sure about his little sister taking his attention away. Carlee Lynn Englebretsen was born September 20, 2007. She weighed 9 lbs. 3 oz. and is a growing healthy girl. Russell and Charla are trying to adjust to having a girl. We also saw the passing of our sister-in-law, Eileen Redeker. She had a massive heart attack, a shock to us all. Eunice's High School Class celebrated their 55th reunion. We are getting old, but still had a wonderful time. We had a lot of reminiscing to do!

October – Charla and Russell moved to a bigger house in Westmont. It was a lot of work to move but it's nice to have more room. Good news also is that Charla was voted in as a partner at her law firm, Barnes and Thornburg. We praise God for all blessings. We celebrated Thanksgiving yesterday and as ever had so much to be thankful for. Since we were with our children and grandchildren last Sunday, November 18, 2007, for Carlee's baptism, we didn't go back for Thanksgiving but instead had our sister, brother, and other relatives over. Turkey and dressing were the main dish.

Ray is still a Bible class teacher at church and still does a lot of building of items for our children, some friends and us. Building his workshop a few years ago has been worth it. Eunice is still serving on the Board of Governors for CHI, the archives where the history of our church are kept. We are in a Building and Museum Expansion project at present. She also serves as an election judge when we have national, state, and local elections. We are both on the Southern Illinois District Partners of the South Africa Board which has proved to be very interesting. We'd like to go there and work for several months but grandchildren, age and funds keep us here.

God bless you all and keep you in His loving care. In this world of turmoil, we need to feel our Lord's presence more and more. We say with the apostle, John, in Revelation, "Come quickly Lord Jesus." In the meantime, we get strength and faith from reading His Word daily.

With love in Christ,
Ray and Eunice Hausler

(On October 19, 2008, Eunice presented a Prayer lecture at Messiah Lutheran Church, Carlyle, IL. The content of that lecture is summarized as follows:)

The Importance of Prayer-I talked about "prayer" being our life-line. God gave us the privilege to talk directly to Him. This has been my source of strength and joy my whole life. Every time I had a problem or needed encouragement or needed wisdom to do a task, I talked to my Heavenly Father. I started my days with Him and ended my days with Him. In my school religion class, I learned that when you pray-first, thank God for all your blessings, second-Praise Him for His great love for you in sending His Son to save you, then-Ask for forgiveness of all your sins, then-ask for needs you have, and end with- "for thine is the kingdom, and the power, and the glory forever and ever. Amen." Then I talked about prayer in the Bible: Jesus always talking to His heavenly Father; plus the many people who prayed in the Bible, like the disciples, Paul, Hannah (she prayed a long time for a child), and so many others. What an uplifting morning it was!

(Eunice presented a lecture for CHI on Nov. 14, 2008 at Marquette State Park. The content of that lecture is summarized as follows:)

I talked about "prayer being my Lifeline, and the importance of CHI where the history of the LCMS is kept. Having served on the Board of Governors for 9 years, I could give some firsthand experience. History is so important to see the mighty works God has performed of old and which our fathers told. Hymn #629 in the Lutheran Hymnal says it well: "Let children hear the mighty deeds which God performed of old, which in our younger years we saw, and which our fathers told. Make unto them His glories known, His works of power and grace; and we convey His wonders down through every rising race."

Christmas 2008

Dear Relatives and Friends,

Grace and peace to you from God our Father, and our Lord and Savior, Jesus Christ. As we again celebrate the birth of our Lord in Bethlehem's manger many years ago, we pray you are all praising Him as well. As we grow older and nearer the time when God will call us home to Himself, we appreciate more and more the great love God had for us sinners in sending His only Son to redeem and save us. May God keep us in faith, His grace, love and favor this Christmastime and forever.

Our family has had a good year with only minor colds and illnesses. Ray celebrated his 70th birthday, May 18,2008, with Anna, his granddaughter who was three years the same day. A special cake with Australian memorabilia on it was made for Ray by Paula's friend. A monkey cake (Anna called it a "munkey cake") was made for Anna by Ray. Ray always decorates the cakes for each of our grandchildren and they get their requests in early. Aaron had a Kungfu panda, Evan had a flower, Nathan had Elmo and Carlee had a princess cake (requested by brother, Aaron). Eunice and Ray spent time in Chicago often babysitting during the year and Aaron and Nathan had a week at our house the last week in July and Evan and Anna had a week with us the first week in August. Each one of them caught a 21" or 22" bass or catfish in our friend, Orville Heseman's Pond. What a thrill that was!

During January, February and March, Ray and Eunice were privileged to help Barbara Marquart Johnson organize her deceased husband, Kurt's papers. Kurt was truly a gifted and wise professor and was used by the Lord mightily. We spent one week of each of those months helping Barbara.

In July we went to Branson, Missouri, to see the show "Noah's ark," a fantastic production in a special theater.

Our Vietnamese friends, who we helped settle in America in 1979, from Vietnam, visited us in July and the rest of their family visited us on Thanksgiving Day. They are very dear to us and attend Memorial Lutheran Church in Houston, Texas. They and we were saddened by the sudden death of our dear friend, Dorothy Lehner, Lincoln, IL, the day before Thanksgiving. She did so much in helping our Vietnamese friends to settle in the U.S.

Our godchild, Sarah Pitney Martin, was installed as a Lutheran teacher at Memorial Lutheran School, Houston, Texas, September 7, 2008. What a "praise the Lord" day that day was! We enjoyed the wonderful reunion with the Pitney family also. We also visited Steve Deo, our Vietnamese boy who graduated from Rose Hulman University now working as an engineer in Austin, Texas. At that time, we visited our good friends, Jim and Betty Herzog, such a faith lifting time. Jim shared many of his wonderful Scripture writings with us.

We celebrated sister Wilma's 85th birthday on August 10, 2008. We treasure our family get togethers. Out of seven children, only three are left in Eunice's family.

We were saddened during the year by the death of some of our fellow missionaries who worked with us in PNG. Especially close to us were Peg and Ralph Bleeke. Everyone who worked with us in PNG is like our family so their passing leaves a hole in our heart, but we know we will see them in heaven.

We look forward to the 40th wedding anniversary, December 14, 2008, of Charla and Garry Wolff, who served with us in PNG.

We are happy at this time to have Ray's sister, Thora, here. A lot of celebrating is going on. December 12-26, 2008, we'll spend in Chicago babysitting and attending the Christmas programs of Aaron, Evan, Anna and Nathan, plus celebrating Christmas with them. We thank the Lord for all His goodness and the joy family times give us. Paula and Scott, and Charla and Russell are still in their same pro-

fessions and doing well. So far, the economy has not taken their jobs away. The Lord will take care of His children even if hard times come.

We pray God's rich blessings on each one of you. God bless and keep you in His grace and favor in 2009.

With love in Christ,
Ray and Eunice Hausler

P.S. Wendi and family and all our family were together Nov 29, '08.

Christmas 2009

Dear Relatives and Friends,

Greetings to you all at this Blessed time of the year. It is with thanks and praise to God for sending His only Son, Jesus, to save us from our sins, that we rejoice and celebrate as the world tries hard to rob us of the message. To celebrate Christ's birth, we pray ever more diligently to our Father in heaven to forgive our sins and help us to grow ever stronger in our faith in Jesus. He has promised that He will never leave us or forsake us. So may He keep us in the true faith until we enter His heavenly kingdom forever, safe and secure from Satan and His luring, and all earthy woe.

We had a wonderful Christmas celebration last year with Ray's sister, Thora, here, it was a happy time. We were all in Chicago at Paula and Scott, and Charla and Russell's homes. Our five grandchildren are full of life and bring a lot of joy.

We are in Chicago a lot to visit and help with the grandchildren, especially when they are sick and they have celebrations. Every birthday is a special celebration and Ray decorated a cake of their liking. We'll try to get up for Christmas programs if weather permits. They will all be at our home for Christmas.

A highlight this year was traveling to the PNG staff reunion in Minneapolis, Minnesota. We travelled up and back with Garry and

Charla Wolff: that was a good time for us to get a visit with them. The Reunion was inspiring as usual. Just seeing fellow missionaries is so uplifting and sharing memories is wonderful. Several of our staff had been back to PNG last year so we had the latest news from there. The Ralls did Evangelist's training and the Schaches did needed carpentry repair work at the hospital and evangelist training school at Birip. (The Ralls go to PNG to work at the Birip Seminary to help the pastors with preaching the Bible in its truth and purity. Rev. Rall also goes out every week to preach at a church in the area. The Schaches go to help with remodeling and keeping buildings at the Seminary in good condition. A lot of the men working with them learn woodworking skills in this manner). *We had special visitors from PNG, Ezekiel Peter (President of the Gutnuis {Good News} Lutheran Church) and Jacob Luke (who was one of the original students Ray/Eunice worked with and became quite the business man, establishing the Jacob Luke Foundation in PNG). It was wonderful to see how God is working amongst these people and they are praising and working for the Lord. A sad note was that we had lost several of our former mission staff since our last reunion, but we know they are Asleep in Jesus.*

In August we had a week in Branson, Missouri, with Charla's family. It was a special time, as we could enjoy the grandchildren and parents in a relaxed and fun setting. A lot of the entertainment there is still Christian oriented.

In August, we also had the Twenhafel reunion. This is Eunice's mother's family. We always enjoy hearing many stories from the past and getting to know new people who come. We also hear from cousins in Germany, since they were here one year for the reunion.

In November we lost our neighbor, Lily Eickmeyer. She was such a dear friend and so much a part of our lives for 29 years. Since she lived next door, she always looked after our house when we were gone. In October we also lost a dear friend, Wilmer Kuske. He became principal at Hope Lutheran School, Levittown, PA when Eunice left for PNG to teach there. (A letter from him was included earlier in this book, see Chapter 2.). *He served there until his retirement. His wife, Bess, and I taught together several years prior to that. Wilmer and I also worked together at Peterson's Ice Cream shop during our college years at CTC, RF.*

Ray and I keep very busy also with our church activities: Bible classes, altar duties, choir, and helping where needed when we can. We have special Bible studies with dear friends as often as we can and we use Rev. Jim Herzog's material. We also take care of our godson, Peter Ngo, as he attends Rose Hulman University, Terre Haute, Indiana. His parents are in Houston, Texas, but they were some of the Vietnamese our church at Lincoln, Il, sponsored to come over from Vietnam in 1979. They are part of our family as we grew close to them by helping them when they came here with practically nothing. We also try to help our friend Hecham Chehab, a converted Muslim who is working hard as a missionary to the Muslims in Chicago. He needs our prayers also.

We pray God richly to bless all of you and keep you in His loving care.

With love in Christ,
Ray and Eunice Hausler

P.S. Anne Marie Hoover came in Sept. '09; Eunice had shingles Oct. '09; Eunice got off of CHI Bd Feb '10. Saw Sharon Brandt Willweber and husband Oct '09 (Sharon was a Lutheran teacher in Richmond, Virginia, when Eunice was in Levittown. They visited each other when possible); *Aaron had pneumonia Dec '09; Carlee swallowed Charla's thyroid pills Dec '09; Carlee and Nathan had strep throat Dec. '09. They all recovered well.*

CHAPTER 7

The 2010's

Christmas 2010

Dear Relatives and Friends,

Greetings to you at this Blessed time of year when we contemplate the great love God had for us in sending His only Son, Jesus, to live for us, to die for us, and to rise for us. In Him, we have the hope and zeal to live each day knowing that He is by our side: leading us, guiding us and will finally take us home to our eternal home in heaven. May the Holy Spirit forever keep us in this true faith unto life everlasting. Amen. Come Lord Jesus. Revelations 22: 20.

Can hardly believe 10 years have passed since we entered the year 2000. There were so many predictions. Now life just rolls on again. We do pray for our country, that God will keep it strong and free.

The year 2010 has gone very quickly, with trips to Chicago to visit our children and grandchildren making it fly by. We celebrated all five birthdays of the grandchildren which is very joyous. They are at the age where it's all very exciting.

In February, Eunice's term on the Board of Governor's for CHI ended. After being on it for 11 years it was hard to leave, but I also am happy not to have to make the trips to St. Louis and since I was Secretary, write the pages of minutes. It was, however, a very rewarding experience. Preserving our church's history is very important for our children. Staying doctrinally pure is critical.

In April, Ray and I took a Caribbean Cruise for 5 days. It was very beautiful and relaxing. We spent a few days in Florida and enjoyed the sights. We took a wrong turn one afternoon and found out how expansive the Everglades are. We couldn't turn around on the Interstate until we were half way across the Everglades. They are a beauty all their own. On the way home we stopped in North Carolina and visited friends from New Guinea days, Clarence and Ruth Budke. We reminisced and it was so good to see them.

We still take care of Peter Ngo, our Vietnamese friend from Houston. He is an American citizen. He is a student at Rose-Hulman Institute of Technology in Terre Haute, Indiana. So we take trips over there occasionally to make sure he is doing okay.

In June and July, we were invited to 3 weddings of former students. That's always a joy.

July 2-7, we were thrilled to have Greg and Elenore Hausler from Brisbane, Australia, here. Greg is Ray's nephew. He and Elenore were delightful guests and we took them around to see the sights in this area—mostly St. Louis. We even got in a Cardinal baseball game. We also went to the July 4th celebration at memorial park and sat on the steps by the river to see the fireworks. It was exciting for all of us. After they left here they went up to Chicago and saw sights there with Paula and Charla. A highlight was visiting the Willis Tower (formerly the Sears Tower) and walking out on the glass ledge on the top floor. I think it's over 100 floors tall. Also exciting was a cruise on the Chicago River. Ray keeps in contact with his family in Australia via phone and letters, but a visit from relatives or friends is very special.

In August we took Paula, Scott, Anna and Evan to Branson, Missouri. We had such a good time. It's a real family place. They especially enjoyed Silver Dollar City and the go-carts.

In September we celebrated a friend in Lincoln, Illinois 80th birthday—Daris Knauer. Was great to see many of our friends from our days in Lincoln.

Our grandchildren all stayed a week in the summer. A highlight was going to Rainbow Ranch where they have exotic animals. They even saw a baby goat being born. Aaron got to name it and he named it Aaron.

My sister, Wilma, has been ill a lot this year so I spent a lot of time caring for her. Taking her to doctors and dentist was part of all. I feel like I know most of the Doctors at our Centralia hospital after all the testing they put her through. She's doing well at the moment. My brother, Luther, also had two knee surgeries and is doing well. Wilma, Luther, and I are the only three left of seven children in our family.

This month we are going up to Chicago every weekend to see the grandchildren in their Christmas programs. Aaron also has a piano recital. We enjoyed last weekend immensely so am sure the rest will be the same.

We pray this finds all good your way and we wish you God's richest blessing in 2011.

With love in Christ,
Ray and Eunice Hausler

Christmas 2011

Dear Relatives and Friends,

Greetings to you at this Blessed time of year when we join the angel choir in singing praises to our God, who sent His only Son to save us from our sins, and believing in Him, we have the peace, love and joy that sustains us here until we can live forever with Him in our eternal home. We pray, even so, come, Lord Jesus.

We praise God that He has given us good health which helped a lot as we spent the year driving back and forth to Chicago helping Paula, Anna and Evan, and also several weeks taking care of the Englebretsen three: Aaron, Nathan and Carlee while Charla and Russell went on short trips, one being a mission trip to the hill country in Tennessee. Charla works for J P Morgan Chase Bank. Paula has her own Architecture firm, Batir Architecture Ltd. and has been doing some work internationally. We thank God that they have work as so many people are suffering from not having work.

A highlight in July was when two of our former students, Dian Roo and Jacob Luke, from PNG came to visit us for a few days. Also, at this time we had our former missionary staff of PNG reunion. Four more leaders came to the reunion from PNG. What an exciting and wonderful two days we had together! All six of the men who came are Christian men and we thank God for their strong leadership in PNG.

In September, we were happy to have Phillip Thiele from Melbourne, Australia, with us. He is the husband of Rita Wiebe, our good friend, from PNG days. He stayed with our good friends the Graens, from Iowa, and they brought him here. We toured Southern Illinois, seeing one spot the "Garden of the gods." It is a little "Grand Canyon," and we hiked down it and had a great time. There are beautiful spots in Southern Illinois.

Of course, all our grandchildren's birthdays were special occasions. They love being special on their day. Ray again made some of their cakes.

On November 26, 2011, our great niece was married at Old Trinity Lutheran Church, in the Soulard area, St. Louis. This is where the LCMS began in STL, with immigrants from Germany about 1847. Carissa is a teacher and her husband, Evan, just finished his residency in St. Louis, and is now a Doctor. Ray and I enjoyed all as we celebrated our 45th wedding anniversary that day as well. We left after the wedding for a few days in Branson, Missouri. We saw a few good shows, "The Miracle of Christmas" was so wonderful and put you back in Bethlehem as it was when Jesus was born.

Also, one of Eunice's former students was married, November 19. He is the grandson of Wayne and Marlene Maschhoff, our good friends. Joshua works at the Maschhoff pig industry, one of the top ten in the U.S. His wife, Angela, is teaching at our Lutheran School in Nashville, Illinois.

We now look forward to Christmas with our children and grandchildren and the Gorneys, who are part of our family as well. We also look forward to hearing from all of you and of your happenings during the year.

God bless you all and grant you a very happy and Blessed new year, 2012.

Love in Christ,
Ray and Eunice Hausler

Christmas 2012 & New Year 2013

Dear Relatives and Friends,

Greetings to you at this Blessed time of year when we celebrate God's great love for us in sending His one and only Son to live a life of sacrifice for us and which culminated in His death for our sins and then his glorious Resurrection. Now you and I can live in the peace of knowing that our sins are forgiven, and living and believing in Him, we look forward to eternal life with Him forever. May this joy fill us in the New Year.

I'm sorry our Christmas letter is late this year but I'll reveal the reason to you later in this letter.

The year 2012 was a good year as were able to spend time with family and friends. We visited Paula, Evan (9), and Anna (7), and Russell and Charla, Aaron (10), Nathan (7), and Carlee (5), and celebrated their birthdays on their special days also.

In June we were privileged to be in Evansville, Indiana, for the graduation from High School of Stephen Kieser. Eunice was the graduation speaker. He is attending Hillsdale College in Michigan, which is a very good school. His father, Rev. Steven Kieser was the seventh and eighth grade teacher in Hoffman, IL, when Eunice was principal there. He moved on to become a Pastor. He and his wife, Julia, have seven children and they are a great family.

We had planned a trip to Australia in March and were able to do this July 17-August 22. We had a wonderful trip. The time with Ray's family and friends was a lot of fun and precious. We played a lot of cards, had delicious meals and celebrated birthdays and anniversaries that were past or coming. When we first arrived at our nephew Greg Hausler's home, our good friend from PNG, Dian Roo was in Brisbane, and we had a good visit with him. We also were able to visit our PNG friends and fellow missionaries in Melbourne and Adelaide. We spent time with the Thieles and Collyers in Melbourne. Then on to Adelaide where we stayed with Jan and Clive Schubert. Betty Feist, whom we worked with in PNG, planned a reunion for us with fellow missionaries in Goolwah, South Australia. Over 20 were present and we had such a good time just seeing each other again and reminiscing from noon until 7:00 P.M. We are so filled with joy and remembrances of this trip. There was only one drawback, Ray got an infected foot while on the beach at Coolum and it turned into a few complications due to diabetes. He has a drop foot and pinched nerve which are still healing and left him with a limp. It didn't dampen our spirits on the trip, however.

During the year we also spent time helping Eunice's sister Wilma, who is ailing and niece, Marcella, who is handicapped and looks forward to our visit each week. We also enjoy visits from our Vietnamese friends in Houston. All these families are very dear to us, and we have Peter Ngo, Jr., in Terre Haute, Indiana, Rose-Hulman Institute of Technology: we try to see him as often as possible. He graduates in May so we won't see him so often after that.

In September, Eunice and her friend since High School days, Marilyn Michael, planned our 60th High School Reunion. We had a very good attendance and missed those who have already departed and a few who couldn't come. At our age, reminiscing and enjoying our past years brings lots of pleasure.

In October, the opportunity came up for Eunice to go to South Africa, December 6-17, 2012 to help start a Lutheran School in Soweto. This is why you are getting this letter late. Anyway, it was a whirlwind trip and I can't believe how much you can fit into 10 days. South Africa is a beautiful country, hills, mountains, valleys, and big cities and lots of people. The first two days we stayed with Bishop William Weber and his family in Praetoria. I had traveled there with Rev. Timothy Schaar, Southern Illinois District President of the LCMS. He was the speaker for the Lutheran Church of South Africa Synod to be held for 4 days. The Weber's took us to a Diamond mine, which was very interesting. I am very impressed with the Weber family. Grandpa and Father Weber were missionaries among the people of South Africa since 1847, and now three of Father Weber's sons are working amongst the people of South Africa, William is Bishop, and Christof and Peter each have a congregation. After this I stayed a night with Carl and Debra Rockrohr, who are teaching at the Lutheran Theological Seminary in Praetoria. Debra started a Deaconess program.

With the Rockrohrs, I traveled from Pretoria to Wartburg, near Durban, about a 5-hour drive, for the Church Synod (convention) *and the scenery was beautiful. The Synod was very enlightening and I enjoyed getting to know many of the delegates and how they think and feel. I stayed with the Ortmanns' who are of German descent and it was delightful. They helped me with lots of insights and also took me to see their family home: the brother who lives there had large sugarcane fields. On the last day of Synod, Thursday, A.M., three Seminarians were ordained at a very special closing Communion service. What a bond in Christ we have with people all around the world.*

Then I traveled to Soweto with Pastor David Tswaedi and two Seminarians. We spent 6 hours conversing and again I was the learner. We stopped for lunch at a fast-food place (yes, they have them too) and I bought them all lunch. We made it a celebration for Pastor Jeremy, who had been ordained that A.M. We had big hot fudge – caramel sundaes, after our plate lunches. Pastor Jeremy was so excited and said, "This is the best day of my life." When we got to Johannesburg, we dropped the two men off at the bus stop and Pastor Tswaedi and I went on to Soweto. I stayed with a lovely family, the wife is a lawyer and husband is in marketing. Grandma was there getting home care and I had good visits with her, lots of insights into her life in South Africa. Then I met with Pastor Tswaedi on Friday: I saw his church and met the 14 confirmands who were cleaning the church for their special service on Sunday. Pastor Tswaedi and I talked about opening a Lutheran School, which he has wanted for a long time. There are 3 empty public schools. We are working on getting one as our school (but secretly I'm asking God to give us all three) as the field there is ripe unto harvest. So many, many children, and they are bussed out of

Soweto at 5:00 A.M. to another township, and they have to pay for bussing and taxes so to have schools in their neighborhoods with good teachers would be a blessing for them beyond measure. I'm praying God to grant us a miracle and let these schools open—imagine 1000 children hearing God's Word every day and parents being involved, Soweto could become a Christian bulwark against other religions trying to move in. Anyway, please pray to God with me that great things will happen there. This is God's will that His Word be taught to the ends of the earth as He told us just before He ascended in to heaven, so this will happen.

Then Sunday came and we got to church at 9:15 A.M. It started at 9:30 A.M. We couldn't get a seat (of course they got me one immediately) and they were singing and praising God. They sing and dance and what a praise session it was. Then we had Christian witnessing from members, the delegate to Synod made his report, many more testimonies and witnessing. I was asked to speak. Then we all walked up to the front (I didn't know what it was for) but it was to drop our offering in the three big baskets at the altar. Well, I didn't have my money so sheepishly I walked back and came up again. Then Pastor Tswaedi gave a very dynamic sermon for 45 minutes. Then the confirmands were confirmed—much like at our church in New Minden, except they wore black and very fashionable hats for the girls. Then we had communion and they wear black when they have communion to show sorrow for their sins—well I wore a red suit that day and stood out like a sore thumb—but Pastor told me later, "Don't worry, they understand because you are not acquainted with our customs."—which made me feel a little better. I asked the lady I stayed with, Mapolo, for her black hat when I went up to communion and she gladly loaned it to me. Anyway, after 5 hours the service finished at 2:00 P.M. Then a big dinner, cooked by the ladies, was served. Time was fleeting as I had to be at the airport by 6:00 P.M. to fly back to the U.S. Well, at 4:00 P.M. Pastor Tswaedi said, "Let's go, we've got to get you to the airport." He told me on the way what he had preached about as it was all in Tshwane, which of course, I could not understand. Anyway, I got on the airplane that evening on angel's wings. I had so much to think about and so much to praise God for that I got to Atlanta a lot faster than the flight to South Africa. So now you know why you're getting this letter late.

After I got home, December 17, we went up to Chicago to celebrate Christmas with Charla, Russell, Aaron, Nathan, and Carlee. We got to see Carlee's preschool Christmas program which was delightful. We missed Aaron's band concert and their Christmas program at Bethel Lutheran Church. They were leaving on Sunday for Canada to visit with Russell's family.

Then Paula, Evan and Anna came home with us and spent the week which was a lot of happy times. Sister Wilma had an accident, December 26, so was in the hospital till December 31, so we had trips to the hospital. That brings us to now when I could write this letter. So next year pray I don't have so much excitement to write about so you won't get such a long letter!!!!

Anyway during 2013, may God's richest blessings be with you. Praise Him with all your heart, soul, and body as I saw the South Africans do. It will bring you peace and joy beyond measure.

Much love to you all,
Ray and Eunice Hausler

Deaths, Injuries Reported in Washington CountyNovember 17, 2013 WSILTV

Original Story

One person was killed and others injured as strong storms and tornadoes swept across southern Illinois Sunday.

Major damages were reported in Washington County, particularly in and around the community of New Minden.

Rick Greten Washington County EMA coordinator, tells News 3 that one person was killed south of New Minden. Greten says there were also injuries reported in that area.

Several homes and a church were damaged in the community. Eastbound lanes of Interstate 64 in Washington County were closed for a time after two semis overturned.

Trooper Joey Watson with Illinois State Police says Route 177 just west of New Minden is expected to be closed "for an extended period of time."

UPDATED 4:30 p.m. Sunday, NOVEMBER 17,2013

Washington County Coroner Mark Styninger says two people were killed in Sunday's storm.

According to Styninger, the victims were an 80-year-old man and his 78-year-old sister. The two were in a house south of New Minden.

UPDATED 10:05 p.m. Sunday, NOVEMBER 17, 2013

The small town of New Minden is another area cleaning up from storm damage Sunday night. A reported EF4 moved through Washington County around noon killing two people.

The victims were an 80-year-old man and his 78-year-old sister.

The strong winds also flipped semi-trucks on Interstate 64 and destroyed multiple homes.

Eunice Hausler saw the tornado coming early Sunday afternoon. She took shelter with her husband in the basement of their New Minden home.

"We heard a big crash," said Hausler. "We knew the top of our house was going."

When the couple climbed out, they discovered their roof and entire rooms missing.

Many of their belongings were tossed across the street, "I knew because of the crash," said Hausler. "Still when you see it, it just kind of takes your breath away."

However, the damage to their stuff can all be replaced. Hausler feels what was left behind is far more important. Her wooden "Trust in the Lord" sign was untouched.

"The cupboards were blown off the wall," said Hausler, "But see that sign up there, that's what gave me hope. I can go on."

Residents in New Minden say the storm came up suddenly. It was so powerful that it knocked over huge trees and tore the roof and steeple of the town's historic church.

"A little baby had been baptized this morning," said Pastor Timothy Mueller. "A very joyful occasion."

Mueller had just walked the last family out of St. Johns Lutheran Church, wrapping up the service of about 130 people.

"Couldn't have been five or ten minutes later when the storm hit," said Mueller.

The congregation dates back 150 years and has seen its share of rough weather. The church was damaged by tornadoes in 1896 and 1907.

"The steeple has gone down in storms two other times," said Mueller.

St. John's will now add 2013 to their history. The congregation is just thankful Sunday night that the church was empty when this tornado touched down.

"If God wills it, we'll hopefully be able to rebuild again," said Mueller. "We'll see."

Emergency crews did set up a help center at the ballpark in New Minden. Members of the Red Cross and Salvation Army came in to make sure every resident had a place to sleep.

Police are asking drivers to stay away from the area to give utility workers time to clear any power lines from the roadways.

Christmas 2013

Dear Relatives and Friends,

Greetings to you at this Blessed time of the year. As we contemplate the mystery of the Son of God becoming flesh – a human being, so He could rescue and redeem us from our sins – may we with grateful hearts thank Jesus this Christmas and always thank Him for His great love for us in that He suffered and died for us so we can be His own and live in His kingdom now and forever. Christmas is truly a Blessed time when we celebrate our Savior's birth and the arrival of angels and shepherds to greet Him.

January was a month of prayer for the schools in Soweto, South Africa. This whole year we are continuing to pray for this venture. So far, we have not moved forward, so keep this in your prayers. As you maybe saw in the Nelson Mandela death news, Soweto is a very poor area. The schools we are planning are much needed.

February, our nephew, Charles Redeker, had a very serious knee infection, which was not diagnosed for a week and got very serious. He still needs our prayers as he still has a lot of pain.

April, Paula got a very serious infection which also was not diagnosed for a week even though we went to the doctor every day. By Sunday she was so bad that we took her to the emergency room at the hospital and they diagnosed her with sepsis. Things started happening fast and if we had not gotten her there when we did, they said she would not have lived till morning. So, we keep thanking God for leading us. We thank God she recovered although her kidneys are still recovering.

May, brother Luther had open heart surgery and after 5 days, had a heart attack which made his condition very serious. He was hospitalized for three months. He is doing well now with dialysis three days a week.

May 25, sister Wilma had a brain hemorrhage and died five days later. She had always been like a mother so we miss her very much.

June 6-Lisa Redeker (our niece) and Andy Schmitt were married at St. Paul's Lutheran Church, Troy, IL. They went to a St. Louis hospital to see her father, brother Luther, after the wedding. Then followed a wonderful reception and dinner.

June, early June, Evan (10) and Anna (8) Price came to visit for five days. We had a good time going fishing at the Heseman's pond, visiting Grant's farm in St. Louis and the zoo. Anna is playing the cello this year and loves it a lot. Both of them take piano lessons.

July, Nathan (8) and Carlee (6) Englebretsen came to visit for 5 days. We again visited the same places in St. Louis. They loved swimming at the Rec center in Centralia, also Aaron (11) couldn't come this year as he had sports activities and also was at Camp Walcamp (a Lutheran camp) for a week. Both Aaron and Nathan still play on hockey teams.

July 30 and 31, we had 17 of our PNG friends here. They came to thank all the missionaries who had come to PNG years ago to bring the Gospel to them. They came for our PNG reunion which we have every two years. This year it was in Monroe, Washington. We couldn't go but they came to St. Louis. It was truly a highlight for us. Some were former students and they have done well. We had a doctor, lawyer, pastor, businessman, government leaders, teacher, housewives, both men and women. This was truly a "Praise God" time. Each day is a "Praise God" day!!

August 3-10 we were with Paula, Evan & Anna in Disney World.

November 17, 2013, we just got home from church about 20 minutes and we were hit by an EF5 tornado: it blew our house away. We just made it to the basement and were safe. It was devastating to see our material things blown away for miles in less than 2 or 3 seconds but it certainly brought us in close contact with God's Almighty power. Never doubt that our God is Almighty and has all power. It also reminded us not to put our hearts on earthly things. As we came up from the basement, one plaque was left on the dining room wall. It was made for me by a 90-year-old friend, Adolph Rebstock, about 10 years ago. It had been scrolled out with his saw and had Jesus over the words, "Trust in the Lord." I said, okay Lord, I got the message. That has given us both a lot of strength and courage as we know the Lord is in charge and "all things work together for good to those who love Him," Romans 8:28. We were so blessed with a community coming out to help us. Our good friends the Maschhoffs gave us a home to stay in. It was the home they use for their interns at the Pork Farm in the summer, so it was empty now. How blessed we were to move into a furnished home the first night and they also loaned us their car for two weeks till our one was repaired. Both were badly damaged. God gave us three days of sunshine to get everything we could rescue packed up and no rain. It is in sheds at Maschhoffs and Hesemans. We plan to rebuild, but it will take at least 6 or 7 months.

Our three neighbors on our block also lost their homes and our beautiful stone church across the street was badly damaged. It will be repaired in 6 to 8 months. Our organ was completely damaged (a beautiful old pipe organ), the steeple fell on it. Our bell fell on the left side of the church and the cross and steeple on the right side. Tornadoes do strange things.

So, 2013 was quite a year. All in all, we bow before our Lord and say, "Your will be done in all things." He is in charge. So, we praise and thank God each day for His mighty wonders and power and most of all His great love for us in sending His only Son, Jesus, to save us from our sins.

God bless you all richly in 2014.

In our Savior's name,
Ray and Eunice Hausler

Christmas 2014

Dear Relatives and Friends,

Greetings to you at this Blessed time of year. Thank God that He loved us so much that He sent His only Son, Jesus, and that He willingly suffered and died for our sins. As we daily sin much, we need His forgiveness each and every day. So, our prayers of thanks and praise rise to Him each day, and many times each day.

This letter will be different from any other we have ever written, as this year has been so different and filled with the unusual and yet filled with so many blessings we can't count them or even believe it ever happened. We have a wonderful God and we know He never leaves His children, but works all for good for them.

January started with us getting settled in the Maschhoff house, that they lent us after the tornado. We were so thankful to be in a furnished house and so close to our old home. This was a great asset while we were building.

In February, construction started on the rebuilding of our home. It seemed like every day we had to make decisions, architectural decisions, electrical decisions, appliances, furniture, carpet and flooring, paint, cupboards, etc. etc. This lasted through March and April. During this time, we were cleaning insulation out of everything that was rescued from the tornado. What a job that was!!! It was a cold winter and lasted longer than usual so what a blessing that our builders were able to work and get us into the house by April 30.

We did take a little vacation the first week in April with Paula and family, Charla and family, and Paula's friend Val Shoger and her daughter and mother. We went to Hebron, Kentucky, to see the Creation Museum. It was a wonderful four days and assured us of the wonderful God we have and the beautiful world He created for us. It was started by Ken Ham, who is from Australia. (He grew up about 35 miles from where Ray lived!). He is at present building an ark that will be the same size as the one Noah built.

In May, we were busy moving and cleaning—we both said, "we don't want to see anymore pieces of insulation!" It was in everything. We had wonderful people helping us with this all so we thank and praise God for all the help we got: physical, mental, and financially. We are still sorting, mostly because we can't stay at it because keeping up with daily activities also takes up our time. It will all get done eventually. Our new home is much like our old one with a few changes. We are so thankful for our insurance company, State Farm, as they took care of us very well and paid for our house and contents. We added a couple of things which we had to pay for.

In May, June, and September, we celebrated grandchildren birthdays which is always a delightful time. Aaron is 12, Evan is 11, Nathan and Anna are 9, and Carlee is 6. They all got to spend a week with us in July. We went to an animal farm, Science Center—where "Build a Bear" was a hit. We also saw Concordia Seminary and other points of interest, most of this being in St. Louis and the surrounding area.

In August, Ray, Paula, and Charla, planned Eunice's 80th birthday party. They took us to Branson, Missouri for 4 days, and it was a fun time. Then on Sunday they had a surprise party with about 80 friends and relatives present. I didn't want any celebration but it was a fun time anyway. The joy was seeing everyone and out of town guests like my brother-in-law, Roger Thusius and his wife, Linda; my niece, Ann Hoover and husband Steve, all from Maryland. Also, nieces and nephews from Chicago all the way down to New Minden. A nice group of friends from my High School class of 1952 were there. A big surprise was that Rev. Jim and Betty Herzog came from Texas. The Garry Wolf's and the Dick Adler's who were in our wedding and with us in PNG also came. God is good to let us enjoy such happy moments.

In October, CHI opened a wonderful display of the Mission work in PNG, which Ray and I were a part of 1959-1972. They did a wonderful job and if you have a chance to go see it, it is worth your time. It covers the story of mission work in PNG very well. One of our missionaries Bob Kroenke, painted many pictures, portraits of New Guinea men and women, and they are in the display.

We thank and praise God always for His goodness. The tornado interrupted our life some—but God's grace and goodness through it all is evidence of what a great God we have. We tell our young people—"give your life to the Lord and let Him lead you and you will be blessed beyond measure—especially with a closeness to Him that gets you through whatever life holds for you." On November 17, 2014, the anniversary of the tornado, we were asked to be on Radio Station, KFUO, our church's radio station in St. Louis. It took an hour and we kind of relived the tornado. Pastor Mueller, our pastor, and Edie Grote, who was also hit by the tornado joined us.

For Thanksgiving we were at Charla and Russ's home. It was a great family time, and we all ate too much turkey and trimmings. For Christmas they will all be at our house. Ray and I celebrated our 48th wedding anniversary on Thanksgiving Day. A great day to celebrate with all the family. We never dreamt it would be that long when we were married in PNG in 1966.

We pray all is well your way and your year has been blessed. We also pray rich blessings for you in 2015. Keep Jesus in your heart and it will be well.

Love in Christ,
Ray and Eunice Hausler

Christmas 2015

Dear Relatives and Friends,

Once again, we are privileged to be in the wonderful advent season when we prepare our hearts to receive our Savior, Jesus Christ. As our world changes, we Christians must tell of Jesus more and more. He is the only God and through Him only will we gain eternal life. We must read God's Word daily so the Holy Spirit can increase our faith in large measure. "God so loved the world that He gave His only begotten Son, that whoever believes in Him shall not perish but have eternal life." John 3:16.

We have had a busy year. We tried to get our home organized again. There was a lot of cleaning, shopping and organizing. We still have some to do. Our insurance company, State Farm, was very good to us and we have a nice home, fully furnished once again.

Paula, Evan and Anna are doing well. They are busy as Paula works, Evan is in Grade 6 and Anna in Grade 5. Charla, Russell, Aaron, Nathan and Carlee are also doing well. Aaron in Grade 8, Nathan in Grade 4, and Carlee in Grade 1. Charla just changed to a new job with Discover. They were all here for Thanksgiving and we had a wonderful four days together. We played a lot of games and cards. Worship and devotions times were also a highlight.

Ray was fortunate in March, his friend Herschel Kasten, took him to Australia to be his guide. They had a good time visiting Ray's family and doing some sightseeing.

In April we made a trip to Killeen, Texas, for the funeral of Rev. James Herzog. It was sad to let him go as he has done so much for our family. He married us in PNG, married our girls here in New Minden, and came for our special family occasions, preaching for some of them. His wife, Betty, was also a dear friend. He kept building our faith with many writings he did which always was a boost for our faith. We miss him but know he now has his reward and is enjoying his beautiful home in heaven.

We also saw Evan perform on his drums in a school concert and Anna plays the cello.

In May, we celebrated Ray and Anna's birthdays. These are joyous occasions.

In June we took Anna and Evan for a week to be with Aaron, Nathan and Carlee at their VBS at Bethel Lutheran Church, Westmont, IL. They do a great job of bringing the children into a closer relationship with Jesus. We celebrated Evan and Aaron's birthdays and we also enjoyed seeing Nathan and Carlee in their dance routines.

Darrell, Susan and Sarah Valentine, our Vietnamese friends now in Houston, visited in June. We ran all over Chicago, and stayed with Charla and Russ.

In July 24, 25, & 26, we had a wonderful time at our PNG reunion in Peoria, IL. We had 21 people come from PNG; some were our former students. They all have a profession and we are proud of them. They came to thank us for bringing the Gospel to them, and brought joy and tears to our eyes. We did a lot of singing, praying, and praising God. We also took them to CHI in St. Louis where they were able to see the wonderful display of the mission work in PNG.

All summer we had tickets to the Muny, outdoor opera performances in Forest Park, St. Louis. Our dear friend, David Wiedenhofer from California has given us tickets for two years now and we are grateful as sitting under the summer sky and hearing wonderful singing and acting is uplifting.

In August, all five grandchildren were here for a week. We had a wonderful time. We went to the St. Louis Science Center, Grant's Farm, Concordia Seminary and CHI. Life is exciting when they are here.

August 9, we had the rededication of our church across the street, St. John's Lutheran, which was heavily damaged by the Tornado, Nov. 17, 2013. The church was packed and the singing and music wonderful. Our daughter, Charla, sang a beautiful song she had written.

August 23, we had a birthday party for brother Luther. Of course, our nieces and nephews included Eunice as she and Luther were born a day apart. Our niece from Baltimore, Maryland was also here.

In August we visited Bryan and Vera Pitney and went to Gatlinburg, Tennessee. Great time!

In September we had the ADT security system put in our home, (don't try to break in, the alarm is very loud!). With a lot of crime around, we decided to do this. We also celebrated Nathan and Carlee's birthdays.

In November we had the whole family, dear friend Wendi and family, Pastor Mueller and his son Jacob and family, brother Luther and friend, nephew David and family, here for Thanksgiving. We thanked and praised God and had a wonderful meal, turkey and all the trimmings. These times are precious.

Ray had two bouts in the emergency room in November. He lost strength in his legs and was very weak. He has neuropathy. They boiled it down to a new medication he was given. He is doing much better since he no longer takes it.

December 19, we will go to Chicago to hear our grandchildren in their Christmas program. They always have a wonderful presentation of Jesus birth at Bethel Lutheran Church, Westmont, IL.

We pray this finds you all in good health and wish you a very Blessed year in 2016.

With love and greetings,
Ray and Eunice

November 2016

Dear Relatives and Friends,

Greetings to you at this Blessed time of year. We thank God that He had mercy on us sinners and sent His only Son, Jesus, to fulfill the Law for us so that now if we believe in Jesus, we have eternal life.

John 3:16 says, "For God so loved the world, that He gave His only begotten Son, that whosoever believes in Him shall not perish but have eternal life." This verse makes it very clear, so we celebrate His birth with great joy.

This year has been rather quiet after two and a half years of being very busy recovering from the tornado. We enjoy our new home and thank God for His goodness every day.

Some highlights: Our grandson, Aaron Englebretson was confirmed on May 16, 2016. We thank God for his strong Biblical confession. We pray his faith will sustain him to life eternal.

We have been helping with a new mission at Aviston, Illinois. We pray for God's guidance for this mission. It is proceeding well, but we need to start service every week instead of once a month.

The end of May we had to give up our last sibling, Luther Redeker. There were eight children in the Redeker family, and Eunice is the only one left. Luther had complications with dialysis and couldn't go on anymore. He is now with Jesus which is far better.

During the summer we had tickets to the Muny, an outdoor opera production almost every week in St. Louis—Forest Park. Thanks to our good friend, David Wiedenhofer, we had tickets. Some of the productions were "Wizard of Oz," "Music Man," "Fiddler on the Roof"—there were seven all together. All very enjoyable.

In June we again took Evan and Anna over to be with Aaron, Nathan and Carlee for Vacation Bible School. Aaron was part of a skit every day and did a great job. They do a great job at Bethel Lutheran Church and the grandchildren have a great opportunity to learn more of God's Word. Anna won a basketful of candy for being the first student to memorize the 23rd Psalm. Of course, she was encouraged by the other grandchildren so they could all share the candy!

Another highlight is the celebration of everyone's birthday. We start in March, then May, June, August, and September. Each one is special. For Eunice's birthday the grandchildren found out a little late that day that she had a birthday also in August as we only said we were celebrating Paula and Charla. So, they said, "Oh my, we need a present for Grandma." They had no money but Evan said, "I have $20.00 in my pocket." Carlee said, "I know where there is a garage sale down the street." So, they all took off and found a beautiful wall plaque that says, "A House is made of Walls and Beams, a Home is made of Love and Dreams." Well, it is the best present ever!

You are getting this greeting early because our daughter, Charla, gave us tickets to go to Australia and celebrate our 50th anniversary there. We go in November and return in December, gone for four weeks. Our daughter, Paula, is also going with Evan and Anna and they will give a dinner for us with our Australian family and friends on November 26, 2016, the exact day of our wedding 50 years ago in Amapyaka, PNG.

Paula has just been engaged to Jerry Meister, and he and his three daughters will all be with us at the celebration.

We pray you are all doing well. The Lord bless you and keep you! We pray you have a very Blessed Christmas and rich blessings in 2017.

Love to you all,
Ray and Eunice

Christmas 2018

Dear Relatives and Friends,

Greetings to you at this Blessed time of the year when we celebrate God's great love for us by sending His only Son, Jesus, to save us from our sins and assuring us of eternal life with Him if we believe in Jesus according to John 3:16. We pray God to grant us strong faith in Jesus whose birth we celebrate. It happened about 2018 years ago. Praise God for loving us so much.

Our year has been a little more quiet than some years. Since Ray's walking is slow, we haven't travelled very much. That's okay at our age, we enjoy being at home more. We have God's creation all around us here in the country. Looking out our patio window we see fields of growing grain and a forest of trees in the distance.

In May we went to St. Charles, IL where our daughter, Paula, and family live. We heard Anna's cello concert, beautiful music! All the grandchildren play an instrument in their school bands except Anna in the orchestra. Aaron plays the tuba, Nathan the trumpet, Carlee the saxophone, and Evan the drums.

In May we also celebrated Anna and Ray's birthdays. Since Ray was 80 this year, he got the big celebration with about 90 guests to help him celebrate at a dinner at our church-school basement. It was a happy day! We sang "For he's a jolly fellow" many times. Our brother-in-law, Roger Thusius and his wife, Linda came from Maryland for the occasion. They helped Eunice so much to get ready for the party. The Knauers were here from Lincoln, IL, our children and grandchildren from Chicago, and relatives and friends from around our area.

Several days later, Eunice was bitten by a tick and got Lyme disease. She was very ill but found the tick, so was able to get the proper medication. She still has some after effects from it but nothing serious.

Early June our good friends from Houston, Texas, visited us. Mike and Hoa Cheng and their four little daughters were here 5 days. They were a lot of fun to have here and Hoa made a large container of egg rolls for all of us that were so delicious.

The last of the month, June 22 and 27, we celebrated Aaron and Evan's birthdays. They are both tall and towering over us. Both are driving and Aaron is 16 and Evan is 15.

June 30 we were at Caitlyn Fuehne's wedding to Christian Egger. Both of them are Lutheran teachers in our Lutheran School in Las Vegas. Two great children and good friends.

July 8, Eunice had the privilege of helping serve a wedding reception for Jael Trinklein and Levi Karth. Jael and her parents are missionaries in Seoul, South Korea. Levi is a missionary in Paraguay and Jael will be joining him there. Their wedding was a Mexican theme so we had a challenge cooking and decorating. It was a beautiful and happy occasion.

July 20-27 we were privileged to have Evan and Anna with us, so we all went to Branson and had a great time. Saw some good shows, Silver Dollar City and rode the Go-carts.

August 19, we celebrated Paula's 50th birthday. Jerry organized a wonderful surprise party for her at a nice restaurant in St. Charles. A lot of her friends were there and it was another fun party. Next year we will celebrate Charla's 50th birthday on August 30.

October 27, we celebrated our great nephew, Luke Redeker's 4th birthday. He is my brother Luther's only grandson. Luther would love to have seen him but he is happy in heaven.

October 17-20 was a happy time, as Jeffry and Helen Ost were here from Brisbane, Australia. They flew into Chicago so we went up there. Jeffrey's father was a very good friend of Ray. Jeffrey has taken his father's place. We had many happy evenings and one day at Morton Arboretum together.

November 17, we remember 5 years ago when the tornado blew our house away. We sponsored the day at our Lutheran Radio Station KFUO. We thank God for granting us a swift and wonderful recovery. Thursday of that week was Thanksgiving Day in America. We had much to thank God for. Charla and her family were here, as well as, the Gorneys, our friends that are our adopted children.

November 24, we helped Gerry and Charla Wolff and Todd and Janet Luedtke celebrate their 50th wedding anniversaries. They served with us in PNG – so lots of reminiscing.

Now we look forward to Christmas when Paula, Jerry, Evan and Anna will be with us, and later in the week Charla, Russell, Aaron, Nathan, and Carlee will also arrive. It's the best when we can all be together. Our good friend, David Wiedenhofer, who has been very good to us will be here during the week. He helps Evan a lot on the drums as he is a big band man. Christmas dinner we will be at our friends the Gorneys.

We pray God to bless all of you and keep you in His loving care in 2019.

Love you all,
Ray and Eunice

CHAPTER 8

The 2020's

Christmas 2020

Dear Relatives and Friends,

Greetings to you at this wonderful time of year when we celebrate the birthday of our Lord and Savior, Jesus Christ. Praise God that He loved us so much that He sent His only Son, Jesus, to save us sinners so that living and believing in Him, we have peace and joy. John 3:16 says "God so loved the world that He gave His only Son, that whoever believes in Him should not perish but have eternal life." This message we need to tell in this sinful world.

After a year of recovery, for Eunice, who had two surgeries, we are now doing well. Sorry we missed getting a letter out last Christmas. I fell and broke my hip on November 25th, 2019, so was in surgery the day before Thanksgiving and in recovery at Carlyle Nursing Home for 3 weeks. I was so thankful to come home just before Christmas. The surgery caused my right leg to be crooked so July 6, 2020, I had surgery again-knee replacement. It went well and I'm walking good again. God was good to me and so were my family and friends. Paula and Charla came and stayed for a week or more after my surgeries. Ray started getting "meals on wheels," so that kept him going. It was before the pandemic so thank God for that.

Our grandchildren are grown and doing well. We'll be glad when they can all get back into school full time. Aaron is now in college. He is at ISU, Normal, IL. He stays at school for hockey practices.

Evan is a Junior in High School. He still plays drums and has a job at Chicken Shack. Anna is a sophomore and is working on driving skills. She also works at a Play Station store on weekends.

Nathan is a freshman. He was confirmed on September 29, 2020. We all enjoyed being together for this Blessed event. Carlee is in eighth grade and doing well. She is a soccer player.

Our children are now coming down here as we don't drive to Chicago. Ray's legs are not good for driving as he has neuropathy.

We are ready for this pandemic to end. It certainly has messed up many lives. Lots of prayers are needed daily for all those hurting in any way. We have always gone to church and now have to listen over the air or stream. Hopefully we will have Christmas services in church.

So, we look forward to 2021 and pray God to grant us and all of you His grace, strong faith in Jesus, protection and care. May it be a Blessed Year.

With love and blessings to you,
Ray and Eunice Hausler

June 22, 2022

My Dearest Friend Eunice,

Thank you so much for your special story. I am honored to receive your book. I have not been here in Kempner (Texas) *for over seven months so I did not know about your book until now. I will be reading it soon. My plans now are to move back to Kempner permanently. There are no relatives nearby but this is where I want to live. I weigh 100 lbs. now because of health reasons. I believe the Lord will heal me at the right time.*

Sam is still living in the Dallas area. He has fallen in love with Jesus and that is all he wants to talk about.

I hope you and Ray are doing good. I have many good memories of you. God bless you both.

Love you both,
Betty Herzog (Jim Herzog's widow)
(She died shortly after this letter)

Christmas 2022

Dear Relatives and Friends,

What a joy to again celebrate the birthday of our Lord and Savior Jesus Christ. Thanks to God the Father for sending Him to suffer and die for our sins so we can go to heaven when we die believing in Jesus. Jesus was willing to do what His Father asked, he suffered and died for us so that now we can look forward to our beautiful home in heaven. With the eyes of faith when reading Gods' Word, we can see heaven.

This letter will answer many of the wonderful cards and letters we have received from you. Our prayer is that the book I wrote will continue to bring many to see and believe in Jesus. The years go by so quickly at our age but it brings joy that each day brings us closer to our home in heaven.

Ray and I are doing as well as possible. Ray's legs are still not working well due to neuropathy but he can still get around with his walker. I am thankful to have made a good recovery after the lack of oxygen episode last November. (Eunice was in Breese hospital for 10 days, her oxygen level was very low. The hospital staff kept telling the family each day that I wouldn't make it-but on the seventh day, my oxygen came back. My room was swarming with people so I asked, "What's wrong?" and the nurse came, held my arm and said, "Honey your oxygen went from 48% this A.M. to 95%. It has stayed there all day. You are well. You can go home soon." God miraculously did it! That's our wonderful God!).

Our family, Jerry and Paula, Evan and Anna, and Katarina, Brianna and Mikala (Jerry's daughters) are all doing well. Katarina, Brianna, and Mikala have all graduated from college and are busy at their jobs. Evan is at Iowa State studying Architectural Engineering, as his mother did. Anna is a senior in High School and busy with leadership responsibilities, no decision on where she will go to college. Russell, Charla and their children Aaron, Nathan and Carlee are all doing well. Aaron is a junior in college at Illinois State University, and still plays hockey. He wants to be a geography teacher. Nathan is a junior in High School, and still plays hockey. He works at Oberweis, a sandwich and delicious ice cream restaurant. Carlee is a freshman in High School and plays soccer. We were able to get up to be at her confirmation at Bethel Lutheran Church in Westmont last May.

In March I was well enough to have the Book Launch for my book, "Thank You Lord for the Privilege." It was a joy-filled day. Our children were all there: nieces, nephews, and many friends, all helped with the program and it was a "Praise God Day!'

In June one of our Vietnamese families, Mike Cheng and family, came to visit. They have five children ages 3-12. We had lots of fun. They are our grandchildren, as the Vietnamese family the congregation brought from Vietnam when we were in Lincoln, has always been like our family. Then in July, Darrell and Susan, another Vietnamese family, who have one daughter, Sarah, came; the daughter is also our grandchild. They live in Houston, so they love the freedom of this country.

In October, our very good friend's daughter, Pauline Humphrey came to visit us with her two children. Her mother, Reta Wiebe Thiele and Eunice traveled around the world when they were in PNG. Charla came down also and took us all to a hockey game that Aaron was playing in.

We are enjoying all your letters and cards. Just think what a joy it will be <u>when we all get to heaven</u>. There is a song by that name and it has become a special one as it reminds me of the prayer groups who *were in the hospital or outside my window when I was in the hospital last November.*

God bless you all and keep you in His loving care. We pray you have a Blessed Christmas and a Blessed 2023.

With love and prayers,
Ray and Eunice Hausler

Epilogue

And, as a final addition to this book, Eunice was approached by Marquis Who's Who of Top Professionals for 2022. It is with mixed emotions that we share this. Eunice has been crystal clear throughout the writing of both her books that she wants only the Triune God credited with "her" successes: that she takes no worldly pride in her accomplishments and attributes all glory to God for her life. However, we feel it noteworthy that members of a secular organization have taken note of these accomplishments. A short biography of her life will be shared in a future press release and in their publication. Once again, it is Eunice's sincere prayer and hope, that if one additional person be pointed to God through this means, then to God be all glory.

In 2022, Eunice was presented with a plaque inscribed as follows:

TOP EDUCATORS

The Marquis Who's Who

Publication Board is pleased to recognize

Eunice Redeker Hausler

As a

TOP PROFESSIONAL

an honor reserved for Marquis listees

who have achieved career longevity and demonstrated unwavering excellence

In their chosen fields.

And in 2023, the following plaque was issued:

THE MARQUIS WHO'S WHO PUBLICATIONS BOARD

is pleased to recognize

EUNICE REDEKER HAUSLER

as a recipient of the

Albert Nelson Marquis Lifetime Achievement Award

an honor reserved for Marquis Biographees who have achieved career longevity and demonstrated unwavering excellence in their chosen fields.

Erica Lee, President 2023

And as this book was going to final publication in the late spring of 2024, we were highly surprised to receive the Marquis Who's Who Magazine, 15th edition (published every few years) listing hundreds of recipients, with a picture of Eunice on the cover and a brief biography included, in which Eunice attributes her earthly success to her faith. Again, a worldwide witness to God's almighty hand at work in her life.

Used with permission by Marquis Whos Who Ventures LLC © 2024.

Author Bio

Eunice was born into a sibship of eight children on a small farm in Illinois. She then achieved a grade school, high school, and college diploma, which led to a life spent teaching elementary students in the United States, elementary and high school students in Papua New Guinea, and English to adults in China. Along the way, she married an Australian and had two children (and five grandchildren). She has traveled extensively, and shared the love of God with hundreds, even thousands of people, with joy, gratitude, and a heart full of love. Eunice has shared her story in her first book, *Thank You, God, For the Privilege*. This is the expanded story of that life.

Other Books by Eunice Redeker-Hausler

Thank You, Lord, For the Privilege: Eunice Redeker-Hausler grew up on a small farm in Southern Illinois, a child born into a family of eight siblings. Hard work was expected. A one-room school was commonplace and being the first in her family to go to high school which opened up the world. College became possible with hard work. A teaching degree in Lutheran Education led to teaching in the US, Papua New Guinea, and China. Marrying an Australian gentleman fulfilled the great adventure.

Westcliffe, CO-House on the right is where Eunice lived with two widows.

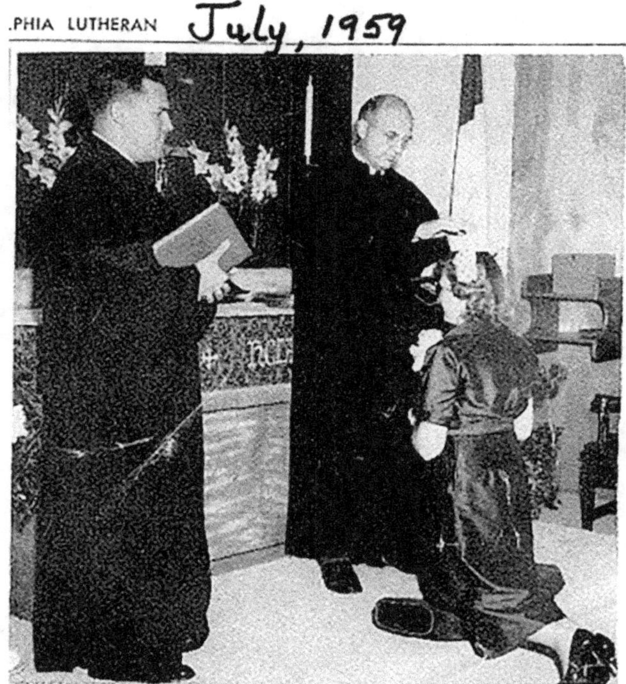

.PHIA LUTHERAN July, 1959

Above is Miss Eunice Redeker kneeling before Rev. Doctor Herman H. Koppelmann of St. Louis, Acting Executive Secretary of the Board for Missions in Foreign Countries, Lutheran Church-Missouri Synod, during the rite of commissioning Miss Redeker as missionary-teacher to New Guinea. To the left stands Rev. W. A. Maier, Jr., pastor of Hope Lutheran Church whom Miss Redeker recently served as instructress of grades one and two and acting principal of Hope Lutheran School since the fall of 1956.

Commissioning Service, May 23, 1959, Hope Lutheran, Levittown, PA
Rev's Walter A. Maier (L), Herman H. Koppleman (R) Eunice kneeling.

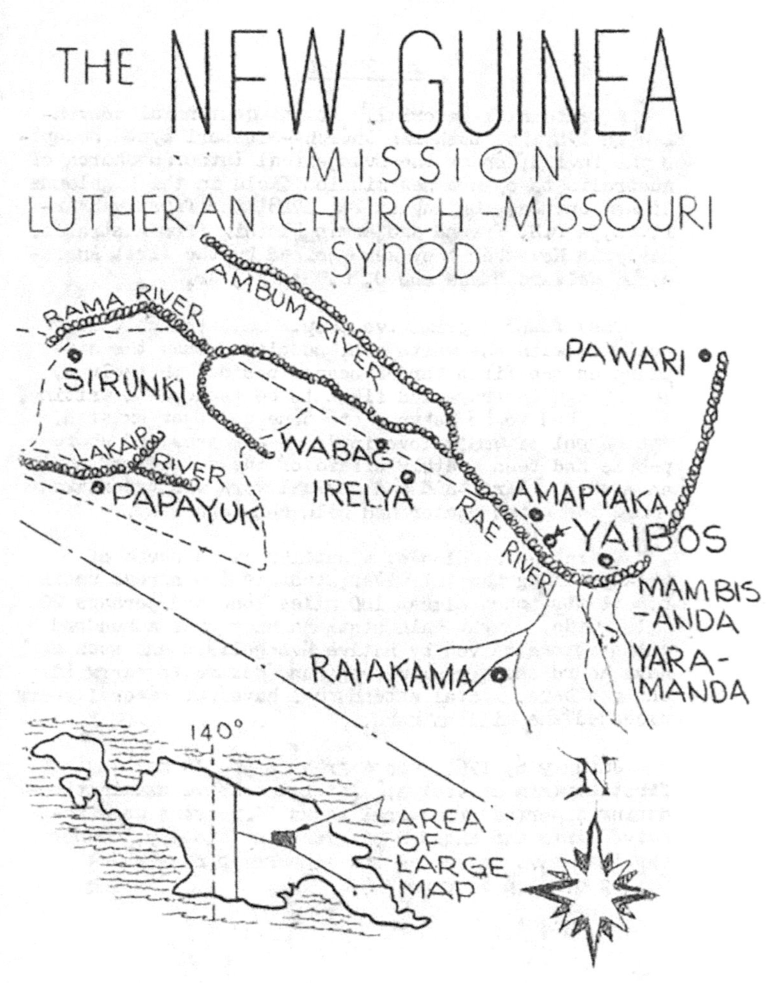

Papua New Guinea Map- The area where Eunice and Ray served.

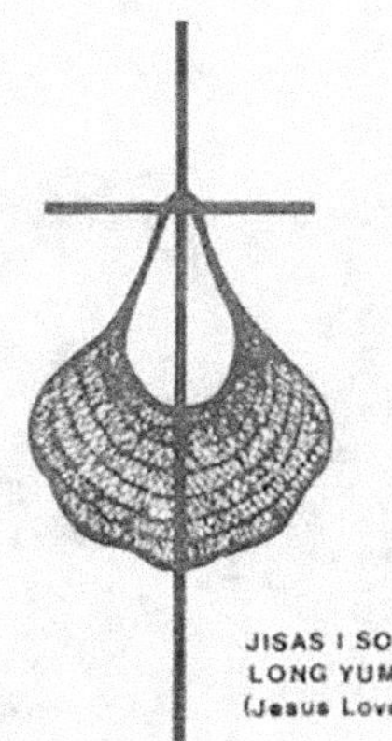

JISAS I SORI
LONG YUMI
(Jesus Loves Us)

Jesus loves us and carries our burdens. The bulging bilum, used throughout New Guinea, hangs on the cross to symbolize the bringing of all our problems and cares to Jesus.

THE LORD'S PRAYER
(Enga Language, Papua New Guinea)

Naimanya Takage ketae kaitinya katege doko. Ebanya kege doko auu pyoo laapa lape. Ebanya isigi mate doko epena lape. Ketae kaitinya ebame masigili pigima. Dopaka pyoo isa yuu dakenya pyepa laape. Idupaka natamano nee dupa diipi. Ebame naimanya koo pigi yanu dupa kayape. Dokotekee ijoo naimanya koo pyekelyamino dupanya koo pigi yanu dupa kaetelyamano. Koo pyepa lao makade pigi dupanya naima laminao napupi. Koo dupanya ebame naima pyoo nyepe. Isigi mate dokopi pupu lapae dokopi tii pipae dokopi, dutupa tata tagapi ebanyaka lamo. Kiniaka.

Compliments,
Ascension Lutheran Church
St. Louis, Missouri

The bilum on the cross.
As Jesus carries our burdens, so the women carried all their burdens in their bilums (from their heads).

The staff during Eunice's first year in PNG (L to R): Teoc (coastal teacher), Teacher Busse, Eunice, Principal Bauer, Kandenge (cookhouse manager).

Aerial view of the St. Paul's Lutheran HS Campus-1959. From the top: two classrooms and a chapel; two dormitories on the left, with a cookhouse on the right; in front of that, a hill carved out for a playfield and gardens.

Rev. Ian Kleinig officiating at a baptism.
Over 600 were baptized at this one at Yaibos, 1960.

Eunice directing the school choir.

A native trade store, 1969.

Eunice buying vegetables, 1969.

The Hausler wedding party-November 26, 1966.

Ray's handiwork: He made (L to R): Lectern, Palm stands, Altar, Baptismal Font, and Pulpit for Grace Lutheran Church, Redcliffe, Australia.

Houseboy Ipatasa with Paula and Charla.

The entire staff of the LCMS in PNG in approximately 1964.
At one time there were 95 staff and family members in PNG.

Aerial view of St. Paul's Lutheran High School, Pausa, 1972.

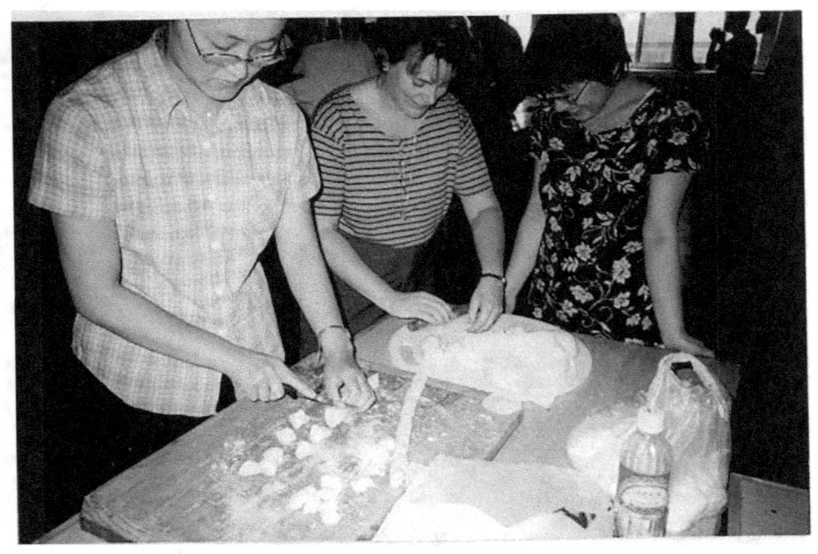

Chinese students showing Ray and Eunice how to make dumplings.

A portion of Ray's Chinese medical students.

Eunice's Chinese high school students.

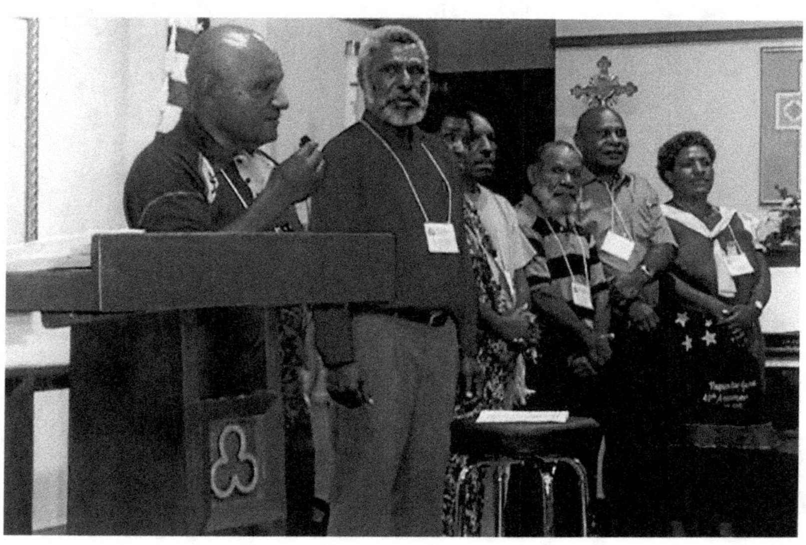

PNG reunion in Peoria, IL. Ezekiel Peter, President of the GLC in PNG (L), along with fellow workers from PNG.

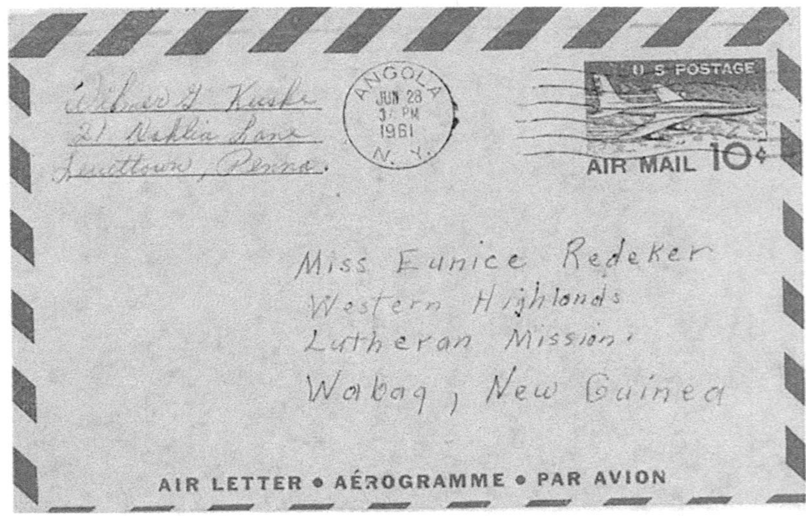

Examples of Air Mail envelops and stamps of the 1960's

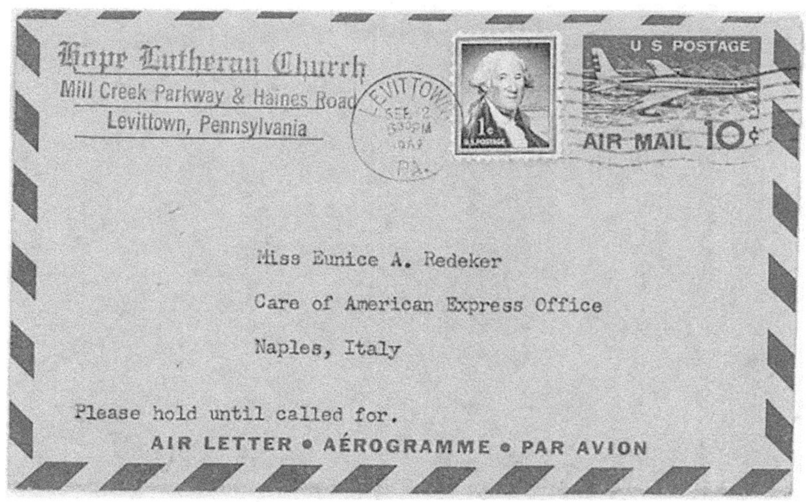

An example of a letter mailed from Hong Kong. Also the blue Aerogramme style was actually about an 8.5 x 11" paper, that when folded, formed the envelope. All the folded sides could be written on.

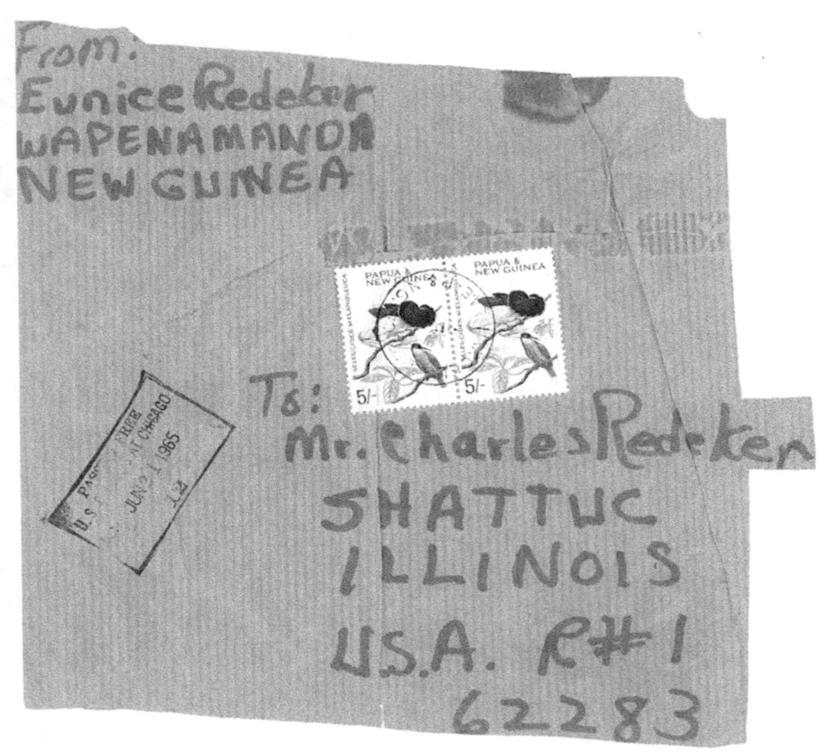

An example of the colorful birds of PNG as conveyed by their stamps.

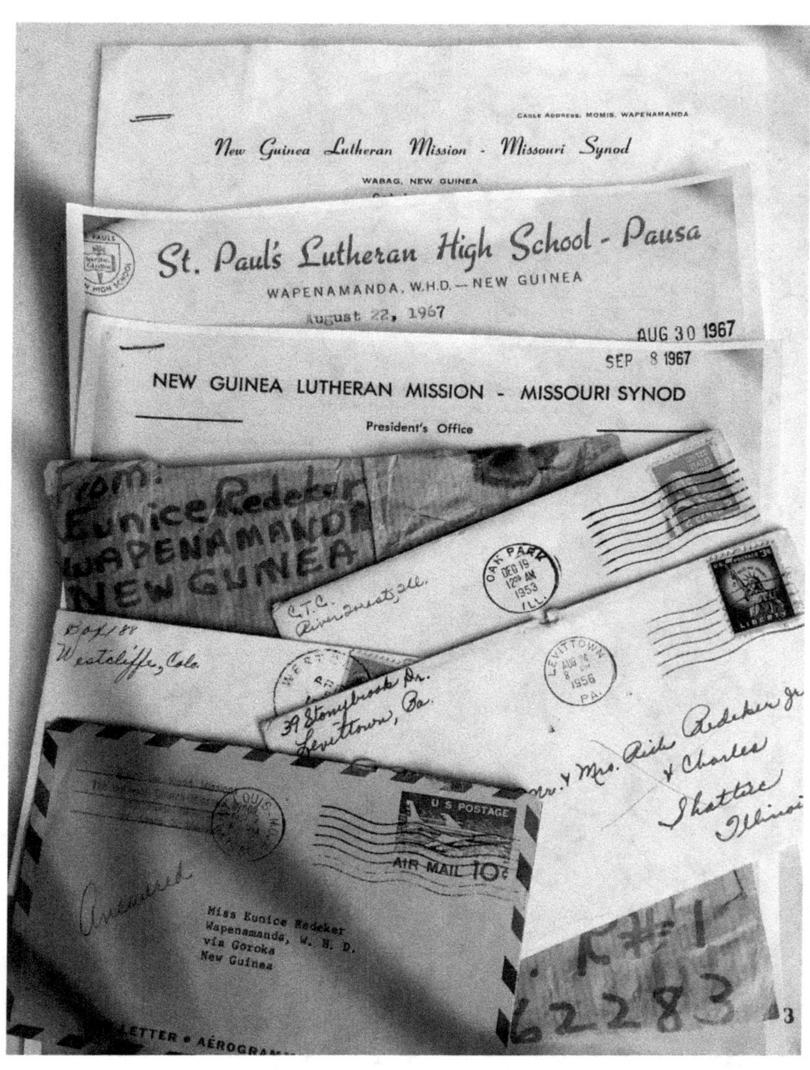

Examples of early letterhead from the New Guinea mission field and some of Eunice's return addresses on mail from the 1950's. (Note the postage stamps for 2 and 3 cents!)

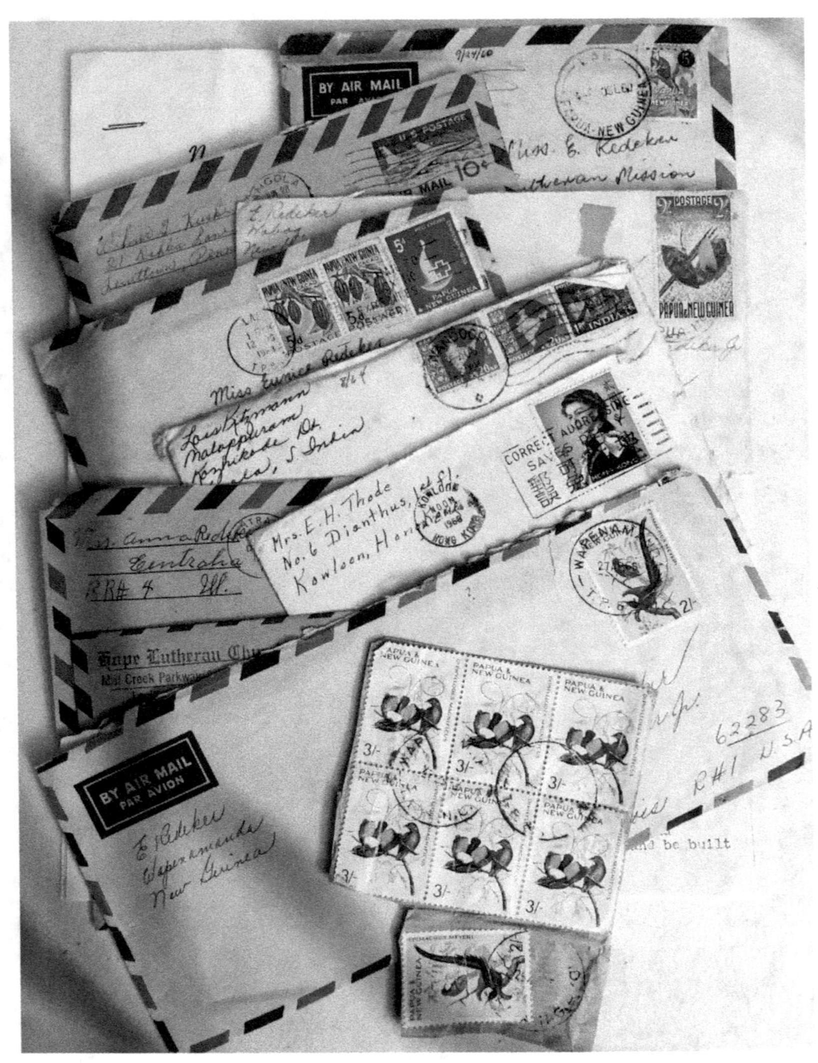

Postage stamps/letters from around the world sent via "Air Mail" in the 1960's.

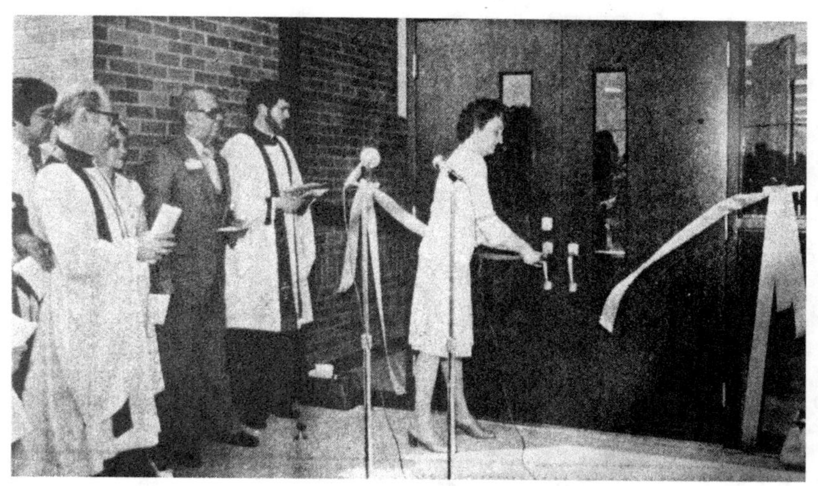

Eunice cutting the ribbon to open the doors of Zion Lutheran School, Lincoln, IL. April 20, 1980.

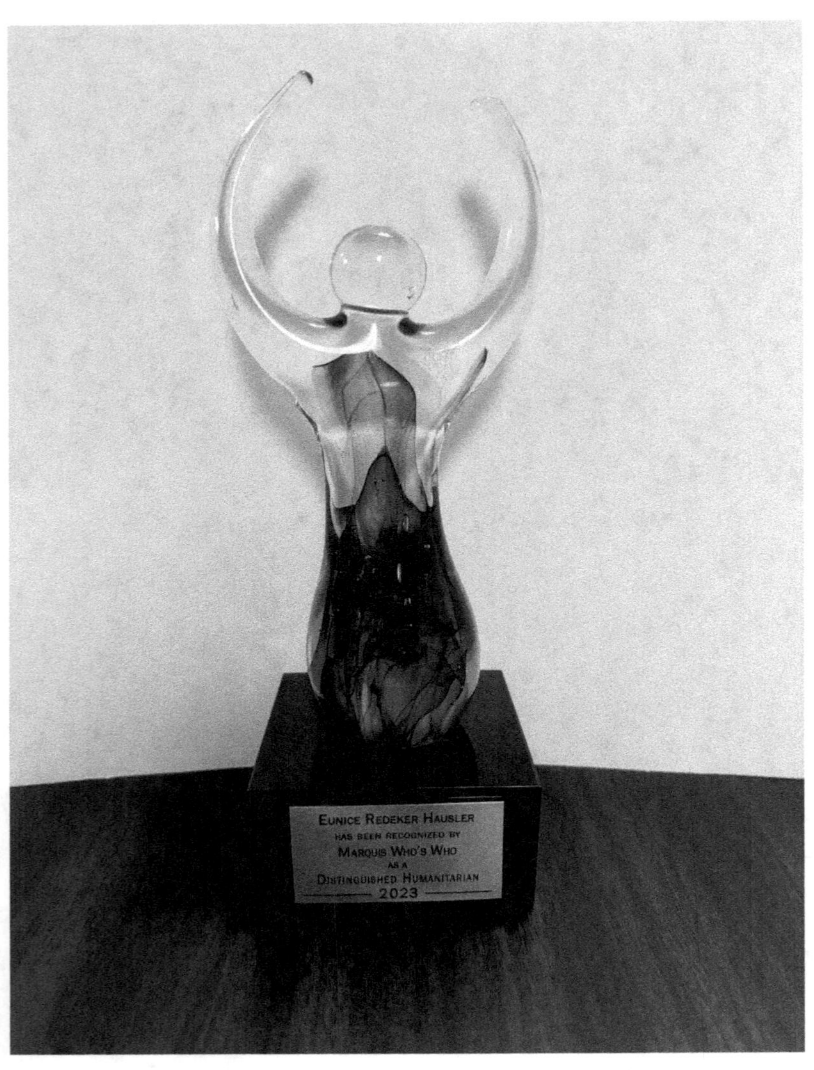

Eunice Redeker Hausler has been recognized by Marquis Who's Who as a Distinguished Humanitarian 2023